# The Complete Idiot's Refere

## Reading Group Rules of Thumb

➤ *The time must be spent discussing the book!*

➤ Be respectful of your fellow book clubians by always doing the following:
1. Arrive on time.
2. Call ahead of time if you can't make it.
3. Finish the book!

➤ Come prepared to say more than, "I liked it!" or, "I hated it!" As you are reading, take note of *what* you found effective or ineffective. For instance, are the characters realistic in the setting presented? Do you care about them? Did you find yourself skimming or were you hanging on every word? Do you think the author's style had something to do with this? How? What did you take away from this book? If nothing, why did the tome fall flat for you? How does this book relate to real or modern life, if at all?

➤ Taking turns leading discussions is the most effective way to keep all things equal.

➤ Humankind can't live on words alone: Make sure some food is available during your meetings. If folks are passing out from hunger, the discussion isn't going to be all that lively.

➤ When starting a book club, family and friends are the most convenient source for reading group members. However, you can form a group through your local bookstore, put up fliers around your neighborhood, or find a few colleagues who want to stretch their minds beyond the 9 to 5.

➤ Comfortable surroundings are of great importance to great discussions.

➤ Book clubs should encourage debate, but discourage competition; there are no winners.

➤ Being too negative or too positive isn't conducive to healthy debate. Don't be afraid to state your opinions—that's what a book group is all about. But if you find that you're the only one saying anything at your reading group anymore, maybe you've beaten your fellow members into submission with too much negativity.

➤ The key to discussing films of books is to analyze their merit as an adaptation. *Do not* substitute the film version of a book for the book itself, and always read the book before seeing the movie.

alpha
books

## Great Fiction Titles to Choose as a Jumping-Off Point

- *Beloved*, by Toni Morrison

- *Last Exit to Brooklyn*, by Hubert Selby Jr.

- *The Great Gatsby*, by F. Scott Fitzgerald

- *A Room of One's Own*, by Virginia Woolf

- *My Antonia*, by Willa Cather

- *Invisible Man*, by Ralph Ellison

- *All Quiet on the Western Front*, by Erich Maria Remarque

- *The Portable Dorothy Parker*, by Dorothy Parker

- *One Hundred Years of Solitude*, by Gabriel García Márquez

- *A River Runs Through It*, by Norman Maclean

- *Where the Wild Things Are*, by Maurice Sendak

- *The Snapper*, by Roddy Doyle

- *A Widow for One Year*, by John Irving

- *Emma*, by Jane Austen

- *The Country Doctor*, by Sarah Orne Jewett

- *The Lone Ranger and Tonto Fistfight in Heaven*, by Sherman Alexie

- *The Intuitionist*, by Colson Whitehead

- *The Talented Mr. Ripley*, by Patricia Highsmith

- *Dracula*, by Bram Stoker

- *Animal Dreams*, by Barbara Kingsolver

- *The Trial*, by Franz Kafka

- *Catch-22*, by Joseph Heller

- *Where I'm Calling From*, by Raymond Carver

- *The Moviegoer*, by Walker Percy

- *Almanac of the Dead*, by Leslie Marmon Silko

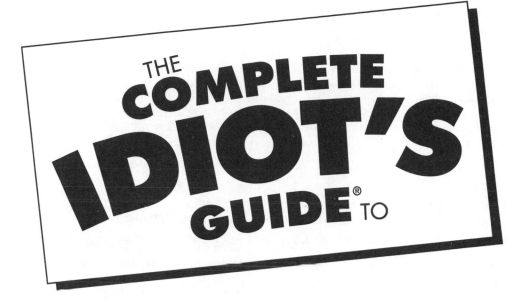

# THE COMPLETE IDIOT'S GUIDE® TO

# Starting a Reading Group

*by Patrick Sauer*

## alpha books

Macmillan USA, Inc.
201 West 103rd Street
Indianapolis, IN 46290

A Pearson Education Company

International Standard Book Number: 0-02-863654-6
Library of Congress Catalog Card Number: Available upon request.

03   02   01   00      4   3   2   1

Interpretation of the printing code: The rightmost number of the first series of numbers is the year of the book's printing; the rightmost number of the second series of numbers is the number of the book's printing. For example, a printing code of 00-1 shows that the first printing occurred in 2000.

*Printed in the United States of America*

**Publisher**
*Marie Butler-Knight*

**Associate Managing Editor**
*Cari Shaw Fischer*

**Acquisitions Editor**
*Randy Ladenheim-Gil*

**Development Editor**
*Amy Zavatto*

**Production Editor**
*Christy Wagner*

**Copy Editor**
*Faren Bachelis*

**Cover Designers**
*Mike Freeland*
*Kevin Spear*

**Illustrator**
*Jody P. Schaeffer*

**Book Designers**
*Scott Cook and Amy Adams of DesignLab*

**Indexer**
*Tonya Heard*

**Layout/Proofreading**
*Juli Cook*
*Terri Edwards*
*John Etchison*
*Michael J. Poor*
*Gloria Schurick*

# Contents at a Glance

## Part 1: Reading Groups: Singles Bars for the Next Century — 1

**1  To Read or Not to Read? — 3**
*Learn what book clubs and reading groups have to offer, why they have become one of the cultural benchmarks of modern society, and how they make life worth living once again.*

**2  The Reading Kind: Where to Find Your Fellow Bibliophiles — 15**
*This chapter deals with the issue of the makeup of your reading group and the pros and cons of selecting members. It tells where you can find enthusiastic book clubians and how to settle the age-old dilemma of familiarity versus homogenization.*

**3  Where Art Thou, Reading Group? — 31**
*A consideration of the proper locale for your reading group and a consideration of costs and comfort level.*

**4  Ground Rules, to Thine Own Self Be True — 43**
*Discover why setting ground rules is vital to future reading group gatherings, and what exactly to do with that certain guy who never reads the book.*

## Part 2: Behold, the Beauty of Discussion — 57

**5  Take Me to Your Leader, Reader — 59**
*Understand the importance and role of the discussion leader, the various styles that can be implemented, including professionals, and the influence of Oprah.*

**6  It Takes *All* the Members of a Village — 71**
*Learn how to deal with every personality type in the book, because you will encounter them all at some point.*

**7  Questions for Fire — 85**
*Explore ways to enhance your cranial powers, use outside resources, and facilitate challenging, intellectual reading group experiences.*

**8  Somebody Tell Me If We're Doing This Right — 95**
*What are the secrets to a successful reading group meeting? Only your reading group members will be the ones in the know.*

**Part 3: Have We Got the Group for You**     **109**

9   We're #1: The Classics Group     111
*The top 100 novels of the century were recently ranked, and the best of the best offer deep waters for diving into your maiden selection.*

10   Women's Groups—Our Miss Books     125
*Women far outnumber men in the reading group universe. Find out why that is, as well as how a feminist angle can be beneficial, and the joys of mother/daughter groups.*

11   Men's Groups—a Rare Species     143
*Explore ways to get more men involved in the reading group revolution through the grand old game or the ol' anglin' hole.*

12   Multicultural Musings—Exploring Cultural Identity     157
*Learn different ways to examine multicultural literature and the difference between a melting pot and a salad bowl.*

13   That's Kids' Stuff     173
*Your kids are never too young to get in on the ground floor of a reading group, even if it's around the dinner table.*

**Part 4: Tailoring Your Group Like a Fine Suit**     **187**

14   Regional Book Clubs     189
*No matter where you go, there you are. Why not pick up a monthly selection from one of the brilliant, distinctive regional authors?*

15   Molls, Snoops, Dicks, Dupes, and a Bunch of Rotting Corpses     207
*Don't let the label "genre fiction" keep your reading group from selecting certain titles because you might miss out on classic mysteries.*

16   Oh, the Horror ... the Horror     221
*From the undead to the soon-to-be murdered: how to choose the perfect horror tome.*

17   Get Real: Nonfiction     235
*Learn how your reading group can unearth the treasures found in works of nonfiction.*

18   People Are People, So What Should I Read?     253
*Explore why fascinating biographies can offer tales to rival the most twisted of fiction, and why your life might be worthy of a bestseller.*

**Part 5: My Group Wants to Party All the Time**    **267**

   19  Food for Thought    269
*Now that your book club is firmly established, it is time
to throw those literary parties of which you have always
dreamed, including the delightful combination of eggs and
oysters.*

   20  The Moviegoers    285
*Learn how to expand your reading group world by exam-
ining cinematic adaptations of written works.*

   21  The Play's the Thing    301
*Reading plays aloud, taking a trip to the local theater,
analyzing Shakespeare, or becoming living room thespians
are all unique ways to enjoy classic plays.*

   22  Of Tender Verse and Narrative Terse    315
*Poetry and short stories are often overlooked because of
stylistic differences to their lengthier cousins, but your
reading group is missing out, so why not open the literary
floodgates?*

   23  Take a Vacation ... Bring a Book ... and the Book Club    329
*There are all sorts of day trips, historical outings, or lazy
days at the beach to consider when planning a special
book club date.*

**Appendix**

   A  Further Suggested Book Club Kinda Books    341

      Index    343

# Contents

**Part 1: Reading Groups: Singles Bars for the Next Century**     **1**

**1 To Read or Not to Read?**     **3**

Dinner Party Disaster.................................................4
An Intellectual Workout ...........................................5
   *Personally* ........................................................6
   *Publicly* ...........................................................8
   *Calm Among the Storms* .....................................9
It's Good for You (and Tastes a Lot Better Than Broccoli) ..10
   *Surprise! It's Fun* ............................................13

**2 The Reading Kind: Where to Find Your Fellow Bibliophiles**     **15**

Those We See Everyday ...........................................16
   *Family* .............................................................16
   *Friends*.............................................................18
Those We See a Lot ................................................20
   *Co-Workers* ......................................................20
   *Community Members* ..........................................22
   *Classmates* .......................................................23
Those We See a Little...............................................24
   *Bookstores* .......................................................24
   *Local Merchants*.................................................26
   *Gyms*...............................................................26
Those We Never See.................................................26
   *Newspaper Ads* ..................................................27
   *Internet Postings* ...............................................28

**3 Where Art Thou, Reading Group?**     **31**

Location, Location, Location ....................................31
   *Home Sweet Home* .............................................32
Around the Neighborhood .......................................35
   *Schools* ............................................................35
   *Community Centers* ............................................36
   *Library*.............................................................37

*Follow the Money*......................................................38
*Bookstores* ............................................................38
*Offices* ..................................................................39
*Eateries and Drinkeries*..........................................40

### 4 Ground Rules, to Thine Own Self Be True    43

Mark Your Calendar..................................................43
Set Your Watch ......................................................45
What Price Books? ..................................................46
*Buying* ..................................................................47
*Borrowing* ............................................................52
Food, Glorious Food ..............................................52
Procedures ............................................................54
*Absenteeism* ........................................................54
*Late Birds* ............................................................54
*Situational Illiterateeism* ......................................55

### Part 2: Behold, the Beauty of Discussion    57

### 5 Take Me to Your Leader, Reader    59

Going for the Goal ..................................................60
*Personal Progress* ..................................................60
*Group Goals*..........................................................62
*Group Charters* ......................................................63
Follow the Leader ..................................................63
*Dictatorships* ........................................................64
*Democracies*..........................................................65
*Socialists* ..............................................................66
*Professionally Led* ................................................66
*Celebrity Led (a.k.a. Oprah-Fi)* ..............................67
*Talk of the Nation* ................................................69
*Internet Led* ..........................................................69

### 6 It Takes *All* the Members of a Village    71

The Runner-Offer-at-the-Mouther..............................72
The Interrupter ......................................................73
The Aggressor..........................................................74
The Digressor ..........................................................75
The Regressor ..........................................................76

The Professor ..................................................77
The Wallflower..................................................78
The "Good" ..................................................79
The "Bad"..................................................80
The "Ugly" ..................................................81

**7 Questions for Fire**     **85**

Where the Wild Things Are..................................................86
Curious George and the Unopened Novel ..........................87
   *Preread Warm-Up* ..................................................87
   *Mental Stretches*..................................................88
   *Have a Game Plan* ..................................................90
   *Be the Book* ..................................................90
The Cat in the Hat Stays on Track ..................................91
   *Author Biographies*..................................................92
   *Scholarly Journals/Lit Crit* ..................................93

**8 Somebody Tell Me If We're Doing This Right**     **95**

And the Winner Isn't ... ..................................................96
   *The Great Debate*..................................................97
The Mention of Tension ..................................................98
The Glory of Story ..................................................99
Let It Flow, Let It Flow, Let It Flow ..........................101
   *Doctor, I Have a Pulse!*..................................................102
   *Okay, Break Out the Nametags Again ...* ..................103
But I Read Bob Uecker's *Catcher in the Wry*..................104
   *On Your Mark* ..................................................104
   *Get Set*..................................................105
   *Read!* ..................................................105
The Party's Over..................................................106
Getting into the Groove ..................................................106

**Part 3: Have We Got the Group for You**     **109**

**9 We're #1: The Classics Group**     **111**

The Top Ten Tomes of Our Times ..................................111
The People Have Spoken ..................................................122

## 10 Women's Groups—Our Miss Books 125

Girl Power .......................................................125
  *Staples* .......................................................*128*
Feminized Slant ................................................133
Mother/Daughter Reading Groups .........................137

## 11 Men's Groups—a Rare Species 143

Where You At? .................................................144
Guy Stuff .......................................................145
  *Fishing*.......................................................*146*
  *Baseball*......................................................*148*
  *Tough Guys* ..................................................*150*
  *Fathers and Sons* ............................................*152*
Get the Men Out ..............................................154

## 12 Multicultural Musings—Exploring Cultural Identity 157

Identity, Who Am I? ..........................................158
The Great American Reading Group Melting Pot............158
  *African-American Tomes* .....................................*159*
Not Just Black and White ....................................161
Asian Voices....................................................165
The Forgotten Ones ...........................................168
Thy Cup Runneth Over.......................................172

## 13 That's Kids' Stuff 173

The World o' Kiddie Lit.......................................176
  *Young 'Uns* ..................................................*176*
Middle 'Uns ....................................................178
The Terrible Teens ............................................181
The Kids Are All Right .......................................185

## Part 4: Tailoring Your Group Like a Fine Suit 187

## 14 Regional Book Clubs 189

Country Roads Take Me Home ..............................189
When Irish Eyes Are Reading ...............................190

English McGuffins .................................................193
A Lit-tle Italy ....................................................195
Living in America .................................................197
Going Out West Where I Belong....................................198
New England of Books ...........................................200
Gotham Greats ....................................................203

### 15 Molls, Snoops, Dicks, Dupes, and a Bunch of Rotting Corpses — 207

Becoming a Genre Genius...........................................208
There's No Mystery About It ......................................211
*That's Mr. Mystery to You* ......................................*211*
*The Glory Days* .................................................*212*
Modern Murder and Malaise.........................................214
Mystery Masterpieces..............................................215
Where to Get the Skinny on Mysteries.............................218

### 16 Oh, the Horror ... the Horror — 221

Evil Is Goin' On ... .............................................221
Bloodsucking Banshees ............................................222
Weird, Wild Stuff.................................................225
Friendly Neighborhood Sociopaths and Lil' Devils .........227
The Sounds of Science.............................................230
*If You Think Blood, Ghosts, Monsters, and Aliens Are for You ...* ...........................................*233*

### 17 Get Real: Nonfiction — 235

Why Finding a Book About a Chiropteran Is Simple........235
The ABCs of Nonfiction ...........................................237
*A:* And the Band Played On: Politics, People, and the AIDS Epidemic, *by Randy Shilts* ................*237*
*B:* Bury My Heart at Wounded Knee: An Indian of the American West, *by Dee Brown* .........*237*
*C:* The Communist Manifesto, *by Karl Marx in Collaboration with Friedrich Engels* .............*238*
*D:* Darkness Visible: A Memoir of Madness, *by William Styron* ........................................*239*
*E:* The Education of Henry Adams, *by Henry Adams*......*240*
*F:* Backlash: The Undeclared War Against American Women, *by Susan Faludi* ........................*240*

*G:* The Guns of August, *by Barbara Tuchman* ...............241

*H:* A Brief History of Time, *by Stephen Hawking* ...........242

*I:* In Cold Blood: A True Account of a Multiple Murder and Its Consequences, *by Truman Capote* ...............242

*J:* The Undisclosed Self: With Symbols and the Interpretation of Dreams, *by Carl Jung* ........................243

*K:* Savage Inequalities: Children in America's Schools, *by Jonathan Kozol* ........................................243

*L:* The Lives of a Cell: Notes of a Biology Watcher, *by Lewis Thomas* ........................................244

*M:* The Prince, *by Niccolo Machiavelli* ............................244

*N:* Beyond Good and Evil: Prelude to a Philosophy of the Future, *by Friedrich Nietzsche* ..........................245

*O:* The Origin of Species, *by Charles Darwin* ...................246

*P:* Parting the Waters/Pillar of Fire, *by Taylor Branch* ....246

*Q:* Red Lobster, White Trash, and the Blue Lagoon, *by Joe Queenan* ........................................247

*R:* The Rise and Fall of the Third Reich: A History of Nazi Germany, *by William Shirer* ..........................247

*S:* A Bright and Shining Lie, *by Neil Sheehan* .................247

*T:* The Mole People: Life in the Tunnels Beneath New York City, *by Jennifer Toth* ..............................248

*U:* Up from Slavery, *by Booker T. Washington* ..................248

*V:* Very Special People, *by Frederick Drimmer* .................249

*W:* Working: People Talk About What They Do All Day and How They Feel About What They Do, *by Studs Terkel* ........................................250

*X:* The Autobiography of Malcolm X, *by Alex Haley, Based on Interviews with Malcolm X* ...........................250

*Y:* Young Men and Fire, *by Norman Maclean* ..................251

*Z:* A People's History of the United States: 1492–Present, *by Howard Zinn, and* A History of the American People, *by Paul Johnson* ........................................251

**18 People Are People, So What Should I Read?**  **253**

The Big Cheeses ........................................254

Oh, Those Arty Types ........................................257

Memoirs, All Alone in the Spotlight ...............................260

The One and Only Interview ........................................261

## Part 5: My Group Wants to Party All the Time   267

### 19 Food for Thought   269

A Final Reminder ..............................................................269
Cooking Up Some Good Reading .....................................271
   *Books for Cooks and Food-Lovers Alike*............................271
   *Books That Cook* ............................................................273
Call Me Ish-*Meal* ...........................................................273
   *The Great Gatsby Roaring Soiree* ...................................274
   *The Joy Luck Club Feast*.................................................275
   *All the Pretty Horses Smokeout Barbecue* .......................278
Seize the *Holi*-Day .........................................................280
   *A Bloody Good Halloween Party*......................................280
   *Yule Have a Great Time* .................................................282

### 20 The Moviegoers   285

I Found It at the Movies ...................................................286
There's No Place Like Home .............................................286
Rules to Read (and Watch) By ..........................................288
   *Edward Scissorhands Snips Again*....................................288
   *Who's That Girl?*............................................................289
   *The End*........................................................................289
There's No Place Like the Movie Haus, Either ..................290
Books for the Movie Fan in All of Us ...............................291
Viewing/Reading Lists .....................................................293
   *Let's All Go to the Movies* .............................................294

### 21 The Play's the Thing   301

Literature with Legs........................................................302
 Why Not Godot See a Production? ..................................303
Great Theaters Around the Country ..................................305
Drama Queens (and Kings) ...............................................306
Always Go with the Favored Heavyweights ......................307
Bill, Bill, Bill, and More Bill.............................................309
   *Book Club Kinda Plays*....................................................311

**22  Of Tender Verse and Narrative Terse**                    **315**

    *To Rhyme or Not to Rhyme—That Is the Question* ............*316*

    *Living Room Laureates* .....................................................*317*

    *Slam It Home*....................................................................*318*

  Poets You Should Know.........................................................*319*

    *Langston Hughes* .............................................................*319*

    *Emily Dickinson*...............................................................*319*

    *William Blake* ..................................................................*320*

    *Walt Whitman* ................................................................*321*

    *Carl Sandburg* .................................................................*321*

    *William Carlos Williams* ..................................................*322*

    *Sylvia Plath* .....................................................................*323*

  America's Concise Contribution ...........................................*324*

    *O. Henry* .........................................................................*325*

    *Raymond Carver* .............................................................*326*

    *Alice Munro* ....................................................................*327*

**23  Take a Vacation ... Bring a Book ...
and the Book Club**                                           **329**

  Beach Blanket Book Club ....................................................*330*

    *It's Too Darn Hot*............................................................*330*

    *Pass the Hawaiian Tropic and the
Tropic of Cancer, Please* .................................................*331*

  Day Trippin' .......................................................................*333*

    *Music, Maestro: Symphony in the Park* .............................*333*

    *Drivin' Down a Country Road* .........................................*334*

    *Around the Pool* ..............................................................*334*

    *Museum Musings* .............................................................*335*

    *Take a Walk on the (Literary) Wild Side*..........................*336*

    *It Starts at Home* ............................................................*338*

**Appendix**

**A  Further Suggested Book Club Kinda Books**        **341**

  **Index**                                                     **343**

# Foreword

You may already be thinking, "A foreword, okay, I usually skip those and jump right into the book. But why him? What does a news guy have to tell me about starting a book group?"

In a way, that's a neat expression of what book groups do in the first place. They take literature away from the experts. They bring the pleasure and privilege of judging, dissecting, assessing the work of writers back to the place those tasks should always belong: with readers.

Book groups are hot because they let you share something not easily shared with others. What could be a more solitary occupation than reading? All the voices, images, and characters project against a screen inside your head. Digesting a book can be the most personal of experiences. The book club rescues that singular experience from its enforced solitude. It has the ability to deepen the impact of that initial experience by bouncing your own set of impressions against the movie projected in everybody else's heads.

In the early '90s, book groups had started to zoom, especially in Washington, D.C., where I had come to work. Everyone I knew seemed to be joining one, or in the hunt for one that suited him. A member of the staff talked one morning about the meeting she had attended the previous night. It brought together friends and friends of friends to wrestle over what the club had agreed was a difficult book to read.

We got to talking about what makes a good group and a good meeting and realized that these were many of the elements that made for a great hour of radio. There was sharing of perspective, accord, disagreement, humor, pleasure, and disappointment. It was spontaneous, energetic, and a place where people didn't feel they needed a Masters in Comparative Lit or a cozy berth at the New York Review of Books to hold forth.

From that conversation came *Talk of the Nation's Book Club of the Air,* a nationwide, unrehearsed, lightly structured, one-hour monthly meeting to pull apart a book.

Keeping with this foreword's theme of giving power to the nonexpert, I might have been the perfect choice as host: a man who rarely read fiction (and had no time to belong to a real book group where people actually saw each other face to face). Through this monthly get-together in the Virtual Living Room built by phone lines and computers and hundreds of thousands of listeners, we tried to capture what makes book clubs so compelling to so many book lovers around the country.

Over the months and years, we read fiction ancient and modern, in English and from translation, written by men and women, along with plays, poems, short stories, and—gasp—nonfiction works. We read books that audiences had never heard of, like Milorad Pavic's *Dictionary of the Khazars,* and books whose titles are almost universally known, although the books are read less today, like Harriet Beecher Stowe's *Uncle Tom's Cabin,* and Edith Wharton's *House of Mirth.*

What became music to this book-lover's ears? As someone who had to travel a great deal in connection with my work I found many contradictory reactions downright thrilling:

"I struggled with last month's book and in the end, decided I really didn't like it. But I'm glad I read it and glad I heard what other people thought about it."

"I've seen that book in the library a hundred times and never would have considered even pulling it off the shelf for a look. So the club forced me to grow."

"I heard you announce that book at the end of last month's meeting and figured it wasn't for me. Then I was out doing errands and heard the meeting, and the book sounded so good I'm reading it right now."

The book you have in your hands is a potent tool for taking back the love of reading from the experts. In a clear, forthright, and often very funny way, it walks you step by step through the process of setting up a successful group. This book is "eyes-open" about the pitfalls, and warns you about them. But being realistic about reading groups should never be discouraging. Instead it should give you confidence to have a handy reference in hand, for all those "but what about?" questions sure to arise when you start from scratch.

Book clubs, book groups, reading circles—whatever you want to call them and wherever you do them—increase the amount of goodness in the world. And that can't be a bad thing. At a time when our lives are rushed, they force us to create a space in our heads—and our calendars—to see other people and do a little work together. They have become a humane, mind-expanding feature of the American landscape and remind folks that they are pretty smart after all. And that can't be a bad thing, either.

Ray Suarez, Senior Correspondent, The NewsHour, and author of *The Old Neighborhood: What We Lost in the Great Suburban Migration* (Free Press, 1999).

Ray Suarez joined The NewsHour in October 1999 as a Washington-based senior correspondent responsible for conducting newsmaker interviews, studio discussions, and debates, reporting from the field and serving as a backup anchor.

Suarez has 20 years of varied experience in the news business. He came to The NewsHour from National Public Radio where he had been host of the nationwide, call-in news program "Talk of the Nation" since 1993. Prior to that, he spent seven years covering local, national, and international stories for the NBC affiliate WMAQ-TV in Chicago. Suarez was also a Los Angeles correspondent for CNN, a producer for the ABC Radio Network in New York, a reporter for CBS Radio in Rome, and a reporter for various American and British news services in London.

Suarez penned the recent book *The Old Neighborhood: What We Lost in the Great Suburban Migration: 1966–1999* and contributed to another, *Las Christmas: Favorite Latino Authors Share Their Holiday Memories.* His essays and criticisms have been published in The News York Times, *The Washington Post, The Chicago Tribune,* and *The Baltimore Sun,* among other publications.

Suarez shared in NPR's 1993–1994 and 1994–1995 duPont-Columbia Silver Baton Awards for on-site coverage of the first all-race elections in South Africa and the first 100 days of the 104th Congress, respectively. He has been honored with the 1996 Ruben Salazar Award, *Current History Magazine's* 1995 Global Awareness Award, and a Chicago Emmy Award.

Suarez holds a B.A. in African History from New York University and an M.A. in the Social Sciences from the University of Chicago, where he studied urban affairs.

A longtime member of the National Association of Hispanic Journalists, Suarez is a founding member of the Chicago Association of Hispanic Journalists. A native of Brooklyn, New York, he lives in Washington with his wife and two children.

# Introduction

Do you ever feel like Scrooge when he is tooling around with the creepy mute Ghost of Christmas Future? You know, when old, crotchety Ebeneezer can see the toothless scalawags divvying up his earthly items, followed by his dark, lonely funeral? Do you feel like everyone around you is leading more interesting, fulfilling lives while you are stuck in a dead-end existence?

Or do you just feel like you don't read enough?

Either way, have I got the solution for you. Step right up and join the literary craze that is sweeping the nation in ways unseen since the *Disco Duck* mayhem of the late 1970s. Become one of the few, the proud, the members of the book club juggernaut.

Maybe you have always wanted to join, or start, a reading group. Maybe you are in one, but it's stagnating. Maybe you want ideas on how to make the meetings more exciting and dynamic. Whatever the reason, it is apparent that you are just the type of person whom the reading group universe needs. So, pour a glass of your favorite beverage, kick off those shoes, put the dogs up, and start bettering your life right now. It all comes down to one simple word that scares off all but the truly remarkable: *reading*.

## What You'll Learn in This Book

*The Complete Idiot's Guide to Starting a Reading Group* covers everything from soup to nuts in the life of a book club. We will start with the organizational details, travel through the vast world of literary choices, and end up at a rip-roaring party. Sound like your cup of tea? Please peruse the following five parts to get the bibliophilic juices flowing for your reading pleasure:

**Part 1, "Reading Groups: Singles Bars for the Next Century,"** provides all the necessary information for getting underway, including the reasons why a book club is better for you than broccoli. We will get into the makeup of your reading group, how to select the perfect locale, and why ground rules early on will pay huge dividends down the road.

**Part 2, "Behold, the Beauty of Discussion,"** answers everything you have always wanted to know about asking questions but were afraid to ask. The various types of reading group leaders are covered, as well as how to handle more personality types than Sybil ever dreamed of, and ways to boost your cranial capabilities.

**Part 3, "Have We Got the Group for You,"** examines the various types of groups out in the reading group galaxy. We will also start going through literary works to expand your mind and blow the roof off of your standard book club gatherings.

**Part 4, "Tailoring Your Group Like a Fine Suit,"** gets to the bottom of why the label "genre fiction" might keep your group from enjoying a brilliant tome. It also opens up the literary arena to include monsters, ax-wielding psychopaths, and good old-fashioned real folks.

**Part 5, "My Group Wants to Party All the Time,"** is for those groups that are now firmly established and want to throw themselves a little congratulatory soiree. It also delves into other ways to enjoy meetings, be it through movies, plays, or other literary formats.

## More for Your Money!

In addition to all the explanation and information, this book contains other types of wisdom to make it even easier for you to unleash all of the passion and power of your book club. Here's how you can recognize these features:

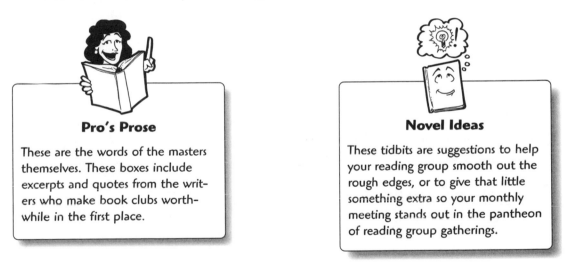

### Pro's Prose

These are the words of the masters themselves. These boxes include excerpts and quotes from the writers who make book clubs worthwhile in the first place.

### Novel Ideas

These tidbits are suggestions to help your reading group smooth out the rough edges, or to give that little something extra so your monthly meeting stands out in the pantheon of reading group gatherings.

**Jane Err**

This is Novel Idea's polar opposite; it offers hints on what to avoid in your reading group. Here you'll find ways to help you dodge uncomfortable situations or awkward moments and keep the reading group engine purring like a kitten.

**Biblio-Trivio**

Biblio-Trivio boxes contain the lesser or unknown facts, anecdotes, and literary lore that can be dropped at meetings or saved for when you attempt to win your fortune on *Jeopardy*.

## Acknowledgments

To the four women who were instrumental in the creation of this book: Jessica Faust for ignoring past deadline/best-effort malfeasance; Amy Zavatto for authentic, first-hand, insight; Mom for raising me to be an idiot; and Kimberly for the motoring skills that got me here in the first place.

## Special Thanks to the Technical Reviewer

*The Complete Idiot's Guide to Starting a Reading Group* was reviewed by an expert who double-checked the accuracy of what you'll learn here, to help us ensure that this book gives you everything you need to know about starting a reading group. Special thanks are extended to Rachel Jaffe.

Rachel Jaffe, a court reporter in Washington, D.C., has maintained a Web site discussing online book clubs and online resources for book clubs since early 1997. Rachel's Compendium of Online Book Discussions, et al. (http://www.his.com/allegria/compend.html) has been cited in national publications, such as *The Wall Street Journal,* the *L.A. Times,* and *The New York Times.*

## Trademarks

All terms mentioned in this book that are known to be or are suspected of being trademarks or service marks have been appropriately capitalized. Alpha Books and Macmillan USA, Inc. cannot attest to the accuracy of this information. Use of a term in this book should not be regarded as affecting the validity of any trademark or service mark.

# Part 1

# Reading Groups: Singles Bars for the Next Century

*"All good books are alike in that they are truer than if they really happened and after you are finished reading one you will feel that all that happened to you and afterwards it all belongs to you; the good and the bad, the ecstasy, the remorse and sorrow, the people and the places and how the weather was."*

—*Ernest Hemingway*

*In the end, all it takes for a successful book club is a brilliant text and curious readers, but it's the little things that ensure your book club will be a triumph. If God is truly in the details, then this section of the book is the most holy.*

*This part of the book will help you to get the wheels in motion; it provides the framework for the reading group adventures to come. It covers all the basics, but it also has hints and ideas to assist in the formation of a book club of the highest order.*

# Chapter 1

# To Read or Not to Read?

---

**In This Chapter**

➤ Reasons to start reading

➤ The basics of a book club

➤ Reading groups as self-improvement: personal and public

➤ How to improve your dialogue and make friends

➤ The positive influences of reading groups

---

Does it seem that every time you turn around lately, another friend or acquaintance has joined a reading group? Everyone seems to be in on it. You walk into a bookstore and begin perusing the shelves. You pick up an interesting-looking softcover, and, lo and behold, there's a sticker on it that says "A perennial book club favorite!" You go to your favorite little café for a cappuccino, head to the back to your regular couch, and sitting on it is a group of people all holding the same book, looking like they're having a really interesting discussion. Later on, you pick up the phone to call your mother to lament about losing your favorite spot to these crazed readers, but all she says is, "Sorry sweetheart! I'll have to call you back—I'm late for my book group!" You're starting to feel like you are on the outside looking in, like there is a major event taking place and you didn't get invited. Never fear, dear reader. The secret is as simple as picking up a book.

# Dinner Party Disaster

Imagine, if you will, a dinner party. But not just any dinner party. It's *your* dinner party. Its centerpiece is a seven-course gourmet meal that took you a week to prepare. You hunted the pheasants and picked the wild berries in your spare time. You hired a wine expert to match the Pinot Noir with the portobello mushroom/sun-dried tomato pâté. You even broke out your Uncle Pierre's 112-year-old brandy and topped that by hand-rolling cigars from a sweet tobacco leaf you have been nurturing in your greenhouse for the ultimate post-feast celebration.

And the guest list! Oh, what a guest list! You've invited your boss, who's deciding if you should become the youngest senior partner in the firm's history. There's the sexy orthopedic surgeon you've been seeing casually, who wants to take the next step and invite you to spend the week at the chalet in Switzerland. There's your smarmy neighbor, the one with the Ph.D. who always seems to be trying to one-up you. Your brother, the jazz musician/sculptor, is at the table along with your sister, the political science professor/White House strategist. Also invited to dinner are a few of your co-workers, the admiring underlings who are willing to break ranks and join that online investment operation you've been conceptualizing. There are also the guests you've invited for *character,* including Norman Mailer, Toni Morrison, David Halberstam, Gabriel García Márquez, Stephen J. Gould, and even J. D. Salinger is sipping a glass of your vintage vino. Last but not least, you've invited that high school English teacher who gave you a D because you never participated in class.

As the cheese course is served, your boss queries:

"In *Cold Mountain,* was Charles Frazier saying that war is the cause of human isolation, or that military conflicts merely exacerbate what is a natural part of the human condition?"

As your guests take a bite of brie, Toni Morrison chimes in with, "It's your party, why don't you start us off?"

You freeze, nearly choking on a rye cracker. After polishing off a glass of water, clearing your throat, and looking straight ahead, you reply, "I ... I haven't read that one yet."

An uncomfortable silence envelops the room. The tension is broken by your brother, who says, "Well, you should read it soon. It is a fantastic examination of the personal divisions war dictates."

David Halberstam adds, "Not everybody is concerned with modern texts. Why don't you tell us why *The Adventures of Huckleberry Finn* has been frequently misunderstood in terms of its racial politics?"

Your shoulders droop as you stare at the elegant place setting you designed for weeks and respond, "I really don't ... remember. It's been a long time. I haven't read ... it ... lately."

The only sound that rings out through your house is startled forks ringing against fine china. Your shark of a neighbor, smelling blood, sticks his dorsal fin out of the water, opens his salivating jaws, and asks, "What author or novel do you wish to discuss? Hemingway, perhaps?"

You shrug your shoulders in defeat.

"Ellison?"

You shake your head.

"Shakespeare? Anaïs Nin? Vonnegut? O. Henry? Dr. Seuss?"

You cover your eyes in shame as your old English teacher stands and reaches for your jugular.

"Tell us, what book that impacted your life would you like to discuss?"

On the brink of tears, you scan the penetrating eyes of all your guests and say, "I'm not much of a reader."

The next thing you know, the Gouda is stone, the bird is ice, and you are curled up on a futon in the fetal position eating Rocky Road ice cream right out of the carton while watching gorgeous, overpaid, silicon-infected, 20-something television hacks get into another wacky mistaken-identity romance on NBC's Thursday night.

Imagine that.

There is one simple way to avoid this horrific nightmare: Join a, or better yet, start your own, reading group.

## An Intellectual Workout

You probably take good care of your body. You hit the gym a few times a week and run, in-line skate, do Tae Bo, or play racquetball on the weekends to keep the pounds off and the ticker humming. You don't devour bacon double cheeseburgers for lunch every day, and you eat 10 times as many apples as slices of peanut butter cheesecake. You visit the doctor on a regular basis, get your eyes checked, teeth cleaned, and hair styled. So why do you skip giving the most important organ of all the exercise it deserves?

By purchasing this book, you are obviously someone who wants to increase your brainpower. Kudos to you, but it's going to take some effort. Let's be honest: Reading for pleasure is not something most of us make time for during a regular day. It's a whole lot easier to flip on the tube than to pick up a four-pound tome, but it's a whole lot less rewarding. Between daily office reports, quarterly insurance packets, yearly Christmas letters, and painful memories of mandatory 10-page book reports on *The Canterbury Tales,* reading is commonly viewed as a chore and not a privilege. Most of us want to be readers, but much like shedding excess holiday fat, it is easier said than done.

Others of you are readers, but aren't getting anything out of the books. Perhaps it is because your selections consist of airport fiction or summertime potboilers. It could also be that you are attempting to get through challenging novels, but without a support group, most of your attempts are aborted by page 100.

Whatever holds you back from becoming the full-blooded, inquisitive, probing reader you aspire to be can be solved by becoming a member of a reading group.

First things first: Let's establish a definition of a reading group (a.k.a. book club). Basically, there are two definitions, a concrete one and an ethereal one.

1. **The concrete one.** A reading group is a collection of people who get together to discuss a particular book.
2. **The ethereal one.** A reading group is a collection of people who get together to discuss a particular book in whatever creative manner they decide.

Badha-bing! Badha-boom! There you have it.

Reading groups also have only one mandatory tenet:

> *The time must be spent discussing the book.*

That's it. That's all you need to know. So, what are you waiting for? Call up some friends and select a title. Or, you can keep reading for all the juicy details you might otherwise overlook. But, if you think you've gleaned enough info to get started, please repeat the glorious rule once more for me:

> *The time must be spent discussing the book.*

Now that you understand your mission, let's take a look at what a reading group can do for you.

## Personally

Joining a reading group can improve your quality of life in many of the same ways as a solitary jog through the woods, an early morning swim in an empty pool, a nap in front of a fire built just for you, or lying ocean-side in the sun on a private beach. These are all life-enriching activities best performed alone. Moments of tranquillity are few and far between these days. If your life is too cluttered or hectic because you have to bring work home after a 50-hour workweek squeezed in between shuffling your kids from hockey practice to pizza parties, then a book club will become your solace.

The first, and really lone, requirement of a reading club before the gatherings is simple: Read a book. The process of reading the book will give you the personal space that went the way of the dodo long ago. It takes

**Pro's Prose**

"Books are children of the brain."

—Jonathan Swift

a hefty chunk of time to invest yourself in completing a novel, but you'll be amazed at how easily you can incorporate it back into your daily life. Reading will become a part of your routine, instead of the occasional walk on the literate side. No longer will your kids, spouse, co-workers, or telephone salespeople be able to interrupt your hour of narrative nirvana because you are "just reading." You now have license to enjoy it—you wouldn't want to be the outcast in the group who (gulp) didn't finish. Tell all those folks impatiently waiting for a moment of your time, "Sorry, I really must finish this chapter—I have people depending on me, you know." (Besides, they don't have to know that you're actually enjoying it!)

The reward will come when you dazzle your reading mates with an incredibly original theory on Lewis Carroll's use of the nonsensical poem within the story structure of *Alice's Adventures in Wonderland* and *Through the Looking-Glass*. Of course, if you give in to all the interruptions and don't make time to finish your tome, the punishment will come when the reading group asks you not to come back because you never contribute, and you realize your reading hour was usually devoted to trying to get the stains out of little Myron's jeans.

### Novel Ideas

If getting through books has never been your strong suit (or even a hobby), try it on a reward basis. Reward yourself with a dish of ice cream, a glass of wine, or a small shopping spree (for new books, of course!).

### Biblio-Trivio

Lewis Carroll created the word *chortle*. It appeared in *Through the Looking-Glass* and is a combination of "chuckle" and "snort." It means "to laugh or sing exultantly."

Sure, it's a Pavlovian way of positive/negative response, reading for personal recognition. But once you start, a natural affinity for books will take over. You're not always going to like everything you read, but you'll know *why*. And then there will be those harmonious occasions when you come across a sentence that will seem as if it was written specifically for you. Not only is this good for the soul, but it's not so bad for the ego, either. And who among us doesn't need a good ego stroking? It's self-affirming to be brainy, so, in essence, being a "book clubian" will make you a better person. Your surroundings will dictate that you focus on becoming a more well-rounded individual.

## Publicly

Joining a reading group can also improve your quality of life in many of the same ways as a potluck barbecue with siblings, spending the day watching goofy movies with old friends, or an all-night poker binge with buddies. These are all life-enriching activities best performed with others. Solitaire has its merits, but cards are a hell of a lot more fun with a lively gang. If you are a voracious reader whose best friends run the gamut from A. A. Milne to Émile Zola, or if you find yourself carrying on arguments with Holden Caulfield, maybe a reading group is just what the doctor ordered. Socializing should include more than asking the local librarian what is new in the anthropology section. Dewey Decimal does not count as a compadre.

If you become a member of a reading group, you will be forced to interact with at least one other human specimen. However, if you really are shy or just have trouble meeting people, there is a built-in advantage. All you have to talk about is the book. It is a great way to make friends that share a common interest. Anyone can do it. Rip Van Winkle himself could rub the sleep out of his eyes, grab a steaming latte, and stop at the local bookstore to sign up for one of their book clubs (which we will discuss later). No longer will you, Hermit the Bibliophile, be able to interact with the rest of the literate bipeds merely as ships that pass in the night.

### Biblio-Trivio

The phrase "ships that pass in the night" refers to people whose paths cross for just a fleeting moment. The expression originated in Longfellow's *Tales of a Wayside Inn* (1874): "Ships that pass in the night, and speak each other in passing ... So on the ocean of life we pass and speak one another."

Reading groups are an original way to spend time with friends and strangers alike. If you are always saying, "We don't see our pals so-and-so nearly enough," this is a way to interact in an engaging manner on a regular basis. Reading groups combine the enjoyment of a soiree with a purpose, like league bowling. And make no mistake about it: There may be no medals for first prize, but healthy debate stirs the competitive juices. Plus, you don't have to be able to drain a 20-foot jump shot or pick up a 7-to-10 split to be a standout.

If your group consists of friends only, you will be astounded by what you can learn about the people you thought you knew inside and out. The written word can be a powerful tool (The Crusades and the Bible, the Civil War and *Uncle Tom's Cabin*) and reactions will come in all shades of the emotional color wheel. Public responses to personal experiences are what lies at the heart of successful book clubs, so why not give it a whirl? It has to beat another Friday night of stale, happy-hour nachos and domestic swill with the after-work club.

## Calm Among the Storms

Another advantage to joining a reading group is that it provides an opportunity for folks to relax and have an old-fashioned, intelligent, face-to-face dialogue. What's that you say? You have numerous meaningful discussions throughout the day. Afraid not.

The bulk of our dialogue as busy American beavers falls into two categories: gossip and work talk. Think about it for a moment: Most conversations throughout the course of a day are quick, uninvolving, and often simply a means of *touching base*. At work, you may have numerous lengthy meetings or brainstorming sessions, but how often is it rehashed basic information or repeated topics that were covered the week before? We have all heard somebody utter this nugget of '90s wisdom: "E-mail is fantastic because I don't have to talk to so many people anymore." Ignoring the fact that e-mail has just made it easier for everyone in the company to incessantly remind you to show up at the aforementioned meetings to cover issues you were aware of a month ago, there is truth to the idea that many daily discussions aren't that important or interesting.

Here, try this little experiment:

Take this list and mark down every time you talk to someone over the course of a day. Ignore simple greetings, but keep track of everything else. Keep track during a workday and on a nonworkday, preferably a weekend so that you are following the standard pattern. Some categories will be checked twice; that's fine, this is far from scientific.

**Dialogue Checklist**

❑ Conversations of less than five minutes.

❑ Conversations of less than 10 minutes.

❑ Conversations about TV or movies under five minutes.

❑ Conversations about sports under five minutes.

❑ Conversations regarding family or personal life under five minutes.

❑ Conversations at home about what happened at work under five minutes.

❑ Conversations on the phone with someone you see on a daily basis under 10 minutes.

❑ Conversations about an issue of the day under five minutes.

❑ Conversations of any length conducted while at least one participant is watching TV, playing video games, working on the computer, surfing the Web, or on a phone of any kind with someone else.

❑ Conversations conducted face-to-face about a single topic lasting more than 15 minutes with at least a few moments of reflection or introspection.

Still don't believe me? The survey probably says it all. You may think number 10 is loaded; if so, cut it down to 10 minutes. Any different? This is not meant to be a guilt-inducing exercise. It merely shows that the art of conversation isn't practiced as much as it should be. It's hard to take the time to sit, reflect, and talk about a single topic because we are all so used to concentrating on a million things at once. It's not an American habit, but focusing and thinking is important—ask the Buddhists. A book club will give you the opportunity to participate in reflection and discussion.

Even if it is only a couple of hours a month, it might be the most calm 120 minutes among the storms. We discussed the personal tranquillity that sitting down with a book will bring, and the public gathering will do the same. The level of discourse might become heated, but the setting and the focus necessary for optimum results will provide a thoughtful, relaxing atmosphere. Introspection is pacifying, even when it plunges emotional depths, because it gives you a chance to know yourself. The book club will be your *Walden Pond,* and you your own private Thoreau.

**Pro's Prose**

"Every man who knows how to read has it in his power to magnify himself, to multiply the ways in which he exists, to make his life full, significant, and interesting."

—Aldous Huxley

# It's Good for You (and Tastes a Lot Better Than Broccoli)

Here is the most unsurprising revelation in this entire *Idiot's Guide:* Reading is good for the gray matter. Scientists believe that you learn more in the first three years of life than in all the rest combined, but it couldn't hurt to try and prove them wrong. And if the average person only uses 10 percent of his or her brain over the course of a lifetime, why not be all you can be and aim for 12 to 13 percent?

Setting aside the gender-bias of Huxley's remark, there is truth in advertising. You will be entering your own *Brave New World* of words and wisdom. Well-read, intelligent conversationalists have always held elite status on the cocktail party circuit, but those dedicated souls are actually benefiting themselves in ways outside of lucid points over a highball. Regular reading is good for the cerebrum and aids all other avenues of life.

The average brain contains about 100 billion nerve cells when you're born. This number slowly decreases as you age because neurons can't be replaced. So why not challenge the little suckers to go down in a blaze of glory? Help them help you.

**Five Ways Reading Is Beneficial:**

1. **Compartmentalizing.** In the beginning of *Great Expectations,* Pip lives in a depressing little shanty he calls home. Hundreds of pages later, he has moved to London, met a whole new group of oddballs, and followed a full story arc. The Dickens classic is dense and tricky, but your brain will train itself to store important bits of information so you can remember when and where certain pivotal events happen, such as when Pip first encounters Magwitch. It is a skill that is often lost in this 24-hour-information-sound-bite world, but it is a valuable one that can certainly make your workdays smoother (not shorter, just smoother).

2. **Imagining.** Unlike visual mediums, reading requires the creation of your own pictures. The imagination is often neglected in the never-ending squalor of meetings, appointments, bills, birthdays, and golf dates. If you don't use your imagination, it gets rusty. The more you read, the more active your imagination will become. It will continue the creative process while you sleep. Sweet dreams.

3. **Problem solving.** A natural ability to analyze Sherlock Holmes or Miss Marple like Sherlock Holmes or Miss Marple will shine through after you become a full-time reader. Plots, no matter how experimental, follow a logical progression. You will begin to fill in the blanks and decipher the underlying codes of the stories you read long before you get to the page with the answers. It's a habit that can help in all aspects of daily life, because the one thing you can never escape is problems to solve.

4. **Concentrating.** Reading demands concentration, period. After getting through *Ulysses,* a "complex" business plan will be easy like Sunday morning.

5. **Writing.** Everybody writes everyday. It might be professionally: e-mails, cover letters, monthly reports. It might be personally: e-mails, love letters, birthday cards. Or, it might be creatively: short stories, essays, plays, perhaps even the genesis of a novel. If for no other reason than osmosis, dissecting the masters will improve your prose. Just wait and see, a promotion and a raise might be in order after the CEO reads your concise, brilliant, witty memos.

**Biblio-Trivio**

As of January 1999, 28 American children have been crushed to death by television sets since 1990.

*—Harper's Index,* March 1999

Another major benefit that reading groups provide is the positive effect it will have on your children (if you have them or plan on having them). Kids emulate their parents, and survey after survey has shown that children learn to appreciate the art of reading at home. One clinical study put the number as high as 75 percent. The impact is even greater when a child witnesses both the reading and the follow-up discussion. There is a school of scientific thought that believes regular conversations around the dinner table are even more important than reading to your kids because it teaches listening, cognitive reasoning, processing, and answering skills. The information isn't just absorbed; it is put through the entire ringer of cognitive human linguistics. In *Endangered Minds,* Jane M. Heally, Ph.D., says, "poor readers and poor problem-solvers tend to be passive; they give up if they don't 'get it.'" Your children will learn from both sides of the book club equation.

Do it for yourself, or think of the children, unless you enjoy living in a world of MTV-fed attention spans.

**Biblio-Trivio**

The benchmark of educational television, *Sesame Street,* only runs segments from 30 seconds to the rare cap of three minutes in a constantly shifting context of colors, sounds, locations, Muppets, music, people, and objects.

## *Surprise! It's Fun*

Roger Ebert once talked about how a perfect movie-going experience is when time ceases to exist. The only world that matters is the one up on the big screen, and two hours pass by like the snap of a finger. It could be the characters' perils, or the intricate plot, the unique universe in which the story takes place, or most likely, a combination of all these aspects working in unison.

Guess what: You can experience the same thrills without shelling out $8—$12 if you like popcorn. A great book is absorbing like no other art form. Visual mediums can be life-changing, but they still demand that you see them on their terms. A book is interactive; you decide how fast, slow, thorough, or brief you want your experience to be with the narrative. A friend of mine finished a collection of Raymond Carver stories and started over from the beginning because, as he put it, "I know I missed *something*."

Reading also doesn't require much of anything:

> Step one: Get a book.

> Step two: Read it.

Watch how quickly your hour-long subway, railroad, or bus commute becomes when you're engrossed in Jane Austen. You'll be looking forward to the waiting room at the dentist's office if you're halfway through *Underworld*. Reading for pleasure is, simply put, a hell of a lot of fun.

Reading is only half the fun though: The book club throws a party for you every time you finish a book. It gives you the opportunity to hang with your homies and talk literature.

Reading groups are entertaining, interesting, informative, and probably the perfect antidote to the daily humdrum of life.

**Pro's Prose**

"We should read to give our souls a chance to luxuriate."

—Henry Miller

**Novel Ideas**

Carry a small paperback at all times. You'll be astounded at how many pages can be devoured during the time we all stand in line for things.

### The Least You Need to Know

➤ In a reading group, the time must be spent discussing the book.

➤ Reading provides a calmness that is often lost in our busy lives.

➤ People rarely get the opportunity to participate in lengthy, meaningful, intro-spective conversations.

➤ Your children will benefit by watching and emulating the art of reading and discussion.

# The Reading Kind: Where to Find Your Fellow Bibliophiles

## In This Chapter

➤ The pros and cons of friends and family

➤ Why work–based clubs are a good idea

➤ Finding those fellow readers in the neighborhood

➤ The kindness of strangers

The first thing a successful book club requires, even before the books, is a club. If you are going to be the founder of a reading group, the odds are fairly high that you will ask people you know to be a part of it. This is a common-sense approach, but not the only way to skin a cat. It is entirely possible that most of your close friends and family members view reading in the same vein as Superman sees kryptonite. But fear not, for lit lovers come in all shapes and sizes and from all walks of life. Thanks to that little piece of plastic gathering dust in your wallet called a library card, books are one of the few things that can be enjoyed across all socio-political-economic lines. The written word is the great emancipator, which truly knows no boundaries. Now that you have decided to become one of the few, the proud, the reading group members, it is time to get down to brass tacks.

### Biblio-Trivio

"Get down to brass tacks" means to start discussing important, fundamental facts of the matter. One theory of the source of the expression is that brass tacks were nailed onto a shop counter and used to measure yards of material. This technique enabled measurements to be configured rapidly and efficiently.

# Those We See Everyday

The most obvious place to begin looking for reading group members is right next to you. Or in the next room. Or asleep in your bed. Or downstairs running up your long-distance bill. Or, in the best-case scenario, sitting quietly in at the kitchen table making their way through *The Unbearable Lightness of Being* and eagerly anticipating the opportunity to share their hypotheses regarding Kundera's vision of the *soul and body.*

Just like Ms. Dorothy says, "There's no place like home."

## Family

The first territory to be mined for book clubians is where the heart is: Home.

Starting with the family is an option that is often overlooked because of the odd and always-shifting nature of the relationships we share with our flesh and blood. Most people will choose to meet with their friends, but meeting with family members does have its advantages.

### Pro's Prose

"All happy families are the same, but each unhappy family is unique in their own fashion."

—Opening line of *Anna Karenina*, by Leo Tolstoy

1. **You always know where they are.** If you live in the same general area as your family, it is usually not a major task to get everyone together. The same holds true for friends and peers, but family may consider it an obligation and thus the scheduling will be a whole lot simpler. Family may make time for each other, even to a greater degree than friends.

2. **You always know who they are.** Most people have a pretty good idea of their family members' skeletons, foibles, qualities, flaws, and positive and negative characteristics. There is a familiarity that eliminates the need for pleasantries, small talk, or natural human reservation.

3. **It's a good chance for cross-generational viewpoints.** Peer groups rarely consist of folks outside of a single generation. If you meet with a couple of siblings, a parent or two, a few aunts or uncles, and top it all off with a grandparent, you have a cornucopia of age and wisdom. You will get unique and varied perspectives, which is a major bonus when dealing with major twentieth-century works like *From Here to Eternity* or *Death of a Salesman.*

4. **It could help bring estranged family members together.** It is reckless to overstate the psychological and emotional power of a reading group, but they have been known to be cathartic under the right circumstances. Many classic novels are about the inner lives of families, and you may be able to pick the one that constructs the bridge over the long-polluted waters of your family.

5. **You have to see them anyway.** Maybe you are like the rest of us mere mortals and the regular get-togethers with "the fam" aren't necessarily a cause for celebration. A reading group is the golden opportunity for ongoing powwows with built-in conversation pieces that aren't related to questions of why you would possibly marry that troglodyte or how you could waste all of your efforts and college education on that ridiculous dream to be a writer.

**Pro's Prose**

"If you cannot get rid of the family skeleton, you may as well make it dance. "

—George Bernard Shaw

Of course, families have been known to have their occasional moments of turmoil (see the Kennedys, Cain and Abel, and every other familial unit that has graced God's green earth).

Keep in mind that using the family has plenty of drawbacks.

1. **Sometimes eight is enough; sometimes it's way too many.** You probably have that certain family member who clears the Thanksgiving dinner table faster than cold pumpkin soup. In uglier times these folks were known

**Jane Err**

Do not try to use the book club as a way to get your parents to open their lines of communication with obvious titles like *Men Are from Mars, Women Are from Venus.* First off, they will see through it right away. Second, it might happen naturally, but book clubs should not be disguises for hidden agendas.

as the black sheep. An abrasive member can quickly ruin things for everybody, and if you are going to feel obligated because he's family, it could easily become a futile endeavor with apathetic participants.

2. **Baggage, baggage, baggage.** If you are still obsessed with that "can't-miss" investment in Arctic kiwi bushels your Cousin Waldo got you into, or if Aunt Janey is royally ticked off because your father still plays golf with her ex-husband twice a week, then it ain't gonna work. Family histories can get messier than Hannibal Lecter's cutting board, so why fight a losing battle? The works you select shouldn't have to compete with real life, as if they could anyway.

3. **Mom and Dad's virgin ears.** Advanced reading groups often select material that pushes the envelope in terms of sex, violence, obscenity, and reprehensible human behavior. If your club avoids the cutting-edge choices because you don't want to discuss the raw sexuality in *Lady Chatterley's Lover* in front of your father, or your mother refuses to read past page 10 of *American Psycho* (or vice versa—conservatism crosses all demographics), you will be left with mellower books that might not provide what you were seeking in the first place. In general, different generations have different levels of acceptable material, and peer groups are more likely to meet your needs.

4. **Should Pandora's box be opened?** This is the flip side of the cathartic experience. Certain titles will bring secrets to the surface and that may not be a road worth traveling. If you have a cousin who was a victim of abuse, *A Thousand Acres* or *Affliction* might open the floodgates and cause irreversible harm. This could happen in any group, but it is much less likely with complete strangers, and friends are drawn to people with whom they feel comfortable telling their secrets. Family provides a natural safety net, but since it is first and foremost a biological one, it might not be worth the risk.

5. **Oh, it's just another one of Uncle Joe's zany ideas.** Familiarity can also lead to a relaxed attitude that torpedoes serious literary analysis. You may have relatives sign up strictly because it is an opportunity to see the family. They might join out of bloodline solidarity, but that doesn't mean they give a whit about a book club. Friends who find the idea unappealing are more likely to tell you to beat feet. Don't assume your family is as interested or excited in the idea of belonging to a book club; they may say yes because you are part of the "fam."

## Friends

Many are the friends who have graced the pages of beloved works: Winnie-the-Pooh and Christopher Robin, Robin Hood and Little John, George Milton and Lennie Small.

The majority of reading groups consist of groups of friends. It makes sense—your friends are usually the people with whom you like to congregate the most, be it on the tennis court, at the neighborhood pub, or on a cross-country trip. Unlike family, you get to choose your friends and the baggage is usually much lighter.

Keeping in mind that the rules for family basically apply to all those who might join your reading group, there are subtle differences. Here are three pluses and minuses to starting the literary endeavor with your pals.

**Pluses:**

1. **You should know where you stand (and sit).** True friends don't have a hidden agenda and probably won't insult your new club every time you leave the room to go refill the salsa bowl. You will probably feel more comfortable with your friends, and less inhibited, so kick back on the sofa and let the risqué feelings and fantasies fly.

2. **Birds of a feather …** The odds are good that you and your friends have similar tastes. It's probably got something to do with the fact that you became friends in the first place. This allows for intimate discussions of the subtext of the book, and not its content. If you happen to be a Goth, your friends are probably Goth, and *Interview with a Vampire* will be at the top of your list. Being among friends eliminates many of the petty squabbles and details that bring so many groups to a grinding halt.

3. **Formalities, schmormalities.** Friends won't care at all if you come to the reading group without a shower; or, if they do, at least you can remind them of some past indiscretion that will even the score. Your schedules will probably be along the same lines also. Having friends around means that there won't be as many hard-and-fast rules because you will know who is flexible and who isn't.

Lest we forget, though, Dr. Frankenstein and the monster were the best of friends in the beginning.

**Minuses:**

1. **Remember that time Howie stole that pig?** Friends often like to spend their time in the Proustian activity of *Remembering Things Past.* You know that the time must be spent discussing the book, but that doesn't mean that your friends won't see past events in the pages. *Rabbit* might be just like your buddy Larry, but that isn't analysis of the work. The love triangle in *Hamlet* might be the same as your best friend, Tiffany, but that's irrelevant to the task at hand (not to mention that Tiffany may be in serious need of therapy).

2. **I'll see you tonight at Café Carcass and tomorrow at the beach and …** Reading groups shouldn't feel like the same old thing. If it's successful, you'll anticipate the meetings and consider them special, like a trip to the opera or the county fair. You may see too much of your friends to ever create the energetic atmosphere that book clubs require. If you and Buster do everything together, maybe you should seek another alternative.

### Novel Ideas

If your friends aren't readers, join an existing group before you try to found a new one with them. That way, if your friends don't attempt to expand their minds and it fails, you will still have the other reading group.

3. **Homogenization ain't just about milk.** Variety is the spice of life (and not the Hollywood trade magazine for all you "industry" folks), but it isn't always the main ingredient in a group of friends. If every meeting boils down to a toss-up between Isaac Asimov, H. G. Wells, and Ray Bradbury, you may need to kick the habit. Friend-based groups can rapidly resemble genre groups if the same topic is harvested again and again. This has been known to happen with 20-something males and postmodern coming-of-age novels. Politely ask, "C'mon fellas, let's throw in some Emily Dickinson, Virginia Woolf, or Judy Blume." If they disagree, ditch 'em like that sour milk in the refrigerator of your bachelor pad.

## Those We See a Lot

Sometimes, no matter how admirable your intentions, friends and family just don't *get it.* Either your Aunt Marion thumbed through Norman Mailer's *The Executioner's Song* and found it remarkably similar to cousin Joey's grand larceny stint at Jessup, or the softball gang agrees to join your book club as an excuse to drink all of your beer and mock you for becoming "highbrow."

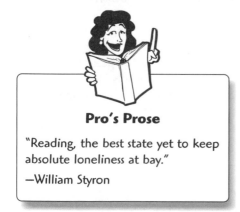

### Pro's Prose

"Reading, the best state yet to keep absolute loneliness at bay."

—William Styron

Or, perhaps you moved clear across the country, away from family and old friends, and are starting over. If you feel like Camus's *Stranger,* you may have to start a club with folks you just met. Don't feel overwhelmed in the quest to feed the literary monkey on your back its fix.

Start with those poor suckers who punch the same time clock as you.

## Co-Workers

One of the fastest growing subsets of reading groups is the workplace club. With the advent of casual Fridays and company volleyball teams, it's clear that the rules have been rewritten. One major benefit has been that companies are always searching for unique perks to keep their employees happy. One song remains the same: Happy employees are productive employees. Company-sponsored reading groups aren't a pipe dream anymore; they are springing up in surprisingly large numbers. If your workplace has an established reading group, more power to you, but if not, what are you waiting for?

If you are blazing new trails and founding a reading group at work, the first thing you should do is ask the boss if you can meet for a couple of hours a month on company time (say, two hours on the last Friday of every month). It might sound like a long shot, but you won't know until you inquire. The worst thing you will hear is "no" (unless it's "you're fired," but you can always reply with "expensive litigation"). If your boss agrees, watch your co-workers flock, anything to get out of a couple of hours of work. If Mr. Slate tells you to get back to the quarry, found a club in the off-hours.

**Novel Ideas**

Choose *The Man in the Gray Flannel Suit,* by Sloan Wilson, as your first selection. It is the definitive story of the 1950s IBM lifer employee. It provides an interesting contrast to modern freedoms and job insecurities.

The primary luxury in founding a work-based reading group is that it is relatively stress-free in terms of scheduling. Interoffice communication is already established, and you know where to find everyone you need, because they are all in the same office. Unfortunately, this has its own "opposite-sides-of-the-same-coin" dilemma.

➤ **Heads.** If you have enough eager beavers, the dam practically builds itself. Find a conference room, pick a date, and let 'er rip. It's a snap to schedule and gives ample opportunity to learn from (and about) your office mates without the normal work-related pressures.

➤ **Tails.** You may not be able to drum up any interest because it reminds your co-workers of, well, working. Lots of office toilers like to completely distance themselves from their job when the quitting whistle blows. A reading group at work is convenient, but uninspiring because of its locale or just impossible because of long hours.

One way to solve this problem is to hold meetings during an extended lunch hour off-site. That way, there will be separation from the office and no worries about post-work commitments. The only concern is getting your boss to allow a two-hour (or more) lunch break. Ask the exalted one to join, and suddenly the entire afternoon might be free.

If you are the boss, though, remember …

➤ Book club members could be reticent to share their honest feelings and emotions with the big cheese. You may want to consider reading with those of equal standing or from a different division altogether. There is nothing more annoying than a room full of parrots mimicking your views of *Treasure Island.*

➤ The openness and familiarity of the discussions could lead to a relaxed atmosphere at work that is inappropriate and undermines your authority. You definitely don't want one of your underlings throwing this out: "Gee, boss. For a woman who identifies with the inherent sexual powers Lolita wields, you sure run a bland sales meeting."

Successful reading groups can have a positive effect on your overall workplace karma. The groups are trust-building entities, and the more you trust your co-workers, the better the results. Book clubs have more depth than the falling-backward-and-having-somebody-catch-you exercise and more complex emotion than the annual golf scramble.

## Community Members

Forming a reading group with members of your community is a nice option because it brings together folks who want to improve their proverbial surroundings through close, intimate contact with those around them. It's hard to find time to meet the neighbors, especially to the depth a book club allows.

They also have somewhat of a shared background, because they belong to the same organizations, clubs, etc. Plus, you have to see the people you work with every day, so it might be a welcome change to feast your peepers on the guy you've never met who lives down the street or across the hall. It might be nice to meet the neighbors or see other churchgoers on the outside or spend time with the PTA members without debating the cost of chalk.

If all politics is local, reading groups can be as well.

➤ **Your block/cul-de-sac/apartment building/condo association.** It's not uncommon these days to have no idea of who the people are living within a five-block radius of you. Forming a group with your neighbors will create a greater sense of belonging in the area beyond the walls of your home. It's also a chance to finally meet that gorgeous woman in the double-wide trailer next to yours.

➤ **Church.** Put an ad in the bulletin or newsletter, and watch the flock flock. Book selections may end up steered toward your denomination and its dogma, but that might be what you want. If you belong to an open-minded communion, a reading group can spark comparisons between literary works and your chosen religious book.

➤ **Community centers.** Most neighborhoods have gathering places that you probably didn't even know existed. They usually have all sorts of activities to participate in and would be a great place to house a reading group. They're inexpensive (often free) and draw from a diverse age range. The elderly are more likely to be found at a community center than hanging out at the hippest coffeehouse, so a community center may have more to offer than the standard club. Along the same lines, retirement villages have a lot of people with flexible schedules and varied interests. With age comes life experience, a godsend to book club conversations.

➤ **Local union halls/political offices/volunteer organizations.** Folks who are members of these groups are already actively participating in the community. If you can avoid the polemic, grassroots headquarters can be a gold mine.

➤ **School boards/PTA/school booster clubs.** Again, it's people who already get off the couch and do something, so why not ask? The additional advantage to educational organizations is that they care about education, a primary facet of the book club experience.

## Classmates

Are you working toward a degree or taking a class or two after work or on weekends for fun? If so, you may have noticed that college campuses have always been a hotbed for book clubs. It isn't going to be a struggle to find those of your bibliophile ilk, because you already know them on a semiliterary basis. Also, starting a group with classmates is a good idea because you will basically know before you start who can carry his literary weight, have a mutual affinity for learning, and are following through on their commitments. If you wait patiently through a few classes, you will also have an idea of which students are best suited to your ideal club.

On the flip side, if you are a high school teacher, it might be professionally exciting and personally encouraging to form an after-school book club.

**Jane Err**

Always feel out a community center before trying to establish a book club. Send around a flier or post a notice to see if there is any interest, and be aware of the overriding views before you begin.

**Pro's Prose**

Iron sharpens iron; scholar, the scholar.

—The Talmud

Teenagers are a vulnerable but valuable commodity, and the only creatures on Earth who feel more alienated and misunderstood than teenagers are teenagers in the pages of great books. Ask who in your class identified with that hunky Matt Damon in *Good Will Hunting.* Give all those who raise their hand a copy of *Catcher in the Rye,* and beg them (well, they are teenagers) to read it and come to a meeting. It will quickly be Good-Bye Hunting, Hello, Holden. Here are five challenging novels to give to a high school group:

1. *The Adventures of Huckleberry Finn,* **by Mark Twain.** One of the best coming-of-age novels ever written. The story of an innocent in a world of madness, a young man trying to escape a deplorable family life. Compare Twain's usage of racial language to a Tupac Shakur album, and you will have several hours of conversation.

2. *The Catcher in the Rye,* **by J. D. Salinger.** Perhaps no book of the twentieth century is as acute in defining teenage alienation. It gets a second mention because it might be even more relevant to today's apathetic, cynical, jaded teenagers than when it was originally published.

**Novel Ideas**

Start with a book that has recently been adapted to a film the group has seen (the Gwyneth Paltrow *Emma* adaptation or the reinvented *Emma, Clueless*). It might seem like cheating, but the first book will be the toughest sale and any extra edge is worthwhile.

3. *A Hero Ain't Nothin' but a Sandwich,* by Alice Childress. Complex, heart-wrenching story of Benjie, a 13-year-old African-American male, well on his way to becoming a full-blown heroin addict. It is a powerful examination of addiction, love, and family told through multiple viewpoints.

4. *The Effect of Gamma Rays on Man-in-the-Moon Marigolds,* by Paul Zindel. A worthy introduction to plays, this is the tale of an eccentric widow and her two teenage daughters, both of whom have a hard time fitting in. This poignant work runs the gamut from pain to hope and will resonate with anyone who wishes he could magically remove the sadness and awkwardness of his mother's (or father's) life.

5. *I Know Why the Caged Bird Sings,* by Maya Angelou. An excellent introduction to poetry, Angelou gives the reader all of the joys and heartbreaks of a childhood that was violently ended before its time. Deals with two of the bigger issues facing young girls: sexual abuse and adolescent pregnancy.

## Those We See a Little

All right, all right, so you don't want to deal with any established groups, you have no friends, and you would just as soon visit the family solely on Christmas Day. You have the perfect disposition for a teenage runaway or a BMV employee. No, you are probably like the rest of us and want to start a book club but don't know enough folks to fill the roster. It is a relatively common scenario, especially for men whose friends equate book clubs with sewing circles. For instance, you might be able to get 30 guys into your basement to watch big, sweaty men throw a ball around, but mention a book club and all of a sudden it's *All Quiet on the Western Front*.

Say good riddance and try one of the following venues to find some fellow bibliophiles.

## *Bookstores*

Bookstores are a great resource for anyone looking to start a reading group. There are two types of stores that you can look to for inspiration: independent booksellers and superstores.

### Biblio-Trivio

The expression "all quiet on the western front" dates from World War I and refers to a lull or respite in fighting. The expression was adopted as the title of the English translation of Erich Maria Remarque's novel *Im Westen Nichts Neues* and was made into a movie in 1930. The popular film quickly added the expression to the American vernacular.

Small, independent bookstores are the heart and soul of the reading group revolution. They normally have numerous groups you could join, or they'll let you hang a flier and start your own. Indie denizens take their literature seriously and may not suffer fools lightly. The best thing about independent bookstores is that the proprietors aren't beholden to a corporation and are often willing to work with you in terms of price and hard-to-find items. Tougher to find, but worth it, because you are guaranteed to find book clubians, many who consider the art of reading to be their number one pastime.

Independent bookstores aren't the only hotbed of reading groups, though. Besides Oprah (whom we will discuss later), the pleasant atmosphere at stores like Barnes & Noble and Borders is one of the big reasons book clubs have become such a trend. Each store decides its own policy on reading groups, but they are very accommodating. You are more likely to find trend-watchers, casual observers, and best-seller groupies. The best thing about superstores is their convenience, comfort, and discounts on new titles.

### Jane Err

Don't try used bookstores for a bunch of copies of the same title for your group. They usually only keep a couple of copies of a book at any given time.

Regardless of whether it's an independent seller or a superstore, you can probably find fellow readers interested in whatever topics you want to cover if you comb enough bookstores.

## Local Merchants

If you simply want to start a club based on convenience, hit as many places as you can think of by your home. If *you* go there, *they* go there. Logistically, people in your neighborhood get their mundane errands done as close to home as possible, so hang a flyer at your local …

- ➤ Barber shop/hair salon/beauty parlor
- ➤ Doctor/dentist office
- ➤ Grocery/drug store
- ➤ Coffeehouse/diner/deli
- ➤ Bank
- ➤ Veterinarian/pet store
- ➤ Dry cleaner/Laundromat
- ➤ Video/record store
- ➤ Train/bus/carpool (if it is the same commute and runs on a regular schedule, this can really help pass the time)
- ➤ Movie theater (independent theaters are frequented by the same crowds as independent bookstores)

## Gyms

Another place not to overlook for potential recruits is wherever you pump iron, burn the fat, feel the pain, carbo-load, or whatever euphemism is being bandied about the ol' locker room these days. It is easy to find recognizable faces at the gym because people work out on a regular routine. The gym rats are already trying to better themselves, so why not guilt them into joining with this simple question, "Sure, you're taking care of your body, but what about your mind? You need an intellectual workout."

# Those We Never See

There is one other subset of readers to consider when putting together your starting lineup: complete and utter strangers, a totally random selection of willing participants. Hanging signs around the neighborhood will give you the opportunity to meet new readers, but in general, they can be demographically similar to you, and, at the very least, familiar faces.

Taking out an advertisement in a newspaper or putting a note on the Internet ensures that you will come in contact with the entire melting pot. And believe it or not, there are definite advantages to dealing with the unknown:

1. **The kindness of strangers.** Be it kindness, unfamiliarity, or lack of excess baggage, it can be easier to open up to those you don't know at all. You may not be able to tell your family how you really feel about Machiavelli or Iago because you want to keep up the choirboy façade, but the reading group gets all the dirty details. You can feel free to cut loose, because this is the only place you'll run into these new confidants.

2. **The fruit bowl.** Unlike a book club whose members are basically homogenous, a ragtag collection of the broad scope of personalities will have completely distinct and idiosyncratic ways of viewing the literary world. Each person will have his or her own taste, ideally complementing the others, but never subverting them. It's possible you will come across the eccentric, the obscene, the crazy, or the out-and-out bizarre, but this can be beneficial as well. Is the point of a reading group to come to a general consensus that Swift's *A Modest Proposal* is a satire, or is it to see how the written word affects varying individuals from all walks of life?

3. **The oasis factor.** It is not at all uncommon for readers to want their book club to be unlike everything in the rest of their hectic (or humdrum) lives. If meeting with friends and family is keeping you from experiencing an intellectual oasis amid the chaos, then start one with new blood. The two hours a month should be unique and important, not just part of the routine.

**Pro's Prose**

"In spite of everything, I still believe that people are really good at heart."

—Anne Frank

**Novel Ideas**

If you are already in a reading group and are satisfied but not stimulated, try a meeting at a bookstore on the other side of town or political spectrum. New ideas might be the shot in the arm you're looking for.

4. **Did you hear about King Lear's children?** The only "gossip" will be related to the text because you have no history with each other except for the books. If you want to dive in and save the family dish for Thanksgiving dinner, then get together with the woman sitting across from you on the subway reading Shakespeare. She knows absolutely nothing about the status of Cousin Merle's workman's comp claim and, better yet, probably doesn't care.

## Newspaper Ads

Newspaper ads are great because you can reach a large cross-section of folks with just one paper.

Try using the smallest local paper you can find, or an alternative weekly newspaper. Small papers often designate plenty of room for community bulletin boards, and their readership isn't overwhelming. This is especially handy if you live two hours from anybody, because you can get the book club together without making the drive to the nearest town. Local libraries always have the regional newspapers if you are accustomed to reading only the closest metropolitan paper. Alternative weeklies are usually found in metropolitan areas and are good sources because the bulk of the paper is focused on the arts. If you want to be part of a large club always guaranteed to have meetings, try one of the weeklies. You can place an ad in the classifieds for a pittance (or perhaps you want to place it in the personals and score a date with a bookworm).

## Internet Postings

Here are a few recommended sites to recruit members. These are not online clubs (we'll discuss those later); they are classified sections to submit open invitations to join your book club.

**Novel Ideas**

The *LAWeekly* Web site (www.laweekly.com) has links to numerous other weeklies from across the country, including the *Seattle Weekly* and the *Cleveland Free Times*.

➤ **www.pw.org.** Poets and Writers Web site has a classified section that is viewed by many in the literary world.

➤ **www.dmoz.org.** Has all sorts of stuff about reading groups, a good place to find preexisting ones in your area, particularly by topic (i.e., literature).

➤ **www.yahoo.com/arts/humanities/literature/ organizations/reading_groups.** Has a link specifically for starting your own book club.

➤ **www.classifiedsforfree.com.** Reaches more than 700 U.S. cities and 60 countries around the world.

➤ **www.sundaypaper.com.** You can post, edit, and delete classifieds for any region of the country.

### The Least You Need to Know

➤ Family and friends are the most convenient source for members, but consider your relationship to them before jumping in.

➤ Workplace groups are great, especially on company time.

➤ Post signs around the neighborhood to meet new readers.

➤ Starting a group with complete strangers has the benefit of members from varying walks of life and with differing opinions.

# Chapter 3

# Where Art Thou, Reading Group?

**In This Chapter**

➤ Understanding why a comfortable meeting spot is so important

➤ Members' homes are easy to use, but there are issues to resolve

➤ Numerous other alternatives available

➤ Why costs will be a concern

Legend has it that William Faulkner wrote his early works in a small shack after long shifts at the local mill. The four flimsy walls and the leaky roof over his head might be excellent material for the legend of a writer as great as Faulkner, but it's no place to start a reading group.

A comfortable meeting place is essential to a productive reading group for one simple reason: People want to spend their time in places they like. Your group should decide the most comfortable spot to hone your craft. It might be an obvious point, but it is a detail that, if overlooked, can run a reading group right off the literary rails.

## Location, Location, Location

Once you've assembled a team of dedicated readers willing to take the plunge and engage in exploring the great books of the world, everything should basically fall into place, right? Well, if the experts are accurate and God really is in the details, then there is plenty of legwork left to be done.

**Jane Err**

Don't assume everyone finds the same places comfortable as you. Rotating venues gives each meeting a distinctive feel, and everyone gets to show you his or her laughing place.

There will be a high level of excitement at this point because the group is starting to take shape. The natural impulse will be to start scouring the libraries and bookstores, working the phones, faxes, and e-mails, or pulling out the literary supplement of *The New York Times* in search of an unheralded, complex novel for the first meeting. Hold back that impulse.

Anybody who has been part of a start-up organization knows that all the good intentions in the world will go up in smoke if the meeting place of the organization isn't set in stone. It is hard enough to find time to read and explore, but think how unfortunate it would be if the brain power you expended were all for naught because the local bus doesn't run through your neighborhood.

It probably seems that finding a location for your reading group would be the simplest and most insignificant detail to worry about, but it should not be overlooked or underappreciated. If you are a member of a group of single-minded bibliophiles who carry *The Sickness Unto Death* in your pocket and discuss Kierkegaard's dissection of the corrupt soul in human nature while riding the subway, then the meeting place probably isn't important. The dedication of a group like that to words and ideas is admirable, but, let's face it, not the type of group most of us would like to join. The rest of us mere mortals want to belong to a warm, friendly, social group that gets together in an inviting location. We want to meet in a safe, comfortable, environment that mirrors the attitude and character of the group.

Ancient Roman churches still stand today because of the solidarity of their foundation. Approach your reading group with the same ideology: A well-built base keeps the walls from crumbling down. And since we're working a theme here, let's decide where your club should hang its proverbial hat.

## Home Sweet Home

The most common gathering place is in the home of one of the members. It is the most logical starting point because of convenience and familiarity. If your group is made up of friends who live in the area, this is probably the route to take, but there are two issues: accessibility and availability.

Accessibility:

➤ Is the house (or houses) centrally located?

➤ Will the accessibility be limited by the weather?

➤ Can all group members get there, even if they don't drive?

These questions are especially important if the same house is going to be the sole meeting place. Although most home-based reading groups rotate every month, it may not be possible if your group has members from a variety of spots on the map. This is common for book clubs comprised of friends drawn from greater lengths such as co-workers at a large company or parents of students at a high school that draws from all over a particular region.

**Availability:**

➤ Is the member's house always going to be available?

➤ If not, will a separate house be available at the same time and date?

➤ Will the availability fluctuate?

**Novel Idea**

If you are founding a new book club that will be meeting in the members' homes, it is a good idea to host the first discussion in your own home.

If you have taken the initiative to start the group, then you have leadership qualities that will work in your favor. You will be able to set the tone for all the meetings in the future. Inviting prospective members into your home establishes a sense of community before a single word is spoken. If the members of a group feel like part of an extended family, they will be more apt to divulge their deepest emotions down the line. Opening your home to others can be metaphorically viewed as opening the gates to the beginning of a path on a soul-searching journey. Or, opening your home to others can be concretely viewed as a place with a cozy sofa.

Another benefit of using a home for the meetings is that it solves the baby-sitting question in one fell swoop. Groups of mothers who meet over lunch are fairly common, and it is easier to bring the baby-sitter to the children than vice versa. Plus, the inverse approach often leads to absenteeism. (Four out of five baby-sitters surveyed prefer minding a larger group as well; they can charge higher rates.) Advance planning will solve the child-care issue most of the time regardless, but having an in-house sitter is one less thing to worry about.

Meeting at home is not without its potential flaws. First among them is the amount of preparation involved in hosting a meeting. If your group is satisfied with tea and cookies, it won't require a whole lot of effort. If your group requires four-star, five-course, homemade gourmet meals, it may take a full month to prepare. Either way, the host will be responsible for more than the others. A basic rotation list should even out the amount of work. If your group is going to hold every gathering at the same house, simply draw up a schedule of whose turn it is to handle the necessary preparations.

**Jane Err**

Not having a baby-sitter will guarantee interruptions. It can be in-house, but the reading group deserves to have "me" time.

### Novel Ideas

Schedule alternate discussion leaders so the host doesn't have to be concerned with both entertaining the troops and readying the topics for analysis.

Another concern is the constant flow of information we receive at our domiciles. A baby-sitter can handle the kids, but who can handle the host if you are expecting an important call, fax, letter, or e-mail? What will happen to the meeting if your long-lost Uncle Howard shows up at your doorstep with a bottle of wine and a photo album? Unlike the office, most of us enjoy the personal correspondences we receive at home. The way to avoid this problem is to strongly vocalize at an early group meeting that the *discussion* time is the *discussion* time. It may sound juvenile, but you never know what patterns people follow in the solace of their own homes. An ounce of preventative medicine goes a long way in keeping those annoying viruses at bay.

Most of us would generally agree that Dorothy hit the cornstalk on the head when she clicked her heels, dreamt of her beloved Kansas, and uttered those immortal words, "There's no place like home." Unfortunately, Dick Hickock and Perry Smith also looked out at the Kansas terrain and saw a home. It belonged to the Clutter family, whose brutal murder was examined in the Truman Capote classic, *In Cold Blood*.

### Biblio-Trivio

Truman Capote didn't use a tape recorder during the interviews for *In Cold Blood*. He deeply immersed himself in the writing process so that he could describe every conversation in detail and give the book more of a novel-type feeling.

The biggest question that will arise comes if your reading group is made up of total strangers. Inviting people you know absolutely nothing about into your home has its inherent hazards. It would be sheer paranoia to assume most strangers are brooding sociopaths, but is it worth the risk? (Lovers of the arts have been known on occasion to be certifiable oddballs. John Hinckley loved *Taxi Driver*.)

It is much more likely that you will have a group member who is too nosy, feels way too comfortable, or decides to drop in whenever she's "in the neighborhood," which seems to be every other day. There is always a decent chance that a group member will invade your personal space, because human interaction is a crapshoot at best. It might be a good idea to hold the first two gatherings with unfamiliar readers at a public venue. It won't take long for you to know whether or not you want to allow all the members into your house, because not everyone is as wholesome and friendly as the Scarecrow, the Tin Man, and the Cowardly Lion.

# Around the Neighborhood

Perhaps *the man* himself said it best: "Won't you be my neighbor?" Mr. Rogers always seemed to know the answer long before he posed the query, but the rest of us mortals have no idea. Starting a reading group provides a great opportunity to meet the people in your neighborhood. Once you have gotten the folks in your community to come on board, finding a spot in the community makes the most sense. Even if your convocations are normally going to be held in various homes, there might be an instance where it doesn't work out and a backup plan is necessary.

## *Schools*

Start with the schools. Reading groups are intellectual organisms, akin to voluntary advanced English courses. Schools usually have vacant classrooms during the course of the day and even more in the hours following the dismissal of classes. It will take some time to get the logistics squared away, but parental groups frequently spring up right before or after children are dropped off or picked up at school. Trying to hold a meeting at night may be more difficult, but it never hurts to ask. High schools are often open at night housing their own numerous clubs and functions, so if your group is flexible enough to coincide with basketball practice, student council meetings, play rehearsal, and jazz quartets, it might be time to make like Rodney Dangerfield and go *Back to School*. The summer months might be hard to negotiate, but with the changing educational standards these days, schools often don't lock their doors during the dog days.

Parents who are active in their child's school activities should know the right person to contact. Otherwise, try the principal's assistant or secretary; they always know the scheduling procedures. Meeting at a school might remind group members too much of their horror-filled high school days, but it might also make them feel like part of the educational community. Parents can teach their children well just by the example they set in the throes of literary passion.

Local colleges are also a smart place to begin. There are always plenty of available meeting rooms at the student union or campus life building. There is often a fee for these rooms, which

**Novel Ideas**

Invite teachers, administrators, janitors, coaches, or any other school employees to join your book club. It never hurts to have someone on the inside.

should be factored in when setting the ground rules (see Chapter 4, "Ground Rules, to Thine Own Self Be True"). If you used your alumni connections as a means to recruit perspective readers, it makes sense to meet on campus. Plus, it gives you another excuse to throw on your old college sweatshirt.

No matter what level, schools are institutions of learning, exploration, and personal growth—which is ideally what your reading group will become. Teachers and educators should be receptive to keeping oral and literary traditions alive.

## Community Centers

Community centers fall under the same umbrella. They all have rooms, but book yours early. Elks Clubs, VFWs, Rec Centers, YMCAs, or any other civic-minded organization should be able to honor your requests. Church basements have been holding functions since the bricks were laid, so they are worth a check. If any of the members of your group are active in their church, it should come off without a hitch.

One unforeseen problem you may come across is being asked to submit a list of selections to the key master of the precious space you long to occupy. Nine times out of 10, it will be strictly out of natural interest (or they're dropping a subtle hint to be asked to join the jamboree). There is, however, that remaining 10 percent. There are those in the world who would deny any requests for a room because of *their* judgment of the content in *your* choices. Instead of calling your tormentor a fascist imbecile, try saying …

➤ "We are all intelligent, reasonable adults here and would appreciate it if we are allowed to evaluate the material as such."

➤ "Please don't tell us what we can and cannot read. It upsets our Constitution."

➤ "If you *have* read the book and find it objectionable, please feel free to come to a meeting and share your feelings. But don't share them with me now, because I hate to talk about a book I haven't read."

➤ "You don't really want to be a leading light of the censorship movement, do you?"

➤ "I'm with you, Goebbels. In fact, let's round up all the copies of the offensive text, take them out back, and burn them to ash so that our children will look upon the demon work no more."

Community buildings house numerous organizations, so know that there will be commotion. It also might not be feasible to use the same room on the same night at the same time every meeting, which can be anathema to startup clubs. There is also the aesthetic quality of the available rooms. Rooms in organization-based buildings are often bland and uninviting (think of the cubicles at the local IRS office). Pleasant surroundings shouldn't be the number-one issue facing the book club, but happy readers are productive readers.

## Library

And who could forget the old standby, Mr. Library?

### Biblio-Trivio

The library as we know it was sprung from the brain of wunderkind Benjamin Franklin, and the original still stands today in Philadelphia, Pennsylvania.

The local library is another option for your new surroundings. A library is always a heady place for a book club's genesis. Librarians are good folk, friendly and accommodating to bibliophiles everywhere. If your group decides to make the library their permanent residence, the librarians may be able to reserve numerous copies of a certain title circulating throughout the system. This can be a money saver (see "What Price Books?" in Chapter 4), unless you are the type of person who likes to take notes in the text. Think of the fines, good reader, the fines. But otherwise, libraries are chock-full of experts—who knows more about obscure titles than those who have dedicated their lives to the science of nonprofit book lending?

The major problem with libraries is the old standby: *"Sshhh!"* It is fairly well known by now that libraries are generally quiet, studious, reserved edifices where folks from all walks of life can seek knowledge (or a nap) in peace. Loud, wild, animated discussions don't fit the bill. Civilized does not necessarily equal low-key. Successful reading groups have moments of high enthusiasm and palatable friction.

### Biblio-Trivio

Hibbing, Minnesota, had the first motorized library bus that patrons could enter. It came complete with a coal stove for the winter. This was the grandfather to the bookmobile.

Even if the local library allows for volume and excitement, you probably don't want random book lovers eavesdropping, staring, or tossing out the occasional uncouth remark.

## Follow the Money

Bookstores have been a home-away-from-home for as long as reading groups have been a part of the American culture. In 1886, Henry James wrote *The Bostonians* about affluent bluestocking lifestyles. Women would gather together to listen to a male lecture on the topic of literature, followed by a discussion of the ideas. A well-known bluestocking, Elizabeth Peabody, owned a bookstore where the women could sit and share their responses, feelings, and insights on the culture of the day. Do the "bluestockings" sound at all different from the "soccer moms" of today who spend the evening at their local book-selling behemoth, talking text?

## Bookstores

Bookstores are, of course, a viable option, but they almost always have to include the general public. Small, independent bookstores house many reading groups and have long been championing complex, cutting-edge fiction. They encourage the exploration of challenging narrative and they need your business, so why not give the little guy a chance? Although they are a dying breed, independent bookstores are worth seeking out, especially if you are looking to start a reading group with a singular focus. There are indies geared toward feminists, gays/lesbians, poets, sports fans, Marxists, animal lovers—you name it. Most of these types of specialized bookstores are found in metropolitan areas or college towns, but they are often accessible on the Internet. There is usually a locally owned and operated bookstore within driving distance, and most owners will be glad to have the business. Group discounts are standard, but give the owners fair warning.

Independent bookstores (or used bookstores, for that matter) rarely have enough room for their inventory, so don't expect much more than a circle of folding chairs. There will also be spillover from the dedicated browsers and opinionated regulars, but they are the type of interesting characters who could energize a new reading group. The advantage of starting a book group at a local bookstore is the diversity and dedication of the indie denizens. Many writers, educators, small press publishers, and serious bibliophiles consider the independent bookstores their reason for being. The breadth and depth of the selections, topics, subject matter, and titles bring out those who truly love the printed word. If you are looking for a new club that probes the text with the precision of a great sleuth, try starting at a local bookstore, Dr. Watson.

**Biblio-Trivio**

Sherlock Holmes was an admitted cocaine junkie who played the violin as his main hobby.

Chain bookstores like Borders and Barnes & Noble also have book clubs, which are generally open to the public. The dates, times, and selections can be found in the company newsletter available in the store. There are no standard policies, and each store can decide how it wants to host reading groups. If you want to join an established setting, or sit in and learn how to run a group, the megastores are a logical starting point. There are a few other advantages to spending time at the larger chains.

Readers who love book clubs often belong to more than one group. They have a personal favorite and public favorite like the clubs at Barnes & Noble. It's a good place to get the lowdown on other established clubs in the area if you don't have time to start one of your own.

Whatever book is being discussed (frequently a current or recent best-seller) is often discounted, so a brand-new hardcover could be yours for a reasonable price.

For whatever reason, if you have trepidation about joining or founding a reading group, it's easy to sit for a meeting to get a feel for how discussions are lead. Intimate groups might expect your input, but you can watch and learn without the hassle at Borders or Barnes & Noble.

## Offices

Another place to consider is an office at your workplace. Empty corporate offices or boardrooms are certainly suitable for discussions and can be reserved during the day. Cleaning crews also come after-hours, so the buildings stay open very late or all night. If your group is made up of co-workers, it might be a necessity. Suppose you work in a Manhattan advertising firm, and the members of your group come from mid-Connecticut to mid-Jersey—well, there aren't many alternatives. Getting pizza delivered to the office *can* be stimulating, but keep in mind that it is human nature to want to get as far away from work as humanly possible when the quitting whistle blows. Office space can also be used if it's your significant other's place of employment and they have the clout to secure the room, although hanging around the better half's workplace might not lead to significant examination of Albee or Woolf.

## Eateries and Drinkeries

Restaurants, coffeehouses, and bars are also home to reading groups around the globe. We will discuss the costs in the next chapter, so for now, let's talk logistics.

Restaurants are primo spots because the meetings become pleasurable outings. It is common for local eateries to accommodate groups in terms of menu, price, and availability, particularly if the gatherings take place during a slow period. If you plan on using the same restaurant month-in and month-out, make sure the choices of food pass everybody's taste and diet regulations.

### Biblio-Trivio

Japanese scientists at the University of Tokyo added extra garlic extract to the diets of mice specially bred to age quickly and found that extra garlic may prevent age-related memory disorder. Keep away the vampires and keep your mind sharp when you're old and gray.

The best reason for having your gatherings at a restaurant is because it adds an instant level of fun and relaxation. Meeting with your book club should never feel like a chore. If dining out gives your group momentum and energy, by all means treat yourself. (You may need it after dealing with a harrowing story like Toni Morrison's *Beloved*.)

Coffeehouses normally don't take reservations or have enough room to house a large club, so it would be hard to plan meetings on a regular basis. Coffeehouses are, however, ideal for the spur-of-the-moment change in plan. If your book club is flexible, ditch the usual location once in a while and head to the nearest java joint. If you're lucky, the comfortable chairs will be open for a thorough examination of an author's motifs, ridding the world of those innocuous conversations the gang of *Friends* always seems to be having. A cup of joe is a lot less to deal with than a full meal, and readers everywhere find a hot mug of coffee and a good novel were made for each other. (Besides, a dose of caffeine might be just what the doctor ordered before delving into Dostoevski's definition of the "extraordinary man" in *Crime and Punishment*.)

Bars should be voted on well in advance. There aren't many startup groups that are going to find the loud, smoky, beer-soaked tavern atmosphere conducive to debating the merits of magical realism, but there are some out there. College campuses are known for their intellectual coteries that find the nearest saloon provides the right ambience for literary exploration. Don't forget, it worked for the Beat Generation, one of the last major literary movements in America. Another reality to remember is that the level of discourse often drops in relation to the number of cocktails imbibed. (A pitcher of beer might be just the ticket to figuring out what the heck William S. Burroughs's *Naked Lunch* is all about.)

Finding the right spot for your book club is most likely going to come down to trial and error. Members' homes will most likely be where you end up, but don't be afraid to shake things up if it isn't working. Sometimes people need a change of venue to stimulate new ideas, but it won't be apparent until you are in the mix. Whatever works, works, and the group will know if it's in the right place at the right time. Finding the perfect house for your club is not the most important aspect of a book club, but it shouldn't be overlooked either. It would be a shame if your club fell apart because somebody didn't like where you put the ottoman or somebody else vowed to never set foot in a library again.

### The Least You Need to Know

➤ Finding the right place to house your group is important because you want the group to feel comfortable.

➤ Using your home is common, simple, standard procedure, but seriously consider the possible ramifications of letting strangers into your house.

➤ There are numerous other spots around the neighborhood, including schools, community centers, or bookstores.

➤ Restaurants can add excitement and enjoyment to your group.

# Chapter 4

# Ground Rules, to Thine Own Self Be True

> ## In This Chapter
>
> ➤ Setting initial ground rules will keep things running smoothly down the line
>
> ➤ Why deciding how much to spend on books is V-I-T-A-L
>
> ➤ How much to spend on food
>
> ➤ How to handle that guy who didn't finish the book

You, my friend, are almost ready to actually start reading. You've committed to taking the book club plunge, found some other eager readers to embrace your quest, and ultimately, decided on a happening spot to house the gang. From here on out, the sky is the limit. But first, it is advisable to lay down some ground rules.

Ground rules are important. You wouldn't try to build a house without a blueprint, right? Even the most experienced tradesmen won't be on the same page if the plans aren't laid out in front of them. The same goes for a reading group: You need to be on the same page as your readers before you are on the same page as your readers.

## Mark Your Calendar

Ground rules are, of course, different from the reading group golden rule, which is, in case you have forgotten:

*The time must be spent discussing the book.*

Just making sure you were paying attention. Aside from that singular nonnegotiable standard, the rest of the operation should be dictated by whatever floats your collective boat. One of the first considerations is when to meet. Most reading groups meet monthly. It's not too soon after the last meeting that finishing the book becomes a late-night cram session, and it is not too far away from the next meeting that you have to worry about forgetting the name of the main character or where it takes place.

Every six weeks is the second most popular option, but anything longer than that and even the elephants will have trouble remembering. There are go-getter book club-ians who may want to meet bimonthly, but leave the gauntlet on the floor.

### Biblio-Trivio

The word *gauntlet* comes from the French *gant,* meaning "glove." A gauntlet was a heavy leather or steel glove originally worn as a part of a suit of armor. To "throw down the gauntlet" was to issue a challenge to fight to the death. If the challenge was accepted, the opponent would pick up the thrown glove or gauntlet.

Even if you're a speed-reader, a bimonthly gathering is too much to ask of the majority of readers, and it will scare potential recruits away before their mission is accepted. At some point in the future, you may decide an occasional extra meeting is necessary to divide the examination of the book into two halves, but only the *Best and the Brightest* bibliophiles need a fix every 15 days; the rest of us in the world with too much to do already will be perfectly satiated by a single monthly seating.

The day of the week you choose doesn't matter, but assume that weekends won't be good for everyone. Sunday nights are a possibility, but weekdays are typically regimented and will entail fewer spur-of-the-moment conflicts and AWOL members.

Many book clubs take the summer months off, which would give you a chance to kick back and enjoy well-earned "light beach reading." It is a good call, because trying to juggle personal vacations, children unbound by the rigors of school, and general, heat-induced, lazy-day blahs can be maddening.

Remember, successful clubs tend to stay together for years, so even if once a month sounds like an easy schedule to you, guilt yourself into feeling you're a slacker. Think of what is best for the group in the long run.

The holiday season is also tough to navigate without a sleigh and some reindeer, so decide early on if taking a month off is necessary or strictly for reasons of convenience. Why not throw yourselves a festive little holiday party as a reward for all of your hard work? It might be the perfect antidote to the crass commercialization that dominates the shopping season.

## Set Your Watch

Selecting a time to meet is, again, completely up to the wishes of your group, but try to keep it consistent. The more leeway you offer in your ground rules, the more likely members' schedules will suddenly start having head-on collisions with the groups. Most clubs meet at one of two times:

➤ Early in the morning, after the kids are off to school. The brain is sharp, the coffee is hot, and the morning is wide-open for a *Breakfast of Champions*.

➤ Early in the evening, just about suppertime. The workday is over, the relaxing has begun, and what better way to cap off the evening than with a Nietzsche nightcap.

Of greater concern is the length of each meeting. As a rule of thumb, there will be a period of gossip before the discussion gets underway. It is to your advantage to factor the Chatty Cathys into the equation and allow for their gab time instead of asking members to come in early to socialize.

A two-hour minimum is your best bet. Leaving the first 15 minutes open for exchanging news flashes and life lessons still gives you a solid block of time to chew the literary fat.

**Jane Err**

Unless your reading group is small and tight-knit, do not agree to meet "whenever everybody finishes." Deadlines serve a purpose—to quell the natural human tendency to procrastinate. It might sound laid-back, but you'll be sorry.

**Novel Ideas**

Choose a holiday-themed short story. They take less time to read, but don't make any less of an impact. Plus, the right selections can reinforce the deeper meaning of the season. Two suggestions: *A Christmas Memory*, by Truman Capote, and *The Gift of the Magi*, by O. Henry. (P.S. They are both life-affirming—not a bad way to feel during the holiday season.)

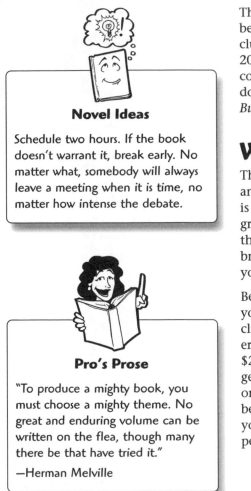

### Novel Ideas

Schedule two hours. If the book doesn't warrant it, break early. No matter what, somebody will always leave a meeting when it is time, no matter how intense the debate.

### Pro's Prose

"To produce a mighty book, you must choose a mighty theme. No great and enduring volume can be written on the flea, though many there be that have tried it."

—Herman Melville

The biggest question concerning length of time must be weighed against the number of members. All book clubians *should* have their say, but common sense says 20 minutes won't give 10 people much of a chance to comment on *Moby Dick,* and two people probably don't need eight hours to spout their opinions of *Billy Budd.*

# What Price Books?

There are always going to be costs involved in the ebb and flow of a top-notch reading group. Sorry folks, it is the way of the world. Well, maybe not. If your group decides everybody has to get their books from the library and that the only refreshments will be cups brought from home filled with water from the tap, you have found yourself a bibliophile bargain.

Before you decide on any other matter of protocol, you should agree on a book-spending limit for your club. It is the one aspect that puts a bad taste in readers' mouths if one member continuously selects a new $25 hardcover, and the rest of the members were budgeting for an $11 softcover. Having the books is the one constant in a sea of variables. Other expenses can be as limited or grandiose as your group desires, but you will need books. Otherwise it's just a room full of people.

### Biblio-Trivio

Book theft goes back to the original Greek libraries. The crime became so rampant in the Middle Ages and the Renaissance that in 1752 Pope Benedict XIV proclaimed that book thieves would be punished with excommunication.

# Buying

The amount spent on books is a topic that must be ironed out right off the bat. Most book clubs purchase their wares for a variety of reasons, including …

➤ You may want to start highlighting and making notes in the margins, which is frowned upon by librarians across the globe.

➤ You will (or already have) want to start your own lending library, to introduce friends, children, Romans, countrymen, and so on to the titles that made a lasting impression on you.

➤ Books become part of the psyche, and having them on your shelves can be a reminder of days gone by. You will remember where, when, and why certain books marked certain occasions in your life. Just like an old song or a forgotten scent, revisiting long-time favorites can open the emotional floodgates.

➤ There is no pressure to get them back to the library anytime soon. This is a problem with current best-sellers, because they are usually available for a shorter length of time, sometimes only a week. Also, books can be recalled if there have been numerous requests for it. If you want to be guaranteed the opportunity to have the book at the meeting, buying it is the way to go.

➤ If you tend to get your head stuck in the clouds, the library fines will add up over the years and you will pay for the books anyway.

Once you have made the decision to purchase your books, you need to decide how you will do this. Will you buy the books as a group, or individually? Book clubs typically purchase their selections as a whole because it is cheaper and everyone is guaranteed a copy. Another advantage of group buying is everyone has the same version, with the same notes, and can refer to the same pages when called upon. I doubt very much if you need instruction on how to complete the transaction for a single book, so let's look at total group purchasing power.

The reason group purchasing is cheaper is because usually a bookseller can be found who will offer discounts. Let your local bookstore know that this will be a regular purchase, and you should be able to score bargain books.

**Novel Ideas**

Appoint a treasurer right away, so no matter how you decide to split the costs, someone is keeping track. Money issues are the number one cause of book club strife, and a meticulous treasurer will help maintain financial order. Not all groups will have dues, but there are always small expenditures to keep in line. Inequality in monies put forth can drive a major stake into the heart of any reading group.

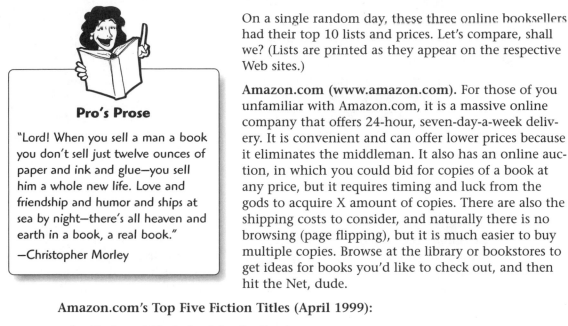

**Pro's Prose**

"Lord! When you sell a man a book you don't sell just twelve ounces of paper and ink and glue—you sell him a whole new life. Love and friendship and humor and ships at sea by night—there's all heaven and earth in a book, a real book."

—Christopher Morley

On a single random day, these three online booksellers had their top 10 lists and prices. Let's compare, shall we? (Lists are printed as they appear on the respective Web sites.)

**Amazon.com (www.amazon.com).** For those of you unfamiliar with Amazon.com, it is a massive online company that offers 24-hour, seven-day-a-week delivery. It is convenient and can offer lower prices because it eliminates the middleman. It also has an online auction, in which you could bid for copies of a book at any price, but it requires timing and luck from the gods to acquire X amount of copies. There are also the shipping costs to consider, and naturally there is no browsing (page flipping), but it is much easier to buy multiple copies. Browse at the library or bookstores to get ideas for books you'd like to check out, and then hit the Net, dude.

**Amazon.com's Top Five Fiction Titles (April 1999):**

1. *Single and Single,* by John Le Carré
   Hardcover, list price: $26
   Our price: $18.20; you save $7.80 (30 percent)

2. *The Testament,* by John Grisham
   Hardcover, list price: $27.95
   Our price: $19.57; you save $8.38 (30 percent)

3. *Tara Road,* by Maeve Binchy
   Hardcover, list price: $24.95
   Our price: $17.47; you save $7.48 (30 percent)

4. *Hush Money,* by Robert B. Parker
   Hardcover, list price: $22.95
   Our price: $16.07; you save $6.88 (30 percent)

5. *Apollyon: The Destroyer Is Unleashed (Left Behind),* by Tim F. Lahaye,
   Jerry B. Jenkins
   Hardcover, list price: $19.97
   Our price: $13.98; you save $5.99 (30 percent)

**Amazon.com's Top Five Nonfiction Titles (April 1999):**

1. *All Too Human: A Political Education,* by George Stephanopoulos
   Hardcover, list price: $27.95
   Our price: $19.57; you save $8.38 (30 percent)

2. *The Greedy Hand: How Taxes Drive Americans Crazy and What to Do About It,* by Amity Shlaes
   Hardcover, list price: $22.95
   Our price: $13.77; you save $9.18 (40 percent)

3. *Something More: Excavating Your Authentic Self,* by Sarah Ban Breathnach
   Hardcover, list price: $20
   Our price: $14; you save $6 (30 percent)

4. *The Courage to Be Rich: Creating a Life of Material and Spiritual Abundance,* by Suze Orman
   Hardcover, list price: $24.95
   Our price: $14.97; you save $9.98 (40 percent)

5. *Business @ the Speed of Thought: Using a Digital Nervous System,* by Bill Gates, Collins Hemingway (Contributor)
   Hardcover, list price: $30
   Our price: $21; you save $9 (30 percent)

**Barnes & Noble (www.barnesandnoble.com).** Barnes & Noble is one of the two leading "superstores," mentioned earlier. They also sell books online, and here are their top 10 (combined fiction and nonfiction) for one day.

1. *The Pilot's Wife,* by Anita Shreve
   Paperback
   List price: $13.95
   Our price: 8.37
   You save: $5.58 (40 percent)

2. *Vittorio the Vampire: New Tales of the Vampires,* by Anne Rice
   Hardcover
   List price: $19.95
   Our price: $13.96
   You save: $5.99 (30 percent)

3. *The Reader,* by Bernhard Schlink
   Paperback
   List price: $11.00
   Our price: $6.60
   You save: $4.40 (40 percent)

4. *The Girl Who Loved Tom Gordon,* by Stephen King
   Hardcover
   List price: $16.95
   Our price: $10.17
   You save: $6.78 (40 percent)

5. *Business @ the Speed of Thought: Using a Digital Nervous System,* by Bill Gates, Collins Hemingway
   Hardcover
   List price: $30
   Our price: $18
   You save: $12 (40 percent)

6. *Bittersweet,* by Danielle Steel
   Hardcover
   List price: $26.95
   Our price: $18.86
   You save: $8.09 (30 percent)

7. *Yesterday, I Cried: Celebrating the Lessons of Living and Loving,* by Iyanla Vanzant
   Hardcover
   List price: $22.00
   Our price: $15.40
   You save: $6.60 (30 percent)

8. *The Pilot's Wife,* by Anita Shreve
   Hardcover
   List price: $23.95
   Our price: $14.37
   You save: $9.58 (40 percent)

9. *The Greatest Generation,* by Tom Brokaw
   Hardcover
   List price: $24.95
   Our price: $17.46
   You save: $7.49 (30 percent)

10. *Healing Back Pain: The Mind-Body Connection,* by John E. Sarno
    Hardcover
    List price: $13.99
    Our price: $11.19
    You save: $2.80 (20 percent)

**Powell's (www.powells.com).** A third hot spot for online buying you will want to be aware of is Powell's bookstore in the Portland, Oregon, area. They are a beloved institution for American bibliophiles and are renowned for their collection of both new and used books and books that are no longer in print. If your group is willing to wait for a couple of years for a particular title, hardcovers can be had at rock-bottom prices.

They list how many used copies they have at any given time as well, so you might be able to mix-and-match and save a couple of bucks each month. Older titles and classics are more likely to be found in the used section. For example, on one particular day, there were no used copies of *Memoirs of a Geisha,* but there were four used copies of *The Sun Also Rises.*

Powell's also offers enormous discounts on honored and respected titles of recent years. Books only have a limited hardcover shelf life, and Powell's scoops up the remaining titles for resale (and not coincidentally, they're frequently book club favorites). For instance, *The Ghost Road,* by Pat Barker, winner of the 1995 Booker Prize and the third installment of Barker's World War I trilogy, lists for $21.95 for a hardcover edition, but costs a mere $5.98 from Powell's.

Let's look at Powell's top five, and a few out-of-print options.

1. *Memoirs of a Geisha,* by Arthur Golden
   Paperback
   New price: $14

2. *The Pilot's Wife,* by Anita Shreve
   Paperback
   New price: $13.95
   Used: $9.95

3. *The Reader,* by Bernhard Schlink
   Paperback
   New price: $11
   Used: $7.50

4. *A Mouse Called Wolf,* by Dick King-Smith
   Children's/Young Adult
   Paperback
   New Price: $4.99

5. *A Widow for One Year,* by John Irving
   Paperback
   New price: $14.95
   Used: $11.95

Although the preceding lists contain best-sellers, they are meant to show what you can generally expect to pay for selections. Mass-market copies of classics in the public domain are a little less, but these prices are standard. The nice thing about shopping online is that you can be sure all of the books show up at your doorstep in a timely fashion. You may be the type of person who loves to scour the shelves looking for titles off the beaten path, but buying them for every group member is easier online. You can buy the requisite number of copies at the store of your choice, but you may find that you end up running all over town trying to find "only" two more. (Try getting 12 best-sellers around Christmastime.) Plus, the cost of the books is consistent with the store, even with the cost of shipping. The elimination of the middleman ensures the nickels and dimes are equal.

**Novel Ideas**

Try online used bookstores as well (such as www.usedbooks.com) to search selection and price.

If you are only buying a copy for yourself each month, check out the used bookstores in your area. They are normally a few dollars cheaper than the prices listed here, but they rarely have more than two or three copies of a particular book.

## Borrowing

Let's assume nobody who pines to be in a reading group needs a detailed explanation on how a library works. If you do, a book club might be out of your league at this point. As far as reserving numerous copies of a book for your club, it is possible, but it would take a conscientious member to keep everything on track. Libraries keep their books circulating, so getting 10 copies of a popular title might take months of advance planning. If, however, your group can't afford to buy books, or if they want to spend their allowance on steak and lobster, give the library at least a 60-day notice, more if you want a current rave.

# Food, Glorious Food

The cost of grub is another factor to consider. Obviously, if your group meets at a restaurant, bucks will have to be shelled out for dinner. Restaurant clubs usually work out a group discount beforehand and just divide up the bill like any other night out for dinner. Home-based clubs have to decide what sort of food to serve and then adjust the payment plan accordingly. Following are a few possible options:

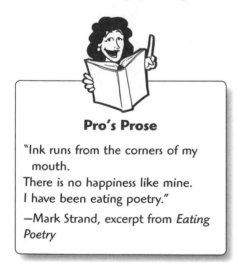

**Pro's Prose**

"Ink runs from the corners of my mouth.
There is no happiness like mine.
I have been eating poetry."

—Mark Strand, excerpt from *Eating Poetry*

➤ **O solo mio.** This will only work if money is not that big an issue to your club, or the snacks are cost-efficient and simple to prepare. If it is cheese and crackers one month, followed by veggies and dip, and so on, then no problem. But, if one reader offers saltines and margarine and the next filet mignon, the discrepancies in time and money will become the focal point and the tension will ruin the book discussion. Some groups only serve coffee, soda, and various cheap, no-frills lit group grub. Others serve their just desserts, which is nice because sweets are relaxing "comfort food" and can be picked up from a bakery on the way over or made the night before if you fancy yourself a baker.

➤ **Community chest.** Set a monthly due (say $5 or $10) and give the money to a different member each month to whip up a feast fit for a king (or the King if you live in Memphis and like fancy fried-peanut-butter-and-banana sandwiches). Or, go with the staple of church picnics everywhere: the potluck supper. This way, everyone brings a different part of the meal and the host won't have to prepare the entire shebang. If you plan on serving dinner, make notes as to who can and can't eat what, so that one vegan member isn't stuck with a bloody side of beef.

➤ **Big nights.** Save all your ducats for the occasional, larger, celebration (maybe Louis Prima will show up, who knows?). Maybe three times a year a big, potluck supper is had and the other meetings are just coffee and doughnuts. Many groups have event/theme reading group parties (which we will discuss later) a few times a year instead of something formal every month. It makes the parties special and keeps the other months simple.

**Novel Ideas**

Don't ask one person to prepare both the food and the book discussion, especially if you enjoy full-course meals. Inevitably, it will be the literary preparations that suffer. Rotate, rotate, rotate.

**Novel Ideas**

If one member of your club loves to entertain and wants to prepare the food every month, let him. Some folks thoroughly enjoy the kitchen, and why burden those who consider warming a can of Chef-Boy-R-Dee ravioli *cooking?* Just make sure the costs are split evenly (this includes provision of paper plates and beverages, too).

Here are a few other costs you may need to keep in mind when figuring out your initial budget:

➤ Baby-sitting. If even one member has a young child, it will be necessary to ensure there are no disruptions.

➤ Postage. Many groups end up sending out dates, times, etc., because it is easier than phone tag.

➤ Transportation. This probably won't be much, but should be noted nonetheless.

➤ Birthday/holiday/anniversary/graduation gifts (after a year these tend to become automatic)

➤ Leader fees (which we will cover in the next chapter)

Don't get scared off by the potential costs. For the first few months, keep your meetings very basic and see how it plays out. You may find that it ends up being the best possible way you could blow $20 or so a month.

# Procedures

There are an infinite number of ways to run a book club, and we will cover a few of them in the next chapter. But, before you sit down, there are two definite policy decisions to be made. They should stand pat because they are two situations that could derail your book club faster than a speeding bullet.

## Absenteeism

What do you do with a repeatedly AWOL member? Absenteeism can really damage a small group and lead to resentment during the odd months that said phantom shows up. Naturally, give the person a couple of chances, because there may be legitimate excuses. Don't ask what they are, though, because this isn't junior high civics class. If it reaches a third offense, however, have a member pull the delinquent aside and politely mention that the group misses his or her monthly insights. If the problem persists, consider whether it is a big issue or a minor inconvenience. The absolute last thing you want to deal with is battle lines drawn over procedural issues. If numerous book clubians fail to show month after month, it might be time to start anew.

### Novel Ideas

If you are the one who comes to the meeting without finishing the book, don't, I repeat, don't be the one who asks questions that you would have known the answer to had you completed the reading. Only discuss what you read, and if that's almost nothing, sit down and shut up.

## Late Birds

The same holds true for punctuality. Sure, we all run late every now and again. You don't have to stand at the front door with a stopwatch, but being more than 15 minutes late on a regular basis can become irksome to other members who manage to show up on time. A member who is constantly late *is* disrupting the meeting and may have to be confronted on the spot. No need for a firing squad, but a gentle reminder from the group as a whole that the lateness is seriously cutting into time that would be better spent discussing the book is completely within the realm of understanding.

If the problem persists, you may consider one of two things: 1) begin the discussion on time and do not wait for the late bird to arrive, or 2) ask the Johnny-come-lately to gracefully step out of the group. The latter is a last resort and will be discussed later.

# Situational Illiterateeism

Unfortunately, various calamities keep members from *reading* the assigned text. The problems arise when it is the same slacker each month who just wants to socialize. Again, it is up to your group, but make sure the person knows that you *will* be discussing the ending. It will affect members' moods if one or two never finish, so you may want to adopt a California prison mentality: "three strikes and you're out."

As Tom Cruise's mother said in *Risky Business:* "Use your best judgment, Joel. Your father and I trust you very much."

---

### The Least You Need to Know

➤ Procedural consistency in terms of dates, times, and monthly costs will keep things running smoothly.

➤ The amount of money spent on books has to be established early on, but there are ways to purchase them on the cheap.

➤ Food isn't essential, but it sure adds to the comfort level.

➤ Don't be the one who never shows up on time, or shows up never having read the book.

---

# Part 2
# Behold, the Beauty of Discussion

*This part of the book will help your reading group in its quest for the ultimate discussion. It delves into the thorny issue of assigning leadership and gets to the bottom of all the personality types for which you'd best be prepared. It also offers the inside scoop on upping the 10 percent of the gray matter that's used to 12 percent, or even 15 percent, and settles once and for all the question of how to know if you are doing it right.*

*Oh yeah, it also goes where few book club books fear to tread and addresses the question: Did Oprah invent these things or what?*

# Chapter 5

# Take Me to Your Leader, Reader

## In This Chapter

➤ Why jotting down some general goals is important

➤ How to choose a leader

➤ Do you need to hire a professional?

➤ Did Oprah invent book clubs?

At this point, all of your organizational *t*'s should be crossed and all of your foundational *i*'s should be dotted. The details have been attended to and the ducks are in a row. It is time to start examining a book, page by page, word by word, discussion by discussion.

Every book is an island of intrigue unto itself, but a plan of attack can be developed to ensure that you get the most out of your meetings. There is no magical formula for success, but there are patterns that emerge and ways to recycle the methods for digging up the discussion diamonds, to get to the meat of the matter, to pull the rabbit from the literary hat. Basically, this chapter will help you prepare and pull off a proper, positive, productive, prose-probing powwow.

### Biblio-Trivio

*Powwow* is an American Indian word that originally meant a medicine man or sorcerer. Later, the word came to represent a conjuring ceremony and, eventually, a council or conference.

# Going for the Goal

Ideally, your reading group will become a source of pride, inspiration, and intense introspection. The other members will become shipmates on your journey, but it will be the personal *Odyssey* that resonates the deepest. And, as a bonus, there won't be any Cyclopes to battle along the way. As I stressed in an earlier chapter, though, it's best to work out the particulars ahead of time before you dive in. One way to do this is to set some goals for yourself and for the group.

## *Personal Progress*

Before you sit down and open the virgin text, jot down a simple set of personal progress goals. Reading groups are inherently devised to be the antithesis of everyday goal-oriented entities (staffs, teams, parties, organizations), because they are crafted around the process, not the results. Loving the process more than the product is easier said than done in American society. It may take a while for your group to grasp the concept of reading and analyzing strictly for the sake of reading and analyzing, so start by preparing yourself. Write up a progress sheet without stressing concrete goals. Your progress sheet should reflect the hopes you have for inner development, not a "must do" list. Before the first meeting, everyone in the group should do the same.

### Pro's Prose

"But words are things, and a small drop of ink,
Falling like dew, upon a thought, produces That
Which, makes thousands, perhaps millions, think."

—Lord Byron

Write down a few personal goals and put them in a safe place for six months. Take it down from the fireplace after half a year with your book club and see if the group is helping to fulfill the goals you set for yourself.

Remember, this is not a laundry list of items to be scratched off as they're accomplished. You should take some time and think about what you really want to get from your reading group experience. Go ahead—light a fire, fill a bubble bath, whip up a chocolate shake, walk through a park, ride a bike, choose whatever activity is perfect for you to relax and think. You have the opportunity to create something truly special, an intellectual safe haven, an oasis of reflection and growth, and a personal goal sheet is the first step. You may even choose to write down open-ended questions, so that there will be room for analysis whenever you take the list down.

Here are a few suggestions for your personal goal sheet:

➤ Do I see myself differently in any way? Why?

➤ Have the books opened any lines of communication or any new strains of internal reflection?

➤ Finish this sentence: "I never realized that …"

➤ Have any of the books truly affected me? If not, why? And if so, how?

➤ Finish this sentence: "I saw myself in (insert character's name) because of the way …"

**Jane Err**

Don't list "read *War and Peace*" (or any other book for that matter) as a personal goal. The selections will frequently be out of your hands, and, more important, the goals should be geared toward individual expansion, not setting a record for the number of pages read.

A personal progress sheet is all about you, so tailor the questions/suggestions/ideas to your personal, emotional, and intellectual needs.

Don't out-think your personal goal sheet, though. There is no correct way to write one, and if it doesn't flow naturally, write one suggestion. It could be as basic as, "I will take notes and pay attention to the books I read, so that my time is well spent." The goal sheet is just a way to prepare yourself for the exciting new experience.

**Novel Ideas**

If you find that your personal progress sheet doesn't hold water after a year, update it by adding a new goal, changing the tone of the questions, or deepening the heart of the queries. It is a simple way to keep challenging yourself and strengthening your approach.

# Group Goals

At your first meeting, after the organizational mumbo-jumbo, it might be helpful to inscribe a few group goals. It can aid in setting the appropriate mood, and it is also a way of getting everyone involved at the beginning, to strike while the iron is hot, as they say.

### Biblio-Trivio

"Strike while the iron is hot" refers to a blacksmith's iron, not a domestic iron. When the blacksmith hammers the horseshoes into shape, the iron must be very hot to bring about the required form. The expression means to act at the precise moment to garner maximum results.

### Pro's Prose

"Let us not look back in anger or forward in fear, but around in awareness."

—James Thurber

The group goal sheets are probably not going to be as ethereal, meaningful, complex, or introspective as the personal goal sheets, but they can be useful in their own right. They are commonly more concrete and practical than their personal sister sheets, but they can clarify your group's initial vision.

The "vision thing" is important because all groups are unique organisms, but their cells are composed of the same DNA: books and readers. Again, don't sweat the smallest of stuff, just get some general, attainable goals down on paper.

Here are a few suggestions for your group goals sheet:

➤ To accept the selections with an open mind.

➤ To read with diligence and focus.

➤ To allow for everyone's opinions and viewpoints, no matter how divergent from each other.

➤ To accept members for who they are and their individual likes/dislikes.

➤ To avoid allowing personal issues to get in the way of group discussions.

## Group Charters

I know of a few groups that have gone as far as incorporating what they hope to achieve into a charter. It is certainly not necessary, but it can be an important physical manifestation of your enterprise: a concrete symbol of the intangible rewards your group wants to garner.

Here is a basic example of a group charter that you may want to draw up:

> We, the members of this reading group *(insert your names here)*, founded upon *(insert date)* will work toward becoming a cohesive, open-minded, thorough club of readers. We will listen to and respect each individual's views, opinions, reactions, and feelings. We will leave our daily personal trials and tribulations at home and check our egos at the door. We will strive for focused examinations of a wide variety of selections. We will spend the time discussing the book.
>
> Sincerely,
>
> *(Members' signatures)*

If you don't care for this example, write your own. It's your group, for Pete's sake! You make the rules.

## Follow the Leader

All reading groups will have a leader. Like it or not, small group (not to mention human) dynamics dictate that somebody will naturally assume the leadership role. The trick is to make sure that members don't feel like their collective toes are being stepped on by a power-hungry zealot. Or, in English, you don't want your group divided from the get-go over who gets to run the show.

Most groups will meet and try to give everyone a fair shot at leading a particular meeting. But, there are as many ways to run your group as there are books from which to choose, so if you want to march to the beat of a different leader, feel free. Your mantra should never waver from a plain truth: Whatever works,

**Novel Ideas**

Print up your charter on thick bond paper and pass it around at your first (or next) meeting to get each member's signature. Make copies for everyone in the group, frame the original one, and proudly display it each month. It becomes a formal representation of your group and a fine keepsake.

**Pro's Prose**

"Of the best rulers, the people (only) know that they exist; the next best they love and praise; the next they fear; and the next they revile. When they do not command the people's faith, some will lose faith in them, and then they resort to oaths! But (of the best) when their task is accomplished, their work done, the people all remark, 'We have done it ourselves.'"

—Lao-tzu, *The Wisdom of Laotse*

works. Period. Don't assume that because one elderly woman prepares every aspect of your meetings, you're doing it wrong. It's not likely that one member would be happy looking after every detail, but it's in the realm of possibility.

## *Dictatorships*

Some reading groups crave a strong, forceful, all-powerful leader—a literary Louis Philippe. This is a typical scenario when one book clubian has to enlist the services of friends who aren't as gung-ho on spending an afternoon on the sofa hashing out the comparison between French culture and American politics in Carole Maso's *An American Woman in a Chinese Hat.* If the book club is working, but you instinctively know that the wheels will come off if somebody else has to take the mantle for even a single meeting, so be it. Dictatorships are often used for the first few months and then abandoned when the group becomes more cohesive and familiar. There are a few other instances in which this is the best-case scenario:

➤ Dictatorships can work if one member is significantly less busy than the others. Say, for instance, one member is a swinging bachelor and the rest of the members all have a couple of rug rats.

➤ They can also be quite successful if one member leads, but is assisted by a different member each month. This might take place over the course of the first year if one member has substantially more reading group experience than the others.

➤ Dictatorships are standard in publicly held book clubs that have open admissions and are designed to have a single leader.

➤ A final way that dictatorships can be the way to go is if there is a literary expert among novice, or inexperienced, readers.

The problem with dictators is, of course—well, they're dictators. Even the most thoughtful and conscientious ruler will cross the line at some point. Grade-A reading groups invariably use a tremendous amount of give-and-take, which runs on an opposite track than a despot. Here are four warning signs that one person is wielding too much power:

1. If your leader automatically chooses the selections and they are all similar, it won't be good for discussion. You'll know it is time for a leadership shift if your selection "leap" goes from Louis L'Amour to Zane Grey.

2. If the members vote unanimously for a coup or they're seceding, it's probably not working.

3. If your reading group Xerxes "decides" who gets to speak, when they get to speak, and for how long, it's time to say you want a revolution.

4. If the members of your group dread showing up to (or frequently skip) the meetings and privately tell you that the leader is the reason, think about the future. If you don't say something to the power-hungry lord almighty, you will be stuck discussing *The Art of War* one-on-one.

Dictatorships rarely last for more than a couple of months because it doesn't work for either side. Said leader will burn out from having to do all the work, guaranteed. The other members will also want to do their share, and part of the fun is picking a complex book and preparing the discussion questions. Sometimes, dictatorships are necessary in public settings, but private reading groups normally want an equal, communal setting.

## Democracies

Our democracy is, in political theory, the reason you and I are able to have reading groups wherever we want and to read whatever book we choose. Democracies are fair and equal and attempt to give all of society an equal opportunity to vote. They encourage individual liberty and cultural freedom, so why are democracies not always the best choice for book club leadership?

Our usage of the term *democracy* is defined by the idea that each book clubian is an equal member and has an equal vote. Ballots will be cast and the majority rule will become the law of the land, or at least, the formulation of the convocation. It is a fair system that can be utilized from the outset.

Voting democratically is always effective and will most likely be the route your club takes. Just be aware that there are a few potential pratfalls.

Majority rule works well for organizational details, places, times, means of transportation, and so on, but can be tricky when it comes down to picking titles and the subsequent examinations. The first method that comes to mind to put book-clubian democracy to work is the good ol' show of hands. There are five primary reasons why a show of hands may not work:

**Novel Ideas**

If you find yourself as the initial designated leader, try to get others to lead discussions and preparations within a couple of months. It will help the overall growth exponentially, and you won't fall into a permanent role that will become stale in a hurry.

**Pro's Prose**

"Only a company that is rich and safe can afford to be a democracy, for a democracy is the most expensive and nefarious kind of government on earth."

—H. L. Mencken

1. Prospective titles will be chosen by members based on whether or not the group will vote yes. Subconsciously, it may leave worthy titles on the shelf. For instance, if you happen to know that a few of your fellow book clubians aren't partial to nonfiction titles, you may avoid suggesting some books that you've been curious to read. Thus, you and your cohorts may miss out on some great discussions spurred on by a title in this genre.

**Novel Ideas**

A great way to collectively decide book selection is for each member of your group to put the name of a book on a piece of paper and put it in a hat. The person whose book is selected hosts the next meeting. At that next meeting, that person's name doesn't go in the hat, and so on at each meeting until each member has had the opportunity to have his or her book read.

2. Voting on issues brings an inherent division to every meeting. If certain members feel like they are always on the losing side of the vote, they might feel like a lesser part of the unit.

3. Democratic voting still doesn't answer the question of leadership. If you choose to vote in a leader, that person is still going to make the bulk of the decisions like a dictator. The majority rule ends up giving one person the bulk of the workload.

4. As a practical matter, holding votes takes up time that could be spent analyzing great political tomes like *The Federalist Papers* or *Common Sense*.

5. Voting may wipe out an author that you had one unfortunate experience with earlier in the life of the reading group. Nobody knocks it out of the park every time at bat, so just because your group hated the *Iliad* doesn't mean they won't love the *Odyssey*.

## Socialists

For all intents and purposes, socialism tends to work well for reading groups. By our definition, socialism simply means that everybody has the same task, to select a book and prepare the monthly discussion of the book. This setup will inspire your fellow members to come to the meetings fully prepared, giving each meeting the potential to be outstanding. This method also affords the closet sci-fi nut to upend the norm and throw *The Time Machine* or *The Hobbit* into the mix, the classics fanatic can suggest *Emma,* and the lover of modern fiction can check out Alice Munroe's latest endeavor. Sharing the workload eases the strain on members and makes each meeting a standout. A single leader is not going to put forth maximum effort every month, but twice a year, it's gangbusters. Plus, the democratic model will always be a part of your group because voting is often essential to decisions.

There may be an issue if the member hosting isn't a great speaker and has trouble articulating all of the questions and information he or she brought for show-and-tell, but another group member can always step in and assist.

## Professionally Led

The raging book club market has given birth to a whole new commercial enterprise: the professional reading group leader. We are going to assume that the rotating member-led system is successful most of the time because the designated leader goes all out in preparing the discussion material for the monthly meeting. But, what if nobody in your book club really has a clue? It might be time to call in the experts.

Professional leaders know how to facilitate a discussion. They know what to look for in your selections and how to find it, different techniques for jump-starting debates, and of course, the best titles in the literary universe.

So, what's the drawback? They don't lead for free. There is no set standard or pay scale, but it might be an extra expense your reading group members aren't willing to incur. Especially considering that professional leaders are most effective if they attend a series of meetings, even up to a year, because it takes that long for all of their wisdom to sink in with all the members. It's a tough call, because many start-up reading groups aren't sure what they're in the market for and need time to see what they're all about and weigh their options.

The trick is to take turns leading your meetings as thoroughly and intellectually as possible. Photocopying pictures of the Globe Theater from an encyclopedia and watching Leonardo DiCaprio in *Romeo and Juliet* to describe the love scenes doesn't count as "preparing" for Shakespeare. A professional leader can set you on the right track, but enthusiastic members are the key to a successful operation.

If you want to find a professional leader try looking at an independent bookstore. You might get lucky with the price if your group agrees to meet at the store the first few times and promises to purchase their selections there. The other places to look are the Internet, the phone book (usually in big cities), community centers, and college bulletin boards. The best way is through word-of-mouth, because professional leaders usually build their reputations and careers by asking friends to pass their name along. Hit the closest campuses and start asking around the English or creative writing departments; it won't take long to find an expert.

**Novel Ideas**

Hold a few meetings before deciding whether or not to bring in a professional. You might already have a couple of readers who lead with clarity and intelligence, and thus, it would be money wasted. Or, on the other hand, you will know what your group's glaring weaknesses are after a few sessions, and a professional can come in to observe and fix whatever ails you.

## Celebrity Led (a.k.a. Oprah-Fi)

Contrary to popular belief, Oprah Winfrey did not invent the book club. She may have brought it to the masses and packaged it for the average Joe or Josephine, but she is not the almighty creator.

It can't be denied that Ms. Winfrey has spread reading fever across the land. Her critics argue that she has helped push the cause of mass-market entertaining books at the expense of deeper literary works. First off, her selections aren't all pabulum; a woman named Toni Morrison carries a bit of literary weight. Second, and most

### Pro's Prose

"I find television very educational. Every time someone turns it on, I go into the other room and read a book."

—Groucho Marx

important, is that it is hard to fault someone who promotes literacy in any form, even from the idiot box. The major drawback to basing your monthly meeting on Oprah's selection is that thematically, many of her books are similar, and once in a while it is good to throw your group a curveball.

The only thing is that Oprah's book club isn't a book club if you are sitting at home with the remote in your hand. She can't hear you, but the other possible members will. Follow her lead and start your own.

Here is the list of past selections from Oprah's book club, starting with the latest offering. (Note that most of these books are on both Barnes & Noble and Powell's top 10 lists in Chapter 4, "Ground Rules, to Thine Own Self Be True.")

➤ *The Pilot's Wife,* by Anita Shreve
➤ *The Reader,* by Bernhard Schlink
➤ *Jewel,* by Bret Lott
➤ *Where the Heart Is,* by Billie Letts
➤ *Midwives,* by Chris Bohjalian
➤ *What Looks Like Crazy on an Ordinary Day,* by Pearl Cleage
➤ *I Know This Much Is True,* by Wally Lamb
➤ *Breath, Eyes, Memory,* by Edwidge Danticat
➤ *Black and Blue,* by Anna Quindlen
➤ *Here on Earth,* by Alice Hoffman
➤ *Paradise,* by Toni Morrison
➤ *The Meanest Thing to Say, The Treasure Hunt,* and *The Best Way to Play,* by Bill Cosby
➤ *Ellen Foster,* by Kaye Gibbons
➤ *A Virtuous Woman,* by Kaye Gibbons
➤ *A Lesson Before Dying,* by Ernest J. Gaines
➤ *Song of Solomon,* by Toni Morrison
➤ *Songs in Ordinary Time,* by Mary McGarry Morris
➤ *The Heart of a Woman,* by Maya Angelou
➤ *The Rapture of Canaan,* by Sheri Reynolds
➤ *Stones from the River,* by Ursula Hegi
➤ *She's Come Undone,* by Wally Lamb
➤ *The Book of Ruth,* by Jane Hamilton
➤ *The Deep End of the Ocean,* by Jacquelyn Mitchard

## Talk of the Nation

National Public Radio also hosts a book club of the airwaves if Oprah isn't your cup of tea. The discussion includes authors, historical experts, Ph.D.s, and other intellectuals. The selections tend to be deeper and cover a much wider arena of topics. They have had classics, mythology, experimental works, nonfiction—you name it. Plenty of selections you won't find on that televised book club with the 800 million viewers.

## Internet Led

Internet-led reading groups are very popular and there are three good reasons for their rise in popularity:

1. You don't have to make any sort of a commitment.
2. There is a massive, diverse, eccentric, sometimes frightening amount of book clubians.
3. They are good for those in isolated areas of the country, people who are housebound, and people whose schedules preclude face-to-face clubs.

The reading groups are done via e-mail, Web board, or chat rooms, so naturally there is no face-to-face give-and-take. The responses also tend to be unregulated, and it may take a little while to find a group dedicated to complex discussion. Still, if you zoom around your search engine long enough, you might find a small, dedicated, intelligent, international (another benefit of the Internet clubs) group that meets online once a week to discuss Chaucer's *Canterbury Tales*.

Here is a list of sites to try so you can find that online spot of your dreams. This is but a drop of water in the cyberspace ocean, so if these aren't to your liking, by all means plug in and drop out. Most of these addresses have links to other sites as well:

➤ **www.Powells.com.** Almost always something being debated.

➤ **www.Adlbooks.com/.** A Different Light bookstore, the premiere gay and lesbian bookstore out of San Francisco.

➤ **www.randomhouse.com/resources.** Along with Random House, most major publishers similar resource pages.

➤ **www.sfwa.org/.** Sci-fi and Fantasy Writers of America.

➤ **www.horror.org.** Horror Writers Association.

➤ **www.talkcity.com/mystery/.** Mystery Place chat.

➤ **www.getset.com/writers.** A hodgepodge of topics is available.

➤ **www.bookwire.com.** All about the book business, but has links to all sorts of bibliophile hot spots.

➤ **www.simonsays.com.** Simon & Schuster homepage has an online reading group.

➤ **www.readinggroupies.com.** Great place for give-and-take with global reading group members.

➤ **www.bb.com.** Biblio Bytes has many books that can be read online for free.

➤ **www.bookspot.com.** Links galore with an online reading groups section and tips for starting a book club online.

No matter what you want to find, whether it be an online reading group devoted to books with talking walruses or angry midgets, keep trying. It's out there.

---

### The Least You Need to Know

➤ Outlining goals will be beneficial in the end.

➤ Taking turns with the leadership mantle is the most effective way to keep all things equal.

➤ Oprah didn't invent the book club, but she sure can popularize it.

➤ There are more online reading arenas than the beach got sand.

---

# It Takes *All* the Members of a Village

> ### In This Chapter
>
> ➤ Know that you'll deal with every personality type in the book
>
> ➤ Suggestions on handling the obnoxious types
>
> ➤ What wallflowers bring to the table
>
> ➤ Identifying the rest of the wacky Homo sapiens

Kurt Vonnegut once said, "People are too good for this world." Well, that may be so, but even the cagey veteran Mr. Vonnegut would have his patience tried by the infinite number of personality types that one can encounter in a reading group. Public clubs open a door to folks from antsy to zesty and every adjective in between. You will be surprised (one hopes in a pleasant manner) by the unexpected dynamics of the private book clubs as well. It takes a village to raise a book club, and that village includes every individual hut. To be human is to be a conglomeration of strengths and weaknesses, and since reading groups are essentially human, well, you can imagine the interesting possibilities.

There is no reason to cover accommodating personality types in this chapter, because such people generally bring about harmonious relationships. There are, however, common personality types that can thwart a profound reading experience faster than a massive overdue library fine.

**Biblio-Trivio**

One of the leading lights of the modern book club genesis were freed African-American women living in Eastern cities in the 1830s. It was the only way to get any schooling; the group served as the educational epicenter.

# The Runner-Offer-at-the-Mouther

You'll recognize this person by the end of the first meeting. This is the type of member who only knows two gears from which to run his or her mouth: full-speed ahead and maximum overdrive. Think of the incessant warbling of Martha and George in *Who's Afraid of Virginia Woolf?*

**Biblio-Trivio**

Edward Albee's classic play *Who's Afraid of Virginia Woolf?* has nothing to do with renowned author Virginia Woolf. Mr. Albee thought it sounded like something pretentious an English professor would say at a cocktail party or some such occasion.

On the other hand, excessive talkers can help your group if it keeps the discussions moving along. Try to monitor the offender's speech. Does it open avenues to other paths of debate? Or does it throw barriers in the middle of the informal give-and-take highway? Usually, the verbosity comes out of excitement over the material and a head full of ideas trying to pass the lips simultaneously. This isn't a problem. Just let the member know that there will be plenty of time to share all ideas.

The greatest obstacle occurs when one member yaks incessantly but says absolutely nothing. In the worst-case scenarios, the person doesn't talk to anyone in particular and doesn't have a planned stopping point to the barrage of banality. It is a defense mechanism, so somebody is going to have to pull the person aside and say …

> ➤ "You make interesting points, but the others felt you gave them the short shrift in terms of allotted time."

> ➤ "You have good ideas, but next meeting why don't you write down them down and pick the strongest ones?"

> ➤ "If you disperse your arguments slowly, over the course of a meeting, we can all digest and comment on their individual merits."

> ➤ "You talk too much! Shut up!"

**Novel Ideas**

If nonstop chatter becomes a problem with more than one book club-ian, put everyone on a 10-minute time clock. It's formal and stilted, but it will keep order and give equal time. After a few meetings, Pavlov's dogs will stop speaking at 10 minutes on their own.

# The Interrupter

The interrupter. You know this cat. Easy to distinguish by some of these favorite expressions: "But, but, but …" "You're wrong. No way that would happen." "I just want to jump in with …" "No. No. No." "Yes. That's what I'm trying to say." Or, about any of the five million other interjections you have been cut off by in your lifetime. The serial interrupter has trouble with common courtesy, and it is virtually impossible to right past wrongs. It may come down to a forceful: "Please, stop interrupting!"

The normal cause of chronic interruption stems from a high level of enthusiasm. Be mindful that a skillful interrupter can be a tremendous asset to reading group dynamics. Too often, gentility keeps the flow of the discussions on a calm and orderly level, which shouldn't be your goal all the time. Lively debate, strong opinions, fiery emotions, and manic interruptions are a heck of a lot more fun and lead to memorable meetings. It's why members of Congress flood the floor of the House to spout their feelings on issues like flag-burning, gun control, or arts-funding and they take naps during dissertations on funding for bee-pollination experimenting. A crafty interrupter adds a healthy dose of energy, so don't look a gift horse in the mouth.

### Biblio-Trivio

"Don't look a gift horse in the mouth" is an ancient saying that means never refuse a gift that is offered. It's rooted in the way that a horse's age is calculated, by looking at its teeth (i.e., don't check out a horse's teeth and figure out its age, which equals value, if it's free).

If the constant interrupters are a headache, it will be up to the group leader to reign in the culprit and keep the gabby group geysers gushing.

### Pro's Prose

"He won't get to the root of his problem, because the root of the problem is himself."

—Carrol O'Connor, describing his character, Archie Bunker

# The Aggressor

Aggressors demand that you accept their argument basically because they're making it. They believe (or at least forcefully pretend) that theirs is the only one that matters. Oftentimes, aggressors mask the lack of a strong, intelligent, clear point through blind determination and/or intimidation.

The highest hurdle with a constant aggressor (as opposed to your average know-it-all) is that he is rabid in defense of his hypotheses, and defending the position is more important than the theories it incorporates. In the extreme cases, aggressors prey on the weaker arguers like a hostile Headless Horseman on Ichabod Crane. There have been reading group members who have come to blows, and we all know that fisticuffs is never the answer, unless of course you make your living as a boxer.

There is no simple way to deal with those who think they know no wrong, so ask yourself these questions:

➤ Is the aggressor ruining the meetings for other members?

➤ Are the aggressor's arguments (and said defense of) so far off-base that they crush any opportunity for debate?

➤ Has there been an increase in truancy among members?

➤ Does the aggressor do most of the talking during the session?

If the answer is yes to any of these questions, it may be time for a group decision about whether or not it is appropriate to bring the aggressor's behavior to his or her attention or, as a last resort, revoke the aggressor's membership card. Whatever you do, don't let the behavior pattern go unchecked. It will become a cancer that spreads very quickly. Book clubs are voluntary, don't forget, and if members feel uncomfortable, they will stop coming to the meetings.

**Novel Ideas**

Many times, an aggressor is seeking a yin-to-the-yang, a big-fish-to-Ishmael, a Henry-to-Cato, so aggressively take up the challenge and give the culprit some of his or her own medicine. It might turn out to be the two polar tent poles upon which vibrant discussions will flourish.

# The Digressor

There are two classic types of digressors. See if either of these arguments rings a bell:

1. "I loved William Kennedy's *Ironweed*. That guy, Francis Phelan, it was so sad that he was, like, an alcoholic and a bum and all. I had this great Uncle Buster who was a drunk, and he got bombed one night, like, 50 years ago and passed out with a cigarette in his hand and burned himself to death. The firemen came and everything, just like in that movie *Backdraft*. I love that movie; Kurt Russell is so hot. I went out with a fireman once. He was fun, but he had issues with his mother. She used to knock on his door every Sunday morning to see if I was staying there, sinning before church. I'm not much of a churchgoer, I'm more spiritual than religious. Hey, has anyone tried the Sunday buffet at O'Flanagans in Clarksville? They have carved ham, personal omelets, fresh strawberries, muffins …"

2. "*Beloved* is such a powerful novel. It's brilliant. The ghosts of slavery are all around us. How do we deal with the past? Especially, the violent past? What about sexual issues? Does the intimate sexual abuse overshadow the external violence of society? Do you think Morrison's work resonates deeply with the roots of modern race relations? Was the use of the ghosts necessary? Is slavery America's original sin? Is there such a thing as ghosts? What did everyone think of Oprah's performance in the movie? What is the most horrifying passage? How does *Beloved* compare with Morrison's other books?"

### Novel Ideas

Pay close attention to any group member who focuses on the same problematic theme meeting after meeting (i.e., a failed marriage, abuse, depression, grief over a death). A book club is not professional therapy, and it is improper to treat it as such. Kindly suggest that the member seek outside help, because it isn't your responsibility or area of expertise.

### Jane Err

Don't embarrass a regressor by telling him or her to pick a side or take a stand. A lot of people are nonconfrontational, content to dwell right in the middle. Let 'em be, they're absolutely harmless.

A strong leader can solve either situation without too much effort. For the former digressor (1), let the member tell a short, irrelevant anecdote from his or her life. But don't give this individual too much rope. Head it off at the pass with a gentle, "Let's try to get focused back on the book." The key word here is *relevance*, because personal stories of life experience can lead to vibrant sharing by other members. Make sure to allow for plenty of leeway. You will instinctively know who is seeing him- or herself in the book and who wants to use the meeting for story hour.

The latter digressor (2), might also be called a rambler, because this person just has trouble focusing. The leader should select a couple of the topics this type of digressor mentioned, and streamline the high points into the group discussion. Most of the ideas will probably be brought up at some point anyway.

## The Regressor

The regressor (also known as the equivocator) tries to avoid conflict and will always sublimate his or her arguments to the majority or the domineering personality.

These wishy-washy Type Bs aren't hurting anyone, so why rock the boat? Every group needs a mixture to gel properly. A problem arises if you have too many regressors, but that would be extremely rare, because the format is meant to be encouraging and supportive. An overabundance of politeness, civility, and/or equal sharing will go right out the window the first time a member says, "I didn't think the violence in Cormac McCarthy's *Blood Meridian* was all that big of a deal."

Keep the regressors of the world around, because too many Type A personalities might lead to bloodshed. Charlie Brown never bothered anyone.

# The Professor

On *Gilligan's Island,* the Professor was more than welcome because he was the only one who could wire together a coconut radio. In many reading groups, however, the professor is unwanted and unwelcome. Arrogant readers (even if they are knowledgeable) are probably the single greatest pox upon the book club movement. If you come across a member who starts sentences with one of the following phrases, grab the other members and run to the nearest deserted island:

**Pro's Prose**

"I'm developing a new philosophy—I only dread one day at a time."

—*Charlie Brown,* by Charles Schulz

➤ "Well, I have a Ph.D. in English from Vassar, and I think the character symbolizes ..."

➤ "When I was in Paris studying the Lost Generation, which is the only way to truly understand the Lost Generation, I connected with the novel on a higher plane and found it to be ..."

➤ "I am going to go out on a limb and guess that there is only one person in this room who wrote their dissertation on the poetry of Robert Frost ..."

➤ "What could you possibly know about it? I had a fellowship to study in Prague ..."

You know the type and will almost certainly cross paths with them at some point if you expand your book club horizons. Unfortunately, reading groups are like Muscle Beach for the average, narcissistic, would-be avid reader. Know-it-alls are par for the literary course, and you should expect to deal with them somewhere along your journey.

Even if your group doesn't have a braggart of letters, individual titles will bring a professor out of the woodwork.

➤ "You're not gay, how could you possibly relate to Allen Ginsberg?"

➤ "I grew up in Montana. I understand the fly-fishing metaphor in Norman Maclean's *A River Runs Through It* in ways you could never be expected to."

➤ "I am an orphan. *Oliver Twist* is me."

**Pro's Prose**

"It is only when we forget all our learning that we begin to know."

—Henry David Thoreau

Now, unless you have a small boy who was a thief in nineteenth-century England in your club, the last statement is a spot of hyperbole. Be prepared. People respond strangely to books that make an impact, even the family and friends you know well.

In addition to the know-it-all professors, you may also encounter moralistic professors who want to "convert" you and the rest of the reading group to their views on God, humanity, sex, love, religion, death, life, love, and so on. It is different than pushing an argument; they are using whatever moral high-ground they possess to espouse an ideology. In both cases, remind the professors that there is no prize for first place. There are no winners. A reading group is a forum for ideas and debate, emotions and sharing, feelings and beliefs, but there is no reason to try to outshine the others. Professors gain nothing and cut themselves off from the greater rewards. The only way anyone could possibly "lose," is to be kicked out of the group, which is a distinct possibility with the condescending professor who doesn't play nice or never offers to wire together a coconut radio.

# The Wallflower

Wallflowers, with the exception of Bob Dylan's kid, tend to keep the same behavior patterns in all aspects of their daily lives. Some wallflowers are naturally shy, but as adults, it isn't normally the same fear of rejection that permeates junior high dances. Many adult wallflowers are simply quiet by nature (a concept that's certainly foreign to you and me).

**Biblio-Trivio**

Silent reading was not a common practice in Western culture until the tenth century. St. Ambrose was an avid reader, who scanned the pages with his eyes and didn't present the words aloud. St. Augustine noted the strange, new practice in his *Confessions*. It is the first definite instance recorded in Western literature. Hard to believe, but St. Ambrose was the oddball eccentric of his day. As a contrasting experiment, try reading a Danielle Steele novel aloud at your local Borders and see how fast the security guards come running.

Reading is an intensely private hobby, and many bibliophiles reflect that reality. Wallflowers might just be contemplating the ideas and meanings, or maybe they don't have anything to say and understand that it is a good time to keep the lips zipped (a lesson we should all learn). Unless a member is so reserved that he or she makes other members nervous or uncomfortable, don't worry about it. At the very least, wallflowers tend to be forgotten or ignored more than anything else, which won't leave your group in shambles. It's always good to solicit their comments, and oftentimes wallflowers wait to speak until they have a salient point.

Wallflowers have no ill effect on the discussion because they opt out of it—except for the fact that you might be missing out on some great insights that are kept locked away out of pure shyness.

Wallflowers bring with them the most important, yet neglected, skill to possess in a book club: the skill of listening. It is the one aspect of book club life that always falls short. Too many members are thinking only of what they are about to say and don't hear what came before them. The most intelligent among us is the one who knows when he or she knows nothing.

**Jane Err**

Do not try to bring out a wallflower by constantly putting him or her on the spot with a direct question. Once in a while is fine, but singling the person out repeatedly will make him or her feel uneasy in ways other group members don't.

## The "Good"

Reading groups aren't meant to be professional wrestling matches, but nor are they intended to mirror a Pollyanna picnic. The "good" in this case are those types of members who want to sugarcoat all that they see and hear.

As Mr. Ginsberg so kindly demonstrates, literature rarely provides a sunny walk in the park, and the brutal nonfiction tomes of war, death, and neglect aren't the Sunday comics. It is one of the primary reasons reading groups exist, to try to understand the dark sides of humanity and beyond. "Good" members want to whitewash the ugly truths, or gloss them over with cheap happy endings.

**Pro's Prose**

"I saw the best minds of my generation destroyed by madness, starving hysterical naked, dragging themselves through negro streets at dawn looking for an angry fix ..."

—Opening lines of *Howl*, by Allen Ginsberg

Like our cold, white friend Mr. Snowflake, each book club is different, but if its members are afraid to tackle the tough subjects and are only looking for warm fuzzies, it isn't going to be worth the time and effort. "Good" members are also the type of people to go way overboard worrying about the other members' sensibilities.

Ideal reading groups are open to wildly divergent points of view, open-minded dissections of human failure, and a wide array of challenging titles. The "good" members will try and keep the meetings on the same mental plane as an episode of *Barney*. Don't let them win.

Book clubs shouldn't be like a box of chocolates, or a soft, mushy center is all you're gonna get.

**Jane Err**

Do not let the content police dictate your selections. There will be the occasional title that offends one (or all) of the people in your group, but being offended can be a boon to conversation. If members are split right down the middle on whether the key party in Rick Moody's *The Ice Storm* is an appropriate game for adults to engage in, get ready for the fireworks.

**Pro's Prose**

"Books are the best things, well used; abused, among the worst."

—Ralph Waldo Emerson

# The "Bad"

No matter how clear and concise your discussion questions, no matter how much advance planning is put into arguments everyone can participate in, no matter how basic the analysis of structure, plot, or character, no matter if you ask people to describe their reaction to the work, no matter what you do: Some folks just won't get it. On any level. It is an indisputable fact of life that you will have to come to terms with, because there are always those who don't process information very well. Think back to your high school days with some classmates who always seemed to have short attention spans and not much to add to any discussion. Well, it is no different in the adult world.

Here are a few examples of ways in which "bad" reading group members miss the point:

➤ (Plot) "Now, who did Oedipus sleep with?"

➤ (Theme) "The Joads sure were lucky; I've always wanted to move to California wine country."

➤ (Character) "That Jay Gatsby, man I envy his carefree attitude."

➤ (Setting) "*Bonfire of the Vanities* is the quintessential look at inner-city life."

➤ (Purpose) "I don't care what anybody says, Kafka was a hopeless romantic."

Like the preceding examples, ridiculous statements will (we hope) never cloud the airwaves of your book club, but there may be a certain member who doesn't understand anything. A "bad" member's typical response is, "I don't get it." If the person is well-liked and doesn't monopolize the time with inane questions or comments, let him or her slide. If the "bad" member refuses to see the forest for the trees and constantly brings the meetings to a grinding halt, well, you know what to do. Keep in mind that if your group decides they have had enough, you will basically be telling the "bad" member that he or she isn't brainy enough to be in the book club. Try one of these things:

➤ Find out why this person joined in the first place. If it is a close friend who likes the camaraderie, it won't be too tough to tell him or her to try to step it up a bit. Even if it is an acquaintance, tell the individual to call you about the book and have mini-discussions over the phone to clear up any big misreadings.

➤ Suggest the reader pick up Cliff's Notes, old reviews, or literary analyses. Take the extra step and meet your friend at the library to review material, including downloads off the Internet.

➤ Try to find a tailor-made book for the "bad" individual, and then go back to steps one and two.

When dealing with "bad" members, it is best to remind yourself that you may be acting like the professor. The offender might not be adding anything worthwhile to the group, but there are no winners and the "bad" member might be trying harder than anyone. If the material comes easy to you, who is climbing the higher mountain? You might have to tell the person to try to focus on a single, identifiable nuance of the book to help him or her get into the flow, but at least it promotes positive reinforcement and learning instead of negative reinforcement and snobbery.

**Novel Ideas**

Ask the "bad" member to lead one of the meetings. Hammer it into his or her head to come thoroughly prepared, knowing the book from cover to cover. In theory, the "bad" member will work twice as hard to be prepared and avoid being on the spot, so you can always tactfully remind this member down the road of how hard he or she worked and how vital the individual was to the discussion.

**Pro's Prose**

"Everyone carries around his own monsters."

—Richard Pryor

# The "Ugly"

If you join a public group, you may encounter some unfortunate souls who still project their fears and hatred onto others. However, even if you are part of a private group, you still may encounter one of these folks. The selections of your reading group will more than likely encompass all sorts of characters with complex life stories. The reactions to some of these controversial, hard-edged works can be a lot more horrifying than the words on the page, because they are real and in the moment. Authors examine the human species and its frailties, but they rarely live that way in life. Did Dostoyevski pen *Crime and Punishment* as a blueprint for sociopathic behavior? No, he wrote it to show who is out there, but in the hands of a

### Novel Ideas

Hand out a questionnaire at the first meeting asking everyone to write down the five works of art that have made the greatest impact on their lives. If one person's list includes 10 variations of mass murder (i.e., *In Cold Blood, Helter Skelter, The Shining, Badlands, Henry, Portrait of a Serial Killer*), that could be a warning sign. But it could be just that most people indulge their dark fantasies and impulses strictly through works of art.

### Pro's Prose

"The more I see of man, the more I like dogs."

—Mme. De Staël

lunatic it could become a how-to book. Is the *Great Santini* a child-rearing manual? No, but there are parents who might find his abusive tactics as the key to discipline. These are exaggerated examples, but ugly reactions are much more common than you probably realize or expect.

I heard a story about a couples' reading group consisting of people who had known each other for many years. One month they selected the Randy Shilts non-fiction tome that looks at the history of the AIDS crisis, *And the Band Played On,* which is extremely critical of the lack of effort to combat the disease by the Reagan White House. One male member was a long-time Republican and rabid supporter of the Gipper who uncorked a torrent of vulgar antigay sentiment for the better course of the meeting, much to the surprise of his wife and the other members. It led to the collapse of the group, because nobody wanted to spend time with the man, but they also didn't want to have to ask his wife not to be a part of the group either. In a perfect reading group world, you won't have to combat this problem, but there is no such thing as a perfect world—and you should never assume that everyone thinks the same way you do or holds dear the same principals.

The odds of coming across truly "ugly" members—racists, homophobes, misogynists, and their ilk—are slim to none. You may well come across opinions that differ vastly from your own and that you think are ugly, but as far as dealing with an intensely warped individual, it's not very likely. If it does happen, your group may consider asking the person to leave.

Reading groups are one of the best arenas for delving into the mysteries of the human psyche. If you are lucky, you won't have to worry about the mystery of why one of your book clubians acts like such a jerk. Keep in mind that sometimes knee-jerk reactions can paint the wrong picture. Occasionally, members will say something offensive, but that isn't who they are. If, however, a member has a pattern of constantly harping and espousing an offensive theme, idea, world view, etc., you probably aren't alone in wanting his or her removal. Voice your concerns at an appropriate time, preferably the end of a meeting, and see if the behavior is modified. If not, your group may have to ask the offender to drop out, because an "ugly" will cause the group to rot from the inside out.

Personality types will always be challenging to deal with, but don't overlook the intriguing, beguiling, and unmentioned subject of reading groups—the members themselves.

---

### The Least You Need to Know

➤ You will deal with every conceivable type of human behavior.

➤ There are specific tricks to handle the various types.

➤ Too much negative or positive opinion isn't conducive to debate—don't be afraid to rock the boat.

➤ If a member of your club is outright offensive and making other members feel uncomfortable, don't be afraid to let him or her know.

---

# Chapter 7

# Questions for Fire

## In This Chapter

➤ Reasons why reading isn't a snap

➤ Ways to boost the cranial power

➤ How to be the book

➤ Does knowing an author's background help or hinder the reading experience?

One of the most difficult habits for novice reading group wanna-bes is learning how to approach an unopened book. If you are like the majority of casual readers trying to take it to a higher level, you have a plethora of half-finished books marinating in dust on the shelf or living a vampire's existence in a dark basement. Almost everybody wants to read, but only those with practice know the secrets. If the last memory you have of completing a long work is when Fielding's *Tom Jones* was assigned chapter-by-chapter in freshman year English Composition, you have a workload coming down the pike.

Like any worthwhile endeavor, reading is not easy. In fact, it is a pastime that can be maddening, frustrating, and exhaustively draining. Plus there is always the overall "I'm-an-idiot-because-I-have-no-idea-what-*Slaughterhouse Five*-is-about" feeling that emerges during thorny afternoons on the couch.

### Novel Ideas

Before your virgin gathering, start reading for a half-hour a day. Don't worry about the length of the selection; it's important to get into the habit. Selecting an entertaining page-turner like John Grisham's *The Firm* or Elmore Leonard's *Rum Punch* will ease you into a daily read, which will become a necessity down the line with thick, dense classics.

Relax.

Take a deep breath.

Look upon your book as a treasure to embrace, not a burden to shoulder.

Realize that reading takes guts and it is going to be tough to become a productive reader. It will take time, but think of how good it will make you feel in the long run. Compare it to losing weight: In six months you will have added 20 pounds of muscle to your brain.

# Where the Wild Things Are

The first (and most important) lesson to learn is that everything you need will be found in the text if you look hard enough. It sounds obvious, but it is a natural human impulse to inject ourselves onto the page (i.e., looking for our own meaning), but that can lead to missing what the author wants to tell us.

The deeper the level of concentration on the printed words, the greater the benefits down the road. Eventually, the text will become all-encompassing, and you'll go the whole hog every time you crack open a fresh book.

### Biblio-Trivio

To "go the whole hog" might refer to the purchase of an entire pig instead of bits and pieces of it, but some linguists believe that hog was slang for shilling, so to go the whole hog meant to spend a whole shilling at once.

By putting a little extra sweat into understanding the text you are also doing your gray matter a big favor. If you always retain information (even useless information) you learn at the office but can't remember a single article from this morning's *Washington Post,* you need to approach the text in a task-oriented frame of mind. If you are the kind of person who can drop the state capitals on demand, but never concoct any abstract dimensions to anything, you need to approach the heart of the text in a slow, exploratory manner, trying to visualize scenes in the book.

You know what works for you and what doesn't, so read your books in a way that emphasizes your strengths. Just make sure to concentrate on the actual events in the book and before too long they will become part of your base cortex like phone numbers and *Happy Days* reruns.

Save the evaluation of the deeper concepts like subtext or theme for later, after you have mastered the art of productive reading. Once you have, though, you will look forward to the private time with your novel as much as the Saturday morning golf game or the weekly visit to the antique stores.

# Curious George and the Unopened Novel

Like the silly monkey, you have to view the unopened selection as a potentially life-altering adventure. Don't be the cautious Man in the Yellow Hat; let your inhibitions down and revert to the child-at-Christmas state of mind. Why not? Expecting that the book in front of you might be the one to make a miraculous dent in your very being will raise your excitement and expectation level without glancing at a page. To paraphrase a famous quote: "Today is the first book of the rest of your life."

It won't be long before you are wandering through bookstores like a five-year-old in Toys-R-Us.

## Preread Warm-Up

Having everything in place for a good read is important. Your physical surroundings could be the make-or-break point for a successful half-hour. Go through this checklist before reading time:

❏ Turn off the television.

❏ Get off the Internet and turn off your computer.

❏ Turn the ringer on the phone off.

**Novel Ideas**

If you get into a book and forget earlier details, go back and reread the relevant pages. It's slow going, but you won't set the book down and wonder what it was you just finished.

**Jane Err**

Don't, however, emulate Curious George and leave banana peels all over the house. The book club members could slip and fall, and we all know household accidents are no laughing matter.

❑ Make sure the kids will be fine for 30 minutes (or if they're young-uns, make sure they're asleep).

❑ Tell your significant other that you'll be AWOL for the next half-hour.

❑ Find a designated spot that isn't within a bird's-eye view of the tasks you need to finish (mopping the kitchen, paying the bills, ironing shirts).

❑ Walk/feed the dog or cat.

❑ Prepare a small snack like cookies, apples, or carrot sticks.

❑ Pour a glass of your favorite beverage.

❑ Use the restroom.

❑ And, whenever possible, lock the door behind you.

This might seem like an obvious checklist, but if you aren't in the regular habit of reading, these distractions will take precedence. Finding a comfortable setting is important, but don't get too relaxed. If you tend to catch zzz's within five minutes of sitting on the bed, try sitting at your kitchen table.

**Pro's Prose**

"In reading, a lonely quiet concert is given to our minds; all our mental faculties will be present in the symphonic exaltation."

—Stephane Mallarme

Another important warm-up not to overlook is actual physical exertion. Exercise is as important to the mind as it is to the body. A long walk or a brisk jog gets the blood flowing to the brain, and you will be amazed at the difference it can make. If you don't exercise on a regular basis and find you have trouble concentrating, consider the correlation. Even moderate exercise can stimulate the brain.

Now that you have the blood flowing and you're comfortably situated, it's time to clear out the cobwebs.

## Mental Stretches

All written works follow some kind of logical progression. It might be hard to unlock the mystery in Beat poetry, but there is an answer in there somewhere. Solving the riddle becomes easier with practice, and practice always includes drills of some kind.

Brain scientists have established that repetitive challenges to the cortex open up the processes of stimulation and information. You wouldn't run a 5K without stretching the leg muscles, so why pick up *Roots* without stretching the brain muscles?

Here are a few suggestions:

➤ Play a game of chess, cribbage, or Boggle.

➤ Choose a couple of short poems and analyze their structure. This works especially well with the Japanese haiku.

➤ Do 10 math problems or diagram 10 sentences.

➤ Work on a jigsaw puzzle or a model airplane.

➤ Paint, sketch, or draw a quick picture.

➤ Open an arts-and-crafts book and start a simple project.

➤ Try to solve a crossword puzzle, a word scramble, or a riddle out of a magazine.

Brain exercises might sound silly and time-consuming, but they are neither. It's a fact that brain exercises increase productivity, and you only have to do them for a few minutes. Painting for 15 minutes before you read might not amount to much on the canvas, but it amounts to plenty under the skull.

Listening to soothing music is also a common practice. Pearl Jam and the Clash are probably not the prime choice to mesh with *The Portrait of a Lady* or *Washington Square,* but different folks have different strokes.

Scientists have recently been debating whether classical music helps in infant brain development. True or false, who cares? Music is relaxing and here are a few records I throw on the old quadraphonic stereo before my reading commences:

➤ *Kind of Blue,* by Miles Davis

➤ *The Best of John Coltrane*

➤ *The Midnight Blues,* by Wynton Marsalis

➤ *Clowns,* by Pagliacci, performed by the Nuremberg Symphony Orchestra and Chorus

➤ *The Barber of Seville,* by Rossini, performed by the London Festival Orchestra

➤ Mahler: *Symphony no. 1,* Lieder/Kubelik, Fisher-Dieskau

➤ Mozart: *The Six Haydn Quartets nos. 14–19*/Julliard Quartet

➤ Rachmaninov, Tchaikovsky: *Piano Concertos*/Richter

If these suggestions don't grab you, just mosey over to your record, tape, or CD collection and pick out a few that you think will be conducive to hunkering down with a good book.

**Novel Ideas**

If you have dual passions, why not combine them? Put together a reading group that gathers for a bike ride or a flag-football game followed by a meeting.

**Jane Err**

Try not to do your mental stretches digitally. Computer screens often open a different mindset altogether, one of glassy-eyed hours in front of the monitor at work.

## Have a Game Plan

Having a game plan simply means that you have a goal in mind when you read. Time, place, setting—it doesn't matter which parameters you want to set your daily goals by, but try to give yourself marks to reach in the beginning. This may sound formal, but it can really help.

Up to this point, we have used half an hour at home at night as the standard, but whatever works for you is the best plan of attack. Until you become a reading addict, factor it into your daily plans. Write it in your organizer if you have to: "Today I will …"

➤ Cover 20 pages after the kids leave for school.

➤ Read one chapter on my lunch break.

➤ Spend an hour in the library before hitting the tennis courts.

➤ Finish 15 pages every night before bed on the weeknights and 30 pages a day on the weekends.

The point is to make reading part of your routine like eating dinner and getting dressed. That way, you won't fall behind and end up with the annoying chore of catching up.

**Pro's Prose**

"Whether I am being shaved, or having my hair cut, whether I am riding on horseback or taking my meals, I either read myself or get someone to read to me."

—Francesco Petrarca

## Be the Book

Becoming one with your text requires that you do a little investigative work. Do a bit of snooping around the backdrop of the book so that you don't get lost in a sea of foreign concepts.

Following are a few examples, if I may:

➤ If your monthly selection is David McCullough's *Truman,* it would help to research the political climate during his ascendance to the presidency and following World War II. If nothing else, you should know why the names *Hiroshima* and *Nagasaki* are crucial to his legacy.

➤ Reading *Amazing Grace* by Jonathan Kozol will be a considerably more enriching experience if you peruse newspaper articles and look at statistics of crime rates, income levels, birth rates, death rates, and so on of inner-city residents.

➤ *Three by Flannery O'Connor* is a collection of her finest work, including the brilliant short novel *Wise Blood.* Her mixture of Catholicism, dark humor, and twisted characters jump off the page, but it will be heightened if you take the time investigate the mores and standards of the Southern landscapes she roams.

➤ Ionesco's play *The Lesson* is an acclaimed staple of the absurdist milieu. If you don't understand that absurdist theater is based on the inherent irrationality behind efforts to try to understand the human experience, the Nazi armband the maid bestows on the professor will be extremely hard to grasp.

Although it isn't necessary to connect the fictionalized world the author creates with the real one he or she inhabits, it is overwhelmingly gratifying. It will also help you to see the power behind the words you are reading.

To prove to you why researching the book's subject will enhance the reading group experience, try this trick. Go to a small bookstore in your neighborhood and ask for a novel by a local author. If it is any good, you will become provincial about it in a hurry because you share a common background. You know of what he speaks. It's the same general principal as knowing what world the book lives in.

**Novel Ideas**

Buy yourself a small desk encyclopedia to keep by your side during reading time. It can quickly clear up historical, geographical, or sociological questions that may arise in your struggles to relate to the text.

# The Cat in the Hat Stays on Track

Pick up a hardbound copy of a 500-plus page book like John Irving's *A Widow for One Year* and visualize finishing it. Not as easy as it sounds, is it? That's because you know that it is a mammoth task to be able to focus on a colossal text with all the junk that floats through your noggin 24 hours a day.

Staying on track means keeping your head in the material, not just zipping through pages. This is where the compartmentalizing skills come in handy, but until they are honed as fine as President Clinton's, try the following handy-dandy helpers.

**Novel Ideas**

Ease into your reading life with great short, concise books like *The Red Badge of Courage*, *Heart of Darkness*, or *Cannery Row*. Let it become an addiction before you go after the big boys.

➤ Jot down important phrases that define the main characters.

➤ Highlight passages that mark a major passage in time or a new setting.

➤ Write in your own shorthand the questions and answers you expect will come up in the reading group.

➤ Skim over the previous chapter before you indulge the daily reading bug.

➤ Map out a rough sketch of the important plot developments as you go along (flow charts are always nice this time of year).

Again, it may sound like overkill, but getting the most out of your reading is as important as the book club meetings themselves.

## Author Biographies

Another facet of staying on track involves keeping abreast of interesting items to stimulate discussions at the next meeting. It is absolutely imperative if you have the monthly crown of designated leader, but rare is the book club that doesn't encourage all its members to bring in provocative material.

**Biblio-Trivio**

When Mark Twain was asked whether or not he liked books, he is said to have answered: that he liked a thin book because it would steady a table, a leather volume because it would strop a razor, and a heavy book because it could be thrown at a cat.

One way to gain information for upcoming meetings is to scan authors' biographies. There are two schools of thought on knowing a lot about an author, so you be the judge.

1. **Pro.** Understanding the background of an author opens up the written work because the reader gets a better sense of what shape the author's mental state was in when the text was penned. For instance, Hemingway's protagonist in *The Sun Also Rises,* Jake Barnes, becomes a confessor for the great author when you know of all his marital troubles and personal woes.

2. **Con.** The work is separate from the author and the words belong to the reader. Knowing Hemingway's life story muddies the reader's relationship to Jake Barnes. If you see Barnes as Hemingway, is it acceptable to assume that Barnes would have committed suicide? Books are meant to uncover universal truths, not basic realities. Besides, who's to say the biographies are even accurate? There is a long-standing myth that Lewis Carroll was a pedophile (he wasn't) and *Alice in Wonderland* is a twisted sexual dream or something (it isn't).

My two cents on the issue is: Read the book first and then research the author. This is separate from understanding the climate in which the book exists; it is simply learning the author's life story. Some events are universally known (if I spilled the beans about Papa Hemingway's suicide, I apologize), but wait to study the writer's background until your initial thoughts and impressions have been filed on disk.

If you don't have a lot of time to dedicate to researching an author, try going online for an hour or so. There are a seemingly infinite number of sites constructed around the lives of authors, especially those of the twentieth century. Colleges and universities often publish material (with numerous links) about writers both past and present. There are also research institutes dedicated to the study of literary heavyweights, like Faulkner, Joyce, Eliot, etc., that aren't too hard to find. Even a routine stop at Amazon.com's reader reviews might have notes of interest, although get a second source to ensure accuracy.

**Jane Err**

Don't be afraid to bring whatever dirt you dig up on the authors to your next meeting. Great debates often stem from the difference between the members' perceptions of the authors compared to the realities.

## Scholarly Journals/Lit Crit

The same basic arguments hold true for using scholarly journals and literary criticism (past and present). The main question to ask yourself is, "Is it really necessary?" Ninety-five times out of 100, your group will do fine without the highbrow analysis because the members come up with theories equal to the level of their book club. If your book club resides in a low-key, casual atmosphere, a 10-page dissection of the detached male predator as the post-Vietnam drifter in Denis Johnson's short story collection *Jesus' Son* probably isn't all that relevant.

If your group is deadly serious about literary analysis, the odds are high that you aren't reading this *Complete Idiot's Guide*. However, a couple possible reasons for adding lit crit to the soup are if you find that the same topics are covered meeting after meeting, or if the discussions are stagnating.

If you would like to take a look-see, here are a few starter sources, which should be found at your local library:

➤ Contemporary literary criticism

➤ Twentieth-century literary criticism

➤ Nineteenth-century literary criticism

➤ Literary criticism from 1400 to 1800

➤ Classical and medieval literary criticism

➤ The *New York Review of Books*
➤ American literature
➤ Amazon.com (to read the amateur critiques)
➤ Magazines such as *The New Yorker, Harper's,* or the *Atlantic Monthly.*

---

### The Least You Need to Know

➤ There are numerous ways to improve your reading life.

➤ Exercising the brain and the body will help improve your skills.

➤ Solving puzzles is a way to keep the brain sharp, along with playing music, creating art, and critiquing poetry.

➤ Researching the time and political climate in which a book takes place will only add to your enjoyment.

➤ There are an infinite number of sources for lit crit.

# Chapter 8

# Somebody Tell Me If We're Doing This Right

**In This Chapter**

➤ Why everyone's a winner in a reading group

➤ Why a little friction is good for you

➤ How to handle acquisitions and defections

➤ How to know if the group is progressing in the right direction

One of the biggest concerns of book clubians around the globe is that, for some reason or another, members don't feel like they're "doing it right." They may not even know what the "it" is that they are sure they aren't doing right, but they know for a fact that some other uber-club is outreading, outdiscussing, and outthinking their amateurish configuration.

Get over it. Now. You are doing just fine.

There's your positive reinforcement for the day, but you don't need your ego stroked by little old me. We're all united in our desire to get more from those dusty books on our shelves. As long as your group follows the golden rule, you have got no worries:

*The time must be spent discussing the book.*

Problems will arise if your club tries to live up to some phantom idealized model. Book clubs are like books themselves, each wholly unique, individualistic, and idiosyncratic. Believe in your club, let it evolve naturally, and you will have years of productive, thought-provoking meetings. If you fall into the trap of presuming other reading groups are light years ahead of yours, the book club will be as dead as a doornail.

**Biblio-Trivio**

For many years, it was thought that the doornail was the metal plate against which a door-knocker was banged "dead" from years of repeated abuse. Now, the door-nail is thought to refer to an actual nail, used to provide a fastening for a door by turning over the point of the nail. The bending of the nail's point makes the joint secure and the nail "dead."

**Pro's Prose**

"Your family sees you as a lazy lump, lying on the couch, propping a book up on your stomach, never realizing that you are really in the midst of an African safari that has just been charged by elephants, or in the drawing room of a large English country house interrogating the butler about the body discovered on the Aubusson carpet.

Reading is an escape, an education, a delving into the brain of another human being on such an intimate level that every nuance of thought, every snapping of synapse, every slippery desire of the author is laid open before you like, well, a book."

—Cynthia Heinel

There are some basic guidelines to keep in mind, but remember, book clubs are like your own can of Play-Doh, to be shaped and reshaped as you all see fit.

# And the Winner Isn't ...

No reader will be presented with a gold medal. No reader will be handed a gold trophy. No reader will be handed the keys to a shiny new Cadillac or walk away with big prize dollars. No reader will be declared MVP and sign lucrative deals selling hot dogs, high-tops, or a neon-green sports drink.

No reader is *the* winner. That's the beauty of book clubs. And of books. And of reading.

In the highly competitive American society that worships at the capitalistic dog-eat-dog altar, enlightening the mind for enlightening the mind's sake is a tough concept to get your head around. Even on campuses, grades and future job prospects are a bigger focus than educating oneself to be a well-rounded individual. Perhaps reading groups have become popular as the anecdote to the pervasive winner-take-all mentality in modern society. Or, maybe people just have too much time on their hands—or they just want to do something better with the time they have.

If you've created an open, comfortable environment, conducive to the sharing of thoughts and feelings, then things are probably coming along just swimmingly. But, if you want to make a mental checklist, there are definite patterns that should emerge.

## The Great Debate

Your group should be engaged in lively debates, which fill the room with energy and vitality. The back-and-forth between members is essential—otherwise the meetings will feel like boring, standard ... well ... meetings.

Oratorical jousting always opens up new avenues of discussion, and a fascinating debate will leave you wondering just where did the time go? It's the Zen state a successful club will attain once it gets into an intellectual groove, and it will only deepen each member's commitment to the next gathering.

And don't feel like every meeting has to be a series of the same static questions (i.e., Did you like/dislike it? What do you think of the main character, plot, setting? Does the author create an original world?). There are an infinite number of ways to view a text, and ideally your group will have a couple of members who see things differently. A couple of basic questions are necessary to get the ball rolling, but try to go outside the box to add unique angles to the topics of debate.

**Novel Ideas**

Use parliamentary procedure for initial reactions, but then let the debate become more free-form. Different books will provoke different readers, so don't worry about letting everybody get his two cents in every time around.

Examples of the possible variety of questions are as numerous as the pages in Joyce Carol Oates's hard drive. Here is a line of queries for E. L. Doctorow's novel *Ragtime*. There are the obvious ones:

➤ Were Coalhouse's violent actions justified?

➤ Were times better or worse for the average immigrant at the turn of the century?

➤ How does Doctorow use real-life characters like Harry Houdini in his fictionalized tale?

Or, there are other, more elliptical questions to ask:

➤ Has television diluted the importance of pre–World War II American history, when there weren't televisions in every home and a lot less recorded video?

➤ Is violence necessary for the underclass to grab its piece of the American Dream?

➤ Does Doctorow cross an ethical line by creating dialogue and scenarios with real people, or are all nonfiction books that retell stories from the past guilty of the same thing? (You could really spice it up and point out that there is no eyewitness reporting in the four Gospels.)

Original questions keep the meetings from getting stale, but they also probe varying facets of the human intellect and emotional center. Working in questions related to science, math, history, psychology, sociology, or any other subject can only have positive results. Even if the particular query is a flop, it was worth the chance that it might beget an unorthodox colloquy.

# The Mention of Tension

Tension is good. Tension is our friend. Tension is the Reggie Jackson of the World Series–winning Yankees of the late 1970s. Tension is the straw that stirs the drink.

I recently heard a story of two soccer moms who were transformed into professional wrestlers, grappling on the living room floor over a disagreement stemming from the chosen text. It would make for a better story if I heard that Hulk Hogan and "Stone Cold" Steve Austin were caught discussing Amy Tan's *The Joy Luck Club* in the dressing room, but life isn't that tasty. Most book club experts wouldn't advise following the lead of the suburban sisters of the sweet science, but at least the ladies were passionate about their literary theories.

All kidding aside, tension is healthy and shouldn't be squelched. Keep in mind that there are two kinds of tension: good and bad.

1. Bad tension is personally driven and can be identified when a member is making others uncomfortable through his personality, attitude, demeanor, and actions. If it is allowed to fester over the course of a few months, the presence of said member will be enough to ruin the atmosphere.

2. Good tension comes from differing perspectives of a text; it isn't an attack on another member, it is a deep conviction in your intelligent ideas. Complexity breeds complexity, and somewhere in the mix there are going to be strong adversaries. It is the difference between debate in the Senate by thoughtful representatives who don't always see the world in the same light, like Sen. Bob Kerry (D-Nebraska) and Sen. John McCain (R-Arizona), and all the other shoot-from-the-hip-at-the-top-of-your-lungs yahoos who dominate C-SPAN. Let the tension develop, because it is the strongest arguments that give birth to deepest thinking.

Obviously, if there is too much tension, your reading group has deeper issues to confront. Good tension, however, keeps the fires burning. Anger, vulgarity, and obscenity are the backbone of many a brilliant yarn, so why not allow for a little of the dark side in your club? Who is more interesting: Luke Skywalker or Darth Vader? Tension is your ally as much as love and happiness. Embrace it.

# The Glory of Story

Understanding the nuts-and-bolts of how stories are written can be a valuable asset to leading a discussion. There are distinct patterns to look for, so let's dust off those seventh-grade English class buzzwords. Keep an eye out for the following:

1. **Motifs.** Reoccurring images, elements, or circumstances inserted by the author to relate to the theme. The use of the sea in Kate Chopin's *The Awakening* as a mirror to Edna's sexual liberation is a prime representation.

2. **Antiheroes.** A staple of post–World War II novels, an antihero is a protagonist who doesn't perform heroically. The lead character in William P. Kennedy's *Ironweed*, Francis Phelan, is a homeless, alcoholic failure at life who still manages to maintain his integrity.

**Jane Err**

Don't choose a staid title for the first meeting because you want to avoid offending the members of your new group. Don't dip your toe in the literary waters; do a cannonball off the high-dive. Start with *Lolita*. Nabokov's classic novel of illicit obsession always sparks intense reactions. The beautifully crafted longings of a pedophile will stir emotions like no other book in the English lexicon. Plus, Amazon.com has a lengthy, detailed list of complex reading group questions so you can start off sounding like a professor after a 10-second download.

3. **Climax.** The whistle on the tea kettle, the point where all of the plot boils over. It is the moment of the highest intensity and energy, and leads to the fallout of the narrative. It is the moment in Charles Dickens's *A Christmas Carol* when Ebeneezer Scrooge sees his cold, lonely corpse and realizes the empty legacy he has created for himself. Sometimes it is difficult to pick out the single moment in a long, dense work, but rest assured, it is in there. Keep digging.

4. **Irony.** The incongruity between actual results of a sequence of events and what would normally be expected. Jonathan Swift's famous essay *A Modest Proposal*, encouraging the eating of children as a solution to famine, is a brilliant illustration of irony.

### Biblio-Trivio

*A Modest Proposal* was written in 1729, and it makes a revoltingly logical argument that Irish poverty can be eliminated if the peasantry fatten up their infants as food for the elite. Legend has it, acclaimed actor Peter O'Toole chose the essay as his reading at the reopening of the Gaiety Theater in Dublin in 1984 and sent many in the audience to the nearest exit doors.

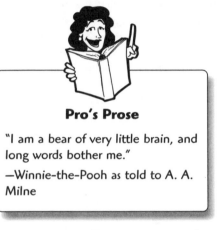

### Pro's Prose

"I am a bear of very little brain, and long words bother me."

—Winnie-the-Pooh as told to A. A. Milne

5. **Allegory.** Stories that have a literal meaning and a larger meaning. The author uses plots, characters, etc., to represent a larger concept. George Orwell's *Animal Farm* is an allegory of the perversion of socialism he saw in the postrevolution Communism of the former Soviet Union.

6. **Symbolism.** Authors use items to represent something else in or out of the narrative. What exactly do the things the soldiers carry in Tim O'Brien's outstanding short story collection *The Things They Carried* stand for? Humanity, for starters.

7. **Hubris.** Exaggerated pride or self-confidence that usually leads to a protagonist's or antagonist's downfall. The Aesop favorite *The Tortoise and the Hare* features a rabbit with a hubris problem. It is a clear-cut example of letting one's ego take control at the expense of reality.

8. **Magical realism.** Use of "magical" or fantasy elements in realistic stories. The elements usually aren't central to the plot (or else it becomes a fantasy), but are rather used sparingly to add a unique, outside element to the world the author creates. Gabriel García Márquez is a veteran practitioner of the format.

9. **Minimalism.** The equivalent of a single-guitar, acoustic folk song in relation to a symphony. It is the stripping down of a story to its most basic element. It is a way to get to the raw nerve of human experience, unencumbered by details and intricate plotting. Short-story virtuoso Raymond Carver's collection *Where I'm Calling From* includes examples like "Intimacy," in which the characters aren't even assigned names. It can be maddening to virgin readers raised on action and particulars, but the base depiction of human nature can pack a wallop.

10. **Stream of consciousness.** A technique that spits out everything flowing through a character's brain. It mixes memory, theoretical minutiae, cognizant responses, and a running commentary without adding differentiating dimensions. Basically, it is the human mind spilled onto the page. Punctuation and other such standard formats are usually abandoned. James Joyce is often considered the father of the form, in books like *A Portrait of the Artist As a Young Man,* but there are other authors who use stream of consciousness. If the format interests your group, pick up John Edgar Wideman's *Philadelphia Fire,* which features the method in the first section.

There are many other literary designations that can be extracted from basic college textbooks if you so desire. Some groups prefer not to use the fancy-schmancy grad school stylings because they are too academic and the readings feel like assignments. However, the scholarly modus operandi does have its benefits. The terminology has been in place a long time, and it can provide topics otherwise unmentioned. If your meetings are all starting to sound alike, or they hover on the surface like a manta ray, meet the English profs halfway and use the bookworm techniques.

Oh, by the way, "deus ex machina" is a contrived scenario in which a person or a thing suddenly appears out of nowhere and provides some sort of solution or resolution to what was an apparently insoluble difficulty. It comes from the gods who would come down in Greek and Roman drama and dictate their will on the outcome of the play.

**Novel Ideas**

Make a list of literary terms, and hand it out at your initial meeting. Your group may never use it as a reference tool, but it will help out if one member uses a more erudite approach. It's preventative medicine so the group doesn't look like the aliens from *V* if one of the members drops the term *deus ex machina.*

# Let It Flow, Let It Flow, Let It Flow

However you decide to run your book club, try not to break up a good thing. This holds true for both the group as a whole and for individual gatherings.

You will know a meeting is going well if Calvino's question for the ages becomes irrelevant in your den. A meeting isn't going well if you've covered the ups-and-downs of the stock market, the NFL playoffs, the cost-effective nature of solar energy, or the greatest Go-Go's song ever recorded (my vote, "Head Over Heels").

**Pro's Prose**

"Where shall we find the time and piece of mind to read the classics, overwhelmed as we are by the avalanche of current events?"

—Italo Calvino

Another sure sign that your meeting isn't going the way it should is if the responses have ranged from "Loved it" to "Hated it."

One distinct sign that your reading club is doing it right is if the round-tables are so engaging that the time evaporates like a sneeze in the breeze and nobody wants to go home. This should be your aim, a literate wave that you can ride until it bucks you off. Try not to let your meetings run on too long past the designated time though; it is better to follow the comic's mantra and leave 'em begging for more.

**Jane Err**

Don't be too formal in the setting and presentation. A relaxed, pleasant surrounding tends to help people open up. It's the reason psychiatrists' offices have comfortable furniture and a plethora of greenery.

## Doctor, I Have a Pulse!

If you have a productive reading group, it is probably worth the time and effort to take the club's pulse every six months or so. Ask a few questions to make sure the other members are as pleased with the direction in which the group is headed as you are. This is important for groups of friends because they might not be getting much out of the books, but enjoy spending time with their pals, and the books should be the main priority. It is equally important for groups comprised of folks who only see each other at the meetings because oftentimes people are afraid to reveal their true feelings to those they don't know very well.

Here are a few questions to ponder now and again:

➤ Have the book selections been varied enough that everyone has been pleased at least once?

➤ Does everyone feel that the group is open to his or her opinions, feelings, and ideas?

➤ Does everyone feel that his or her voice is being heard?

➤ Has anyone been offended by other members, and, without naming names, why?

➤ Are dissenting opinions respected equally by the book club?

➤ Is the reading group meeting your expectations?

➤ Is the level of discussion deep enough to satisfy the collective intellect?

➤ Would everyone please write down a few titles they would like to read?

➤ Does anyone have any suggestions on how to improve the meetings?

➤ Where would you like to see the group go from here?

These questions certainly aren't essential, and you will probably be able to anticipate the answers. There are cases, however, that mirror the best of Victorian literature, more complicated and sinister than they appear on the surface. The occasional checklist gives the book club the opportunity to ward off cancers before they spread.

## Okay, Break Out the Nametags Again ...

One way that the flow of your club will inevitably be interrupted is through the addition and subtraction of reading group regulars. Adding new members is always easier than subtracting them. A warm hug is simpler to administer than a harsh kick in the behind, but desperate circumstances call for desperate measures.

If your group is together for a long time, eventually some folks are going to call it quits. Be it work related or strictly personal, people are going to vamoose. Don't be surprised if Uncle Earl springs the news that he's joined a NASCAR fantasy league that meets on the same night and he won't be able to make it anymore. More often than not, members lose their lust for a literary life. If you feel the loss won't make a huge impact, then hold the status quo. But if you think that one lacking voice is going to put a damper on things, the best solution is to find a new member. Ask the remaining members if they know of anyone who might be interested. However, ask them to keep the following in mind:

**Novel Ideas**

The first time you take the temperature of your reading group, pass out bookmarks with a relevant phrase, design, or passage. If you are handy with the arts and crafts, a homemade bookmark will always impress. Either way, the gesture will endear you to the other book clubians and they might ignore small, petty, whiny *issues* they have with your leadership. Never underestimate the universal power of free stuff.

➤ Will the person fully commit to the group?

➤ Will the person potentially add something interesting to the mix?

➤ Is the person reliable?

➤ Does the person love to read?

The one potential problem you may run into is several members wanting to bring in a new person. If there's only room for one more, the best thing to do is one of two things:

➤ Have the members describe their candidates and the rest vote on who sounds like the best addition.

➤ Put the names in a hat and pick.

Although seemingly simplistic, the latter tends to be best way to go about this dilemma. It's fair, completely impartial, and no one will end up with bad feelings, as the only place to put blame is the luck of the draw.

### Jane Err

Don't let random friends come and sit in at your meetings. Unless the reading group (and the individual friend) are considering making it a permanent arrangement, there is no reason for people to "hang out" with the book club. It will throw off the established rhythm, members won't feel as comfortable as usual, and since the friend or friends probably haven't read the book, what's the point? You are only asking for trouble if it becomes a social function.

### Pro's Prose

"There's man all over for you, blaming on his boots the faults of his feet."

—Samuel Beckett in *Waiting For Godot*

Asking members to leave is a much more difficult task, but it will become necessary somewhere down the line. The first thing to be sure of is that the majority of the reading group is in agreement that so-and-so has got to go. If you're the only one with a problem, tough cookies. It is possible that you best "check yourself before you wreck yourself" as the wise poet Ice Cube once said. It will be apparent from the get-go if one soldier is dragging the rest of the army into the muck, and that situation is not hard to handle: Ask the offender to stop coming.

Dealing with an uncomfortable and potentially explosive situation like this is never easy. The thing to remember is that the group will not survive if members start dreading their monthly meetings. Addition through subtraction may be the only way to tame the beast. Losing two parts, even if one has been a valuable asset, is preferable to the sum than a drawn-out erosion. Hack off the useless limb, don't slowly bleed to death.

## But I Read Bob Uecker's *Catcher in the Wry*

It's almost go time. The runners are in the starting blocks. The gentlemen have started their engines. It's the moment we have all been waiting for: the first meeting.

## On Your Mark

Some groups like to include a book discussion in their first meeting, others like to have a brief organizational powwow before the first official meeting. Whatever you choose, make sure everyone knows what the first book to be read is. It sounds silly, but the first discussion is very important. You want to come firing out of the gate with a pronounced statement about the high level at which you expect others to perform.

Oftentimes, the numero uno assembly can make or break a book club, because a faulty beginning will cause it to malfunction before it has a chance to get off the ground.

Many reading groups have members that were coaxed into joining by their significant other or best friend, so don't allow an apathetic virgin voyage to be the excuse they use as a way out.

## Get Set

Take the time to be completely sure that all details, no matter how insignificant, have been accounted for well in advance of the initial con-gregation. It is up to you to set the tone, relaxed but thorough. It is your responsibility to present a professional, working model of how the meetings should be constructed. Unorganized meetings are a consistent complaint of book clubians everywhere.

Plus, if you lead a lazy, slipshod meeting clearly reeking of a half-hearted effort, others will do the same. You will reap the benefit of the hard-earned example when another member strives to reach the level of the bar you set. Subliminally challenge the reading group to match your outstanding model of a well-oiled book club machine.

You are free to create and facilitate a reading group in any manner you see fit. Take pride in the opportunity.

Lead by example, young literary lion.

## Read!

The part of the reading group that should be obvious is that it requires a certain amount of reading, but as hard as it is to believe, not everyone follows this precept. It is easy to get people to sign up for something, anything, if they are warmed by a blanket of an encouraging crowd, but when the time comes to put their money where their mouth is, they're broke. Empty lip service is paid

**Jane Err**

A more delicate situation will arise if a replacement member is brought in by a long-time member and the friend proceeds to stink up the joint, alienating the formerly harmonious throng. If this happens and the rest of the group is in agreement, take the longtime member aside and tell him or her of the group's concerns. Chances are, he or she will already have noticed, but if not, pointing it out will help nip the problem in the bud.

**Novel Ideas**

You may want to take care of providing copies of the maiden book choice. People don't always listen to directions, so handing each member a text will eliminate the clouds of confusion. It might set you back a tidy sum (which can be recouped after dues are collected) or force you to visit every library in the tricounty area, but it will be worth it. You want to ensure that nobody has the opportunity to say, "I didn't know what we were supposed to read."

**Pro's Prose**

"Liberty means responsibility. That is why most men dread it."

—George Bernard Shaw

**Novel Ideas**

Give every member a call under the guise of making sure she is aware of the schedule, and slyly slip in questions about how she's enjoying the book. You can even say something like, "I can't believe that Suzy Q already finished it. She said she just couldn't put it down." Avoiding embarrassment and guilt, saving face, and keeping up with the Tom Joneses are all impulses that will drive members to crack that novel. It's a bit backhanded, but it's only for the first meeting. After that, the natural enthusiasm of the group should keep everyone on task.

to book club leaders all the time by people who fancy themselves bookworms, but the actual time spent reading puts them in the category of television moths.

Frequently, nonreaders join book clubs out of guilt or a desire to get into the habit of polishing off at least one book a month. It is up to the leader, you in this case, to create an encouraging, supportive atmosphere that allows slower readers to feel like they're on equal footing. New readers often bring fresh energy and an original perspective because they don't have the egotistical baggage of seasoned veterans.

Keep close tabs on the book clubians' page progress before your initial meeting, so that it is a raging success and everyone can't wait for the following month. Otherwise, you may end up with an unmitigated disaster and the following meeting will consist of you, a Walkman, and Jackie Collins as read by Keanu Reeves.

## The Party's Over

The last point to address before we jump into the fray of book selections, genre favorites, and party ideas is what to do if it just ain't workin' out.

The answer is jump ship. If you have put forth 100 percent of yourself and all the group members have managed to do is figure out who is in the current cast of *Days of Our Lives,* get out while you can.

Reading groups should be stimulating, exciting, and entertaining. If you tried your best and the group doesn't match the standards you envisioned, find another one. Go back to the beginning of this *Idiot's Guide* and follow the steps to joining a book club that meets your ideal model. Or, skip the part about going back to the first chapter, get out there, and carpe the diem.

## Getting into the Groove

The main point of this chapter is that you have to have all your *p*'s and *q*'s in place for the first meeting, or else you run the risk of destroying the seed before the flower blooms. Once everything is in place, allow the group to grow organically and spontaneously. Don't fall under the spell of whether or not you're "doing it right," or asking the "correct" questions. However, some book clubs like to have a few sample questions to fall back on, so here are some general examples. These are broad, basic queries, though, and whatever you come up with that relates to the monthly selection is almost universally going to be more challenging and thought-provoking.

**Pro's Prose**

"I don't know which *is* more discouraging, literature or church."

—E. B. White

➤ What is the relationship between the title and the text?

➤ Does the opening scene set the proper tone for the rest of the book?

➤ Why do you think the author chose this subject matter, and can you find a character that may be the stand-in for him/her?

➤ Who is more complex, the protagonist or the antagonist?

➤ Why (or why doesn't) the author use ambiguous characters? Is this realistic or phony?

➤ What would the book be like if another character were the narrator?

➤ Does the setting enhance the story, or is it too generic?

➤ Is there a noticeable difference between the portrayals of the male and female characters?

➤ Was this a tough book to get through? If so, why?

➤ For those who hated it, what was the main reason?

➤ Has anyone read a book that compares to this title?

➤ Has anyone read another book by this author, and if so, how do they match up?

➤ Is the conclusion satisfying, or are there loose ends that should have been addressed?

➤ Why is this book so popular? Considered a classic? An undiscovered gem?

➤ Why would anybody consider this a worthwhile selection?

No matter what path your group follows, it's the right one as long as all the members are getting something out of their literary life that they weren't getting before. If it works, it works—damn the outsiders who claim they're "doing it right."

If your reading group is the right one, you'll just know.

### The Least You Need to Know

➤ Each reading group creates its own world, and if it feels good, don't worry about the way outside clubs operate.

➤ There is no competition; there will be no winners.

➤ Rousing debates and a certain amount of tension are essential.

➤ The scholarly approach can be effective in breaking the monotony.

➤ The first meeting has to be planned down to the most minute detail, which includes making sure members are reading the book.

## Part 3

# Have We Got the Group for You

*"You can lie to your wife or your boss, but you cannot lie to your typewriter. Sooner or later you must reveal your true self in your pages."*

—Leon Uris

*You must also reveal your true self in your reading group, and the best way to reach that goal is to select challenging, thought-provoking works that tap into those parts of the human psyche usually kept hidden. In simpler terms, a book with no guts won't offer anything.*

*This part breaks down various groups and looks into the reasons that men's groups are only slightly more common than the woolly mammoth. This part is by no means meant to say certain groups should stick to certain material, but it offers a quick reference guide when you go-a-hunting for tomes of staggering sagacity.*

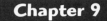

# Chapter 9

# We're #1: The Classics Group

**In This Chapter**

➤ What's so great about the classics?

➤ Where to begin: the top 10 classic books of all time

➤ Checking out other opinions on the top 10

➤ Why variation is key

Classic literature is often passed over in the book club world for current best-sellers, which can be a grave mistake. The reason books become recognized as classics is because the search for universal truths stands the test of time. This chapter is going to start at the top and list great literary works your club can always fall back on in the quest for the ultimate title.

## The Top Ten Tomes of Our Times

A group of literary experts was selected by the editorial board of the *Modern Library*, a division of Random House that has been publishing classic literature since 1917. The voters, Daniel J. Boorstin, A. S. Byatt, Christopher Cerf, Shelby Foote, Vartan Gregorian, Edmund Morris, John Richardson, Arthur Schlesinger Jr., William Styron, and Gore Vidal, spent a year deciding on the best English novels of the twentieth century. They were given a compilation of 400 titles from which to choose.

The list caused quite a stir in bibliophile circles and sparked more debate than a book-burning convention. Many columnists weighed in with the opinion that the selections were too white, too male, and too old. There was, after all, only one woman on the actual panel: English novelist A. S. Byatt. Another question that remains insufficiently answered is, why were English-language books the only ones eligible? Doesn't that taint the process? Other critics were, however, impressed with the depth and intelligence of the choices, an impressive collection of dense, challenging books that avoided the trap of pandering to the pop culture favorites. One indisputable fact is that the top 10 books rank with the finest ever penned, regardless of whether there are other novels that deserve equal consideration. Any of these 10 books would be a great place from which to embark on your reading group adventures.

And without further ado, let's start at the top:

1. *Ulysses,* **by James Joyce.** In this colossal work, Joyce plays the English language like a bebop saxophone. It is the story of two men, Stephen Dedalus and Leopold Bloom, in Dublin, Ireland, on June 16, 1904. It's a typical day, a standard 24-hour period of banality. But Joyce's stream-of-consciousness style allows the reader to spend the time inside the heads of the characters as they attend to their separate businesses. They each meet up with unforgettable Dubliners as they take care of nominal tasks like eating, walking, arguing, and playing with themselves (well, Leopold anyway).

**Biblio-Trivio**

*Ulysses* was the centerpiece of a renowned 1933 court decision. Judge John M. Woolsey ruled that the book was not obscene and allowed it to be imported into the United States. It had been burned by the U.S. Post Office in 1918 and seized en route to be published by the same organization again in 1930.

It is not a book of plot, story, or action; it's the human experience under a literary microscope. Joyce takes us into the thoughts, opinions, memories, feelings, loves, hates, and emotions that run through the characters' cortex. It is a hard novel to describe, other than to say Joyce captures the complexity of simply living through an unremarkable day.

Many readers flat-out hate the book. This synopsis barely scratches the surface of the density and fragmentation of the twentieth-century giant. Does it have universal appeal, or is it only worthwhile for Ph.D.s? That is for your book club to decide.

2. ***The Great Gatsby,* by F. Scott Fitzgerald.** In 1922, F. Scott Fitzgerald penned a book that is to the Jazz Age what *On the Road* was to the Beat generation of the 1950s; that is, the whole era in a nutshell. It is the story of Jay Gatsby, self-created millionaire, and the decadent times in which he lives. It encompasses the glam life, the nonstop parties, and the enormous excesses of the Roaring '20s, which eventually ran smack into the Great Depression. The novel is concise in its depiction of all the things that make America great: cash, unchecked greed, blind, obsessive ambition, and the classic rise and fall of man and his ego, or as we like to call it, hubris.

The story is narrated by Gatsby's neighbor, Nick Carraway, a detached soul who describes the events without pomp and circumstance. His detached narration helps capture the emptiness of the life that Gatsby creates for himself on the Long Island Sound. You see, Jay Gatsby is in love with Daisy Buchanan, who lives across the water in ritzy East Egg. She is married to Tom Buchanan, a self-involved snob who gained her affection with hedonistically priced jewelry.

Eventually, the tragedy that is Jay Gatsby's life comes to a head. He is murdered, and for what? The world he lived in didn't allow for honest emotion, just superfluous wealth. Only three lonely souls attend his funeral.

**Jane Err**

Don't attempt *Ulysses* right out of the box. It is truly a glorious monster that will take a massive commitment. It is long, thick, and rambling, and many readers find it impenetrable. Your group will have to go above and beyond the standard call of duty to penetrate Joyce's opus, so spend a year working up to it.

**Novel Ideas**

A worthy topic to ask if your group decides to delve into Joyce's masterpiece is if *Ulysses* can only be understood by 1 percent of the world's population, how much practical influence does it really wield?

### Biblio-Trivio

Fitzgerald spent the last two years of his life drinking Coke by the case as a substitute for the excessive boozing that ruined his life. He wrote his last book, *The Last Tycoon,* in bed, but never finished it. In an eerie coincidence to his most famous Mr. Gatsby, no one attended his funeral.

Unlike *Ulysses, The Great Gatsby* is an entirely accessible novel with exquisite, pithy prose and plotting. Most groups enjoy this book, and I highly recommend giving it a whirl at some point during the first year of your book club. Fitzgerald portrayed (in his work and life) how living only for today will haunt your tomorrows.

3. *A Portrait of the Artist As a Young Man,* **by James Joyce.** Maybe your book club has got that Joyce fever, but *Ulysses* is simply too time-consuming an endeavor. Fear not, ye' Gaeliophiles, for just as McDonald's surely offers the Shamrock Shake for those who can't handle their Jamesons', the Irish litterateur offers the less taxing *A Portrait of the Artist As a Young Man,* written in 1916.

*A Portrait of the Artist As a Young Man* is the tale of a young Stephen Dedalus as he grows from a toddler to an adult. Joyce uses his amazing stream-of-consciousness technique to elaborate on the growth of a human mind. The novel parallels the development of Stephen's perceptive levels of personal awareness with various revelations that occur throughout his life. A major highlight is the intense religious conflict he experiences at a day school in Dublin. And, if you enjoy the character, Dedalus reappears as a player in *Ulysses*.

Dedalus reaches college and challenges the standards of Irish society he has been saturated with since childhood to create his own tapestry of faith and intellectual sovereignty. In the end, he leaves for Paris and the chance to free his mind and become a true artist. Joyce brilliantly uses simplistic prose for the years of Stephen's childhood, and his writing becomes more advanced as Stephen ages.

This book has the additional benefit of trying to encapsulate why art is so important for humanistic development, which is also a function of book clubs. Maybe not all the time, but you will certainly have discussions about how art explains reality. Start off with his question, "Is Joyce the artist he describes?"

**Pro's Prose**

"By far the most important living and convincing picture that exists of an Irish Catholic upbringing."

—H. G. Wells on *A Portrait of the Artist As a Young Man*

4. *Lolita,* **by Vladimir Nabokov.** Perhaps no other book of the twentieth century provokes its audience quite like Nabokov's weird, twisted work that is, no matter what you think of the subject matter, a work of absolute genius. It is the story of a European intellectual named Humbert Humbert, who comes to America and falls in love with a 12-year-old "nymphet" named Dolores Haze, a.k.a. Lolita. Humbert Humbert is haunted by the memories of the lost love of his adolescent life. He will do anything to seduce Lolita, including marrying her mother and plotting her murder. (I won't give it away.) One of the most interesting aspects of *Lolita* is that Humbert Humbert's lasciviously gorgeous prose is so glorious to read that the actuality of what he is saying can slip the reader's mind. It would be much easier to despise Humbert Humbert if he weren't a master with language; he sees himself as a man in love, with a poet's heart.

**Biblio-Trivio**

Vladimir Nabokov was an accomplished, enthusiastic lepidopterist (butterfly specialist) who identified and named at least one new species of butterfly. There is a literary theory that proposes Humbert Humbert's obsession with Lolita is a metaphor for Nabokov's love of the butterfly.

Nabokov was born in St. Petersburg, Russia, but moved to America in 1940. In *Lolita,* he clearly revels in the meeting of old-world European Humbert Humbert and New World Lolita. The metaphor of Humbert Humbert as aged, proper, educated Europe and Lolita as youthful, crude, energetic America has been a topic of conversation since its publication, so feel free to continue the debate. Nabokov seems to love the clash of cultures, especially at such a base level.

*Lolita* is without question a rumination on love, no matter how bizarre, illicit, loathsome, yet possibly pure it may be. Plus, there is a school of thought that Humbert Humbert hallucinates through the bulk of the narrative, so you decide what's what. Start off with this query: Why would Nabokov pen this work in the first place?

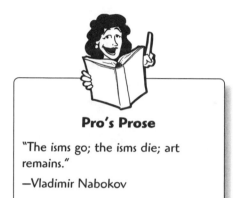

**Pro's Prose**

"The isms go; the isms die; art remains."

—Vladimir Nabokov

5. ***Brave New World,* by Aldous Huxley.** "Community, Identity, Stability" is the motto of Aldous Huxley's utopian World State, which is his dystopian masterpiece. Huxley creates a world in which artificial births lead to a genetically engineered populace without familial connections. The state monitors the growth of society and decides what level of intelligence human embryos will be able to reach. The masses swallow daily doses of Soma, a drug that fights depression, and enjoy feelies, films that recreate the senses. The human cattle need the feelies to experience sight, hearing, and touch.

**Biblio-Trivio**

Huxley was a proponent of the positive effects of LSD and mescaline, and his essay *The Doors of Perception* (taken from a William Blake poem), was about his experiences with drugs. Musician Jim Morrison used it as the name of his band, the Doors. In a related story, political outcast Lyndon LaRouche believed Huxley was a British intelligence agent sent to revive the ancient Egyptian Isis cult, centered around the use of drugs. Huxley died on November 22, 1963, the same day, coincidentally, as President Kennedy's assassination.

In Huxley's world, everybody is provided for and violence is nonexistent, but Bernard Marx knows that something is missing from his world. An error at the Predestination Centre has made him brilliant, but weak. He is a loner until he meets Lenina and takes her to a Reservation, where she falls in love with John, a savage who is unfamiliar with the ways of her society. They break the established rules of the utopian community and John meets with disastrous consequences.

This tome definitely relates to the cyberage, because it probes the effects of dehumanization in a world of science and technology run amok. Genetic engineering, anyone?

**Pro's Prose**

"Maybe this world is another planet's hell."

—Aldous Huxley

6. ***The Sound and the Fury*, by William Faulkner.** *The Sound and the Fury,* published in 1929, was William Faulkner's favorite: He called it his "most splendid failure." He followed Mr. Joyce's lead and used the stream-of-consciousness motif to great effect, although a standard criticism of the novel is that he went overboard with the technique.

The novel is one of many set in Faulkner's fictional Yoknapatawpha (*Yok-nuh-puh-Taw-fuh*) County, Mississippi. It is the story of the decline of the aristocratic Compson family, told from four differing points of view in four separate sections, the first three from the three Compson sons. The lead-off narrator is Benjy, a 33-year-old "idiot." He regales the reader with flashback tales of his family, and the trick is to determine which aspects of his yarns are in the past and which are in the present. He tells of his castration, his brother Quentin's suicide, and when his sister Caddy lost her virginity (in many ways, Caddy is the main character).

The story shifts back in time, and the second narrator is Quentin, on the day he kills himself. He is a freshman at Harvard, wandering around Boston preparing to die. He, too, is obsessed with Caddy and can't handle her burgeoning sexuality.

The last of the Compson brothers to weigh in is the eldest, Jason, a sadistic man who details the blooming sexuality of Caddy's daughter, Quentin, who came to live with the Compsons after Caddy's divorce. Many of the mysteries of his brothers' lives are revealed in greater detail.

### Biblio-Trivio

Faulkner worked a string of odd jobs while he chased his dream of a writing life. One of his jobs was as a postmaster at the University of Mississippi. Faulkner was by most accounts a horrendous postmaster who was known to throw mail in the trash, take his sweet time delivering the outgoing mail to the train, and write and play cards with his pals for hours on end. Eventually, a postal inspector came to snoop around and Faulkner resigned. Another time, his drinking cost him a position as a scoutmaster.

The final section takes place on Easter Sunday and is told from the point-of-view comments of the Compsons' black servants, a woman named Dilsey in particular. The servants have watched the Compsons for years and managed to endure their sad lives. The last part is a commentary on the Compsons' poisoned existence.

Faulkner can be as inaccessible as Joyce, but he is the preeminent southern writer in the American index. Literary criticism abounds for *The Sound and the Fury,* including the theory that Benjy is some sort of ironic Jesus figure. The use, meaning, and differences of the four varied perspectives will provide plenty of fat upon which you can chew.

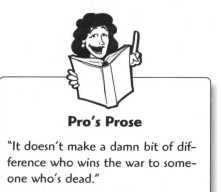

### Pro's Prose

"It doesn't make a damn bit of difference who wins the war to someone who's dead."

—Yossarian in *Catch-22*

7. *Catch-22,* **by Joseph Heller.** Heller's masterpiece is a powerful mix of comedy and horror that has defined the utter insanity of war like no other book written in the bloodiest century on record. It is a jab to the gut of the results of the so-called "good war." Soldiers died. Soldiers went crazy. Civilians were massacred. Bureaucrats tallied the numbers and smiled with their acceptable success rates. And keep in mind that Heller's book was published in 1961, before the first troops were sent to Vietnam.

*Catch-22* is the story of Yossarian, a cynical bombardier who is manic over all the people he doesn't know who want to kill him. World War II is coming to a close, and Yossarian and his squadron are biding their remaining time on a Mediterranean Island off Italy. Yossarian seems to be the last sane person left, and his singular goal is to stay alive. The book is a symphony of the frustrating absurdities of language, especially the ridiculousness of military, religious, and political spin. Every character is a confounding mess, including Milo, the resident capitalist who is making a killing off the selling of morphine during the war.

### Biblio-Trivia

Joseph Heller flew more than 60 missions in World War II. He was a bombardier for the U.S. Army Air Forces in Europe. He earned the rank of first lieutenant.

The phrase *Catch-22* was created by Heller and has become one of the most frequently used allusions in all of the American art forms and a standard English phrase. In the book, the "Catch-22" is a military regulation that says a soldier is insane if he willingly flies perilous combat missions, but if he formally asks out of such missions, then he has to be sane, thus rendering him ineligible to be relieved of the duty of flying the dangerous missions. Originally Heller called it a "Catch-18," but the publisher already had a book with "18" in it so they changed it, which was fortuitous, because the symmetry of a duplicate digit, "22," does a better job of capturing the circular ideology behind the meaning. Heller's novel became an antiwar staple in the 1960s; reading it was a rite of passage for the counterculture and influenced such powerful protest films as *Dr. Strangelove* and *M\*A\*S\*H*. It hasn't lost any relevance and will always mirror whatever violent conflict in which America is currently engaged. As Yossarian said to Doc Daneeka, "that's some catch, that Catch-22."

8. ***Darkness at Noon,* by Arthur Koestler.** Koestler's work is a tale of the endurance of the human will set against the backdrop of the Moscow purges and treason trials in 1930s Russia. The protagonist, Rubashov, is a disillusioned revolutionary, thrown into jail for crimes he did not commit. Rubashov is psychologically tortured by two investigators, Ivanov and Gletkin, eager to get a phony confession out of him. Their sinister methods work, and Rubashov

admits to doing things he has not done. Confined to solitary anguish, Rubashov reexamines his life as a member of the totalitarian regime that would use any means to achieve their ends.

### Biblio Trivio

In the Kenneth Starr report, Clinton told friend/advisor Sidney Blumenthal that he was "surrounded by an oppressive force that is creating a lie about me and I can't get the truth out. I feel like that character in the novel *Darkness at Noon*." Who wants to discuss hubris?

### Novel Ideas

Contrast Rubashov's epiphanies with Koestler's personal example of the human spirit. He was a firm believer in euthanasia. In 1983, while battling Parkinson's disease and leukemia, he took his own life. Is it the ultimate example of individual will, or is it a cop-out of the human spirit from the man who turned his back on the Communist party in 1937 because he was disenchanted?

Amid the madness, Rubashov is able to come to some sort of understanding of his role in the illegalities and immoralities of the regime in power of which he was once a loyal follower. It is in direct contrast to his tormentors who toe the party line. Rubashov knows what his blind support of iniquitous leadership has wrought. The countries and claimed ideologies change, but the horrific stories of unchecked power around the globe remain, as does the strength of Koestler's novel. It is a story of politics versus free will, which is a question for all time.

*Darkness at Noon* is the least-known of the top 10, but is not lesser in its ideas and prose. In *The New York Times Book Review,* Harold Strauss wrote, "It is the sort of novel that transcends ordinary limitations ... written with such dramatic power, with such warmth of feeling, and with such persuasive simplicity that it is as absorbing as melodrama."

9. ***Sons and Lovers,* by D. H. Lawrence.** D. H. Lawrence has long been a controversial figure for the frank sexuality depicted in his books.

### Biblio-Trivio

The first version of *Lady Chatterley's Lover* was written in 1928. An expurgated version was published in America in 1932. The third version, which was the most explicit, was not published in the United States until 1959, almost 30 years after Lawrence's death. It had been withheld until a court ruling allowed for its publication. *Sons and Lovers* was also edited down somewhat before its publication.

*Sons and Lovers* is one of Lawrence's earliest novels, a largely autobiographical work that deals with life in a Nottingham mining town. Paul Morel is a son whose life is defined through his mother. He is starting to realize that his attachment to his mother is stifling his emotional development; he can't get together with another woman to save his life. His obsessive love and sexual yearnings mark this as one of the great examinations of the Oedipus complex in modern works of fiction.

Paul's possessive feelings come to a head when his mother is stricken with cancer. He is resentful of her, because her death will leave him without an identity. Control through sexual power is the primary staple of Lawrence's writings. Sex is always a hot topic at book club meetings, and D. H. does not disappoint. Lawrence might be the man who extracts the most ribald reading group roundtables on record.

### Pro's Prose

"I'd wipe the machines off the face of the earth again, and end the industrial epoch absolutely, like a black mistake."

—Attributed to D. H. Lawrence

10. ***The Grapes of Wrath,* by John Steinbeck.** John Steinbeck won the Pulitzer Prize in 1940 for *The Grapes of Wrath,* his famous tale of the Joads, a family of migrant farm workers struggling through the Great Depression of the 1930s. The Joads pack up and flee Oklahoma after the Dust Bowl renders the land barren. They have heard of the steady work and glorious riches in California and embark on the journey in hopes of a secure future. What they encounter—power-hungry police, hostile locals, slave wages, deplorable living

### Pro's Prose

"The ancient commission of the writer has not changed. He is charged with exposing our many grievous faults and failures, with dredging up to the light our dark and dangerous dreams for the purpose of improvement."

—Attributed to John Steinbeck

### Novel Ideas

Before discussing *The Grapes of Wrath,* listen to a selection of songs from the 1995 Bruce Springsteen album *The Ghost of Tom Joad.* At a time when the pundits uniformly trumpet the strength of the American economy, the Boss recorded a sparse, acoustic reminder that thousands of our citizens have been left behind and struggle to put food on the table. For your group, try to answer the following question: "Have things changed at all since Steinbeck penned the saga of the Joads?"

arrangements, drunks, violence, and general human cruelty—is a far cry from their original dreams.

The book brought to light the hardships migrant workers face and is considered one of the stronger daggers to penetrate our collective moral compass written this century. The Joads stick together and maintain their dignity and basic human grace in a world of poverty and despair. Steinbeck constantly reworked the theme of how the underclass survive in America's ruthless, dog-eat-dog economic system, and his main conclusion seems to be that they lean on one another.

All of these books will spark serious conversations at your next meeting, but so will hundreds of other titles. These books certainly rank with the best ever written, but it is an awfully long list, considering stories have been around since the dawn of humankind.

# The People Have Spoken

Here are two other versions of the best books of the century. Powell's "unscientific but pretension-free" list includes titles that weren't on the modern library list. The Radcliffe publishing class list was compiled by 100 students at Radcliffe in response to the modern library list.

**Powell's Books Top Ten:**

1. *Their Eyes Were Watching God,* by Zora Neale Hurston
2. *Beloved,* by Toni Morrison
3. *Blood Meridian,* by Cormac McCarthy
4. *To Kill a Mockingbird,* by Harper Lee
5. *The Color Purple,* by Alice Walker
6. *My Antonia,* by Willa Cather
7. *Wise Blood,* by Flannery O'Connor
8. *The Handmaid's Tale,* by Margaret Atwood
9. *The Foundation Trilogy,* by Isaac Asimov
10. *Gravity's Rainbow,* by Thomas Pynchon

**Radcliffe Publishing Course Top Ten:**

1. *The Great Gatsby,* by F. Scott Fitzgerald
2. *The Catcher in the Rye,* by J. D. Salinger
3. *The Grapes of Wrath,* by John Steinbeck
4. *To Kill a Mockingbird,* by Harper Lee
5. *The Color Purple,* by Alice Walker
6. *Ulysses,* by James Joyce
7. *Beloved,* by Toni Morrison
8. *Lord of the Flies,* by William Golding
9. *1984,* by George Orwell
10. *The Sound and the Fury,* by William Faulkner

In addition to all those previously listed, there are as many worthy titles as there are remaindered copies of *Monica's Story,* and it is up to your group to decide what suits you best. These books will offer benefits that others might not; for example …

➤ They are all influential in terms of format and style, which is not the case for 99 percent of current popular fiction.

➤ There will be a ton of lit crit, author history, and question guides available for in-depth analysis.

➤ They will definitely challenge the members of your group, which is not always the case with simpler titles, so a healthy debate is almost ensured.

➤ Discussions about how overrated the books are can be equally stimulating.

➤ Each member of your book club (including you) will feel a strong sense of accomplishment after having completed one of the heavyweights, which is always a pleasant experience.

**Jane Err**

Don't rely on lit crit as you are reading a novel from the top 10. Try to get your own ideas of the author's intent, no matter how basic, down on paper first. Otherwise, your understanding of the book will be heavily influenced by some unknown Ph.D. Literature is for everyone. Your ideas are valid.

I think the best way to use the classics is to incorporate a couple into your group over the course of a year. There are reading groups that dedicate themselves solely to the analysis of novels that are commonly regarded as the best ever written. However, a healthy mix will keep your book club on its toes, so do *The Great Gatsby* one month and The Great Grisham the next. Don't ignore the classics outright for fear of not understanding them or simply because they have been co-opted by academics. They have too much to offer.

## The Least You Need to Know

➤ Don't be intimidated by the classics—they're still around for a reason.

➤ If you're interested in getting your group started on a classic tome, a good place to start is *Modern Library*'s top 10.

➤ Although *Ulysses* is one of the greatest books of all time, you might want to get your reading group started with a few other books to get those muscles of intellect flexing and in shape before diving in.

➤ Variation is key: Keep a good mix of books circulating, so that one month you read a classic and the next a modern work.

# Chapter 10

# Women's Groups—Our Miss Books

---

## In This Chapter

➤ Why do women rule: a plethora of theories

➤ Feminist angles to ponder

➤ The joys of mother/daughter clubs

➤ The first list of many

---

As in just about every other facet of the predominately male-dominated societies that dot the globe, women were not always encouraged to participate in the macho experience of learning stuff. Reading was not always open to the fairer sex; it was considered inappropriate for a woman to engage herself in activities unrelated to the home.

Perhaps it is this long, submissive history that has been the primary factor in the overwhelming number of female book clubs. In this chapter, we're going to take a look at women's book clubs, why they've been so successful, and how you can start one—you go, girl.

## Girl Power

Theories abound as to why there are so many more women's groups than men's, but there is no single, definitive reason to explain the phenomenon. For every intriguing possibility, there is an inverse scenario that throws the heart of said idea off-balance.

It is most likely a combination of a variety of reasons, dependent on the individuals in the book club. But, for sociological purposes, here are a few hypotheses on why women are king in book club numbers:

**Pro's Prose**

"Once made equal to man, woman becomes his superior."

—Socrates

➤ **The Masculine Socialization Theory.** Even in this day and age, so-called manly pursuits are still the be-all and end-all ingrained into young boys' minds and carried through to adulthood. God forbid that young men spend their time in noncompetitive, mind-enriching enterprises. The incessant drumbeat of being "the best" makes rewards more important than the process. As book clubs are a process of self-improvement, the only prize gained is not shiny, is non-monetary, and is basically intangible. The ironic thing is that it is an attitude perpetuated by such literary heavyweights as Ernest Hemingway and Norman Mailer, even though it is the very attitude that keeps other men from reading (and buying) their works.

**Biblio-Trivio**

The legend from Oak Park, Illinois, had a tragic ending to his incredible writing life. Ernest Hemingway killed himself with a shotgun blast to the head. It was reportedly the same weapon his father had used on himself.

➤ **The Sheer Numbers Theory.** There are more women than men in the United States, so maybe it's an accurate reflection. This theory doesn't explain why the numbers are so one-sided, though, or why there are almost universally more women than men even in co-ed groups. It is a simplistic theory, but sometimes the most obvious answer has as much merit as a detailed, probing investigation. (Okay, okay, it is quite frankly a bad theory—but is it that much worse than the others?)

➤ **The Freedom Factor Theory.** Just like men, women want to get out and join their peers in organized events. Book clubs are open to anyone, unlike, say, sports leagues, and they are easy to found if there isn't an established reading group available. Book clubs give women a chance to expand their intellect in a challenging yet warm social setting. Maybe too many men see it as a squishy, "feminine" pursuit. It is a woefully unrefined way of looking at book clubs, because a heated discussion over a tough book like Jane Smiley's *A Thousand Acres* is anything but cuddly. Most book clubs become lively, engaging, joyful entities, and maybe women need to help men understand what an enriching opportunity they are passing up.

➤ **The No Sweating Theory.** This theory is that men mainly join groups that guarantee the excretion of the sweat glands. This why beer-league softball games, lumberjack contests, and YMCA recreation hoops are dominated by men, but men view book clubs the same way Dracula views garlic. This theory is bunk. First off, it plays heavily into standard male/female stereotypes, and, more important, it doesn't answer this question: Why are there equal numbers of men and women at gyms across the country at any given time? If women can sweat with the boys, why can't men discuss with the girls?

➤ **The Trend-Watcher Theory.** This is the one theory that has obvious merit, but it still doesn't hold up as the main reason that women far outnumber men in the reading group universe. Trend-following certainly isn't gender specific. However, some factions might point to the influence of the all-mighty Oprah as the proliferator of this trend among women, since her audience is predominantly female. However, national radio personality Don Imus is the host of a popular morning show that doesn't have a regular female talker in the booth. Imus's show originates from a male-dominated all-sports radio station in New York City, but they discuss books on a regular basis and even give out yearly awards. Titles have had significant sales increases after being featured on the show, showing that men are indeed interested in trendy books. So, are they buying the books but avoiding the book clubs?

**Novel Ideas**

I heard a rumor about a reading group/aerobic class that meets at a local gym. They work out, shower, and have a biweekly discussion over breakfast in the juice bar afterward. This would take a hefty commitment from group members, but it must be an extremely gratifying experience to enhance the body and the mind in a two-hour stretch.

➤ **The Empowerment Theory.** This theory takes into account the long history of treating women as second-class citizens. Education was not always an equal-opportunity proposition, so many women chose to educate themselves, even if it had to be a covert operation. In the early nineteenth century, "study clubs" flourished that discussed political issues as well as literature. There was also an upswing after World War II with the Great Books movement, albeit in more equal terms. Founded by educators at the University of Chicago, the movement preached that classic literature was accessible to anyone who could read and discuss the works. The masses could open their minds just the same as the campus denizens. The movement was popular with housewives, aiming to improve themselves through reading discussion groups. Women have historically used learning to become more empowered, because nobody can regulate what is in the interior cortex. Modern reading groups could be theorized as an outgrowth of past oppression.

### Pro's Prose

Despite my 30 years of research into the feminine soul, I have not yet been able to answer ... the great question that has never been answered: What does a woman want?"

—Sigmund Freud

### Jane Err

Ironically, one of the major criticisms of today's book clubs is that the majority of them don't aspire to read the most challenging literature, but rather politically correct, sentimentalized, unambiguous pop fiction.

➤ **The Just-Because Theory.** This is my favorite theory. It adheres to the concept that there are more women than men in book clubs and who cares? If women are smart enough to realize the personal value in book clubs and men aren't, more power to them. This isn't a sociology lesson; let us say it is "just because," and get on to bigger and better topics.

I think the father of psychoanalysis would have to agree: Women want book clubs.

## Staples

Here are five titles that are staples of many women's reading groups and are definitely worth including in yours.

1. *Beloved,* **by Toni Morrison.** If someone were to ask you what is the single book that best represents today's reading groups, this would be it. Morrison's seminal work won the Pulitzer Prize in 1988 and uses all sorts of literary devices to spin this tale of what slavery wrought on the souls of its victims. *Beloved* is the story of Sethe, an escaped slave who is vexed by the spirit of her murdered child, Beloved. The ghost both haunts and comforts Sethe as the circumstances of the baby's death unfold, connecting the brutal past to the frightening present.

### Biblio-Trivia

In 1993, Toni Morrison was the first African-American woman to win a Nobel Prize for Literature. It was a long journey for Chloe, who reportedly changed her name to Toni because it was easier to pronounce.

*Beloved* is a fractured narrative that mirrors the fractured lives of slaves in America. The experimental style, coupled with the incredibly powerful subject matter, has made *Beloved* an important book about the aftermath of slavery. Its lyrical prose defines the souls of those African Americans who kept their dignity amid unspeakable horrors.

Oprah is dead-on in her cheerleading of Morrison's body of work. Regardless of what you think of the validity of her attempt to bring *Beloved* to the big screen, it was a labor of love about one of the finest, multifaceted novels of the century.

2. ***The Portrait of a Lady*, by Henry James.** Many scholars consider this novel the high point in Henry James's remarkable career. It is the story of Isabel Archer, a headstrong American girl who has been brought to England by an eccentric aunt to reach her potential as a well-rounded woman. She becomes involved with a British aristocrat and an ugly American and is confronted by a nasty villainess.

### Pro's Prose

"Counting on the stillness of her own soul, she had forgotten the other one: the soul of her baby girl. Who would have thought that a little old baby could harbor so much rage?"

—Excerpt from *Beloved,* by Toni Morrison

### Biblio-Trivio

Henry James was born into a family of profound intellect and influence. His father was a renowned religious philosopher and his brother, William, was the author of *Pragmatism* and the first notable American psychologist. Henry studied all over the world, including France, Germany, and Switzerland; he eventually settled in England and wrote consistently about the differences between the American and European experiences.

James's deeply psychological novel examines the interpersonal ramifications of Isabel's innocence and vulnerability in an entrapment of deception, backbiting, and treachery. It is an intense, psychological work that relies more on the slow revelation of character than overtly dramatic incidents.

### Pro's Prose

"Under certain circumstances there are few hours in life more agreeable than the hour dedicated to the ceremony known as afternoon tea."

—Opening line of *The Portrait of a Lady*, by Henry James

Isabel is a complex protagonist who will split your group down the center with those who love and hate her motives. It will be a book your group doesn't forget anytime soon.

3. *Animal Dreams,* **by Barbara Kingsolver.** This is another book club favorite, a layered story with numerous issues and lively characters. It is the story of a woman, Codi Noline, who returns to her roots in a small town in Arizona to take care of her father, who is diagnosed with Alzheimer's. Codi also reconnects with her sister, Hallie, and with the issues that affect her hometown community.

### Biblio-Trivio

Kingsolver received a Masters of Science from the University of Arizona and went on to write features for journals and newspapers including *The Nation, The New York Times,* and *Smithsonian.*

*Animal Dreams* is a moving story about a woman who is able to come back from the brink of desperation. It is a familial love story that ends on a saccharine note.

4. ***Bastard out of Carolina,* by Dorothy Allison.** This is the story of the Boatwright family, who try to maintain their dignity while refusing to submit to the baggage of the label "poor white trash." It takes place in 1950's South Carolina, as young Ruth Anne (a.k.a. Bone) deals with the outside stereotypes of her family and the ugly, unwanted advances of her stepfather. Ruth was born to her unmarried mother, Anney, 15 at the time, and the big red stamp of "ILLEGITIMATE" graces the birth certificate. Anney spends years trying to get a new certificate and trying to raise her daughters in a loving home. She seeks a father figure for her girls in the form of the local grocer, Glen, with disastrous results (he beats and molests Bone at will).

### Novel Ideas

*Animal Dreams* contains powerful prose, but it also features a checklist of politically correct components. Evil corporate policies, Native American culture, the soulful powers of the desert, and ecological issues are threaded throughout, but are they too overt? Are the hot-button topics manipulative? One of the main criticisms of modern narrative is that every story is a rehashed version of redemption, with all issues in simple black and white. Is that the case here, or should storytelling reward its audience with a happy ending? This is a good title to stimulate a discussion of these questions.

**Biblio-Trivio**

Up until the age of 24, Allison burned everything she wrote: stories, letters, journals, you name it. She was living in a lesbian-feminist collective in Tallahassee, Florida, and the women encouraged her to hold on to her writings and to examine why she was so intent on destroying her works. Allison began to hold on to material for longer periods of time, and six books later everybody has benefited.

Allison treats the material with compassion and a slight hint of nostalgia, an interesting choice considering the subject matter. She vividly captures the rural South and takes her time to explore all the elements of the Boatwright clan. The drinking, poverty, sorrow, and brutality are a central theme, but no more so than family love and inner-strength. Allison's book is a powerful story of child abuse in all its forms and has been known to invoke very personal, intense book club discussions.

**Pro's Prose**

"'What?' Ignatius thundered. 'Do you think that I am going to perambulate about in that sinkhole of vice? No, I am afraid that the Quarter is out of the question. My psyche would crumble in that atmosphere. Besides, the streets are very narrow and dangerous there. I could easily be struck down in traffic or be wedged against a building.'"

—From *A Confederacy of Dunces,* by John Kennedy Toole

5. *A Confederacy of Dunces*, **by John Kennedy Toole.** This Pulitzer Prize–winning novel came out of nowhere in 1980 (the author killed himself 11 years earlier) and has become somewhat of a comic prose landmark. It is the story of Ignatius J. Reilly, a brilliant, obese, self-absorbed, scholarly misfit who gets picked up by a cop in New Orleans for nothing more than looking suspicious. Reilly and his mother deal with the situation by getting blind drunk, crashing their car, and sliding into the dark, twisted vortex of the depths of the French Quarter of New Orleans. As they wander through the insanity of the night, Reilly keeps up a running correspondence with his horny girlfriend and delivers a barrage of rantings and ravings, simultaneously twisted and insightful.

Some readers find Toole's work to be glorified trash, with the depth of a kiddie pool. It also has a huge cult following of readers who consider it a masterpiece, a lucid depiction of the madness of modern society. Either way, it is one of those books that always brings out strong opinions. One question: Was Toole's success dumb luck, or would he have become a literary giant?

These are five books that your group will revel in, and if it's your maiden voyage, they will probably pop up early in the life of the book club.

# Feminized Slant

Another role that reading groups provide for women is as a format for feminist examination. Some groups are militant in their approach, while others are more relaxed in their analysis of women's issues, but they will definitely come up again and again. The depiction of the interplay between men and women, between women and women, and between both sexes and society is the centerpiece of innumerable works of art. Women protagonists are often fighting the standards placed upon them by outside forces, and these battles are at the heart of inequality.

The direction of the debates in your book club will, of course, be heavily influenced by the makeup of the members, but there may come a time when you instinctively know that the group needs to be pointed in a new direction. Perhaps all of your discussions revolve around the accuracy of the dialogue or the hidden symbolism in the characters' furniture, and a feminist analysis is just what you need to fan the winds of change.

Here are a few questions that might work with your monthly selection, especially if things are starting to get a little stale around the edges.

➤ Is the Madonna/whore complex a factor in the depiction of the female protagonist's sexual awareness?

➤ Are the female characters treated with equal depth as their male counterparts?

➤ How would the narrative be different if the protagonist (or antagonist) were a male? Or vice versa?

**Pro's Prose**

"A woman without a man is like a fish without a bicycle."

—Gloria Steinem

**Jane Err**

**Feminism** is a word that has been co-opted in the last few decades and been assigned a negative connotation in many circles, but it's an inaccurate presumption. *Webster's Dictionary* defines it as "the theory of the political, economic, and social equality of the sexes," and "organized activity on behalf of women's rights and interests." Who can argue with that?

➤ If the author is a male, does he accurately capture the voices of women? If not, where does he go off the rails?

➤ Can a man write a feminist work?

➤ If the author is a female, are the characters honest or are they polemic stand-ins?

➤ Are there any double standards in the text? If so, are they essential to the story or a misunderstanding of the female psyche?

➤ Which is worse, psychological or physical violence?

These questions might not work—after all, I am a guy—but it is a way of viewing the texts. Here are five titles that will spark debate over the role and meaning of feminism.

1. *A Room of One's Own,* **by Virginia Woolf.** Who's afraid of Virginia Woolf? Certainly not women of intellect. This epic essay states that in order for women to become great artists, they must have complete financial autonomy and a private room in which to work. Surprisingly, this long essay about society and art and sexism is one of Woolf's most accessible works. Woolf, a major modernist writer and critic, takes us on an erudite yet conversational—and completely entertaining—walk around the history of women in writing, smoothly comparing the architecture of sentences by the likes of William Shakespeare and Jane Austen, all the while lampooning the chauvinistic state of university education in the England of her day. When she concluded that to achieve their full greatness as writers women will need a solid income and privacy, Woolf pretty much invented modern feminist criticism. Woolf celebrates other women authors including Jane Austen and the Brontës, while employing the stream-of-consciousness technique that Joyce used so well.

**Biblio-Trivio**

Virginia Woolf struggled with mental illness all her life and wrote about it in *Moments of Being.* After trying to commit suicide a number of times, she was finally successful when she filled her pockets with rocks and drowned herself in a river near her home.

Woolf was one the original modernist writers; her graceful prose and eclectic, conversational style were visionary. She was also a woman of strong ideas, and one of the more intriguing thoughts in the essay is that all brilliant minds are androgynous. A good query to ponder: Was she able to create a room of her own in light of her mental instability?

2. *The Woman Who Walked into Doors*, **by Roddy Doyle.** This might seem like an odd choice to find in the feminist section, but it begs the very important question, can a man write a feminist novel? Doyle is a book club favorite, and this is the story of Paula Spencer, a 39-year-old Irish woman who is looking back on her hard life a year after the death of her abusive husband. Doyle's familiar tough, foul-mouthed characters litter the pages of this book, but it is a much more moving story than some of his other books. Is it perhaps because he chose a female protagonist? Paula recounts stories from her life as a young girl proud of her early development and the attention it brought her from local boys to her beautiful courtship and honeymoon to the violent reality of her loathsome husband.

One interesting thing about Doyle's work is that the book isn't overwrought with abuse, but it always feels omnipresent. The way Paula's heavy drinking becomes both a literal and emotional excuse for the beatings she takes is another discussion-worthy tangent. The humanism in Paula's dignity and self-determination is very provocative. So, ask yourselves, is this a feminist novel?

> **Novel Ideas**
>
> Compare/contrast *The Woman Who Walked into Doors* with *Bastard out of Carolina*. How is the abuse in each novel treated? Does the author's gender play a part? Is one or the other more realistic? Harrowing? Contrived?

3. *The Portable Dorothy Parker.* Parker is an icon for many reasons, not the least of which is the breadth and depth of her writings. During the 1920s and '30s, when the majority of women were still relegated to "womanly" professions, she became an intellectual force all on her own, which ranks her right up there with any feminist author. She was a poet, a drama critic, a book reviewer, a writer for the stage and screen, and she covered the Spanish Civil War for the *New Masses*. Her sardonic, sarcastic wit dealt with love, sex, and the role of women in the ridiculous mess that is American life.

### Biblio-Trivio

Parker met with other intellectuals of her time, including Robert Benchley and George S. Kaufman, for boozy discussions of, among many topics, politics, culture, and literature (a distant cousin to your book club, perhaps). They met at the Algonquin Hotel in New York City and were known as the Algonquin Round Table. Parker was said to have often ended the gathering with her line, "One more drink and I'll be under the host." The group was brought to the big screen in the 1994 film *Mrs. Parker and the Vicious Circle*, which starred Jennifer Jason Leigh, Campbell Scott, and Matthew Broderick.

### Novel Ideas

A **novella** is defined as "a story with a compact and pointed plot." There isn't a standard page length, but novellas generally run 50 to 100 pages. Examine the format in relation to the standard novel or short story. Does it serve a different purpose? Is it effective?

This fulfilling volume contains many of Parker's best stories, poems, and reviews. She has been criticized for being too sentimental, but her sophisticated irony, caustic humor, and experimental efforts were ahead of their time. She excelled and persevered in a masculine world, and most amazingly, she was self-taught. Parker's intelligence and acerbic tone were developed through her voracious reading and writing habits; she never graduated high school.

4. *Julip*, **by Jim Harrison.** This is a collection of three novellas, the first of which features a quirky, original, feminist woman named Julip. She has spent her entire life surrounded by lunatics and has to find comfort in her individualistic pursuits, training dogs and reading (how apropos). She tries to get her brother declared mentally incompetent so that he can be released from prison. He murdered three of Julip's former lovers, even though she slept with them willingly.

The second novella is the story of a man named Brown Dog who ends up entangled in a mess with a group of radical American Indians. The last novella is the story of an English professor who has a spiritual awakening amid a sexual harassment scandal. Harrison creates characters who are foolish, selfish, bizarre, and oddly uplifting and who often live by the dictates of their libidos. Julip is a conversation piece all on her own, but when discussing her with your group, ask each other if she is a champion of women's rights.

5. ***How the Garcia Girls Got Their Accents Back,*** **by Julia Alvarez.** This is the story of the four Garcia girls and their journey from a life of privilege in the Dominican Republic to the streets of the Bronx. The family is exiled from the Dominican Republic after taking part in a failed coup attempt, but the readers are taken on a journey of stories that works backward. The book opens in the late '60s and the Garcia girls are fully Americanized, with all of the positive and negative connotations immigrants face. The girls are educated and assimilated, but they are also growing up in the wide-open Age of Aquarius and losing their relationship with their heritage. It is a search for identity through 15 interrelated stories.

One of the most interesting aspects to Alvarez's book is the way she portrays the flaws and strengths of each country. From a feminist standpoint, she examines how each country deals with the question of equality. America certainly has more basic freedom, but it is also the consumer culture that leads Sandi Garcia to become obsessed with her weight and unsatisfied with her life. It is an engaging book that covers all sorts of topics in the sisters' growth to adulthood.

**Novel Ideas**

This is a great book to examine how style affects content. Some readers find that working backward with disjointed connecting stories takes away from the narrative and becomes the focus instead of the text itself. Your group will probably have members in both camps, so take the time to discuss how style can add to, or overshadow, content.

# Mother/Daughter Reading Groups

A rapidly emerging subset of the book club experience is the mother/daughter group. I have frequently heard that the groups have opened the lines of communication in ways that no regular dinner table discussion ever could. The setting is intimate, and a carefully chosen selection can bring out feelings, ideas, and emotions that otherwise might lie dormant.

If your daughter doesn't read, knowing what book to choose can be tough, but there is a story out there somewhere that will seem like it was written just for her. If she is already an avid reader, it will enhance a pastime she already enjoys. Topics that are hard to broach, like sex, violence, drugs, and so on, can be tackled with a book that cuts to the heart of what young people feel but might not be ready to share with their parents at the drop of a hat. *The Basketball Diaries* (albeit the movie more than the book) has been blamed for every school shooting in the last few years, but what gets lost in the hysteria is the notion that the children may also identify with the feelings of abandonment in author Jim Carroll's tome.

**Jane Err**

Don't think for one second that a mother/son, father/daughter, or father/son group isn't a worthwhile endeavor. Unfortunately, most males who join book clubs are brought on board by their significant other, so these clubs are rare, but they could provide the breakthrough you've been hoping for. Keep in mind that to make it work, you will have to choose titles that may not be anywhere near your sensibilities, but it should be worth it over time. Truly great novels transcend their basic plotline.

Being part of a mother/daughter reading group can also be an effective way to open up a closed relationship. Mother/daughter groups are referring primarily to adolescent/adult book clubs. A teenager who wants to involve her mother should try to make Mom understand that her participation is as important as if she came to watch her daughter in a play, concert, or soccer game. Parents are always looking for ways to spend more time with their kids, so let your mother know how important her joining your group is.

Another benefit is that mothers are given the opportunity to hear vivid dreams from their daughters' imaginations and creative spirits and realize that they might not be as grown-up as they fear. It isn't only the bridges over troubled waters that can be crossed; more than one mother has said that she was pleasantly surprised that her daughter is dealing with the same issues she did as a child. Mothers also get the chance to listen to the other mothers/daughters in the reading group, which can remind both parent and child that they aren't the only ones who get lost in a sea of ill communication (ask your teenagers; they'll know).

Last, it is the perfect forum to become better friends with your daughter, especially if she is entering her later teen years. It combines the Norman Rockwell painting feel of the two of you participating in a wholesome activity, but it has infinitely more substance than baking bread or hitting tee shots. Rumor has it there is a mother/daughter group that kept its monthly meetings by way of a conference call after members went away to college.

Here are five titles that are favorites of mother/daughter clubs:

1. *Are You There God? It's Me, Margaret,* by **Judy Blume.** This has been a rite of passage for younger adolescent girls since it was published over three decades ago. It is the story of Margaret Simon, a 12-year-old girl who has moved from New York City to the suburbs just as her body is beginning to blossom. Blume was the first author to have a hit book that dealt with the awkwardness girls endure throughout puberty. Menstruation and training bras were apparently

off-limits for the world of children's literature, even though they are two subjects half of the human race deals with in their lifetime.

### Biblio-Trivio

Judy Blume has been enormously popular throughout her career as an author of books for children and adults. She has sold more than 65 million copies and has been translated into 20 languages. She has also been the victim of censorship: *Are You There God? It's Me, Margaret* has been removed from school libraries because of its *content*.

Angst over the slow growth of her chest is not the only crisis Margaret faces. She has a personal relationship with God, but doesn't really have a relationship with organized religion. Does she have to become Jewish to fit in with her new friends? And, where is God with the answers when she needs them? This is a classic book that will be an instant hit with any mother/preteen reading groups, even if they have already read it 50 times. *Then Again, Maybe I Won't* or *Blubber* are also worthy selections.

2. *Little Women,* **by Louisa May Alcott.** This is the enduring classic that is constantly mentioned by female authors when asked of their influences. It is the story of the four March sisters, Beth, Jo, Meg, and Amy, and their New England lives during the Civil War. Each girl has a distinct personality and a world view all her own. The classic novel captures each of the March sisters' hopes, dreams, fears, fights, loves, and losses.

This story of family love has been a favorite of generation after generation; it is guaranteed to strike an emotional chord of one

### Pro's Prose

"'Girls,' said Meg seriously, looking from the tumbled head beside her to the two little night-capped ones in the room beyond, 'Mother wants us to read and love and mind these books, and we must begin at once. We used to be faithful about it; but since Father went away, and all this war trouble unsettled us, we have neglected many things. You can do as you please; but I shall keep my book on the table here, and read a little every morning as soon as I wake for I know it will do me good, and help me through the day.'"

—From *Little Women,* by Louisa May Alcott

color or another, probably in more ways than one. Alcott's 1868 story of Yankee childhood endures as well as any novel ever published in the United States. Ask your group, did they become "little women"?

### Novel Ideas

*My Antonia* is a wonderful look at life on the plains, and the saga of Americans who lived outside the great cities. It reminds the reader of how America is many different countries, and always evokes strong identification for those who live in smaller towns. It is a great book to use in combination with your town's history or with personal genealogy. Hold a meeting dedicated to sharing hometown or family histories.

### Pro's Prose

"Listen, Paula. I am going to tell you a story so that when you wake up you will not feel so lost."

—Opening to *Paula*, by Isabel Allende

3. *My Antonia,* **by Willa Cather.** This is commonly regarded as Cather's finest work in a remarkable career. It is a story of immigrant farm life at the dawn of the twentieth century on the wide-open prairies of Nebraska. Jim Burden recalls his upbringing on the farm and the love he had for Antonia. It is a touching book with a big heart that never dips into sentimentality.

Antonia is a strong, courageous woman, a natural role model for young women. The pioneer spirit is clear throughout, but Cather still manages to keep the prose honest. It is an outstanding achievement.

4. *Paula,* **by Isabel Allende.** This is the moving story that began as a letter to Allende's grown daughter, who slipped into an irreversible coma in 1991. She started writing their family's history to give to her daughter, Paula, when she came out of the coma, which never happened.

The story of the Allendes is nonfiction, but the author includes magical realism and dreamy fantasy elements to contrast the sad, sober reality. It is also a fascinating family story, because Allende's uncle was elected president of Chile in 1970, but Augusto Pinochet lead a military coup that overthrew Salvador Allende's socialist government in 1973. The family had to escape to Venezuela in 1975, and the saga is as compelling as Paula's death is heart-wrenching. Ultimately, it is a beautiful book about the great love a mother has for her child.

5. *Her First American,* **by Lore Segal.** This is a book that has had a huge following in the literary community and would be a fantastic selection for any mother/daughter group. It is a story with a wide scope, covering everything from immigrant life and interracial relationships to a mother/daughter dance and the effects of alcoholism. It is also a complex, bittersweet love story that shows how people grow, learn, and change from those we love.

The protagonist is 21-year-old Ilka Weissnix, who has arrived in America after surviving the Nazi terrors in Europe. She meets "her first American," Carter Bayoux, a distressed black intellect. Bayoux has a different view of Weissnix's new country and their relationship is remarkable. It is a book that is destined to become a classic, and your group shouldn't miss it.

Following are a few other suggestions for books by women authors for all-female book clubs or specifically for mother/daughter groups:

➤ *The Handmaid's Tale,* by Margaret Atwood

➤ *The House of the Spirits,* by Isabel Allende

➤ *Pride and Prejudice,* by Jane Austen

➤ *The Good Earth,* by Pearl S. Buck

➤ *The Book of Ruth,* by Jane Hamilton

➤ *Mrs. Dalloway,* by Virginia Woolf

➤ *Them,* by Joyce Carol Oates

➤ *My Home Is Far Away,* by Dawn Powell

➤ *Frankenstein,* by Mary Wollstonecraft Shelley

➤ *Save Me the Waltz,* by Zelda Fitzgerald

➤ *In This Our Life,* by Ellen Glasgow

➤ *The Road from Coorain,* by Jill Ker Conway

➤ *Tracks,* by Louise Erdrich

➤ *Who Will Run the Frog Hospital?* by Lorrie Moore

➤ *The War Between the Tates,* by Alison Lurie

➤ *Wuthering Heights,* by Emily Brontë

➤ *The Sea, the Sea,* by Iris Murdoch

➤ *The Prime of Miss Jean Brodie,* by Muriel Spark

➤ *The Accidental Tourist,* by Anne Tyler

➤ *Death Comes for the Archbishop,* by Willa Cather

➤ *Zeely,* by Virginia Hamilton

➤ *Machine Dreams,* by Jayne Anne Phillips

➤ *The Custom of the Country,* by Edith Wharton

➤ *Gone With the Wind,* by Margaret Mitchell

➤ *The Bone People,* by Keri Hulme

➤ *The Wedding,* by Dorothy West

**Novel Ideas**

*The New York Times Book Review* said of *Her First American,* "Lore Segal may have come closer than anyone to writing the Great American Novel." Ask your book club, what is the "Great American Novel"? Is there such a thing, or is it an empty label that everyone loves to throw around? What, if anything, would define the "Great American Novel" (as opposed to the great Icelandic or Egyptian novel)? Have everyone choose one book that they feel comes closest to their view of the "Great American Novel" and let the games begin.

### The Least You Need to Know

➤ For reasons yet to be explained, there are infinitely more women than men in the reading group universe.

➤ *Beloved* is probably the number-one book club staple.

➤ A feminist approach to material can fan the winds of change.

➤ Mother/daughter groups can open dormant lines of communication.

# Chapter 11

# Men's Groups—
# a Rare Species

---

### In This Chapter

➤ Why don't men get it?

➤ The tricks of the trade

➤ Trouts, outs, louts, baddies, and daddies

➤ I got your second list right 'ere

---

As you well know by now, men just don't seem to get it. For whatever reason, book clubs aren't thriving among the testosterone-toting in the same way they do in the estrogen zone.

So, the question becomes, how do you get men to overcome the "female" feeling in the air at a reading group?

One sure-fire way to get men to come to book club meetings is to offer high-quality grub (which we will discuss later), but will they willingly come with an open mind? Fred Flintstone would sit through hours of Betty and Wilma talking about Pat Conrock's novel *The Prince of Stones,* as long as he was able to gnaw on a big ol' well-done brontosaurus burger, but would Fred's heart (and mind) be in the right place?

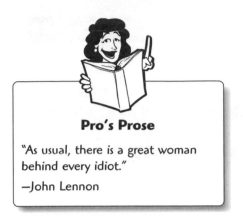

**Pro's Prose**

"As usual, there is a great woman behind every idiot."

—John Lennon

# Where You At?

I don't want to belabor the point, because it isn't a dire situation. Book clubs made up of men and women do exist, but the all-male club is a rarity. And, indeed, some book clubs that encompass an all-female membership like it that way. It's as if the stereotype of men not being sensitive, thoughtful, or patient enough to fit into the introspective milieu may be at hand. The problem with this stereotype is that there are too many men who become poster children for it. Unfortunately, both men and women lose out and are the lesser for it. One ironic twist is that reading groups evolved because women weren't allowed to participate in intellectual and literary pursuits. Another twist is that book club selections aren't normally tilted toward male or female authors; it's one of the few 50-50 gender propositions around. But is the lack of a consistent male presence in the reading group stew going to be an eternal Achilles' heel?

**Biblio-Trivio**

The expression "Achilles' heel" means a weakness or fault, and it comes from Greek mythology. Thetis, mother of the warrior Achilles, wanted to make her son invulnerable by dipping his body in the river Styx. Thetis held Achilles by the heel, and it was thus untouched by the water. It remained vulnerable and was the warrior's only mortal body part. He was eventually brought down by Paris, who shot a poisoned arrow that struck him in the heel. The battle between Achilles and Agamemnon is recounted in Homer's *Iliad*.

Another truth not to be overlooked is that men don't read less than women; they just don't join reading groups. So, the challenge is to recruit those apples who are ripe for picking. If you, or someone you know, fall into one of these categories, please rise:

➤ A guy who would enjoy a book club but is too thin-skinned to withstand the taunts of family or friends.

➤ A guy who wants to join but isn't sure where to look (please return to the beginning of the book and read much slower).

➤ A guy who reads a ton of genre fiction (sci-fi, Westerns, mysteries, horror).

➤ An introverted guy who reads quite a bit but looks down his nose at book clubs.

➤ A guy who reads daily newspapers and monthly magazines and always wants to cover the topics of the day at the dinner table.

Now, look around: There are plenty of men who stood up. All that is needed is a concentrated recruiting effort because normally once men become reading group members, they have a rewarding experience.

Book clubs serve another basic human need for companionship, and the camaraderie often reaches a deeper level than a general civic club. A successful club always leads to the shedding of false personas and a breaking down of defense mechanisms, which is a longing men crave (and need), even if they won't admit it. And I'm not exactly part of the Alan Alda crowd, so you can imagine the verbal beating I am going to endure for that last sentence.

## Guy Stuff

One way to entice the masculine half is to relate to them on their terms. Disguise the high-minded narratives under the guise of generic testosterone-juiced "guy stuff" categories. Give it to 'em straight to get them thinking about a few of their favorite things. Men are simple creatures; use that to your advantage.

If, however, you are a trailblazing fellow and want to found an all-male group, kudos to you. The best attack is to keep it low-key while pushing specific titles. Start by sharing a dynamite book with a few friends and striking up a conversation. Find out if there is any interest in the book and, if so, see if you can get a few friends to meet and discuss the tome. Starting an all-male book club is no different than an all-female or co-ed group, but the stigma of the "book club" label might derail the train before it leaves the station. If you are trying to convince skeptical friends, start with a great book and work backward. If you are recruiting strangers, follow the established standards because there are a lot of men out there who are only looking for the opportunity.

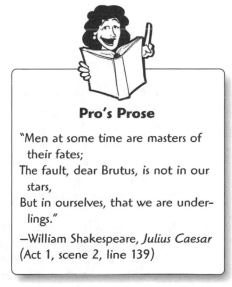

**Pro's Prose**

"Men at some time are masters of their fates;
The fault, dear Brutus, is not in our stars,
But in ourselves, that we are underlings."

—William Shakespeare, *Julius Caesar* (Act 1, scene 2, line 139)

The upcoming suggestions are geared toward women who want to recruit men, but they can easily be revised for men asking men to join the book club universe (just don't let on what it is).

We are underlings, subordinate to those things that make life worth living, so try this approach.

## Fishing

"Honey, you should join the reading group for the next couple of months, we're going to cover books about your favorite pastime: fishing."

"Oh yeah? Sounds like it might be interesting. Okay, I'll come, I should read more."

Now, what fishing books, pray tell, should you attempt? Try one of these:

1. ***The Old Man and the Sea,* by Ernest Hemingway.** One of the man's most enduring tomes. It is the story of a poor, lonely, old Cuban fisherman, Santiago, and his relentless struggle with a giant marlin out in the waters of the Gulf Stream. It takes our hero three days to land the glorious fish, only to have sharks ravage it as he brings it back to the harbor. Santiago's seemingly failed battle becomes a personal triumph as the other fishermen marvel at the enormous skeleton.

**Biblio-Trivio**

*The Old Man and the Sea* won the Pulitzer in 1953 and was a major factor in Hemingway being awarded the Nobel Prize for Literature in 1954. In April 1999, Hemingway's centennial, four Nobel laureates (and numerous other literary heavyweights) met at the JFK library in Boston to honor Papa. The fearsome foursome was made up of Nadine Gordimer, Derek Walcott, Kenzaburo Oe, and Saul Bellow.

Hemingway's masterpiece was his last major work of fiction and manages to have the scope of an epic journey and the directness of a parable. It is a story of courage and fulfillment, and one of the best fish stories ever told. Plus, it isn't all that long, so you can slowly initiate the skeptical male of your choice.

2. *A River Runs Through It,* **by Norman Maclean.** This portrait of a Montana family that is divided by life, united by fly-fishing, has quietly become a modern-day classic. Two brothers, headed in opposite directions in life, and their father, a religious man, learn to understand one another when they are on the river. Fly-fishing isn't a metaphor for life; it is life here.

The time the brothers spend on the river provides the moments that fill the mental scrapbooks we all keep of our siblings. Maclean knows we can't stop the ones we love from self-destructing, so find the ground upon which you can find acceptance and unity—in this brilliant case, fly-fishing on a gorgeous Montana river.

3. *Moby Dick,* **by Herman Melville.** You can call me Al, but a true angler would rather you call him Ishmael. With the possible exception of that Jonah guy and his tale from the belly of the beast, this is the fish story to beat. All right, so technically it's a *whaling* story, but it's still an incredible portrait of obsession. Vengeance is the driving force for Captain Ahab, who roams the sea searching for the great white whale, Moby Dick, who took his leg on an earlier voyage.

In some ways, it mirrors all intense fishing experiences, the will of the human spirit against the magnificent creatures with which we share the Earth. In other ways, it mirrors all of our human experiences, the battles of good versus evil. The question is: Is it Moby Dick or Ahab who defines good or evil? Or is it a combination of both?

Following is another scenario to kick around.

**Pro's Prose**

"In our family, there was no clear line between religion and fly fishing."

—Opening line to *A River Runs Through It,* by Norman Maclean

**Jane Err**

Don't start the fish stories with *Moby Dick.* It is a thick, complex novel that should come somewhere down the road. Start off with one of the other two selections, and then go with Melville's magnum opus. It has layer upon layer to unravel and discuss, but it's not for rookies.

**Novel Ideas**

If your group isn't too big, hold your monthly book club meeting out on a boat. If you choose a book with an appropriate subject (fishing, lakes, summertime), it will be a delightful change of pace.

# Baseball

"Pumpkin, do you remember in *Pride of the Yankees* when Gary Cooper says '... today (today), ... I consider myself (I consider myself) ... the luckiest man (the luckiest man) ... on the face of the Earth (on the face of the Earth) ...'?"

"Of course, it's only the greatest baseball scene in movie history."

"Well, I'd consider myself the luckiest person on the face of the Earth if you would join our book club for a discussion of diamond fiction."

"Ummm, okay."

So, baseball fans, get ready to step up to the plate with one of these favorites:

1. *Shoeless Joe,* by W. P. Kinsella. Most of you will recognize the film adaptation that starred Kevin Costner, *Field of Dreams,* and they both share the wonder and magic that a simple game has provided for our young nation. The story is basically the same: Ray Kinsella hears a voice from his cornfield and proceeds to build a baseball field on his land in honor of baseball icon Shoeless Joe Jackson, putting his family in financial jeopardy.

**Biblio-Trivio**

In the movie, Ray has to take a reclusive, semifamous author named Terrence Mann, played by James Earl Jones, to a Boston Red Sox game. In the novel, the hermitic author is none other than J. D. Salinger. He threatened to sue, so the character was changed in the movie.

The lyrical book is a fantasy for the baseball fan in all of us. It is a story of what makes America great: the crack of a bat, a row of corn, and the love of a family to share them with. "If you push it, they will come."

2. *The Natural,* by Bernard Malamud. This is another book that was turned into a popular movie, the 1984 film that starred Robert Redford. Unlike the previous novel, the filmed version of Malamud's work was vastly altered. In the deeper,

more realistic and nuanced book, Roy Hobbs is not a stoic hero. Hobbs does come back to tear up the league and lead the New York Knights into pennant contention, but hubris leads to his ultimate downfall.

Malamud's story raises questions of greater complexity, the audience roots for Hobbs because of his amazing efforts, but also sees his basic human flaws, which include greed and insatiable lust. The movie is fine escapist fare, but the novel offers so much more. Compare the final scenes in each, one a mammoth home run, the other a man weeping bitterly, and ask your group which has the more humanistic, poetic ending?

3. *Men at Work,* **by George Will.** Will has been criticized in the past for his pompous style and unabashedly one-sided conservative arguments, but his "other" life is irrelevant in *Men at Work.* One thing the man knows inside and out is baseball, and, interestingly enough, there has been more than one cultural pundit who has made the claim that Will writes better essays on the grand old game than on the grand old party.

This incisive book is broken down into four distinct sections: the Manager (Tony LaRussa), the Pitcher (Orel Hershiser), the Batter (Tony Gwynn), and the Defense (Cal Ripken Jr.). Will breaks down each section with succinct, intelligent analysis. It is a book that will appeal to longtime students of the game as they compare their own theories with Mr. Will's, and those who know nothing about the game and want to thoroughly learn what makes baseball so unique. It is also an interesting character study with characters who are dedicated to the game and to being the best every time they take the field. One question to ponder in your group is which is more important: desire or natural ability?

**Pro's Prose**

"In our sun-down perambulations of late, through the outer parts of Brooklyn, we have observed several parties of youngsters playing base, a certain game of ball ... Let us go forth awhile, and get better air in our lungs. Let us leave our close rooms ... The game of ball is glorious."

—Walt Whitman

**Pro's Prose**

"Winning is not everything. Baseball—its beauty, its craftsmanship, its exactingness—is an *activity* to be loved, as much as ballet or fishing or politics, and loving it is a form of participation."

—Excerpt from the introduction of *Men at Work,* by George Will

### Novel Ideas

Offer to take said man to an up-coming ballgame, complete with beers, hot dogs, and peanuts, in exchange for his participation in the next book club meeting. A little good-natured bribery never hurt anyone. Plus, it reinforces the desire to read about baseball.

## Tough Guys

Getting guy into book club sketch, take three:

"Sweetheart, you know how whenever it's your turn to pick the flick it has to star Robert Mitchum, Steve McQueen, Clint Eastwood, or Bruce Willis?"

"Hey, I sat through that Meg Ryan fest you and your sister made me—"

"All I was going to say is that my book club is reading a novel about a guy who kicked a lot more butt than all your cinematic heroes combined."

"Oh, yeah?"

1. *L.A. Confidential,* by James Ellroy. This is a tangled web of murder, sex, blood, tabloids, drugs, tough guys, and glitzy '50s Hollywood showmanship. Ellroy revels in the La-La-Land underworld, and so will you. It has more plot than some authors have in their entire collection. It boils down the story of three cops with tortured souls trying to solve a wide-open spiral of crime that includes heroin dealers, hookers sculpted into movie stars, a twisted land developer, and more crooked cons, cold corpses, and corrupt cops than you can shake a nightstick at.

### Biblio-Trivio

What do respected novelists James Ellroy and Don DeLillo have in common with bombastic filmmaker Oliver Stone? All three have given the masses a take on the JKF assassination; Ellroy in *American Tabloid*, DeLillo in *Libra*, and Stone in the big-screen's *JFK*.

This was made into one of the better film adaptations you will ever see (which we will discuss later), but the novel adds subplots and dimensions the movie couldn't capture in the allotted time span. It rises above the genre because of its unique style and multiple narrative strains. Ellroy's dynamic wordplay, hard-boiled dialogue, and rapid-fire paragraphs keep readers on their toes, but it is definitely worth it. It's a can't-miss for those who love crime stories.

2. *Lonesome Dove,* **by Larry McMurtry.** Like *L.A. Confidential,* this novel avoids the limits and structures of the genre by creating its own distinct universe. McMurtry's turf is the American West and the wide-open terrain it encompasses. It's the tale of two former Texas Rangers, Augustus McCrae and W. F. McCall, who drive their cattle north to Montana. They start out as common hard-scrabble antiheroes of so many revisionist Western novels and movies, but the long journey changes them. This saga has arc and scope, and a sense of purpose far greater and more relevant than the movement of cattle across the shifting landscape.

### Biblio-Trivio

McMurtry owns antiquarian bookstores in Tucson, Arizona, and Washington, D.C., but his largest store is in his tiny hometown of Archer City, Texas. Its 300,000–volume well competes with the larger dealers in the country.

The book is a tremendously engaging read with all sorts of secondary characters, wild animals, and lively settings. A query to debate: Does the cattle rustlers' vision of the American Dream match up with yours?

3. *Population 1280,* **by Jim Thompson.** If there ever was an example of the expression "hard-boiled," this is it. Thompson is a master at digging into the violent, cold-hearted, ruthless underbelly of picture-perfect Americana dreams. He is one of the defining authors of the *noir genera* that permeated American fiction after World War II, but *Population 1280* breaks the mold. It has an injection of black humor that sets it apart from the rest of Thompson's oeuvre. It is the story of Sheriff Nick Corey, a lazy man with a love of booze and illicit sex. The problem is some of the people in and around the town, most notably his wife, are starting to make trouble and the only way Corey deals with trouble is behind a gun.

For all those who root for the bad guy to win, or at least get away scot-free, this book's for you. Corey is no charming rapscallion; he is a cold-blooded murderer, but the wicked soul is often more interesting. Thompson will appeal to the sadist in all of us.

Let's milk this cheesy segue one more time.

## Fathers and Sons

"I know you feel like you don't communicate with Myron very well, but things are fine. It's natural to have a gulf with your teenage son."

"No, I'm pretty sure I am the worst on record."

"No you're not."

"You're just saying that."

"No. I'm not. But you and Myron should join my book club. We're focusing on fathers and sons whose relationships will make you feel like you truly earned that World's Greatest Dad T-shirt."

1. *Affliction*, **by Russell Banks.** Banks grew up in a rough blue-collar family, and this story reflects his tough upbringing. It is the story of Wade Whitehouse, a hard-drinking, middle-aged father in a small town in New Hampshire, devastated by the closing of a local mill. Wade's life is unraveling amid a series of awful deaths. Wade's rage takes over his soul during the final two weeks of his life that crush his hopeless dream of familial bliss. Through a series of flashbacks, the readers are taken back to scenes of Wade's abusive, alcoholic father.

Banks is one of the finest storytellers of the lives of those who live on the fringes of so-called "normal" society: the broke, tired, uneducated, and lonely have-nots who never fulfill their American dream. *Affliction* is a powerful tale of the cycle of violence passed on from father to son.

### Biblio-Trivio

Banks spent time living and writing in a Florida trailer park. His first big success was a book titled *Trailerpark*. It chronicled the lives of the poor "trailer trash" overlooked, stereotyped, or plain forgotten by the mainstream.

2. *The Great Santini,* **by Pat Conroy.** Bull Meecham is a devout Marine and treats his family like his personal battalion. Conroy explores the emotional, volatile relationship with his eldest son, Ben, an athlete who never measures up to Bull's standards. Ben tries to stand up for himself, but that goes against the military code in Bull's twisted sense of loyalty.

   The Southern landscape factors heavily in Conroy's prose, and his use of humor adds a necessary touch of humanity. Conroy's greatest trick, however, is making Bull an empathetic character.

3. *Independence Day,* **by Richard Ford.** This is the second novel about Frank Bascombe, first introduced in *The Sportswriter*. Frank takes his son, Paul, who is still haunted by the death of his brother, Ralph, on a weekend of sightseeing at sports stops that include the Baseball Hall of Fame and a Vince Lombardi rest stop in New Jersey.

### Pro's Prose

"My father's violence is the central fact of my art and my life."

—Attributed to Pat Conroy

### Biblio-Trivio

Richard Ford worked for a time at *Inside Sports* magazine. His experiences were the backdrop for his chronicles of Frank Bascombe.

All of you who think you have trouble relating to your teenagers will quickly identify with Ford and his attempts to know his troubled son better. This book is frequently laugh-out-loud funny, and Ford's use of fate in the mundane grind of life is outstanding.

# Get the Men Out

Parts of this chapter have drifted into stereotypical conceits, but it would be foolish to say that there isn't some truth at work. For whatever reason, women make up a much higher percentage of book clubians, and it is too bad. Most people get much more out of their reading group than they put in, and it offers self-improvement by its very nature. I can understand that all-female groups would be reluctant to throw a man into the mix; people don't act the same in mixed company. But you are missing out on a different perspective, and it is an almost foolproof guarantee against homogenization. Plus, it's important to discuss novels from all sides, and if all sides aren't represented, something is lacking.

I encourage the same sensibility for people of various religions, ethnic backgrounds, and sexual orientation. It is going to take some work, but we need a concentrated effort to include the dudes. Start one at a time, invite a man to your next meeting and see what develops. He may tell a friend, who tells a friend, and so on and so forth, until they're forming their own groups at the rate that Stephen King writes new tales of the macabre. Before you know it, engines won't be tuned, lawns won't be mowed, basketballs won't be dribbled, and fences will remain unpainted as your men lie in hammocks with an icy cold glass of lemonade wiping away their tears as they finish the final pages of Michael Ondaatje's *The English Patient*.

And just to give you some more to think about, following are a few more book club kind of books by male authors that any self-respecting guy would read:

➤ *Underworld,* by Don DeLillo

➤ *Bleak House,* by Charles Dickens

➤ *Les Misérables,* by Victor Hugo

➤ *Something to Be Desired,* by Thomas McGuane

➤ *Purple America,* by Rick Moody

➤ *The Trial,* by Franz Kafka

➤ *Paris Trout,* by Pete Dexter

➤ *All the Pretty Horses,* by Cormac McCarthy

➤ *Rabbit, Run,* by John Updike

➤ *A Prayer for Owen Meany,* by John Irving

➤ *Farmer,* by Jim Harrison

➤ *Herzog,* by Saul Bellow

➤ *Babbit,* by Sinclair Lewis

- ➤ *The Adventures of Sherlock Holmes,* by Sir Arthur Conan Doyle
- ➤ *The Sheltering Sky,* by Paul Bowles
- ➤ *Naked Lunch,* by William S. Burroughs
- ➤ *Rule of the Bone,* by Russell Banks
- ➤ *The Call of the Wild,* by Jack London
- ➤ *Cannery Row,* by John Steinbeck
- ➤ *A Room with a View,* by E. M. Forster
- ➤ *Washington Square,* by Henry James
- ➤ *All Quiet on the Western Front,* by Erich Maria Remarque
- ➤ *A Separate Peace,* by John Knowles
- ➤ *In the Lake of the Woods,* by Tim O'Brien
- ➤ *American Pastoral,* by Philip Roth

---

### The Least You Need to Know

- ➤ There need to be more men in the book club movement.
- ➤ Lots of guys fit the profile; seek them out.
- ➤ There are plenty of books with "guy stuff" at their core.
- ➤ Baseball and fishing are worthy subjects for literature.

# Chapter 12

# Multicultural Musings—Exploring Cultural Identity

## In This Chapter

➤ Why reading groups have a positive effect on cross-culturalization

➤ Jumping into the great literary melting pot

➤ A peak at the African-American experience through literature

➤ Why black and white aren't the only shades that matter—a look at Latino and Spanish, Asian, and Native American writers

One of the truly great experiences of a reading group is that the world of books knows no boundaries. The selections often cross every racial, gender, religious, cultural, regional, sexual, or whatever line (interplanetary?) you can draw in the sand. The fact that *Beloved* is probably the most popular book club title speaks volumes about our appetites for learning about all those who make up this beautiful planet we share. We tend to overlook the strides that have been made in the last few decades; it ain't *Utopia*, but would a book, written by an African-American woman, about the brutal effects of slavery on a poor, scared woman have been roundly discussed by white Americans 50 years ago?

Reading groups aren't going to fix any of the problems we face as a society, but every tome probed by a reader who may know very little about the author's reality has to be a step in the right direction. If nothing else, it leads to a deeper understanding, which is important in these fractured times.

**Biblio-Trivio**

Euripides wrote *The Trojan Women* about 2,500 years ago, but its bitter denunciation of the emptiness of war and its gritty, graphic realism are the forerunner to *Saving Private Ryan* and *The Thin Red Line*. Sophocles himself said that he wrote how men should be, while Euripides wrote how men are, which, coincidentally, is what some film critics claimed was the difference between Spielberg's and Malick's World War II cinematic examinations.

# Identity, Who Am I?

Other than the hard sciences, almost every aspect of writing aims to solve the riddles "Who am I, and how did I get here?" Why do scholars spend their lives researching minute details of history? Because human behavior has long dictated that we will make the same stupid mistakes again and again. It's a cliché, but those who do not confront the past are doomed to repeat it, which will happen until mankind goes the way of the woolly mammoth.

**Pro's Prose**

"From family to nation, every human group is a society of island universes."

—Aldous Huxley

The questions of identification are central to written works of all shapes and sizes, but for bookkeeping purposes we will be dividing groups into varying ethnic, sexual, and religious enclaves. That will make it easier to flip to the individual reading lists anyhow, which is what most of you bought this book for in the first place. Oh, don't think I don't know.

# The Great American Reading Group Melting Pot

The United States has long been called the world's melting pot. In this spirit, I recommend that you choose a wide variety of titles, including selections that may be 100 percent outside the radar of your reading group's collective sensibility. There is a world of books to revel in—enjoy a taste of all the different meals on the literary menu. Grab a ladle and let's get started.

# African-American Tomes

Many reading groups are seeking out books by authors of color, especially because Oprah's book club includes all sorts of writers. Keep in mind that the books that follow are listed in categories as a quick reference point; there are no boundaries. All of the novels in this chapter are worthwhile for any book club. If your group is looking for books that deal with the African-American experience, here are some of the best African-American selections:

### Novel Ideas

If homogenization in the book selections is becoming a problem, write down eight selections: two popular, two classic, two controversial, and two unknown works. To make it even more random, have an outsider make the choices. Draw four, throw the rest away, and you are covered for the next third of the reading group calendar.

1. *Invisible Man,* **by Ralph Ellison.** There is a school of thought that Ellison's work of brilliance, published in 1952, is the best book ever written about a black man's experience in a white man's world, and you will certainly get no argument from me. It is a story told by a nameless narrator of a young black man's journey from the Deep South to the streets of Harlem. His pilgrimage takes him from a historic black college, from which he is expelled, to a key role in the "Brotherhood," a black activist organization, to a lonely basement where he becomes the Invisible Man he always believed he was.

   Ellison uses stream of consciousness, naturalism, surrealism, and the juxtaposition of wide-eyed innocence and grave macabre. It won the National Book Award for fiction in 1953 and was one of the first major works to deal with racial problems in America from a black man's perspective. It struck a cord and remained on the best-seller list for four months. It is an amazing work about how societal pressures create invisible men. Question: Are things different than they were in 1952?

2. *Their Eyes Were Watching God,* **by Zora Neale Hurston.** This is the story of a strong-willed, independent Southern black woman, Janie Crawford, who refuses to live her life under any standards but her own. Crawford's quest is for the most basic of human needs, one that transcends all other barriers: She is looking for herself and someone to love her as such. Her journey spans 25 years and three marriages.

### Biblio-Trivio

Zola Neale Hurston was born and raised in Eatonville, Florida, the nation's first incorporated, self-governing city. In 1960, she died very poor and unrecognized by the literary community and was buried in an unmarked grave. In 1973, Alice Walker successfully led a quest to find her literary idol and give her a proper burial site. Walker was instrumental in bringing Hurston's work back to the forefront and making sure her epitaph reminded folks that she was a genius of the South.

### Jane Err

Don't attempt to read another of Wideman's complex tomes, *Philadelphia Fire,* without accruing information on the 1985 bombing of the MOVE house in Philadelphia. Eleven members of the black, militant MOVE were killed (and 250 neighborhood denizens were left homeless). The irony that the assault was ordered by a black mayor, Wilson Goode, seeps through the prose at every turn. *Philadelphia Fire,* like *Brothers and Keepers,* is a powerful work that honestly questions how we reached the point of military action against our own citizens.

Hurston's masterpiece is a favorite of book clubs because of Crawford's determination to find a rich love. Does she fulfill her quest?

3. *Brothers and Keepers,* **by John Edgar Wideman.** Wideman has written numerous books about the black experience, many of them set in the Pittsburgh ghetto of Homewood where he grew up. His works are challenging and complex, with the influence of the Joycean stream of consciousness. *Brothers and Keepers* is the autobiographical story of the author and his brother Robby, who is serving a life sentence for a murder committed during a botched robbery. It is an introspective work about the bond between brothers, racial identity, and the dichotomy of guilt and pride in his successes and Robby's failure.

This is a raw examination of what family means, the role of fate in personal growth, and the disparity of the racial makeup in our criminal justice system. Ask your group what they would do if one of their siblings, close friends, or children (Wideman's son is also in prison for murder) committed a brutal crime? How would you handle it?

The following are some books by African-American authors:

➤ *Native Son,* by Richard Wright

➤ *Jazz,* by Toni Morrison

➤ *The Color Purple,* by Alice Walker

➤ *Middle Passage,* by Charles Johnson

➤ *The Autobiography of My Mother,* by Jamaica Kincaid

➤ *Disappearing Act,* by Terry McMillan

➤ *The Women of Brewster Place,* by Gloria Naylor

➤ *Breath, Eyes, Memory,* by Edwidge Danticat

➤ *Anthills of the Savannah,* by Chinua Achebe

➤ *Go Tell It on the Mountain,* by James Baldwin

➤ *High Cotton,* by Darryl Pinckney

➤ *Your Blues Ain't Like Mine,* by Bebe Moore Campbell

➤ *Roots,* by Alex Haley

➤ *Finding Makeba,* by Alexis D. Pate

➤ *Philadelphia Fire,* by John Edgar Wideman

# Not Just Black and White

Hispanic Americans are the fastest-growing minority group in America, and population experts have predicted there will be as many as 50 million Latinos in this country by 2025. Latino book clubs have been growing in record numbers, and there seems to be a shift in the publishing world to include more and more Hispanic authors, so it is a heady time to join the mix. There are a few other considerations to bat around the room when reading works from Hispanic authors, such as …

➤ How do the immigrant characters' experiences differ from Jewish immigrants, Irish immigrants, Italian immigrants? Can you think of any similar immigrant stories that match that of this book?

➤ What are the major differences/similarities between various Latino cultures within various novels? (By the way, this same question works well for all groups: Jamaican vs. African American, Korean vs. Japanese, etc.)

➤ In this book, how does Latino culture influence mainstream American culture? Are there any real-life examples that you can draw on to further demonstrate this? These are basic questions, and there are certainly much deeper questions that can be extracted from individual texts. Searching for patterns within a frame of literature is always a challenge worth pursuing. Also, asking questions that cross standard assumptions can open the floodgates of communication as well. For instance, how has the continuing spectrum of slavery, America's original sin,

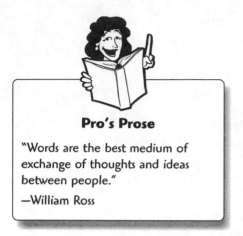

**Pro's Prose**

"Words are the best medium of exchange of thoughts and ideas between people."

—William Ross

affected literature by Latino authors? Slavery is usually viewed through a black/white prism, but consider for a moment its resonance upon Latino writing. Does it have any influence at all?

Try writing down an assumption you have about an unread work and applying that to a book you recently completed. You will quickly find the flaws in the thought process because assumptions about what a novel will entail are often misguided. It's just a quick check to remind yourself that there are great books from all over the spectrum of literature. As my mother always says, "When you assume, you make an ass out of you and me," but examining how those assumptions truly relate to others can be a mind-enriching experience. Here are a couple of brilliant selections by Latino authors:

1. *One Hundred Years of Solitude,* by Gabriel García Márquez. This is the irrepressible tale of the mythical town of Macondo, from its sleepy dawn to its apocalyptic finish, as told through six generations of the Buenda family. This epic yarn is awash in symbolism and fantastical plotting, unending rains and levitating priests, and yellow flowers falling from the heavens.

**Biblio-Trivio**

Always a committed leftist, García Márquez accused the Colombian government of trampling free speech after they shut down his antigovernment television program, QAP, which was a muckraking exposé that often reported on official corruption. QAP was the first to report on political contributions by the Cali drug cartel, even though official channels found no wrongdoing.

García Márquez made the world safe for Latin American magical realism, and it hasn't been the same since. Magical realism blends fantasy and reality until the distinction is vanquished. *One Hundred Years of Solitude* won the Nobel Prize for literature in 1982 and is often cited as the most powerful and universally loved of Márquez's work. The sheer genius is obvious in the mystical symbols, eccentric characters, and surrealistic events that unfold in the town of Macondo, which now ranks up there with Oz and Never-Never Land as places we should all be so lucky to visit. In talking to book clubians, I have learned that *One Hundred Years of Solitude* is frequently cited as a classic, and one they would consider revisiting.

2. *Paradise,* **by Elena Castedo.** This book was nominated for a National Book Award in 1990 and rightfully so; it is an impressive literary debut. The story is narrated by an insightful 10-year-old, Solita, who is a refugee from Franco's Spain. She chronicles the journey her mother, Pilar, takes her on from a run-down Chilean ghetto to an estate called El Topaz—Paradise. Pilar was formerly an aristocrat and yearns for nothing more than the chance to hang around the rich, powerful, important people.

This novel has a bit of a Spanish *Great Gatsby* theme in its examination of the pretensions, mores, shallowness, and the multitude of class divisions between wealthy eccentrics and common folk. Ultimately, Solita yearns to return home to her father. But did she live a safer life in the slums?

### Pro's Prose

"The best way to get where you want to be is to please those who own the road."

—From *Paradise,* by Elena Castedo

3. *Drown,* **by Junot Diaz.** This is a collection of ten stories about a family trying to achieve the "American dream." There are stories of children, teenagers, and adults trying to find their identity and build a substantial family life. The stories weave the Dominican Republic and America into a larger picture of trying to escape despair, external and internal. In "No Face," a young boy with a disfigured appearance tries to maintain his dignity among the torments of other village children. In "How to Date a Browngirl, Blackgirl, Whitegirl, or Halfie," a cocky teenager shares his secrets to getting any girl he desires.

Diaz is one of the most respected new voices, and these stories have a lot to chew on. Maintaining a family and struggling to grasp the "American dream" have been a part of this country's literature since day one, and Diaz's take on the material is a fine addition.

### Pro's Prose

"Dinner will be tense ... A halfie will tell you that her parents met in the Movement ... Your brother once heard that one and said, 'Man, that sounds like a whole lot of Uncle Tomming to me.' Don't repeat this."

—From "How to Date a Browngirl, Blackgirl, Whitegirl, or Halfie," in *Drown,* by Junot Diaz

### Biblio-Trivio

Junot Diaz immigrated from a poverty-stricken area of the Dominican Republic to the supposedly greener pastures of New Jersey.

### Novel Ideas

Reading *The Mambo Kings*, Oscar Hijuelos's enjoyable story of two Cuban brothers who form an orchestra called the "Mambo Kings" and appear as Ricky Ricardo's cousins on *I Love Lucy*, will be heightened if you throw on a couple of Tito Puente albums of the period. The legendary bandleader is of Puerto Rican descent, and he *is* the mambo king. *Cuban Carnival* (1956) and *Dance Mania* (1958) will set the perfect mood for the "Mambo Kings," both fictional and literal.

Now that your interest is piqued, here are some more suggestions by Spanish and Latino authors:

➤ *The Mambo Kings Play Songs of Love*, by Oscar Hijuelos
➤ *The Autobiography of a Brown Buffalo*, by Oscar Zeta Acosta
➤ *Hopscotch*, by Julio Cortazar
➤ *Aunt Julia and the Scriptwriter*, by Mario Vargas Llosa
➤ *The Violent Land*, by Jorge Amado
➤ *Love in the Time of Cholera*, by Gabriel García Márquez
➤ *Dreaming in Cuban*, by Cristina Garcia
➤ *The Adventures of Don Quixote*, by Miguel de Cervantes
➤ *The Lost Steps*, by Alejo Carpentier
➤ *The Old Gringo*, by Carlos Fuentes
➤ *Estampas del Valle*, by Rolando Hinojosa
➤ *Down These Mean Streets*, by Piri Thomas
➤ *The House of Mango Street*, by Sandra Cisneros
➤ *The Shadow of the Shadow*, by Paco Ignacio Taibo II
➤ *Nilda*, by Nicholasa Mohr

# Asian Voices

There has also been an explosion in novels dealing with Asian culture, both at home and in native countries. With the thousands of centuries of writing from the Far East, you could pretty much fill up your reading schedule until the last member buys the farm. If it fits the bill, try comparing and contrasting the use of these topics in the wide variety of titles:

➤ Western religions versus Eastern religions

➤ Democracy versus Communism

➤ Women's liberation versus societal submission

➤ Individual liberty versus governmental control

➤ Marxism versus Communism versus Socialism

➤ Reincarnation versus the afterlife

➤ New World values versus old-world values

➤ Preinternment versus postinternment, or pre-Hiroshima/Nagasaki versus post-Hiroshima/Nagasaki

➤ Permissive sexual attitudes versus repressive sexual attitudes

This list is a simple jumping-off point to help you dip your toes into the literary wading pool of some of the following suggestions:

1. *The Joy Luck Club,* **by Amy Tan.** This is another perennial reading group selection. It is the story of four mothers and four daughters (which coincidentally makes it a good mother/daughter selection as well) and their personal histories. In 1949, four Chinese immigrant women begin meeting in San Francisco to play mah-jongg, eat dim sum, invest, and tell their stories. They are the "Joy Luck Club." It is the commonality of the secrets they share that has made the book a universal favorite. Each vignette reveals truths about their lives and the interconnected strands of existence are simultaneously liberating and intertwining.

**Novel Ideas**

There's no need to limit these questions to books with an Eastern flavor. You can compare and contrast with any two books. It can be the difference in Yossarian's world-view from *Catch-22* to *Closing Time* or the homosexual tendencies in the South in *Other Voices, Other Rooms* and *Deliverance.* Don't limit yourself and your book club by issuing certain questions for certain titles. Try asking them all and see what sticks.

### Biblio-Trivio

The movie version of *The Joy Luck Club* was directed by a man, Wayne Wang, co-written by a man, screenwriter Ron Bass (with Amy Tan), and, most surprisingly, one of the producers was Mr. *Natural Born Killers* himself, Oliver Stone. See ladies: There are plenty of sensitive men out there; they're just conspiracy theorists.

As the mothers share their never-mentioned Chinese experiences, readers in your group won't be able to avoid thinking about the unknown lives of their own mothers. Defining a life is impossible, but examining a life isn't, and this book transcends race, age, place, and time in its luminous prose.

Remember, *The Joy Luck Club* always makes for a fine Mother's Day selection.

### Novel Ideas

Before the gathering to discuss *The Joy Luck Club,* have members write down five questions they would like to ask their mothers and read them aloud to the group. The questions will spark storytelling by all the members that may trigger other buried memories, whether Mom is present or not.

2. ***The Remains of the Day,*** **by Kazuo Ishiguro.** Ishiguro was born in Japan and raised in England from the age of five. He writes about both countries in an elliptical manner. He claims to write of an invented country with a resemblance to Japan and of an England he was never a part of. This is his British story, of the quintessential English butler Stevens, who finds himself working for an entirely different type of boss. After years of loyalty to Lord Darlington, he is in the employ of a sociable American who purchased the hall and kept him.

This is another popular choice because of all the underlying questions regarding class, culture, social roles, self-deception, what's beneath the surface, and what it means to be British. Some ideas to look at are: How does Ishiguro's Asian heritage influence this novel? Which has the major impact, the society in which we live or from which we descend? Is this true for Stevens? What determines a wasted life?

3. *Seventeen Syllables and Other Stories,* by **Hisaye Yamamoto.** This collection features wide-ranging topics, from the personal to the political. One issue that is revisited in Yamamoto's stories is her mother's experiences in the internment camps in America during World War II.

Yamamoto's stories are a tender mix of history and culture, particularly the isolation of Japanese women. The divisions between the Eastern traditions of first-generation parents, the Issei, and Western freedoms of their children, the Nisei, are another focus. Anyone who has ever felt like America is a foreign land will appreciate her works. Yamamoto won the 1986 American Book Award for Lifetime Achievement in 1986, and it isn't hard to see why.

**Novel Ideas**

If your reading group is interested in a couple of oral histories and first-hand accounts of life in the internment camps, consider either *And Justice for All: An Oral History of the Japanese American Detention Camps,* by John Tateishi, or *A Fence Away from Freedom: Japanese Americans and World War II,* by Ellen Levine.

**Biblio-Trivio**

Worried that you haven't finished writing your own Great American Novel? Don't be. It took Hisaye Yamamoto from 1948 to 1987 to pen *Seventeen Syllables and Other Stories.* See? There's no rush.

Other books by Asian authors include …

➤ *The Doctor's Wife,* by Sawako Ariyoshi
➤ *Donald Duck,* by Frank Chin
➤ *Obasan,* Joy Kogawa
➤ *An Artist of the Floating World,* by Kazuo Ishiguro
➤ *The Silent City,* by Kenzaburo Oe

➤ *Sour Sweet,* by Timothy Mo

➤ *The Kitchen God's Wife,* by Amy Tan

➤ *Getting Used to Dying,* by Zhang Xianliang

➤ *Bone,* by Fae Myenne Ng

➤ *The Floating World,* by Cynthia Kadohata

➤ *The Concubine's Children,* by Denise Chong

➤ *Nip the Buds, Shoot the Kids,* by Kenzaburo Oe

➤ *Kitchen,* by Banana Yoshimoto

➤ *Jasmine,* by Bharati Mukherjee

➤ *The Sailor Who Fell from Grace with the Sea,* by Yukio Mishima

**Biblio-Trivio**

Kenzaburo Oe was born into a prominent samurai family but ended up an international, left-wing, antiwar activist. It has been said of his literature that he works through the darkness to get to the light, and he frequently uses grotesque realism, which is the flip side to García Márquez's forte. Oe uses grotesque imagery as a way to define both the ugliness and beauty of the world we share.

# The Forgotten Ones

Because there is a lack of a strong, unifying Native American voice due to the hardships and atrocities they suffered at the hands of greedy land barons and the U.S. government, the importance and relevance of the slaughter of numerous tribes has drifted into virtual oblivion. Fortunately, many of the stories from the oral tradition are available in various collections. I highly recommend *The Last Best Place: A Montana Anthology.* Edited by William Kittredge and Annick Smith, it contains literature of all types from the Big Sky State, and the 130 pages are a celebration of Native American stories and myths.

The decimation of millions of their ancestors at the hands of those who "discovered" North America is important to keep in the back of your mind as you read works by Native American authors. Just as the Holocaust has influenced all aspects of Jewish culture since World War II and slavery is infused in African American culture, the great loss of their homeland, culture, and destruction of family weighs heavily in the Native American arts.

**Pro's Prose**

"I want to have time to look for my children and see how many of them I can find. Maybe I shall find them among the dead. Hear me, my chiefs. I am tired. My heart is sick and sad. From where the sun now stands I will fight no more forever."

—From Chief Joseph's speech before the surrender of the Nez Percés, included in *The Last Best Place: A Montana Anthology*

1. ***The Lone Ranger and Tonto Fistfight in Heaven,* by Sherman Alexie.** If the mark of a great writer is someone who can find a truly original voice, then Sherman Alexie belongs right up there with the best of them. This collection of linked short stories (which will be discussed as a format later in the book) is filled with a haunting power about the sparse existence of the American Indian in contemporary society—sparse in terms of power, wealth, relevance, esteem, and hope. The stories are set in and around the Spokane Indian Reservation, and there are few wasted words; the prose is blunt, direct, and raw. Alexie deals with all of the ugly realities of life on the reservation with naked pain, grim irony, and caustic humor. Alcoholism, basketball, traditional dress, storytelling, movie stereotypes, Indian ancestry—it's all filtered through Alexie's wry microscope.

   The place of the American Indian in modern society is a burning issue in Alexie's work. He has little time for a white America that still sees Native Americans as nineteenth-century noble savages. Keep your dream-catchers hanging from the rear-view mirror when analyzing Alexie; he doesn't suffer fools (of any kind) lightly. His amazing collection does the impossible and finds a poignant balance between abject defeat and soulful humanity. In the words of Alexie, "Let us tell our own damn stories." No argument here.

2. ***Almanac of the Dead,* by Leslie Marmon Silko.** This is an epic, dense, kaleidoscopic narrative of Native American war against the Anglo culture and all its perversions, including heavy drug usage, pornography, the rape and pillage of the environment, and any other shade of evil you can think of (and some I imagine you can't). Silko attempts to create fiction on a grandly dizzying scale. It is not for the faint of heart, but the rewards are worthy indeed.

### Biblio-Trivio

Silko wrote *Almanac of the Dead* after receiving a five-year MacArthur "genius" grant rumored to be in the neighborhood of $175,000. However, the immense undertaking took 10 years to complete.

Silko's book is in many ways a revolutionary nightmare of depravity, vulgarity, obscenity, violence, and unbridled degenerate sex. The lowlifes who traipse through her pages aren't the kind of folks you would want to join the ol' book club, but it is bold, defiant, bravura storytelling with more than its fair share of truth. Take the journey into the brutal, chaotic underbelly of America and ask yourself, why did the Europeans assume they were the only ones who believed in the promised land? And what have they done to it?

### Novel Ideas

Read Silko's *Almanac of the Dead* right before, or shortly after, the turn of the century (2000, that is). It is the perfect apocalyptic tome to help ring in the new world order.

3. *Love Medicine,* **by Louise Erdrich.** This is the first book in an ongoing series that includes *The Beet Queen, Tracks,* and *The Bingo Palace.* The series follows the lives of several Chippewa families and their attempts to honor tribal traditions and culture through the generations of the last century. It is also a series of stories of love and family, led by seven narrators from the Kashpaw and Lamartine families. Erdrich doesn't stick to standard linear narrative; she uses multiple perspectives and haunting language. Her style is often called "poetic," which is also why some readers find her prose confusing. Erdrich takes a little more effort than many writers who don't break from the norm, but her imagery, spirituality, and colorful characters have earned her many devoted fans.

### Biblio-Trivio

Erdrich's wide-ranging depiction of the Argus, North Dakota, Indian Reservation has been compared favorably by more than one critic to Faulkner's Yoknapa-tawpha County. They both use numerous voices, fractured plotting, and nonlinear time passages. What does your group think—are the comparisons accurate or a stretch? Would the residents of Argus and Yoknapatawpha have anything to talk about?

Erdrich, like Alexie, is in tune with the way modern reservations are, so the characters aren't the stereotypes of so many attempts at Native American fiction. Erdrich also has a love for tribal traditions, and her prose is peppered with the beautiful imagery of the native stories. Be warned, *Love Medicine* may spur your group to read Erdrich's entire tetralogy, and that will take up an entire season.

The following are some suggestions for books by Native American authors:

➤ *The Jailing of Cecilia Capture,* by Janet Campbell Hale

➤ *House Made of Dawn,* by N. Scott Momaday

➤ *Seven Arrows,* by Hyemeyohsts Storm

➤ *The Grass Dancer,* by Susan Power

➤ *Mean Spirit,* by Linda Hogan

➤ *Trigger Dance,* by Diane Glancy

➤ *The Death of Jim Loney,* by James Welch

➤ *Black Eagle Child,* by Ray A. Young Bear

➤ *Crow Texts,* collected by Robert H. Lowie, compiled by Luella Cole Lowie

➤ *Indian Killer,* by Sherman Alexie

➤ *Ghost Singer,* by Anna Lee Walters

➤ *Brothers Three,* by John M. Oskison

➤ *From the River's Edge,* by Elizabeth Cook-Lynn

➤ *The Moccasin Maker,* by Pauline E. Johnson

➤ *Raven Tells Stories: Alaskan Native Writing,* edited by Joseph Bruchac

# Thy Cup Runneth Over

Whatever the makeup of your book club, there should be more than enough choices in this chapter to fill a whole lotta calendars. One of the great aspects of the book club is the chance to expose yourself to and discuss new ideas, theories, cultures, beliefs, ways of life, or anything else under the sun. Cultural identity is an all-encompassing topic. Embrace it.

---

### The Least You Need to Know

➤ The essence of the reading group is to explore the unfamiliar.

➤ Going outside the classic top 10 will be a rewarding experience for you and your reading group.

➤ Don't ignore current Native American fiction; there is some powerful stuff out there.

➤ Don't be afraid to explore the literature of other cultures for fear of not understanding—just the opposite will occur.

---

# Chapter 13

# That's Kids' Stuff

---

### In This Chapter

➤ How to juice up your dinner table talk

➤ How to entice kids to view book clubs as party time

➤ Why kids will be dreaming of ways to get out of raking leaves

➤ Why *On the Road* is the ultimate teenage tome

➤ Why the kids are all right

---

In a previous chapter, we discussed all of the influential powers book clubs could possibly hold on today's youth. Get them involved in a reading group, and before long they will be raking the yard without asking, eating cauliflower as snack food, volunteering at a local senior citizens center, and setting aside the money they earn shoveling sidewalks or delivering newspapers to help pay for college "down the line." Well, maybe none of these things will happen, but it can't hurt to try, right?

In some ways, kids participate in book clubs every day at school, so a different approach is essential to getting them excited about outside reading. They really are never too young to start. There was a report a couple of years ago that studied the effects of meaningful dinner conversation as it relates to the development of a child's brain. Surprisingly, the problem-solving and cognitive-reasoning skills were considered more important than the standard practice of nightly reading to a child. Children learn to process information and formulate opinions and arguments, and use their powers of deductive theorizing, which can be lost in the primarily one-sided act of listening to a book read aloud (which has serious benefits to a child as well, and shouldn't be downplayed).

Dinner conversations, however, often run the gamut from self-indulgent gossip to your general pop culture trivia (*ER* plot updates anyone?). My mother constantly complained that we spent way too much time talking about sports, particularly at the expense of my musician brother who didn't associate the word *jazz* with Karl Malone and John Stockton. Why do I share this relatively bland anecdote with you? Because I suspect my family wasn't the only one that let the conversations drift into rehashed triumphs of banality. So, why not get your kids involved in a reading group? And get the best of both worlds.

### Novel Ideas

Dinner table reading groups are a thing of beauty because you're probably already 90 percent of the way there. All it takes is finding a selection that appeals to child and parent alike and you're off. To make it seem like less of an assignment, serve meals that kids will love and make it like a miniparty. If your kids know that pizza and hot fudge sundaes are included with the reading group, they'll finish the book.

Remember, kids want to belong to social groups, and book clubs offer a level playing field. Even if everyone on the Little Guy football team gets a chance to play, the team knows who has athletic skills and who doesn't, and, let's be honest, it will become verbally acknowledged. Same thing with academic pursuits: The mid- to lower-level children will always know where they stand. Besides the intellectual benefits, reading groups offer a social setting for kids on an equal level, where the input of the gawky outcast is as welcome and relevant as the BMIK (Big Man in Kindergarten). Book clubs are much more akin to the Boy Scouts and Girl Scouts or some type of volunteer organization.

Here are a few ways to ensure that kids are active participants:

➤ **Bribe 'em with baked goods.** Just like at home, kids will respond to cake and ice cream, especially if it is served after the 45-minute meeting, right before they go home.

➤ **Choose titles they will actually enjoy.** For whatever reason, warm and fuzzy, politically correct children's books have tended to dominate reading lists. Why? Kids aren't stupid; they know what is out there. Disney's watered-down, cuddly *The Little Mermaid* is a far cry from the Hans Christian Anderson yarn about a mermaid who wants to become human because their souls are immortal. What is true for adults is true for kids—challenging books ask more of their audience, but offer greater opportunities for complex thought. Don't sell your kids short, and don't worry, most children's books have a positive conclusion; it is the stuff in the middle that counts. General rule of thumb: If it makes you nervous, they will love it.

➤ **Lead with leading questions.** This is essential for productive discussions, even with teenagers, because the combination of fear of rejection and being taught to give short yes and no answers will grind things to a halt. Directing the questions as much as possible ensures answers that will provoke other answers; just have enough questions so that the same answers aren't repeated ad nauseam. For instance (to the youngsters), "Did you share any feelings with Wilbur or Charlotte?" Or, (for the teenagers), "Choose two scenes from *Catcher in the Rye* and tell us why you identify with them."

➤ **I have a theme.** Adult reading groups often tailor their monthly selections to an appropriate theme (which we will cover in detail later), but it will have an even greater impact on kids groups. Reading Mary Hoffman's *Amazing Grace* during Black History Month gives the kids a frame of reference and a chance to enjoy a great book about social standards. It's the story of a little girl who wants to play Peter Pan in the school play and how her grandmother works to overcome the standards (white and male) of traditional roles. Why not read J. M. Barrie's *Peter Pan* as well that month and encourage the kids to make theatrical costumes? It takes a lot of work but children will equate reading the book with having fun, and that's precisely the point.

➤ **Markers, and scissors, and crayons (oh my!).** Another way of getting kids excited about reading groups is to ask them to create art projects based on the book they read, or to create said projects after the discussion. Any book can be converted to another symbolic form, and you will be astounded with what the kids dream up. There are obvious activities like discussing *Stone Soup* as the broth boils, or having the kids paint a watercolor picture of the island life described so vividly in Scott O'Dell's 1961 classic, *Island of the Blue Dolphins*.

**Pro's Prose**

"Of all people children are the most imaginative. They abandon themselves without reserve to every illusion. No man, whatever his sensibility may be, is ever affected by Hamlet or Lear as a little girl is affected by the story of poor Red Riding Hood."

—Attributed to J. B. MacAuley

**Novel Ideas**

If you choose to discuss E. B. White's marvelous *Charlotte's Web*, be sure to discuss the circles of life and nature in the text. The constantly changing seasons mirror the relationship between two friends through death and birth.

# The World o' Kiddie Lit

The following are a few choices to consider for younger kids, junior high kids, and the always-frightening teenage kids.

## Young 'Uns

1. *The Giving Tree,* **by Shel Silverstein.** This is a deceptively moving parable about the nature of "giving." It has certainly become a staple in the American psyche, and most readers probably consider it a beautiful story about the fulfillment of sharing what we have with those we love (otherwise why would it be so popular?). For the uninitiated, it is the story of a boy and a tree, and the tree gives everything it has to the boy over the course of his lifetime. When the boy is a child, the tree provides shelter, companionship, and a playground for the imagination. The tree is happy, but things become more complicated as the boy grows, because the tree has less and less to offer after its apples for money, its branches to build a home, its trunk to carve a boat, and eventually, its stump as a resting spot.

**Biblio-Trivio**

Shel Silverstein had a long, rich career. In addition to the millions of books he sold, he was a playwright, guitarist, a lyricist, a journalist. He appeared in a movie in 1971, drew cartoons for *Stars and Stripes* as a private in Korea and Japan, and penned the legendary Johnny Cash tune *A Boy Named Sue.*

Critics have noted that the story is as much about taking as it is about giving. The tree effectively gives up everything, and for what? By scientific principles, the tree kills itself when it gives the boy its branches, and what does the boy give it in return? The boy has no qualms about gutting the tree, which appears to have a severe codependency problem. The narcissistic boy basically uses the tree for whatever he desires whenever he desires it. Is complete self-sacrifice a healthy thing? What many critics fail to recognize is that Silverstein leaves the essence of the story open to interpretation. Remember, the tree is "not really" happy when there is nothing left, and maybe its final actions are out of desperation? Question, for kids and adults alike: Did the tree give too much?

2. *Yertle the Turtle,* **by Dr. Seuss.** This isn't exactly a hidden gem, but when it is the work of the master, why try to get cute? Dr. Seuss created characters that have become wholly ingrained in the modern history of children's books. This one is the story of a power-hungry turtle that will only be happy if he becomes the king of the universe. He is, of course, undone by a simpleton, Mack, one of the lowest turtles on the totem pole.

This simple fable can be used in a discussion about how power corrupts, or how those on top shouldn't ignore those on the bottom. It isn't a story that plays as well for adults as it does for children, but the vivid drawings and witty wordplay will make it a popular selection. You may want to use Yertle as an example of how bullying the weak never works, or as the beginning of a dissertation about the various coups in history that removed corrupt dictators, but that is entirely up to you.

> **Pro's Prose**
>
> "And today the great Yertle, that Marvelous he, is King of the Mud. That is all he can see. And the turtles of course ... all the turtles are free. As turtles, and maybe, all creatures should be."
>
> —From *Yertle the Turtle,* by Dr. Seuss

3. *Where the Wild Things Are,* **by Maurice Sendak.** Again, we aren't blazing any new trails with this outstanding story of the powers of imagination, but it is one of the benchmarks of child literature. For my friends out there who have been living in a cave or a fallout shelter since the early '60s, it is the story of Max, a mischievous young whippersnapper who dons his favorite wolf suit and, as usual, gets himself into trouble. He is sent to bed without dinner and his imagination turns the room into a jungle filled with odd-looking beasts with giant eyeballs where he becomes the king.

> **Biblio-Trivio**
>
> Maurice Sendak won the prestigious Caldecott Medal in 1964, which is the annual award given to the artist of the book voted the most distinguished picture book for children published in the United States during the previous year. Sendak has also designed sets and costumes for numerous operas, including Mozart's *Magic Flute.*

The book is a celebration of the imagination and the wondrous drawings leap off each page. The "wild things" are as funny as they are scary, and it reads like a fantastic dream. Ask the children to tell (or write) one of their dreams, to tell the story of where their wild things are. It would be a delight for adult reading groups as well.

The following are more suggestions for young kids:

➤ *The Meanest Thing to Say,* by Bill Cosby (Little Bill Books for Beginning Readers)

➤ *The Complete Hans Christian Anderson Fairy Tales,* edited by Lily Faowens

➤ *Mrs. Frisby and the Rats of Nimh,* by Robert C. O'Brien

➤ *The Wizard of Oz,* by L. Frank Baum

➤ *Snowy Day,* by Ezra Jack Keats

➤ *The Polar Express,* by Chris Van Allsburg

➤ *Shadow,* by Marcia Brown

➤ *The Wind in the Willows,* by Kenneth Grahame

➤ *The Complete Tales of Uncle Remus,* by Joel Chandler Harris

➤ *The Jungle Book,* by Rudyard Kipling

➤ *Ramona the Pest,* by Beverly Cleary

➤ *Goodnight Moon,* by Margaret Wise Brown

➤ *Harold and the Purple Crayon,* by Crockett Johnson

➤ *Aesop's Fables*

➤ *Swiss Family Robinson,* by Johann Wyss

**Pro's Prose**

"When life is so tiresome there ain't no peace like the greatest peace—the peace of the Lord's holding hand."

—Excerpt from *Sounder,* by William H. Armstrong

## Middle 'Uns

1. *Sounder,* **by William H. Armstrong.** This is a moving story about a slice of Americana—a boy and his dog. The African-American protagonist is a boy who is angry after his sharecropper father is jailed for stealing food: angry at his father, at their poverty, and at the tough, racist, nineteenth-century South in which they live. Sounder is wounded, but both the dog and the boy's father manage to make it back home.

This is a beautifully crafted, bittersweet tale of resilience, misery, courage, hatred, and love. The boy's self-determination against unfathomable odds is poignant, especially considering his singular goal is to learn how to read. It is an intense work that will definitely elicit emotional responses. Why does the author keep the characters nameless? Is it to focus on the details of sorrow and poverty? Does it rob the characters of their individuality? Or, does it strip away the superfluous, to get to the core of humanity? Lots to discuss with this one.

2. *The Adventures of Tom Sawyer,* **by Mark Twain.** One of the most beloved scamps in all of American letters is good ol' Tom Sawyer. Twain's ode to the joys of childhood is full of humor and fun. Tom Sawyer and Huck Finn revolutionized the view of the child in literature. They weren't the goody-goody, all-American boys who dominated the Sunday school standards of the times. Basically, Twain allowed the children to be children. The difference between the two is that Tom is a prankster, allergic to work and always looking for a spirited adventure, whereas Huck lives in a cruel world and does whatever he has to for survival, not for fun.

### Biblio-Trivio

Even though *The Adventures of Tom Sawyer* takes place in Twain's boyhood home of Hannibal, Missouri, it was written at his home on 351 Farmington Avenue in Hartford, Connecticut, near *Uncle Tom's Cabin* author Harriet Beecher Stowe. Tours are available. Be sure to check out his fourth-floor billiards table. Twain was a voracious pool player, and was said to wake his butler for a late-night billiard game whenever he had insomnia.

*The Adventures of Tom Sawyer* is less polished than its sequel, but it is also more appropriate for middle-schoolers. It is side-splittingly funny, and every kid in the book club will dream of a way to use the infamous fence-whitewashing scene that summer when it is time to stain the garage. There is also the innocent love story with Becky Thatcher to please the romantics in the crowd. The foolishness of adults is always relevant to kids, and the racial language is not as prevalent as in *Huck Finn*. There is a reason Mark Twain is considered to be among the greatest American writers, and a story that resonates almost 125 years later with both children and adults is all the proof you will ever need. Have some fun with this one.

### Novel Ideas

Incredibly, there are those who think Mark Twain was a racist writer, which is an absolutely ludicrous proposition. First of all, he used the ugly language of the day to be realistic, and second, his black characters, especially Jim, maintain a strong sense of dignity. He wrote against oppression and his language can be traced directly back to the pre–Civil War South, which is where the slave spirituals were woven into the Delta blues. The Mississippi River unites them all, so throw on some Robert Johnson or Muddy Waters while reading Twain and see if your kids don't feel the connection.

### Pro's Prose

"Fancy thinking the beast was something you could hunt and kill! You knew, didn't you? I'm part of you?"

—From *Lord of the Flies,* by William Golding

Twain saw a wisdom in children that was lost on adults, so who knows what he would have made of the next choice.

3. *Lord of the Flies,* **by William Golding.** Golding's classic book is one of the most haunting stories of youth gone awry ever written. Sadly, the violent elements of the young male psyche captured so brilliantly in his fictional tale have been horrifically on display in the rash of school shootings. Now more than ever, this is a book that needs to be read. What causes young men to give in to their animalistic instincts? It is the story of a group of English schoolboys who are stranded on a deserted island after a plane crash. One of the boys, wholesome Ralph, and his sidekick, nebbish Piggy, try to maintain order and lead a civilized existence, but many of the boys quickly fall under the spell of the ruthless leader, Jack, the leader of the pig hunters.

The brutal ending to an innocent boy's life at the hands of his peers, without any sense of logic or compassion, is guaranteed to provoke debate among preadolescents. Golding's chilling novel is as relevant today as it was at its publication in 1954, and boys and girls alike will have an understanding of it in ways their baby-boomer parents wouldn't have dreamed. Some might say this is a book for the high school set, but in light of recent events it is necessarily suitable for fifth and sixth graders. There is a myriad of appropriate questions, such as: Is violence the only way to personal power? Is Simon a martyr? Does a lack of structure always lead to abhorrent behavior? Is human decency the only line between order and chaos? Will kids allow evil to happen because they want to be with a certain crowd? Are Jack's followers scared of their insecurities? Of the unknown? Of peer rejection? Are we all savages at heart?

Now, here are some more books for middle school kids:

➤ *From the Mixed-Up Files of Mrs. Basil E. Frankweiler,* by E. L. Konigsburg

➤ *The Cay,* by Theodore Taylor

➤ *The Adventures of Robin Hood,* by Howard Pyle

➤ *Anne of Green Gables,* by L. M. Montgomery

➤ *Owl Moon,* by Jane Yolen

➤ *Number the Stars,* by Lois Lowry

➤ *Manic Magee,* by Jerry Spinelli

➤ *Charlotte's Web,* by E. B. White

➤ *The Narnia Series,* by C. S. Lewis

➤ *Danny the Champion of the World,* by Roald Dahl

➤ *The Secret Garden,* by Frances Hodgson Burnett

➤ *Jane Eyre,* by Charlotte Brontë

➤ *I Am the Cheese,* by Robert Cormier

➤ *The House on Pooh Corner,* by A. A. Milne

➤ *White Fang,* by Jack London

➤ *Robinson Crusoe,* by Daniel Defoe

➤ *The Brave,* by Robert Lipsyte

➤ *Oliver Twist,* by Charles Dickens

➤ *The Phantom Tollbooth,* by Norton Juster

➤ *James and the Giant Peach,* by Roald Dahl

➤ *The Little Princess,* by Frances Hodgson Burnett

# The Terrible Teens

1. *Ordinary People,* **by Judith Guest.** This is an important tome for our depression-conscious times. The subject of teenage depression has been a frequent topic on the news magazines lately, and Guest's book is one of the more honest and realistic accounts you will come across. It is the story of an ordinary family and how they cope with tragedy and reconciliation. The protagonist, Conrad, is a troubled teenager who recently witnessed his brother's death. He tries to pretend that everything is fine, but the sadness and confusion are just below the surface, and his pain boils over in a suicidal malaise. He visits a witty psychologist who helps him come to a point of self-realization about his family role. Conrad and his father, Cal, come to grips with the tragedies in ways the mother never does. There are no ordinary people, and that is what makes Guest's book so remarkable.

Robert Redford made an award-winning film out of the book; Timothy Hutton won an Oscar for his portrayal of Conrad, but it probably isn't a movie your teens are familiar with, so give them the written version first. It is timely and universal: There are no ordinary people in the world because of the unordinary situations we are all forced to endure. Teenagers have told me that Conrad is them, or someone they know, trying to deal with the chaos and sorrow in their young lives. It would also be a great choice for any parent/child reading groups. Question: Why do so many marriages dissolve after a child dies (the statistics are quite high)? Or, why do American teenagers feel so vulnerable? And/or suffer from depression?

2. *To Kill a Mockingbird,* **by Harper Lee.** The streets of Maycomb, Alabama, have been ingrained in the national consciousness since Lee's work won the 1960 Pulitzer Prize. Immortalized on screen, the book is as fresh as the first time you read it in ninth or tenth grade. Scout Finch still has some of the funniest and most astute points about the racial attitudes of the Deep South ever put to the page. It is the story of Scout's father, Atticus, who is the appointed lawyer of a black man, Tom Robinson, against a rape charge. Lee's book avoids clichés because of the sharp satirical observations of Scout and the humorous overtones in the story.

### Biblio-Trivio

Harper Lee's novel was incredibly successful from the beginning and was something of a publishing phenomenon. It was chosen by three American book clubs: Reader's Digest Condensed Books, the Literary Guild, and the Book-of-the-Month Club. It sold 2.5 million copies in its first year and went through 14 printings. Lee is still alive, but she has never written another book, only a few essays.

Each rereading of this book brings something new, it is that richly textured. It is an undeniable fact that Scout remains one of the leading voices in the racial discourse that has been the central American debate since the end of World War II. *To Kill a Mockingbird* will always be first thought of as a heroic tale against injustice, but it is the subtle perceptions of the climate in the South from a young girl that makes it such a treasure.

3. *On the Road,* **by Jack Kerouac.** If your teenager happens to be one of the few who lives for: cars, music, partying, the opposite sex, life in the fast lane, and wild times (and if you answered no, it may be time to take a whiff of the java), then this is the book for them. Kerouac's minutely fictionalized yarn of his journey back and forth across the country, from the arty Village in New York City to the old South, from the rough-and-ready cowboy town of Denver to the jazz joints in San Francisco; this is teenage America since the proliferation of fast cars and interstate highways. Narrated by Sal Paradise, the hipster odyssey he takes up with Dean Moriarty has become a rite of passage, be it the ubiquitous college "road trip," or a summer day spent cruising the vehicular veins that keep America's heart pumping.

### Biblio Trivio

For reasons never fully explained, Jack Kerouac created alter egos for himself (Sal Paradise) and his friend/travelling mate Neal Cassady (Dean Moriarty), even though the journal is basically a real first-person travelogue.

Kerouac wrote *On the Road* back in New York in marathon sessions that only lasted a couple of weeks. It has been roundly criticized in a variety of ways, most notably by Truman Capote, who said, "That's not writing, it's just … typing!" The prose has been knocked as some sort of hyperregurgitated journal, but the free-form style matches the kinetic trips he experienced. Although this book is the primary title in the oeuvre of the Beat Generation, Kerouac was much more of a romantic than the other Beats. He was neither political or sociological; he thought that there was a better world than the one in which he was raised. He idolized the "Negroes" who played the jazz and blues, but didn't notice any of the civil rights rumblings that were taking shape in the '50s.

### Pro's Prose

"It was remarkable how Dean could go mad and then suddenly continue with his soul—which I think is wrapped up in a fast car, a coat to reach, and a woman at the end of the road—calmly and sanely as though nothing had happened."

—From *On the Road,* by Jack Kerouac

### Novel Ideas

If you find yourself in San Francisco, head to the North Beach area, the section of the city the Beats called home. Visit City Lights, a fantastic bookstore started by poet Lawrence Ferlinghetti, which publishes its own poetry series and was blocked by an obscenity suit from publishing Ginsberg's *Howl* in 1957. Ferlinghetti was arrested in May, but a judge ruled that *Howl* was not obscene after a long summer trial. It was a landmark free-speech case and set definitions for "obscenity." Then, head to Vesuvio's for a cocktail, which is where the young authors read their works to their enthusiastic peers.

In the book, Sal worships Dean, who is a few years younger and much more raw and unrefined, but again, he completely misses the reality of Dean's hollow existence. Kerouac dreamed of utopia; it just didn't involve a white-picket fence, and of course, like all starry-eyed dreamers, he fell to Earth. As the real world took shape, he became an angry, cynical drunk who died at a young age. Unlike his Beat Generation peers (Allen Ginsberg, William S. Burroughs, Gary Snyder, or even Norman Mailer to a lesser degree), Kerouac gave up on the bohemian beliefs and had less of a cultural impact over the course of a lifetime.

I think *On the Road* is the quintessential book for the post–World War II American teenager. The older I get, the more the flaws in Jackie-Boy's thought process and world view become apparent; but if I looked back on my younger visions of the way life should be, there would be little room to argue. Kerouac's opus is still a vibrant, exciting ode to everything that makes youth grand: love, sex, loud music, and good times. If your teenager doesn't appreciate that, it's time for a long talk.

Interest piqued? Then below you'll find some more suggestions for your angst-ridden teenager:

➤ *Brotherly Love,* by Pete Dexter

➤ *One Flew Over the Cuckoo's Nest,* by Ken Kesey

➤ *The Outsiders,* by S. E. Hinton

➤ *Shizuko's Daughter,* by Kyoko Mori

➤ *The Pigman,* by Paul Zindel

➤ *Clockers,* by Richard Price

➤ *Death of the Heart,* by Elizabeth Bowen

➤ *Dr. Jekyll and Mr. Hyde,* by Robert Louis Stevenson

➤ *The Object of My Affection,* by Stephan McCauley

➤ *Floating in My Mother's Pain,* by Ursula Hegi

➤ *A Death in the Family,* by James Agee

➤ *Trainspotting,* by Irvine Welsh

➤ *Snow Falling on Cedars,* by David Guterson

➤ *Cat's Eye,* by Margaret Atwood

➤ *Billy Bathgate,* by E. L. Doctorow

➤ *After the First Death,* by Robert Cormier

# The Kids Are All Right

The biggest thing to keep in mind when initiating the reading group with, or for, your children is to make sure they see it as a barrel of monkeys. We have a problem in this society that too often we approach reading like it is a chore, which it isn't—it's fun. It isn't as easy as watching TV, or as visually stimulating as a video game or a movie, or as adrenaline-infusing as rap music, but it is as much fun, and that is what kids need to learn.

Don't make television or the computer the enemy: It is that type of "adult" behavior that turns kids off from reading in the first place. If all they hear is, "TV is bad for you. You should be reading a book," then guess what they are precisely going to turn around and not do? Your goal should be to help them get into the habit of reading, so it becomes as second nature to pick up a book as the remote control. Find out their favorite show and pick up a book with similar themes, but whatever you do, don't make reading out to be something they should do. If the book club is fun, they'll respond, but if it's "good for them," it will rank up there with broccoli, dental exams, and curfews.

It might be hard to imagine your hyperactive little girl or apathetic teenage son enjoying a reading group, but don't sell the kids short. If you can sell the first meeting as a good time with friends, that may be all it takes. No matter the personality of your child, there is a book out there that they will identify with like it was written with them in mind. The number of children's reading groups is spotty; it's like once they learn to read, the schools take over—but they are out there. Keep the faith and believe in your child's appetite for experience. And remember, the older they get, the more likely they are to fly solo and have their own self-sufficient book clubs. And wouldn't that be something?

**Novel Ideas**

Keep the reading groups (especially teenage ones) lower in number than yours, so that they will have to participate. Adolescents normally respond better in small-group dynamics, so better to get four kids from the neighborhood than 10. Plus, if the kids can get to the meetings on their own, they will have zero excuses, short of the measles.

## The Least You Need to Know

➤ There aren't many kids' reading groups, but they are a social activity with a completely level playing field that any kid could enjoy.

➤ Dinner table book clubs are a great idea.

➤ Don't tell your kids reading is something "good for them," or an alternative to TV. Treat reading as an equally fun endeavor.

➤ Smaller groups are better for kids of all ages, but especially for teenagers.

# Part 4

# Tailoring Your Group Like a Fine Suit

*Creatures of the night, this blood's for you.*

*The label "genre fiction" gets slapped on particular books faster than MSNBC on a tragedy, and it's just as ridiculous. This part breaks down some of the great works that shouldn't be overlooked because some egghead wants to marginalize them, or because they are stuck in the back section of your local superstore.*

*For all of you who can't get enough of characters with names like Coffin Ed Johnson or Grave Digger Jones (see Chester B. Himes), who salivate at spending time sucking blood through the eyes of a vampire, or don't consider a book a book without a detective solving a bloody murder, this part is right up your dark alley.*

*This part also jumps into the nonfiction fray, with characters and stories that are so outrageous some author would have eventually made them up. There is also a section uniting the hottest of fads, the book club meets the memoir, with an expert who explains why your life might become the next big reading group revelation.*

# Chapter 14

# Regional Book Clubs

## In This Chapter

➤ A few titles to get your Irish up

➤ God save the queen from reading bloody rotten books

➤ Go West, young bibliophile

➤ New England at its literary finest

➤ Start spreading the news, I'm reading today ...

While it would be impossible to list every style of book club that are out there, we here at the *Idiot's Guide* factory want to offer a few more selections from our vast menu. This chapter drifts away from the established standards and throws a variety of items into the stew, digressions if you will. If you don't like what you see right away, don't fret, a topic that suits you is only a page away.

## Country Roads Take Me Home

Book clubs often like to visit other lands that they are either very familiar with, for the gratifying feeling of recognition, or know very little about, for the exciting experience of originality. The following three European countries have long provided the world with first-rate literature and many groups like to delve into the past and present fiction from the indigenous authors. So, I give you a trio of European euphoria.

Let us begin in the land of the shamrocks ...

### Novel Ideas

Make sure to take a look at maps, historical documents, articles, letters, and so on, from the country and era in which the novel you select was written. A refresher course in what the country was like during the period the novel takes place will help remind the group of the differences between the country then and now. It also aids in explaining the current political climate and how that influences the work. For instance, the Holocaust has had an incredible impact on modern German literature in the same way the "troubles" have shaped Irish writings.

# When Irish Eyes Are Reading

Ireland has long been a literary bastion, famous for its downtrodden poets and playwrights, and the numerous heavyweights from the Emerald Isle rank with the best in history.

One of the most celebrated Irish playwrights also wrote some overlooked novels:

1. *Murphy*, **by Samuel Beckett.** The 1969 Nobel Prize–winning author of the benchmark play *Waiting for Godot* penned this work in 1937 with his literary idol, James Joyce, in mind.

   This is the story of the humorously tragic life of Murphy, a man trying to get his financial life in order so his bride-to-be can join him. Beckett sets the book in both London and Dublin in his indelibly individualistic style. One of the major themes in Beckett's works is how there are no answers. Search as the protagonists might, life does not have any answers, it is simply a journey that ends at some point. Murphy is a man who is never going to make his life work out the way he planned and knows very little of the self. It is a wickedly funny, uncompromising narrative of the ideas Beckett visits again and again. How do you make God laugh? Make a plan. That is Beckett in a nutshell.

### Biblio-Trivio

Samuel Beckett left Ireland and, for the most part, permanently settled in his beloved Paris in 1937. A few months later he was inexplicably stabbed while standing on a Paris street. An acquaintance, Suzanne Dumesnil, visited him and became his lifelong companion, and 20-plus years later, his wife. The crime didn't sour his views of Paris; he lived there for the rest of his life and actually began writing all of his works in French after World War II, in part to try and eradicate the heavy influence of James Joyce in his work.

2. ***The Snapper,* by Roddy Doyle.** This is one of
the stories in the *Barrytown Trilogy;* the other
two are *The Commitments* and *The Van.* This is
another tale of the working-class Rabbitte
family from a blue-collar community in
Dublin. The 19-year-old daughter, Sharon,
has an unplanned pregnancy and won't
reveal the identity of the father. She has to
endure the prodding from her overprotective
father and her gossip-hungry barfly girl-
friends. The longer she keeps the identity of
the father of the "snapper" secret, the more
fuel is added to the fire, especially when one
of her father's peers claims ownership. Sharon
takes to spinning her own blarney about a
nameless Spanish sailor, which becomes topic
number one in the local pubs. In the interim,
her father surprises everyone by becoming a
pregnancy expert, a sensitive male, and her
staunchest ally.

**Pro's Prose**

"I've been criticized for the bad
language in my books—that I've
given a bad image of the country.
There's always a subtle pressure to
present a good image, and it's
always somebody else's definition
of what is good."

—Roddy Doyle on his works from an
interview in *The Reading List of
Contemporary Fiction*

Doyle writes in a frank, vulgar Irish tongue that is long on dialogue and short
on description. The back-and-forth between characters raises the routine stakes
into a wonderful humanitarian realm.

Doyle's voice can take some getting used to, but his love of the honest characters shines through on every page.

3. ***The Country Girls Trilogy and Epilogue,* by
Edna O'Brien.** This is a collection of three
novels by celebrated Irish author Edna
O'Brien. The three books in this collection
are *The Country Girls* (1960), *The Lonely Girl*
(1962), and *Girls in Their Married Bliss* (1964).
Many of her fans consider her first book, *The
Country Girls,* to be her best. It is an autobiographical story of a rural Irish lass's sexual
awakening in the 1940s and the subsequent
fleeing from her home. O'Brien tells the story
of Kate in a succinct, matter-of-fact manner
that makes the sexual frankness jolting for
the reader.

**Pro's Prose**

"Hear no evil, see no evil, speak no
evil, and you'll never be a success at
a party."

—An old Irish proverb

**Biblio-Trivio**

Edna O'Brien's first seven novels were banned in her native Ireland due to the graphic nature of her books and the sexuality standards of the time. She was raised in a suffocating Catholic environment in County Clare and broke free from the emotional, physical, and intellectual shackles when she moved to Dublin at age 14. O'Brien has credited her decision to become a writer to her discovery of James Joyce (surprise, surprise).

*The Lonely Girl* picks up the story in Dublin, as Kate and her friend Baba take part in sexual escapades throughout the more liberated Dublin. The last book, *Girls in Their Married Bliss*, allows Baba to take over the narration of their stale marriages and tawdry affairs.

Sex is always a hot topic in reading groups, and O'Brien's frankness is raw, intoxicating, and sometimes dispiriting. This trilogy offers a voice that is an honest, engrossing, look at the traps and freedoms of sexuality.

If you're interested in the writings of the Emerald Isle, here is a short list of some more great Irish books:

➤ *Death of the Heart,* by Elizabeth Bowen
➤ *Breakfast on Pluto,* by Patrick McCabe
➤ *This Side of Brightness,* by Colum McCann
➤ *Hurrish,* by Emily Lawless
➤ *The Lonely Passion of Judith Hearne,* by Brian Moore
➤ *Lamb,* by Bernard MacLaverty
➤ *The Collegians,* by Gerald Griffin
➤ *Fools of Fortune,* by William Trevor

# English McGuffins

Follow the Union Jack to these selections of British brilliance from England's long history of leading literary lights:

1. *Emma,* **by Jane Austen.** Emma Woodhouse is considered by many Austen fans to be her greatest character. She is certainly one of the most flawed, but it is her identifiable imperfections that endear her to generation after generation of readers. Emma's exceptionally large ego leads her to believe she is the perfect woman to remake another woman, Harriet—in her image, of course—to ensure she snares a husband. She sets her sights on an ambitious vicar for her made-over friend Harriet and proceeds to play matchmaker. Austen's wit and wisdom regarding the human chess game called courting is quite astonishing. Her simple dating games reveal the deeper human needs for power and control. The impressive trick Austen pulls off, though, is to keep Emma charming throughout her self-indulgence by allowing her to mature. Emma is a three-dimensional woman, not a device to spit out the author's views of the way life works.

   Austen claimed she was going to write a heroine that nobody would like except for her, but she was way off base. Emma is one of the classic female protagonists in all of literature. *Emma* will more than likely be a hit at your book club, even if nobody is of English or European descent. Question: Does Emma learn (or earn) *anything* in the end?

2. *Money: A Suicide Note,* **by Martin Amis.** Amis's visionary world of darkness shines through brighter than the sun in this outstanding black comedy. The antihero, John Self, is a heavy indulger in booze, drugs, fatty food, tobacco, and cheap sex, all while waiting for his big movie deal to roll in and line his pockets. The gluttonous Self manages to be simultaneously lovable and excessively noxious, and Amis's love of the repulsive is frequently laugh-out-loud funny.

**Pro's Prose**

"With all dear Emma's little faults, she is an excellent creature ... where Emma errs once, she is in the right a hundred times."

—Excerpt from *Emma,* by Jane Austen

*Money: A Suicide Note* is also a sharp look at the obese lifestyles in London and New York in the 1980s, a time when fat cats became role models and investment gurus appeared on magazine covers. It is a layered book that can be enjoyed on any number of levels. Amis's dark sensibilities might not be for everyone, but those unfortunate sods are missing out on savagely funny stuff.

**Biblio-Trivio**

Martin Amis is the son of famous novelist Kingsley Amis, a satirical novelist whose greatest works chronicle British society since the post–World War II fallen empire. It was another author, however, who sparked Martin's enthusiasm. His stepmother, novelist Elizabeth Jane Howard, introduced him to Jane Austen in his teenage years and the rest, as they say, is history.

3. *Amsterdam,* **by Ian McEwan.** This is a slim book from an author who has been referred to as Ian Macabre because of the dark subject matter of books like *Child in Time* and *Black Dogs*. This is the story of two friends, Vernon Halliday and Clive Linley, who enter into a euthanasia pact after a friend's death in her 40s from a degenerative illness. They agree that if one of them faces the same type of disease, the other one will kill him.

**Biblio-Trivio**

*Amsterdam* won the highly prestigious Booker Prize in 1998. The Booker Prize is one of the most important literary awards in the English-speaking world. It was founded in 1969 and is bestowed annually to a full-length novel written in the British Commonwealth and published in the preceding year. Other winners have included Salman Rushdie, Anita Brookner, and the appropriately named David Storey.

McEwan's book is concise and funny as it marches toward its final calamity. The plot has twists and turns as the characters in the book confront their own mortality on the way to finding out who is going to kill whom. It is a book that can be analyzed in terms of its structure, because there is nary a sentence wasted. Why don't more writers cut to the bone? Or, do the characters get the short shrift?

Now, if you want some more from across the pond, this short list of English books ought to get you off to a good start:

➤ *A Tale of Two Cities,* by Charles Dickens

➤ *Waterland,* by Graham Swift

➤ *Middlemarch,* by George Eliot

➤ *Lucky Jim,* by Kingsley Amis

➤ *The Life and Loves of a She-Devil,* by Fay Weldon

➤ *Precious Bane,* by Mary Webb

➤ *Living,* by Henry Green

➤ *Barchester Towers,* by Anthony Trollope

# A Lit–tle Italy

From Europe's boot come plenty of titles that kick butt:

1. ***Reeds in the Wind,* by Grazia Deledda.** This is the story of the Pintor sisters, written by a relatively unknown author. The novel was only recently published in this country, even though it was first published in 1913. It is a story of the peasant beliefs in destiny. The poor sisters are waiting for salvation from their earthly troubles on the harsh land of Sardinia, an island off the eastern coast of Italy.

**Biblio-Trivio**

Grazia Deledda had a limited formal education and learned her craft through avid reading. She wrote 33 novels and many short stories. In 1926, she became the first Italian woman to receive the Nobel Prize for Literature (second woman overall after Swedish author Selma Lagerlof).

Deledda writes poetically of the Italian landscape and the universal familial conditions. The humanity at the core of the bittersweet tale of a family in decline erases the cultural and generational gaps modern audiences might anticipate. The sisters believe in a jumbled mix of witches, theology, black magic, and folklore that may remind some readers of present-day third-world spirituality, but

### Novel Ideas

Opera, which is another form of storytelling, began in Italy in the late sixteenth century. Why not put on Puccini's *La Bohème*, Verdi's *La Traviata*, or Rossini's *Barber of Seville?* Your closest central library should have the operas on CD, and they will brighten up your discussion of Italian literature.

the conviction of their beliefs is sincere and moving. Question: Do the tenets of all religions require human faith in myth and suspension of that which can be proved? If not, what religions do not use an unexplained mystery as a central belief?

2. ***The Garden of the Finzi-Continis,* by Giorgio Bassani.** This is the story of a young middle-class Jewish boy's obsession with the aristocratic Alberto and Micol Finzi-Contini, whom he only sees occasionally at school or at synagogue on holy religious celebrations. It takes place during the days of Mussolini's fascist anti-Semitic edicts, which pushes the Jews to the margins of society. Banished from the local tennis club, the narrator is invited to play behind the all-encompassing walls at the Finzi-Contini estate. Unfortunately, the narrator assumes this means his love for Micol will be returned.

It is a story of one-sided love amid the ever-present horrors of fascism and the Holocaust. It deals with how individuals cope with destruction, both internal and external. It is a tragedy of a time when nobody was safe from the outside world, even on the inside. It has become a well-regarded novel in recent years, and I highly recommend it.

### Biblio-Trivio

*The Garden of the Finzi-Continis* won the 1972 Oscar for Best Foreign Language Film. It was directed by neorealist master Vittorio De Sica (*The Bicycle Thief*, 1948), but at the time, many fans of the book thought he was washed up and would butcher the adaptation. Instead, it sparked major interest in the novel, which had fallen somewhat from public consciousness.

3. ***Unto the Sons,* by Gay Talese.** Okay, I'm cheating on a couple of levels here, because this book isn't fiction and it is the story of the immigration of Talese's family from Italy to pre–World War II New Jersey. It begins in a small Southern Italian town and covers three generations of familial growth. Talese is one of America's best nonfiction artists, and this book should interest all ethnic groups (much like Alex Haley's *Roots*) because it is such an American commonality—the immigrant experience and assimilation of the younger generations. The depiction of prejudice against Italian-Americans during World War II, the struggle to make a living and maintain a business, and the contradictions between Old World customs and New World realities are all different shades of the central tenets in American literature.

Impeccably researched, this operatic narrative, is a wonderful book that gives life to the oft-told and overly mythologized immigrant story.

Feeling the lure of the land of figs and grapes? Try reading one of these great books:

➤ *Mr. Palomar,* by Italo Calvino

➤ *The Land of Cockayne,* by Matilde Serao

➤ *The Woman of Rome,* by Alberto Moravia

➤ *The Name of the Rose,* by Umberto Eco

➤ *The Betrothed,* by Alessandro Manzoni

➤ *History, a Novel,* by Elsa Morante

➤ *The Late Mattia Pascal,* by Luigi Pirandello

# Living in America

Let's drive the tour bus back home and look at three different regional divisions. The categories could be broken down time zone by time zone, region by region, state by state, city by city, town by town, village by village, and so on down the line until there is one room in one house that is

**Pro's Prose**

"That Sinatra was an Italo-American gained no concession from my father, who seemed irrationally resistant to any and all performers who appealed primarily to a youthful spirit or exemplified the latest fad. The objects of his displeasure included not only crooners but also the most celebrated new stars of Hollywood and the heralded figures of the sports world."

—From *Unto the Sons,* by Gay Talese

**Novel Ideas**

At least once a year, your reading group should make a concerted effort to read a book from a local writer, particularly a tome that is set in the common area. Get in touch with the closest small press, check the neighborhood bookstores for "local authors," or try calling an English department at the nearest college. It will give your group provincial pride and help out a fellow New Yorker, Wisconsinite, or Montanan. You may read an author who is going to go on to an amazing career.

**197**

### Novel Ideas

*The Viking Portable Library Western Reader* would be too great an investment for a single-month read, so select X number of selections for the entire group to read for discussion and X number of other selections of the reader's choice. That way, there will be plenty to discuss up front, and the other choices will add contrast and context to the discourse of America's mythological wide-open ranges.

### Novel Ideas

The entire catalogue of *The Viking Portable Library Reader* series is worthwhile. They have everything from *The Portable Oscar Wilde* to *The Portable Medieval Reader*. The books dedicated to a specific genre (as opposed to a single author) are particularly effective at providing a wide array of interesting material. If your group, or you yourself, ever want to spend a few months (or years) covering a single topic, this is a good place to start.

the setting for a brilliant work of fiction, but we don't have that much time. So, for our purposes we will look at three American landscapes, one massive, one large, and one quite tiny (at least by square miles, anyway).

Let's start on the left coast.

# Going Out West Where I Belong

1. *The Portable Western Reader,* **edited by William Kittredge.** This is a fantastic anthology of writings from, of, and about the western half of the United States. The editor, William Kittredge, knows the terrain, both the landscapes and the literature, and he has selected an exciting variety of stories, poems, essays, Native American yarns, and excerpts from landmark novels and nonfiction works.

   Kittredge's highest achievement in this anthology is that he presents an enormous range of voices, and captures the mythology and reality of western life. He includes more than 70 authors, everyone from John Steinbeck and Allen Ginsberg to Joy Harjo, Ivan Doig, and Raymond Carver. It is an original collection of a literary genre that has only taken shape and come to be recognized in the last couple of decades.

   Different selections from the anthology will appeal to everyone in your reading group, and Western culture is ingrained in our collective American psyche through the legendary celluloid renderings.

2. *The Handyman,* **by Carolyn See.** Bob Hampton is that most innocuous of workers, the anonymous jack-of-all-trades, the handyman. He has returned from Paris after he pragmatically decided he couldn't afford to keep his dream of being a painter alive in the City of Lights. Back in Los Angeles, Bob becomes a

handyman to help pay for his art supplies, but his job title doesn't begin to describe his unexpected power to heal people's shattered lives and get their emotional planes flying right again. Bob relishes the role and the perk of bedding some of the dysfunctional women he encounters.

See's book is an examination of where art and love cross paths and what sparks creativity. It is warm and funny, and it has an interesting structural format. Two grant-application letters from 2027 frame the story. An art researcher wants to look into the early works of the renowned painter Robert Hampton and the witnesses to his life. The witnesses turn out to be the folks he healed in 1996, and the reader gets the pleasure of figuring out which testimonial matches their younger, unhappier, selves. *The Handyman* is a book that believes in the basic good of interpersonal relationships and how they are the keys to happiness.

3. ***Dancing at the Rascal Fair,*** **by Ivan Doig.** This is the middle book in the Montana trilogy of the generational experiences of the McCaskell family. The other two books are *This House of Sky* and *English Creek*. The books take place in the beautiful highlands of Two Medicine country in Montana, a suitable land for the homesteading Scotsmen. Doig is a native Montanan who was raised in a family of Scottish ranchers and sheepherders, and he majestically captures the sounds, smells, and atmosphere of the lay of the land.

This book is the story of two friends, Angus and Rob, who emigrate and settle as sheep farmers. Rob marries, but Angus falls in love with a woman who marries another man. It crushes his heart and Angus never recovers, and it ruins his relationship with his great friend. Angus has been criticized for being weak, and some readers find it hard to believe

**Novel Ideas**

If your group is interested in the rhythms and nuances of life in Southern California, See's *Making History* is a must. Her memoir of her family's struggles with money and booze entitled *Dreaming: Hard Luck and Good Times in America* is also a worthy selection. See is a fantastic writer and rapidly becoming a reading group favorite.

**Pro's Prose**

"What do we want with this vast, worthless area? This region of savages and wild beasts, of deserts of shifting sands and whirlwinds of dust, of cactus and prairie dogs? To what use could we ever hope to put these great deserts, or those endless mountain ranges, impenetrable and covered to their very base with eternal snow? What can we ever hope to do with the western coast, a coast of three thousand miles, rock-bound, cheerless, uninviting, and not a harbor on it? What use have we for this country?

—Attributed to Daniel Webster, reportedly from a speech in the Senate

**Pro's Prose**

"Even on the calendar of memory, though, winter must fit ahead of May, and that first winter of Adair and myself outlined us to one another as if we were black stonepiles against the snow. After the first snowfall, the weather cleared, the air was crisp without being truly cold yet. Being outside in that glistening weather was a chance to glimpse the glory the earth can be when it puts its winter fur on ..."

—From *Dancing at the Rascal Fair*, by Ivan Doig

that he would never get over a woman. Ask your reading group if this is accurate, or is it because Doig creates such rich, complex, characters that the audience doesn't *want* to believe that such a man exists?

If you and your group decide to go West, consider this question, no matter which tomes you decide on: Why did we mythologize one section of America more than the others in the first place? While you chew on that, here is a short list of some more Western books:

➤ *The Big Sky,* by A. B. Guthrie
➤ *I Am Lidian,* by Naomi Lane Babson
➤ *Cannery Row,* by John Steinbeck
➤ *Palm Latitudes,* by Kate Braverman
➤ *The Ox-Bow Incident,* by Walter V. T. Clark
➤ *Housekeeping,* by Marilynne Robinson
➤ *Almost Perfect,* by Alice Adams
➤ *Bless Me, Ultima,* by Rudolfo A. Anaya

Now to the other side of the map, if you will.

# New England of Books

Since the Pilgrims landed on Plymouth Rock, literary works have come flowing from the New England waters. From the scarlet "A" Hester Prynne wears to the *Heart Songs* of E. Annie Proulx, it has always been a hot-bed region for great books.

1. ***The Country Doctor,* by Sarah Orne Jewett.** These days, Jewett is not an instantly recognized name in the pantheon of nineteenth-century novelists, but she was a major influence on authors in the first half of the twentieth century. *A Country Doctor* is her first novel and a beautiful portrait of the unblemished Maine countryside and coastline. The theme of the book mirrored the main struggle of educated women of the time, whether to live the standard, confining marital existence, or to follow a professional career path, even though the opportunities were scarce. Should Nan become a doctor or a housewife? At the time, the main quandary in Jewett's life was how to go against societal grain and follow her dreams of becoming a professional writer. Her determination blazed the trail for many female authors and is your reading group's gain.

The realistic details Jewett captures place her among the very best regional authors. The local color is vividly depicted on just about every page, and your book club will have to search the ends of the Earth to find a richer mental painting of the Pine Tree State.

2. *A Prayer for Owen Meany,* **by John Irving.** In the interest of full disclosure, I will let you know that this always gets consideration when somebody asks me, "What's your favorite book?" There is never just one, but this story of a dwarfish boy, Owen Meany, who believes he is an instrument of God, is near the top. Meany accidentally kills his best friend's mom with a baseball and assumes that he will make up for it through God's divine intervention. It is an odd, perceptive, religious fable of immense depth and clarity. Irving's humor and unexpected moments of horror will be familiar to his fans, but his most heartbreaking protagonist is what makes *A Prayer for Owen Meany* such a standout.

The novel can be enjoyed on a seemingly infinite number of levels, including as an indictment of America's undefined role in Vietnam. It is a book with moral arguments that never resorts to preaching or spitting out a dogmatic strain of ethical codes for saintly living. *A Prayer for Owen Meany* isn't awash in self-righteousness, it is simply a tremendous novel about human belief systems.

3. *Outerbridge Reach,* **by Robert Stone.** The theme of man-against-the-sea is a story that has been told since Biblical times, and Stone's book is a worthy addition. It is the story of Owen Browne, Annapolis graduate, Vietnam veteran, and sailboat salesman in Connecticut. Browne's wealthy boss is supposed to sail around the world solo, but he disappears and Browne becomes the man for the job. He is no expert when it comes to sailing, but he feels unfulfilled and takes up the challenge.

**Novel Ideas**

The eloquent descriptions of life in Maine are vivid and put the reader right in the heart of the twenty-third state. Since your book club probably can't afford to load up the bus and head to Cobscook Bay, why not bring a little bit of Maine home to you and boil up some lobsters as you debate the merits of Jewett's prose? A little butter, a little lemon, a one-pound lobster, and a hearty discussion of women's place at the turn of the century sounds like a whale of an evening to me.

**Pro's Prose**

"I am doomed to remember a boy with a wrecked voice—not because of his voice, or because he was the smallest person I ever knew, or even because he was the instrument of my mother's death, but because he is the reason I believe in God; I am a Christian because of Owen Meany."

—Opening lines of *A Prayer for Owen Meany,* by John Irving

### Jane Err

Do not watch *Simon Birch,* the movie "adaptation" of *A Prayer for Owen Meany,* before you read the novel. Whatever you may think of the film on its own merits, it is a completely watered-down and simplistic version of the brilliant Irving tome. He took his name off of the script after he saw what they wanted to do with it, and why wouldn't he? *Simon Birch* is sappier than a Vermont maple in syrup season.

Accompanying Browne on his journey is a hedonistic, cynical documentary filmmaker, Strickland. His movie is about the adventure, but it is augmented by interviews with Browne's sad, lonely, alcoholic wife, Anne. The trip, naturally, doesn't go as planned, and it is Stone's deep philosophical themes that make the journey so fascinating. It is a tragicomedy with big ideas that rises to the level of art. Maybe the man-against-the-sea theme brings out the best in author's psyches, and this book ranks up there with Melville and Hemingway.

If you're craving lobster and the crisp smell of fall foliage, here's a short list of New England books:

➤ *Vanished,* by Mary McGarry Morris

➤ *The Scarlet Letter,* by Nathaniel Hawthorne

➤ *Heart Songs and Other Stories,* by E. Annie Proulx

➤ *The Bostonians,* by Henry James

➤ *Monkeys,* by Susan Minot

➤ *The Funeral Makers,* by Cathie Pelletier

➤ *The Beans of Egypt, Maine,* by Carolyn Chute

➤ *The Secret History,* by Donna Tartt

### Biblio-Trivio

Stone spent six weeks in Vietnam, and his impressions of what a mistake the war was led him to write the National Book Award–winning *Dog Soldiers.*

# Gotham Greats

Our final stop is in the city that never sleeps (most likely because they stay up late reading "one more chapter").

1. *The Bonfire of the Vanities,* **by Tom Wolfe.** This is the '80s. It is the story of a "Master of the Universe" (a popular action figure for boys at the time) named Sherman McCoy, a white, arrogant weasel of an investment banker flush with cash in the heyday of flaunted excess. Sherman ends up in the borough the rich and powerful (read: white) of the Upper East Side had never before set foot in, the Bronx, and runs over an innocent black male. He flees the scene and assumes everything is going to be fine because men in his position are too important to let the consequences of their actions get in the way of business. Before long, Sherman is sweating bullets as a drunken tabloid reporter, racially demagogic politicos, and a restless mistress contribute to his downfall.

   There have been critics who say that this book is too much of a cartoon, but as a satire, it is dead-on. The underlying rage that the have-nots feel toward the vain displays of excess by the wealthy were at a fever pitch in the mid-'80s and haven't cooled down all that much today. Wolfe nails all of the kinds of tensions that float through the Big Apple streets, be it economic, political, racial, sexual, or social. It is a wickedly funny page-turner that spits its venom equally; everyone in this work is out for number one. It is also one of the few books that visits the affluent and the down-trodden without making one or the other the clear-cut heroes. It is a story of greed, greed, and more greed. The intricate plot takes Dante-esque chaos and pulls New York City into a bonfire of its own creation. For those of you out there who hate Gotham (and I know you're out there), it will satisfy every inkling of the moral decay the city revels in (at least in the age of the Gipper). For those of you who just love great American fiction, this is the masterpiece of the Wall Street-worshipping '80s.

### Pro's Prose

"Tonight, with nothing but his hand and his nerve he had fought the elemental enemy, the hunter, the predator ... The time had come to act like a man, and he had acted and prevailed. He was not merely a Master of the Universe; he was more; he was a man."

—From *The Bonfire of the Vanities,* by Tom Wolfe

2. *The Age of Innocence,* **by Edith Wharton.** Perhaps no book in the long history of stories about New York City resonates year after year quite so sharply as *The Age of Innocence.* It is the story of the upper crust, and of Newland Archer's hopeless love for disgraced Countess Ellen Olenska who dared leave her husband. It is a biting social commentary of a time when the well-to-do were still living under Victorian codes and European-influenced manners of decorum that sublimated human passion. It is a costume period piece, but it delves much deeper into the ways humans let others dictate their behavior. Is the supposedly allpowerful emotion of love more important than living by the societal standards imposed upon them?

**Biblio-Trivio**

Edith Wharton, the first woman to ever receive an honorary degree from Yale, is forever linked with New York City for *The Age of Innocence* and other books, like the collection of four short novels, *Old New York.* Ironically, she left there in 1907 and settled permanently in France, primarily because she hated the artificial codes of behavior she was expected to abide by.

It is an engaging tome that almost becomes an anthropological study of the elite. It won the Pulitzer Prize in 1921 and was successfully adapted for the big screen by Mr. *Goodfellas* himself, Martin Scorsese. It is a book club favorite because of its enduring theme of breaking the shackles of the life we are presented. The eternal question is, does Newland make the right choice? Is it worth it to give up everything for love?

3. *The New York Trilogy: City of Glass, Ghosts, The Locked Room,* **by Paul Auster.** One of the best words to describe this book is hypnotic. The three stories are all part of an existential puzzle, an abstract mystery if you will. It is a dense read that, although not an easy book to discuss on standard planes, offers the best of a post-modernist maze without the pretentiousness. The first story, *City of Glass,* is a genre mystery that starts out simple enough: A detective writer is mistakenly hired as a real detective to shadow a recently released mental patient, Stillman. The story becomes a search for identity and in a fascinating strain, the reader finds out Stillman is a linguist trying to uncover the original language of Adam

and Eve. It is the quest for an answer that haunts the characters in Auster's trilogy. In *Ghosts*, White hires Blue, a detective, to watch Black, and the case proceeds to go on for years. Blue gets trapped in trying to figure out why Black needs to be watched because neither of them is doing anything.

The final story, *The Locked Room,* is a little more accessible than the first two because there is a distinct character to follow. The narrator is called by the wife of a childhood friend to finish the manuscripts of a writer named Fanshawe, who vanished and is assumed to be deceased. The narrator eventually takes over Fanshawe's life, going so far as to marry his wife. Out of the blue, Fanshawe sends the narrator a message that puts him in grave danger. Auster manages to tie things from the first two books in *The Locked Room,* and they combine to become a rich noir mystery that will take an investment of thought, but it is worth it. Ask your book club, why is a character in *City of Glass* named Paul Auster? Is it all done to mess with the readers' mind? Or is it part of the complex puzzle of life in Metropolis?

**Pro's Prose**

"The days go by, and once again things settle down to the barest of routines. Black writes, reads, shops in the neighborhood, visits the post office, takes an occasional stroll. The woman does not reappear, and Black makes no further excursions into Manhattan. Blue begins to think that any day he will get a letter telling him the case is closed. The woman is gone, he reasons, and that could be the end of it. But nothing of the sort happens."

—From *Ghosts* by Paul Auster

Now that I've got you humming along to the tune of "New York, New York," here are a few more tales of Gotham to whet your appetite:

➤ *Getting Over Homer: A Novel,* by Mark O'Donnell

➤ *The Victim: A Novel,* by Saul Bellow

➤ *Washington Square,* by Henry James

➤ *Slaves of New York,* by Tama Janowitz

➤ *A Tree Grows in Brooklyn,* by Betty Smith

➤ *Home to Harlem,* by Claude McKay

➤ *In Nueva York,* by Nicholasa Mohr

➤ *Waiting for the End of the World,* by Madison Smartt Bell

Wherever you may roam, stop and buy a book. There's always one around if you look hard enough.

## The Least You Need to Know

➤ Make sure you know the historical and geographical background of the regional book you select to get the most out of the reading.

➤ The Emerald Isle and the United Kingdom have a library of worthy titles unto themselves.

➤ All sections of America have their literary histories.

➤ Select local authors on occasion, even if their books are unknown, because you're helping a neighbor and will get provincial rewards.

# Chapter 15

# Molls, Snoops, Dicks, Dupes, and a Bunch of Rotting Corpses

## In This Chapter

➤ The reason "genre fiction" can be a meaningless label

➤ Things to look for in books of a particular genre

➤ Why Sherlock Holmes is in our homes

➤ The history of the potboiler

➤ A thrilling yarn about an elevator operator?

The purpose of Part 4 is to give those of you who want a specific style of group an opportunity to join the party. All you lovers, killers, monsters, and would-be sleuths, your time has come. The chapters will be broken down into a variety of genres. Too often, quality works of fiction are marginalized because they have been categorized in a way that keeps clubs from enjoying different styles of writing. Great noir crime novels have their view of humanity that may not be as complex as *A Doctor's Visit: Short Stories by Anton Chekov,* but it can still spark probing discussions of what drives the criminal mind.

Don't be scared of books that fall under "genre fiction." Just seek out the generally recognized best-of-the-best of the particular genre. There are challenging Westerns, romances, mysteries, horror novels, and so on, and your book club shouldn't be embarrassed because you want a change of pace. On the flip side, if all that your group reads is genre fiction, simply put, you are really missing the point of exploring literature.

Let's move on to some of the things upon which your reading group should keep their collective (private) eye.

# Becoming a Genre Genius

Becoming a genre genius requires knowing the history, the importance, and the variety of whatever style of books you want to analyze. Since this chapter is going to revolve around detective/mystery stories, we'll use examples from that genre, but they more or less hold true for whatever literary subspecies you want to tackle.

➤ **Main characters.** Oftentimes, a series of books will feature the extended adventures of a single character or characters, be they Sam Spade, Dr. Kay Scarpetta, Encyclopedia Brown, or G. K. Chesterton's crime-solving Roman Catholic priest, Father Brown. The primary reason is so the audience can become familiar with the habits, nuances, views, attitudes, and other defining qualities of the lead character, which shifts the focus from human behavior to the plot. It doesn't necessarily mean that the lead character has less depth; picture it as the difference between an exciting new friend and the old pal down the block. It is a standard practice that fans expect, and they often come to feel as if the fictional character is somebody they know personally. Agatha Christie's two unconventional sleuths, Hercule Poirot and Miss Marple, were the main protagonists in her uniquely prolific career. The main character is important because it eliminates the need for extra details and allows for a tight, concentrated narrative.

**Biblio-Trivio**

Agatha Christie published more than 75 works in her lifetime, including poetry books, a volume of Christmas verse and stories, and a play, *Mousetrap*, which has been running in London since 1952. She started in 1920 with *The Mysterious Affair at Styles* and sold more than 100 million copies worldwide.

➤ **Settings.** Much like you and me, the main characters in these books frequently roam the same territory, or have the same job, or visit the same people, or drink at the same bar, or do the same things day in and day out, so that the uniqueness in the premise of the book keeps the audience interested. Tony Hillerman sets his mysteries in the Southwest and uses Navajo detectives and Native

American culture as an integral part of the stories. J. A. Jance keeps her homicide cop, J. P. Beaumont, busy in and around the Seattle area, which becomes another character, not just a random setting.

### Biblio-Trivio

J. A. (Judy) Jance's agent submitted her first manuscript using her initials because it was written in first person through a male detective's point of view. The idea worked, and, for the first six J. P. Beaumont books, there was no author photo or biographical information.

As in all varieties of fiction, these authors want their locales to be part of the flow of the characters' lives, but the details have to be completely fleshed out and accurate because the die-hard fans are going to be returning again and again. It also adds credibility because most of us could describe the town in which we live more succinctly than someone who has never been there (I hope). Another benefit, particularly in detective stories, is that the sleuths can check old suspects, case files, snitches, and killers that have been previously introduced, like Sherlock Holmes's nemesis Professor Moriarty.

➤ **Patterns.** Another standard practice to be aware of is the use of a basic pattern in a series of books. Patterns can be dictated by the plot; for example, every murder in a particular author's series roughly happens within the first few pages and then the mystery is the identity of the killer. The author may reveal the killer right away and the plot is more of a cat-and-mouse game of trying to establish proof. The point is the pattern is basically adhered to in every book, but there are other aspects as well. This is the one part of "genre fiction" that is usually cited as the main reason that certain selections aren't considered literature. The problem with the argument is that most novels follow the standard three-act structure, be it F. Scott Fitzgerald or Robert B. Parker. There are, of course, experimental works of brilliance, but they are the exception.

*The Great Gatsby* is absolutely more important in the intellectual and psychological realm than the Spenser books, but it has nothing to do with the conventional story patterns, because the books share them. Don't dismiss written works because they follow the established pattern, otherwise say good-bye to Mr. Shakespeare, for starters.

➤ **Styles.** Another facet is the author's style. Elmore Leonard, April Smith, and James Ellroy all use distinctive writing characteristics, which carry over from book to book, even though the plots and characters might be wildly divergent. In Ellroy's fiction, you'll find tough-guy banter, staccato sentences, short paragraphs, newspaper headlines, bloody violence, alliteration, rhyme, onomatopoeia, and a pressure-cooker pace designed to exacerbate underworld life on the fringes.

Unique style is one of the great drawing cards of authors, and it often ends up influencing the next generation. Joyce's stream-of-consciousness is a stylistic benchmark, but more subtle lineage can be made from authors like Raymond Chandler on the works of writers like James Ellroy.

### Pro's Prose

"Sinatra slid on slick black sap gloves. They were wickedly weighted with dollops of double–ought buck. They packed a well-known wallop. "

—From *Tijuana, Mon Amour,* by James Ellroy

➤ **Red herrings.** The last example, the red herring, is primarily a function of the detective genre. It is a mechanism that misleads or distracts the audience from the real issue at hand. It could be a clue that's clueless, a suspect that's innocent, or a note that's meaningless. Red herrings are used to get the audience to look to the left, while the answer is on the right. Surely readers of an *Idiot's Guide* are too sharp to be duped by a standard device.

### Biblio-Trivio

A red herring was originally a herring that had been cured in such a way that it had a pungent aroma. It was used as a hunting decoy, dragged along the ground to throw the dogs off the scent of the fox's trail, because the smell was much more powerful. Thus, the hunting dogs would follow the wrong direction, or in today's terms, be misled.

Now let's look at the history and the stalwarts of the mystery/noir/detective genre.

## There's No Mystery About It

Purists will argue that traditional mysteries belong in a completely different realm than a 1950s hard-boiled noir yarn, which doesn't belong in the same grouping as postmodern tales where cases aren't always solved and the inner lives of the detectives carry the narrative. For our purposes, though, the wide variety of detective stories can be traced in spirit to the originator, Edgar Allan Poe.

### That's Mr. Mystery to You

Poe dreamed up the first of the renowned literary detectives, C. Auguste Dupin, and unleashed him upon the world in *Graham's Magazine* in April 1841 in the classic short story "The Murders in the Rue Morgue." Dupin's combination of odd personal habits and his skills of deductive reasoning became the foundation for legions of mystery writers who followed.

**Biblio-Trivio**

It is believed Poe's detective, C. Auguste Dupin, was modeled after the original real-life detective, Francois Eugene Vidocq, France's *chef de la Surete* (a.k.a. head of the Criminal Investigation Department) in Paris.

The genre lay relatively dormant for years, although two English novelists kept the dark embers smoldering. Charles Dickens penned *The Mystery of Edwin Drood* in 1870 but died before its completion so the identity of the murderer was never revealed. Wilkie Collins is another of the forefathers; his works, *The Moonstone* and *The Woman in White,* appeared in periodicals edited by Dickens. In 1887, the detective story was forever cemented in the collective psyche of the world's readers when *A Study in Scarlet* was printed in *Beeton's Christmas Annual* and a man named Sherlock Holmes was introduced.

**Pro's Prose**

"'Ah! Watson,' said Holmes, smiling, 'perhaps you would not be very gracious either, if, after all the trouble of wooing and wedding, you found yourself deprived in an instant of wife and of fortune. I think that we may judge Lord St. Simon very mercifully, and thank our stars that we are never likely to find ourselves in the same position. Draw your chair up, and hand me my violin, for the only problem which we have still to solve is how to while away these bleak autumnal evenings.'"

—From *The Noble Bachelor*, by Sir Arthur Conan Doyle

Sir Arthur Conan Doyle patterned his detective after Poe's, but he gave Holmes his own bizarre world to inhabit, which included healthy doses of "shag." He also emulated Poe's use of a separate narrator who was part of the protagonist's inner-circle, in Holmes's case, his old naive buddy Dr. Watson. Doyle also gave Holmes a nemesis, the fiendishly criminal genius Professor Moriarty. The stories were enormously popular, and Doyle became somewhat of an international celebrity.

The impact of Doyle's darling dick can not be overstated; the detective story has remained popular ever since. Although there are elements of the gothic novel in many works of mystery, it is the cases of Sherlock Holmes that influenced the genre we recognize today.

## The Glory Days

The 1920s and '30s were a heady time for the genre. The Dame Commander of the Order of the British Empire herself, Agatha Christie, gave the world her snazzy Belgian shamus, Hercule Poirot. S. S. Van Dine introduced Philo Vance, the Ellery Queen series began, and Earl Derr Biggers fostered Chinese gumshoe Charlie Chan upon bookstores everywhere. The decades also brought aristocratic gumshoe Lord Peter Wimsey from the mind of Dorothy Sayers, psychological mastermind Inspector Jules Maigret from Georges Simenon, and hefty hero Nero Wolfe from Rex Stout.

**Biblio-Trivio**

Before his days as an author, Doyle was a practicing physician. From 1882 to 1890 he was a doctor in Southsea, England, and used to write stories while waiting for patients. Within five years of his first publication, Doyle had quit medicine to write. Sherlock Holmes became so popular, clubs formed to read his works, most notably the Baker Street Irregulars, which still prospers around the world today.

During the 1920s another type of mystery novel was taking shape, which we will call the noir novel. The term *noir* comes from "film noir," which was a reactionary strain of crime movies bathed in cynicism with malevolent, double-crossing characters, sleazy locales, and a shadowy, foreboding atmosphere of violence and mistrust of everything and everybody. It is a commonly held theory that the reason these movies took shape was because the horrors and atrocities of World War II had infused some members of that generation with a cynical outlook on life. Emotions that were sublimated in proper company were unleashed on the big screen.

The connection here is that many of the best film noir pictures, including *Double Indemnity, The Big Sleep,* and *The Postman Always Rings Twice,* were adapted from what we call noir novels of prior decades. The 1920s gave rise to "pulp" comic books, most notably *Black Mask,* which featured tough-talking, hard-boiled gumshoes who needed cash, not to be intellectually engaged. Masters of the mayhem were Raymond Chandler, and his creation Philip Marlowe, Erle Stanley Gardner with the ever-present Perry Mason, and Dashiell Hammett and his legendary character Sam Spade.

### Novel Ideas

Nero Wolfe spent two hours in the morning and two hours in the evening tending to his beloved orchids in the greenhouse on his roof with his plant nurse, Theodore Horstmann. If your book club chooses a Nero Wolfe mystery, why not brighten up the gathering with a generous smattering of orchids (or a cheaper facsimile)?

### Biblio-Trivio

After World War I, Dashiell Hammett was a private investigator, which provided material for his popular works. Realism and brutality were his trademarks, and he eventually ended up in Hollywood writing screenplays. Ironically, in the '50s, this writer of classic American tough-guys was alleged to be taking part in pro-Communist activity and was briefly imprisoned for contempt of court in 1951.

These authors were the forerunners of the cynical antiheroes of today's mystery stories, and modern writers have found ways to blur the lines between good and evil while still following the established rules.

# Modern Murder and Malaise

Although the popularity of the detective story has its ups and downs, it is never relegated to the dark, lonely corners of a dusty library, although that may be the best place to read it. Different conventions have appeared in the last couple of decades, including the rise in fans of the police detective series. These titles include the *87th Precinct Mysteries* collection by Ed McBain, and the Lawrence Block books like *Everybody Dies,* featuring the boozy, defrocked New York City cop Matt Scudder. Other popular series include characters like the crafty medical examiner/forensic pathologist Dr. Kay Scarpetta in Patricia D. Cornwell's *All That Remains* and *Cruel and Unusual* (among others), or Spenser and Hawk, the stars of the 26-and-counting collection of Robert B. Parker.

There are also the irony-laced tomes of Elmore Leonard like *Maximum Bob, Get Shorty,* and *Rum Punch* (which was turned into *Jackie Brown* by Quentin Tarantino in a '90s modern deconstructed film noir, much like *Pulp Fiction,* which took its name from the old standbys like *Black Mask*—see how it's all coming together?). And some of the old stalwarts are still alive and kicking and have published works in the last few years; for example, Dick Francis, who published another of his works of fiction, *10 lb. Penalty,* in October 1998.

### Biblio-Trivio

The majority of Dick Francis's books have been set against the backdrop of horse racing. Francis himself was a celebrity jockey in the world of British National Hunt Racing, won more than 350 races, and was the 1953 to 1954 champion. He rode eight times in the Grand National Steeplechase and was retained as jockey to her Majesty Queen Elizabeth. A serious fall led to his pursuit of the literary life.

If it seems like all mysteries are part of a series, well, they usually are. There are the occasional single titles, but most of the time the author has a common thread, which often comes in the form of a repeat character. An explanation for this is that authors fall in love with their characters (or themes, or setting, or style, etc.) and want to continue to watch them grow and explore their familiar worlds. Readers enjoy the journey with a known character who inhabits an unknown world, which in the case of mysteries, is a world of intrigue and murder. It's a clever tool if you think about it, because the author has to create an engaging case and can't rely on the inherent interest in a fresh protagonist. Take time to ask your book club what the challenges are in using familiar characters.

My theory on why mysteries are generally a part of a series is that too many readers only read a certain kind of book, and mystery lovers who become mystery writers follow the same roads as those they wish to emulate. Before authors become "authors," they are readers like you and me.

It may seem that advocating genre fiction is a contradiction to earlier points I made about selecting challenging works, but it isn't. I am purporting that you find the best mix of the best-written books available. You don't want to limit the possibilities available to your book club.

**Jane Err**

Don't overlook the fact that some of the heavyweight literary writers like Joyce and Heller also recycled characters, locations, and so on, just like their genre fiction counterparts.

# Mystery Masterpieces

1. *The Hound of the Baskervilles,* **by Sir Arthur Conan Doyle.** It should be elementary as to why Sherlock Holmes keeps coming up: The importance of this character in the world of the detective story cannot be overrated. But the other reason is that Doyle's stories are complex, engaging, and often very witty. This is one of the best known, although most collections will suffice if you are looking to stay off the beaten path. In this story, the Baskerville family is "hounded" by a beast that might be of the canine persuasion. The most recent casualty is Sir Charles, and giant footprints from the legendary demon are found near the corpse. Was the beast seen roaming the moors at night? Will the new baronet inherit the same grisly fate? Has Sherlock Holmes finally met his match in this unknown terror?

**Biblio-Trivio**

Arthur Conan Doyle wanted to give his new gumshoe an outlandish moniker and seriously considered Sherrinford. He decided to go with the Christian name Sherlock, lifted from a Yorkshire bowler he had played cricket with named Mordecai Sherlock.

Doyle constantly throws readers for a loop, and the intensity grows with every new twist and turn. The Baskerville family curse is baffling to Holmes and Watson, and the shifting levels of deception make this one of the toughest cases Sherlock will ever have to crack, especially when his cunning adversary appears as Holmes himself. *The Hound of the Baskervilles* is generally regarded as one, if not the best, of Doyle's many adventures with Sherlock Holmes, and it is guaranteed to thrill your book club.

Holmes may have had a penchant for drugs, but he is an angel compared to our next shamus.

**Novel Ideas**

Tell every member in your reading group to live by the honor system and abstain from reading the last chapter of this, or any, detective story. At the meeting, go around the room throwing out theories, or write them down, and then read the last chapter out loud. It's a good test of your deductive skills. Maybe the winner could walk out of the meeting with a pipe or one of those cool Sherlock Holmes hats.

2. ***The Talented Mr. Ripley,*** **by Patricia Highsmith.** It is hard to explain exactly what you will be getting into when you crack one of the books from the Ripley series, but the lead character could be described as amorally fascinating. Tom Ripley is a self-indulgent young sociopath with a major sense of entitlement. His parents died when he was very young, and his wretched upbringing by an aunt has shaped him to believe the world is his for the taking in any way he sees fit, including a murder here and there if necessary. He does solve mysteries, but not in the way most readers have been conditioned. In *The Talented Mr. Ripley,* Tom agrees to go to Italy for a wealthy man and bring his son, Dickie Greenleaf, back to the states. Initially, Dickie isn't thrilled with his "old friend," which Dickie's father mistakenly believes was their past relationship; they were barely acquaintances. Tom charms Dickie, and then decides he wants to become him. And what better way than to kill Dickie off and literally take over his former existence?

Tom Ripley is one of the most intriguing protagonists in the entire universe of mystery writing. Highsmith manages to create a clever antihero without a soul who is simultaneously frightening, alluring, and endearing. A question to ask: Do we all have a Ripley inside us? Look for this movie in the near future starring Matt Damon and Gwyneth Paltrow, and directed by the man who brought you *The English Patient,* Anthony Minghella.

3. ***The Maltese Falcon,*** **by Dashiell Hammett.** Who has the golden statue of a falcon created for the Holy Roman Emperor Charles IV? Sam Spade wants to know. He also wants to know who the strange luminous redhead with the sad-sack story is, who killed his partner, and how he is going to put it all together without being pinned as the murderer or winding up dead in a ditch somewhere.

Spade is one of the original private dicks who played by his own rules; he can throw a fist or a move with the same powerful grace.

Spade is the essence of tough-guy cool, and he has influenced two generations of authors and filmmakers. His sparse prose is a tightly constructed web that requires logical thinking by both Spade and his loyal readers. If you find that your group has been overtaken with sentimental tomes and needs a shot of intelligent testosterone, this is the book to choose. Plus it features one of the all-time great shady character names, the sinister fat man, Casper Gutman.

4. *The Intuitionist*, **by Colson Whitehead.** For all those who want a dose of literature in their mystery, or vice versa, here is a stunning debut novel that is layered with architectural, sociological, racial, philosophical, anthropological, and social undercurrents in a crafty, intelligent work about none other than an elevator inspector. Meet Lila Mae Watson, the first black female elevator inspector in an unnamed New York City-ish metropolis. She's smart, hard-working, and keeper of a flawless record, which doesn't sit so well with her old-boy colleagues. They couldn't be happier when "Number Eleven," an elevator in a new high-rise, drops into a free-fall hours after Lila Mae has given it the thumbs-up. She uses the *Intuitionist* method of determining elevator safety (which is a vertical and meditative belief system that can't be given justice here) and the *Empiricists* (mechanical failure belief system) want her removed in this year of the Elevator Guild elections. It may have been sabotage, but Lila Mae is going to make an intense investigation to clear her name. She will come across all sorts of dubious characters, some out for blood, some out for the government, and some out for themselves.

**Novel Ideas**

Just a thought, but noir books always seem to go better with a stiff drink. Maybe your book club abstains, but if not, turning the lights down low, throwing on Rhino Records' *Murder Is My Beat: Classic Film Noir Themes and Scenes,* and sipping scotch during the discussion just feels like Raymond Chandler, doesn't it?

**Pro's Prose**

"The man's lips arch up towards his nose and Lila Mae understands that he's never seen an elevator inspector like her before. Lila Mae has pinpointed a spot as the locus of metropolitan disaffection. A zero-point. It is situated in the heart of the city, on a street corner that clots with busy, milling citizens during the day and empties completely at night except for prostitutes and lost encyclopedia salesman."

—From *The Intuitionist,* by Colson Whitehead

The novel delves deeper into human behavior, both literally and figuratively, as Lila Mae goes underground and makes incredible discoveries about the founder of the Intutionists, who was going to revolutionize urban life forever with his "black box." Whitehead takes her on an odyssey that is sheer literary genius. He balances technical detail with passages of great depth about the racial complexities of the world we inhabit. It is an outstanding debut that has drawn numerous comparisons by critics to Ralph Ellison's *Invisible Man.* There is no higher praise that could be given; it is definitely worth your book club's time, and its reputation is only going to grow in stature.

# Where to Get the Skinny on Mysteries

Many people want to know why writers and bibliophiles are so addicted to independent bookstores. People often say, "Oh, the independent stores and big chain stores basically offer the same experience." To which I say, "No they don't." And here is an example of why.

I had heard a rave review of *The Intuitionist* on NPR and read an equally positive critique in a magazine. Unfortunately, when I got around to purchasing the book, I forgot the title. I called a megabookstore near my apartment in New York City and asked for someone who knew a lot about mysteries. The woman told me she was an "expert." I said, "I am looking for a book, but I don't know the title. It's about an elevator operator, and it came out in the last six months or so to rave reviews. I think it is called *The Institutionalized.*" She asked me if I knew the author; I said no, to which she responded that there was no way to find out. Now, what she meant was that she couldn't enter anything into her computer at work (the author or title), so there was nothing to do. However, if she were truly an "expert," she would know the name (and probably have read) the mystery that had critics raving in a variety of publications including *Booklist, Publishers Weekly, Vanity Fair, Kirkus Review,* and the *Village Voice Literary Supplement,* among others.

The problem is, she is probably a regular retail employee as in any other chain bookstore. There is nothing wrong with that; however, it's not the same as getting help from a devoted bibliophile who is in the business because she loves books. Why look for guidance from someone who doesn't know any more than you?

The next day, I called Partners and Crime at 44 Greenwich Avenue in New York City, and the minute I said the words "elevator inspector" the clerk gave me the name, author, and a brief review, "You'll love it." It is a simple anecdote, but it is an accurate one, and I think people should understand what the little guys have to offer. Oh, by the way, if you have any questions about mysteries, the number at Partners and Crime is 212-243-0440, or visit their Web site at www.crimepays.com.

Now, here are a few mystery/noir/detective books that you can punch into that Web site and read all about:

➤ *I Married a Dead Man,* by Cornell Woolrich

➤ *The Big Clock,* by Kenneth Fearing

➤ *Murder on the Orient Express,* by Agatha Christie

➤ *The Long Goodbye,* by Raymond Chandler

➤ *Nightmare Alley,* by William Lindsay Gresham

➤ *The Daughter of Time,* by Josephine Tey

➤ *North of Montana,* by April Smith

➤ *The Black Dahlia,* by James Ellroy

➤ *The Mystery of Marie Roget,* by Edgar Allan Poe

➤ *The Black Echo,* by Rex Stout

➤ *The Glass Key,* by Dashiell Hammett

➤ *The Boy Who Followed Ripley,* by Patricia Highsmith

➤ *The Alienist,* by Caleb Carr

➤ *An Unsuitable Job for Women,* by P. D. James

➤ *Red Death,* by Walter Mosley

➤ *Blind Man with a Pistol,* by Chester B. Himes

➤ *N Is for Noose,* by Sue Grafton

➤ *The 39 Steps,* by John Buchan

➤ *The Case of the Duplicate Daughter,* by Erle Stanley Gardner

➤ *The Suspect,* by L. R. Wright

---

### The Least You Need to Know

➤ Don't ignore a segment of books because someone says they're "genre fiction" and not "literature."

➤ Main characters, settings, patterns, styles, and red herrings are various angles to look at when reading detective stories.

➤ Stories of Sherlock Holmes revolutionized the mystery writing field.

➤ Hard-boiled noir stories have produced some of the most memorable dicks in literary history.

➤ A good mystery can give your book club a refreshing change of pace once in a while.

# Chapter 16

# Oh, the Horror ... the Horror

---

**In This Chapter**

➤ A variety of ways to view the volumes of violence

➤ Unearthing the undead

➤ The brilliance of a Kafkaesque experience

➤ The Hannibal that might eat an elephant, but would never ride one

➤ The reason nerd persecution must end

---

This chapter is going to be broken down into two halves: horror stories and science-fiction adventures. Let's skip the formalities and pleasantries here, though, and get right to the blood, the guts, the fangs, the dismemberments, the ghouls, the ghosts, the haunted houses, the aliens, the monsters, and all of the other scary beasts that make life exciting, shall we?

## Evil Is Goin' On ...

The best of the lot in both genres—horror and sci-fi—share a common trait: They say more about the nature of human beings than first meets the eye. Mary Shelley's *Frankenstein* is a monster yarn on the surface level, a meditation of man's quest to push the boundaries of technology without regard to morality. On another level, it is a story of the isolation all of us feel in a foreign environment, and on yet another level it is an examination of the opposite halves of a single being. One of the fundamental questions in Shelley's classic is, who is the "human" creature in the story: Victor Frankenstein or his monster?

A few questions to consider when reading tales of the supernatural and wicked are …

➤ Does the setting/backdrop of the novel have a larger significance (i.e., war, famine, oppression) than the story itself?

**Pro's Prose**

"But it is true that I am a wretch. I have murdered the lovely and the helpless; I have strangled the innocent as they slept and grasped to death his throat who never injured me or any other living thing."

—Excerpt from *Frankenstein,* by Mary Shelley

➤ Does the subhuman or nonhuman character represent a common flawed human behavior?

➤ Is the nature of evil filtered through the "monsters," or the reaction of the other characters?

➤ What role does mob mentality/mass hysteria play in the outcome of the story?

➤ What is the author's philosophy toward violence? Is it an exploration, glorification, or excoriation?

➤ What are the bigger issues the author addresses through the "beasts" that don't fit in "normal" society? Complex ideas are timeless (i.e., Victor Frankenstein's amoral scientific creations in terms of the genetic cloning of animals and, theoretically, humans).

➤ Are we all capable of evil acts? And what would it take to get us there?

One major concern with choosing horror/sci-fi stories right off the shelf is that the poor tomes revel in the violence without a hint of subtext. The unchecked brutality isn't going to appeal to the average reading group, and why should it? There is no reason to avoid books with violence at their core—it's human nature; but there are plenty of books that are written strictly to push the envelope of grotesque, gratuitous scenes of torture and death.

The essence of violence is at the core of book club favorites like James Dickey's *Deliverance* or Dorothy Allison's *Bastard out of Carolina,* but they aren't "horror" books per se. Make sure you are aware that if you go searching for unfamiliar titles in the horror/sci-fi departments of your local bookstore, there is always a decent chance you'll pick up a novel ripe with vicious (often misogynistic) behavior without the soul of true literary novels.

# Bloodsucking Banshees

Let's start our parade of evil-types with the old garlic-dodgers themselves.

1. *Dracula,* **by Bram Stoker.** As Keith Jackson would say, this is the "granddaddy of them all." It is one of the most influential books ever written. Count Dracula and vampires in general are a staple of twentieth-century culture. Stoker did not invent the vampire story; there have been tales told for centuries. Stoker's native

Ireland has an ancient tale of Dearg-Due, a female creature who used her beauty to tempt men to her side and then suck their blood. The Slavic regions of Eastern Europe, however, have long been the epicenter of vampire superstition. No other version has had the singular impact of Stoker's classic, though, and its mesmerizing powers are as striking today as the day it was published. Stoker also cemented the image of the Transylvanian noble Count Dracula as a suave, intelligent man and not the roaming zombielike beast of folklore.

Stoker's story of lusts and desires and the undead's quest to fill their craving for human blood can be analyzed on numerous levels. It can be read as a scary yarn of terror, as a basic religious allegory of good against evil, as the inner struggle of a man trying to find the deepest sense of himself. There's a literary theory that it's a questioning of why men both fear and yearn for women who are sexually liberated. You might buy into the subtlety of that particular viewpoint, but however you interpret Stoker's classic, it is a smooth, hypnotic story of human terror that deserves an attentive read.

### Novel Ideas

If the members of your book club have strong stomachs and are interested in reading a thoroughly repulsive, controversial, love-it-or-loathe-it novel of brutal savagery, try Bret Easton Ellis's infamous *American Psycho*. It is as raw and disgusting as any mass-marketed book ever written, and most readers will find it utterly revolting, self-indulgent trash (and probably not finish it). There is, however, a small contingent that finds it an outstanding satire of vapid socialite consumerism. I'm not recommending this book, but it will bring out severe reactions and maybe your group wants to debate what is acceptable to put in print.

2. ***Blood Thirst: 100 Years of Vampire Fiction,*** **edited by Leonard Wolf.** This is an engaging collection of 20-plus vampire stories that looks at the significance of the vampire since the publication of Bram Stoker's *Dracula*. The basic question is why are vampires so alluring to writers and readers alike? His introduction is an interesting look at the way the blood metaphor is what separates vampire tales from other arenas in the horror genre. Blood is life, and Wolf uses the metaphor as the basis for why vampire stories enjoy such a wide-ranging popularity. He examines biblical stories, transubstantiation (the religious ritual in which wine becomes Christ's blood), and the underlying sexuality in the bloodthirsty tales. Do you need more vampirical evidence than this? If so, check out Wolf's thorough collection, which includes both heavyweights and lesser-known scribes.

**Biblio-Trivio**

Many scholars believe Stoker based Count Dracula on a fifteenth-century Romanian prince, Vlad Tepes, called Dracul. Vlad was Prince of Wallachia, bordered to the north by Transylvania. Vlad the Impaler was a ruthless practitioner of unbelievable atrocities. His main method of torture and execution was to impale his victims on a long, oiled, but not-too-sharp stake that was driven through a lower orifice and on up through the mouth. It was a slow, painful death, and Vlad was known to leave the corpses to rot on the stakes—reportedly 20,000 outside the capital of Tirgoviste.

Wolf's book contains authors as diverse as Stephen King, John Cheever, Lafcadio Hearn, C. L. Moore, and Edith Wharton. It is a vampire-lover's dream, but it is also a book that could be used by your reading group to look at the influence of the vampire story on the arts in general. Parts of it could also be read in conjunction with Bram Stoker to get the full Dracula experience.

Got that thirst for blood? Here's a short list of vampire books:

➤ *Interview with the Vampire,* by Anne Rice
➤ *The Hunger,* by Whitley Strieber
➤ *Carmilla and Other Tales of Mystery,* by J. Sheridan LeFanu
➤ *The Darkest Thirst: A Vampire Anthology,* edited by Thomas J. Strauch
➤ *Vathek, the Vampyre,* by Horace Walpole
➤ *Our Vampires, Ourselves,* by Nina Auerbach
➤ *Vampire,* by Hanns Heinz Ewers
➤ *Salem's Lot,* by Stephen King

**Pro's Prose**

"He let out one more gasp and fell sideways onto the carpet. She stood looking down at him. The blood flowed everywhere like water. He was groaning, trying to raise himself, one arm pinned beneath his chest, the other shoving at the floor. And now, suddenly, she flew at him and clamping both arms about his neck, bit deep into him as he struggled."

—From *Interview with the Vampire,* by Anne Rice

# Weird, Wild Stuff

1. ***The Trial,* by Franz Kafka.** Very few writers have had their name come to define an existential state, but "Kafkaesque" has come to refer to the bizarre, tense, anxiety-filled social conditions of the world and its portrayals. Kafka's brilliant works deal with isolation, loneliness, and the utter powerlessness of our lives. He blended surreal fantasy with a claustrophobic irony to produce some of the more highly regarded stories of the last century. He often placed regular characters in horrifying situations and watched their futile struggle. In *The Trial,* an ordinary chap named Joseph K. wakes up and finds he has been charged with a crime that he did not commit. They won't even tell him what he has been accused of, but Joseph K. must report to the court on a regular basis or face possible penalties.

   Joseph K. continues to try and fight the system, but he never gets any answers and nothing is ever resolved. It becomes a maddening quest; his professional life as a bank employee starts to fall apart, and his social relationships begin unraveling. The more he tries to wrest control of the situation and get his life back on track, the quicker the downward spiral picks up speed until Joseph K.'s ultimate defeat. It is a harrowing novel that can be looked at on the level of large-scale governmental intrusion or of petty, mind-numbing bureaucratic problems. Kafka knows what it means to be utterly alone, and so will your book club if you pick up *The Trial.* Question: Is there a rational explanation for what happens? Is there a rational explanation for why anything happens?

2. ***Dr. Jekyll and Mr. Hyde,* by Robert Louis Stevenson.** Robert Louis Stevenson reportedly had a dark, recurring dream in which he was a respectable citizen during the day and a violent drifter in the dead of night. His dream eventually became the basis for the classic tale of the duality within every single person, *The Strange Case of Dr. Jekyll and Mr. Hyde.*

   The theme of duality is at the heart of this story, especially between acceptable and

**Pro's Prose**

"These warders, moreover, were degenerate ruffians, they deafened my ears with their gabble, they tried to induce me to bribe them, they attempted to get my clothes and underclothes from me under dishonest pretexts, they asked me to give them money ostensibly to bring me some breakfast after they had brazenly eaten my own breakfast under my eyes."

—From *The Trial,* by Franz Kafka

**Pro's Prose**

"… when I looked upon that ugly idol in the glass, I was conscious of no repugnance, rather a leap of welcome. This, too was myself."

—From *Dr. Jekyll and Mr. Hyde,* by Robert Louis Stevenson

**225**

nefarious human behavior. The fact that Dr. Jekyll finds the evil acts of Mr. Hyde add a thrilling sense of power to his life is an interesting theory on the nature of evil. Do we all have a killer inside us? Is it possible that the power to take away life could excite any ordinary person given the chance to act upon it? The sins humans commit and their frequent shirking of the responsibility is another area Stevenson delves into. If we all have a dark side, why do we deny that it, too, dictates our actions?

### Biblio-Trivio

When Robert Louis Stevenson entered Edinburgh University, his father assumed he would study engineering and join the family firm. Robert didn't want to, so they compromised with law, but he never practiced it. Robert decided to become a writer and took off on journeys spanning the globe. Literary scholars have noted that the struggle between an authoritarian father and a son is a recurring theme in which he could explore the struggles of his own upbringing. The father/son relationship is true to a smaller degree in this novel, because Mr. Hyde is often portrayed as Dr. Jekyll's son.

This timeless portrait of a man and his agonizing soul deftly precedes modern psychoanalysis in its examination of the complex human makeup. It is not a clear-cut case of good and evil, it is about the light and darkness that resides in all of us and why some allow the monster to win.

Does the horror within the mind have you on the edge of your seat? Following is a short list of freaky books that are sure to leave you screaming for more:

➤ *Dead Souls,* by Nikolai Gogol

➤ *The Metamorphosis,* by Franz Kafka

➤ *At the Mountains of Madness and Other Tales,* by H. P. Lovecraft

➤ *A Clockwork Orange,* by Anthony Burgess

➤ *The Haunting of Hill House,* by Shirley Jackson

➤ *Heart of Darkness,* by Joseph Conrad

➤ *The House on the Borderland,* by William Hope Hodgson

➤ *Best Ghost Stories of Algernon Blackwood,* edited by Everett F. Bleiler

# Friendly Neighborhood Sociopaths and Lil' Devils

I'm sure some of you out there are saying to your-selves, "Hmmm, some of these categories are really starting to overlap. There's detective books with serial killers and some of the weird stuff involves various forms of demons. Just what exactly are you trying to pull here? You can't put one over on me like that. No-siree, Bob."

All I have to say is, congratulations, you caught me.

Since you have so much free time, why don't you keep on trucking down the page of pariahs:

**Novel Ideas**

If you go with one of the ghost story books, hold your meeting around a campfire if possible, preferably in some nearby woods. If that's impossible, sit around your living room with only candlelight and put on one of those CDs that has sounds of horror and haunted houses. The campfire is the best way to go if it's feasible.

1. ***Crime and Punishment*, by Fyodor Dostoyevsky.** Raskolnikov is the alienated star of this infamous tale of murder and its consequences. Dostoyevsky wrote deep, probing, psychological novels that drive right to the heart of human behavior. *Crime and Punishment* is a profound study of the constantly shifting parameters of sin and guilt that people weave into their moral compass. It is a novel that gives equal weight to a violent act and the soul-deadening shame that the perpetrator is forced to confront.

Raskolnikov is a poor desperate student who thinks he is a genius, an "extraor-dinary man." He decides to plan and execute the perfect crime, the murder of a pawnbroker in St. Petersburg. He holds to a theory that evil means justify chari-table ends, and the pawnbroker accumulated wealth through the misfortunes of her fellow man. Raskolnikov believes that total freedom allows him to set the limits of what is right and wrong, and he is doing the greatest good for the greatest number of people by bludgeoning an old woman with the blunt end of an axe, which leads to a harrowing sequence with another victim of the blade end of said axe. Compare this passage with the malevolent glee most killers in contemporary books exhibit as they brutalize their victims.

Panic takes hold of him more and more, especially after the second and quite unexpected murder. In a muddleheaded moment of desperation, he flees and tries to keep the secret of the murders. Dostoyevsky is not interested in hollow nihilism: Raskolnikov pays for his sins through the powerful guilt of his con-science that forces his hand. It is a meditation on the human capability for psy-chotic behavior and a thrilling detective story. It is a fascinating character study and a social commentary. Raskolnikov's battle within is one of the classic confrontations in all of literature. It is intense and dark, yet there is selfless love from a prostitute and eventually an understanding and recognition of the atrocities committed, so it has depth and a level of humanity most stories of murder don't understand. It is the precursor to all modern tales of the criminal mind, but few come remotely close to measuring up to this masterpiece.

## Biblio-Trivio

Dostoyevsky had firsthand experience with the criminal mind because he served time in a Siberian prison. He was convicted along with 23 others who gathered to discuss social reform. Repressive Czar Nicholas I saw their political activity as a threat and didn't want their "revolutionary" ideas to spread. Dostoyevsky spent four years in a prison in Omsk performing back-breaking manual labor with some of Russia's most notorious criminals. His insights into the criminal psyche and the human capacity for evil were essential to *Crime and Punishment*.

2. *Red Dragon,* **by Thomas Harris.** Most everybody is familiar with Dr. Hannibal Lecter and Clarice Starling. *The Silence of the Lambs* was a monster hit in print and the movie was a $130 million juggernaut and one of only three to sweep the four major awards (picture, director, actor, and actress) at the Academy Awards. Harris is the current J. D. Salinger of the macabre; he doesn't do interviews, book signings, or press junkets, and he took 11 years to get around to the third installment. The main thing that separates Harris from the pack is his meticulous research, impeccable details, and lyrical prose.

   Readers often overlook his winning first Lecter novel *Red Dragon,* which might not be as universally read as *The Silence of the Lambs,* but some Harris fans think it's better. It is the story of Will Graham and his hunt for the horrific serial killer Francis Dolarhyde. Graham almost bought the farm when he caught Hannibal Lecter, but he enlists the assistance of the legendary lunatic in his quest to bring in a killer who revels in butchering entire families.

### Biblio-Trivio

Harris peppers his work with references to gourmet cooking. In Lecter's debut, he is lying on a cot thumbing through Alexandre Dumas's *Le Grand Dictionnaire de Cuisine*. Harris may be reclusive with the press, but he is no hermit; he has taken classes at the Le Cordon Bleu cooking school in Paris. Harris is also an oenophile (a wine connoisseur). Lecter drank Ararone, not Chianti, with his liver and beans (they changed that fact for the flick).

Graham hates the standard practice of getting inside the mind of a killer; it's sickening. He quit the FBI, but comes back to track down the epitome of evil, Francis Dolarhyde. Enlisting Lecter may sound like a good idea, but the manipulative genius toys with both the hunter and the hunted. Dolarhyde is obsessed with a William Blake painting and believes a red dragon of the picture lives inside him. His twisted habits, choosing victims from their home movies, were developed at the hands of his sadistic grandmother. Harris uses twisted flashbacks and stream of consciousness to create empathy for the demented killer. It's an odd sensation to root for his love life to work out knowing what his modus operandi is, but Harris manages to pull the rabbit out of his blackmagical hat. It isn't *Crime and Punishment*, but it's a quality read that might offer the perfect bloody tonic if your reading group has been mired in romantic muck lately.

### Novel Ideas

There is a movie version of *Red Dragon*, Michael Mann's 1986 film *Manhunter*. It is a different type of movie than the Foster/Hopkins favorite; it's a visual take on the mind of the killer. It is hypnotic, fractured, and dark, much like the novel Harris wrote. It's less likely everyone in your book club will have seen it, and it could lead to a discussion of which film was a stronger adaptation. You may be surprised.

If your book club doesn't feel it has soaked up enough blood, here's a short list of devilishly good murdering books:

➤ *The Women of Whitechapel and Jack the Ripper,* by Paul West

➤ *Psycho,* by Robert Bloch

➤ *Rosemary's Baby,* by Ira Levin

➤ *Dawn Song,* by Michael Marano

➤ *Zombie,* by Joyce Carol Oates

➤ *The Devil and Daniel Webster and Other Writings,* by Stephen Vincent Benet

➤ *Looking for Mr. Goodbar,* by Judith Rossner

➤ *Prayer for the Dead,* by David Wiltse

# The Sounds of Science

There may be no more loyal fan than the science-fiction fan, as anyone who's ever met a Trekkie knows full well. It is an oft-maligned genre, viewed as the domain of computer nerds, techno geeks, and middle-aged men and women who have never had a date, live at home, and believe The Force is an actual thing. Well, I'm here to say that Dr. Green is right, nerd persecution must stop, and stop right now! Because, hey, you're the one missing out on some fantastic titles.

**Novel Ideas**

Don't be afraid to log on to the Web to search for unheralded science-fiction titles, conventions, reading groups, tours, Isaac Asimov first editions, *Battlestar Galactica* lunch pails, and the like. Whatever you want to know can be found in multiple locales on the Web.

The best of science fiction uses metaphor to examine the numerous shortcomings of the human condition. The authors create worlds of wonder, but the universal problems are the same as in any literary work. Why human beings can't leave well enough alone and the unfettered advancement of technology are two standard issues. A well-chosen science fiction tome can tap into your group's collective imagination in ways the average family dramas can't. Go ahead, try sci-fi on for size, you might find it eye-opening, and you'll be sporting Vulcan ears before you know it.

1. *The War of the Worlds,* by H. G. Wells. They're out there. This is where it all started. From the opening words, Wells makes it ominously clear that we are not alone.

Martians quickly land on the outskirts of London, and before long they put their colonization plan in motion. A giant machine rises up from the landing pit and starts destroying everything in sight. A deadly heat ray wipes out soldier and citizen alike, and soon the Martian army is rolling through the streets. The English denizens panic, the metropolitan area is evacuated in a hurry, and the frenzied crowd starts adhering to an every-man-for-himself credo. Poisonous gas envelops the countryside, and the narrator hides in a cellar. He watches the Martians inject human blood into their veins for sustenance. The human race has become grist for the spacey invader mill.

Wells's classic sci-fi tome is not only worthwhile as the matriarch to the infinite offspring of alien invader stories, it is also an examination of technology run amok and its ultimate submission to ol' Mother Nature. It also deals with the human (and alien) impulse to forcefully take whatever suits the strongest societies. Wells died before the nuclear weapon was readily available to wipe out cities with the push of a button, but he was nothing if not prophetic. It could have been written as an atomic allegory in the mid-'50s. Question: Why is pop culture dominated by hostile alien conquerors instead of peaceful interlopers?

2. ***The Left Hand of Darkness,* by Ursula K. Le Guin.** Science-fiction writing is often mistakenly thought to be male terrain, but there are many fine women authors crafting truly great stories. Thirty years ago Le Guin penned one of the most literary science-fiction stories in the entire galaxy, and it is near the top of a very short list. It is the story of Genly Ai, a representative who has to journey from the human world to the lost planet Winter. He is supposed to bring it back into the alignment of other civilized galaxies. Winter is a strange world populated

**Pro's Prose**

"No one would have believed that his world was being watched keenly and closely by intelligences greater than man's and yet as mortal as his own. Early in the twentieth century came the great disillusionment."

—From *The War of the Worlds,* by H. G. Wells

**Novel Ideas**

Be sure to find a copy of the infamous Orson Welles radio broadcast of 1938. It is readily available on cassette or compact disc, and it still packs a punch. It is fascinating to consider that the images that frightened a nation were created in the minds of listeners from a radio broadcast, not through visual imagery. It is one of the few concrete examples of the power to create human reaction, which seems to be on every pundit's lips these days. Plus, it is just so much cooler than junk like *Independence Day.*

**Pro's Prose**

"Can't you see I'm busy dying!"

—H. G. Wells's words on his death-bed to those gathered around waiting for famous last words

by people without a defining gender. The philosophy of predetermined notions of what people should be subtly permeates the novel. The underlying sexual tensions and sexual roles are astonishingly modern and relevant to life back here on plain old Earth.

This book is not a quick, rock-'em-sock-'em robots kind of a book. It takes its time developing the characters, and the audience learns all about Genly Ai's prejudices, preconceived notions, and world outlook. It is a novel of depth and insight that has more in common with a philosophical treatise than any novelization of anything involving Jedis, wookies, or bad dudes named Darth. *The Left Hand of Darkness* isn't the most familiar title in the science-fiction lexicon, but take a chance on it. It was written at a time when segments of our culture wanted to expand the dimensions of standard thought, and Le Guin's story is right in line with the consciousness-raising books of the '60s. It always sparks engaging discussions.

**Biblio-Trivio**

Le Guin is one of those authors who uses her imaginative powers to break down the wall of limitations a certain genre might hold. It is no wonder, then, that her favorite twentieth-century author has very little to do with galaxies far, far away, but has everything to do with defining roles on her own terms. Le Guin's favorite author of the last 100 years is rumored to be Virginia Woolf.

Now that nerd persecution has become a thing of the past, bring your book club around to one of these sci-fi titles:

➤ *Fahrenheit 451,* by Ray Bradbury

➤ *Kindred,* by Octavia E. Butler

➤ *Jurassic Park,* by Michael Crichton

➤ *Woman on the Edge of Time,* by Marge Piercy

➤ *The Caves of Steel,* by Isaac Asimov

➤ *The Hitchhiker's Guide to the Galaxy,* by Douglas Adams

➤ *The Time Machine,* by H. G. Wells

➤ *From the Earth to the Moon,* by Jules Verne

## If You Think Blood, Ghosts, Monsters, and Aliens Are for You ...

And for all those who can't get enough of a good thing, or who want to become die-hard fans of the topics we've covered, here are a few extras to choose from:

➤ *Watership Down,* by Richard Adams

➤ *The Shining,* by Stephen King

➤ *Journey to the Center of the Earth,* by Jules Verne

➤ *Unnatural Acts and Other Stories,* by Lucy Taylor

➤ *Rendezvous with Rama,* by Arthur C. Clarke

➤ *The Turn of the Screw,* by Henry James

➤ *Dune,* by Frank Herbert

➤ *The Invisible Man,* by H. G. Wells

➤ *The Martian Chronicles,* by Ray Bradbury

---

### The Least You Need to Know

➤ The best genre novels, no matter how macabre or imaginative the story, are the ones that are really speaking about us.

➤ Violence is often a central theme, but there is a big difference between exploration and glorification.

➤ The classic titles of a particular genre (Bram Stoker's *Dracula*) are classics for a reason: They are complex, layered, and intellectual.

➤ Selecting *The War of the Worlds* by H. G. Wells is a good excuse to listen to the brilliant radio play by Orson Welles.

# Chapter 17

---

# Get Real: Nonfiction

**In This Chapter**

➤ Did the band play on?

➤ Does X Marx the spot?

➤ Is the Prince formerly known as Niccolo an artist?

➤ Who exactly are the Mole People?

The best nonfiction is written creatively, succinctly, and intelligently, just like its fictional counterparts. If your book club has never dived into these equally literary waters, it might be time to give it a whirl.

# Why Finding a Book About a Chiropteran Is Simple

Since the enormous volumes of nonfiction books are getting abridged into two short chapters in this reading group book, I would like to try and make it up to you by cramming as many titles as possible into the following pages. It's called the quantity not quality theory. This is due mainly to the fact that fictional tomes dominate the average book club, and specialized groups in history, political science, or economics probably aren't looking for hints on hidden vampire tracts.

With a few notable exceptions, the following list is comprised primarily of nonfiction books written in the post–World War II twentieth century by American authors with American themes. This isn't any sort of cultural imperialism or generational

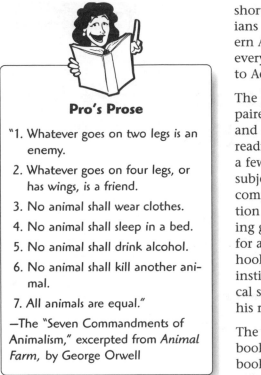

**Pro's Prose**

"1. Whatever goes on two legs is an enemy.

2. Whatever goes on four legs, or has wings, is a friend.

3. No animal shall wear clothes.

4. No animal shall sleep in a bed.

5. No animal shall drink alcohol.

6. No animal shall kill another animal.

7. All animals are equal."

—The "Seven Commandments of Animalism," excerpted from *Animal Farm,* by George Orwell

shortsightedness, but rather, the majority of book clubians I spoke with are interested in the shaping of modern American culture. Certainly academic groups cover everything from Sudanese agriculture to entomology to Aeolian poetry, but that's not us, is it?

The great thing about nonfiction is that topics can be paired down to a specific word, date, place, and so on, and a book can be found to satisfy any interest your reading group may have. Unlike fiction, which covers a few big themes, nonfiction is normally broken up by subject. You may even consider finding nonfiction companion pieces or excerpts to go along with the fiction tome of the month. For example, say your reading group has selected George Orwell's *Animal Farm* for analysis. A quick subject search at the library can hook you up with Orwell lit crit, tyranny in social institutions, Soviet Communism, pigs, farming, political satire, Marx, or Trotsky, all of which are a part of his renowned protest novel.

The point is, it is often much easier to find nonfiction books on original or peculiar subjects, whereas fiction books require word-of-mouth recommendations or trusting the overly fawning book jacket.

Oh, by the way, a chiropteran is a bat, which just might come in handy the next time you sit down for a visit with Lestat.

**Biblio-Trivio**

The bat is the only mammal capable of sustained flight, and there are 850 to 900 species of bats—far more than any other mammalian order except the rodents.

# The ABCs of Nonfiction

Before we get to the list, I would like to apologize to Dewey Decimal himself for violating the alphabetical nonfiction ordering within a particular subject that is a centerpiece of his beloved system. I cheated; I chose to do some by author and others by title in order to get all the letters of the alphabet in there. So sue me.

And they're off …

## A: And the Band Played On: Politics, People, and the AIDS Epidemic, *by Randy Shilts*

This is the first major, and still definitive, work on the AIDS crisis in America. Thoroughly researched and reported, it chronicles every major and minor detail of the 1980s years of the epidemic.

Shilts is critical of nearly every group involved in the crisis. His harshest criticism is lobbed at the Reagan administration, which he claims invented figures and misled Congress, cut medical funding even though the scientific community was desperately clamoring for it and Congress was willing to give it to them, and kept their collective mouth shut until the mid-'80s, by which time thousands were infected with the virus.

This isn't a one-sided tract though; the Gipper isn't the only one who failed to act, according to Shilts. Scientists posture and preen in hopes of winning awards instead of saving lives, the mainstream press whitewashes the information because it's a gay issue, gay leaders bicker and fragment over what message to spread, and other elected officials sit on the data. The evidence in Shilts's book is enraging at times and bewildering at others. It may seem a bit dated, but find a copy of the article titled "The Virus at the End of the World," by Laurie Garrett in the March 1999 issue of *Esquire,* and it won't seem dated anymore, just sickening. Question: Why wasn't the AIDS crisis addressed from the very beginning? And where do we go from here?

## B: Bury My Heart at Wounded Knee: An Indian History of the American West, *by Dee Brown*

This monumental work, first published in 1971, sold over a million hardback copies and almost four million copies in the paperback edition. It is the story of the genocide, the systematic removal of the American Indian in the latter nineteenth and early twentieth centuries. It is not an easy book to read. The torture, execution, and relocation was carried out by the government and civilians alike, often in the name of Christian destiny, or simply for the almighty dollar. Numerous tribes are included (the Crows, the Apaches, the Nez Percé to name a few), but the stories sadly remain

**Novel Ideas**

Many nonnative people live within a couple of hours of a Native American reservation, and a field trip won't be the same after reading *Bury My Heart at Wounded Knee.* It is worth it to see firsthand the lasting effects of the mass extermination of the original Americans. It won't be easy, and shame is the most common reaction to the book, but it will get your book club face-to-face with the ugly reality of the home of the brave.

the same. Brown presents an American tragedy that has been at times glossed over, which is a good jumping off point for a discussion of how authors choose to write about varying sides of an issue. There is a criticism of Brown, however, that she justifies the Indian atrocities.

Brown's work is not preachy or polemic; it is an eloquent encapsulation of the brutal annihilation of the indigenous American peoples.

## *C:* **The Communist Manifesto,** *by Karl Marx in Collaboration with Friedrich Engels*

Any edition of this legendary work will suffice, but the 1998 version with the introduction from Eric Hobsbawm includes the pertinence of the manifesto in the modern world. Considering the way the globe has shifted since the end of the Cold War, it is the edition that will open up all sorts of debate in your reading groups. *The Communist Manifesto* is more than 150 years old, but it still has its influence, which is remarkable in these days of global capitalism. Marx identifies class struggle as the primary dynamic in history and divergent views on the most equitable economic systems should send your book club into a realm of powerful discussions. It's not the type of reading for everybody, but if your book club has members who are interested in politics and economics, why not give Karl a shot?

Marx's work is dry, but the ideas are striking and sure to provoke intense deliberation (wear protective gear for this one). Questions to ponder: In these heady capitalistic days, why do so many feel left out? Why is Marx blamed for the tyrannical practices of Communist leaders who implement their version of *The Communist Manifesto* (Joseph Stalin, for example)? Won't some people always exploit their neighbor regardless of who owns the property? Is violent revolution the only way for the underclass to make substantial gains? What parts of *The Communist Manifesto* could help build a stronger America? Read with an open mind, Marx's book is fascinating and thought-provoking, even if you don't agree with any of it. If your reading group is wary because of the hangover of Cold War rhetoric, read *The Communist Manifesto* in unison with Adam Smith's *The Wealth of Nations,* a brilliant text that outlines the reasons for a capitalist, free-market system. This would be a major commitment on the part of your reading group. If you decide to take it on, your group might want to put aside three to six months for reading and discussion.

**Biblio-Trivio**

In the second part of Marx's work, he advocates the total abolishment of private property, so there is a fundamental change in material existence and the bourgeois class, the benefactors of capitalism, will be unveiled. The ownership of the state will then belong to the proletariat, and eventually all class distinctions will be erased in the communal social order. Try to envision an America without private property—virtually impossible, isn't it? It's hard to fathom the practicalities of a Communist society.

## D: Darkness Visible: A Memoir of Madness, *by William Styron*

Severe clinical depression is a disease, plain and simple, yet many people's response is to "get over it." Nobody would ever say that to a cancer patient, so why is this disease any different? Styron was gripped by a crippling depression, which dragged him from constant insomnia to the threshold of suicide. This slim essay details his descent into "madness" and the long recovery that followed.

**Biblio-Trivio**

William Styron has a book on both the Modern Library 100 Best Novels list, *Sophie's Choice,* and the Modern Library 100 Best Nonfiction Books, *Darkness Visible.* He shares the honor with seven other authors: Vladimir Nabokov, George Orwell, James Baldwin, E. M. Forster, Richard Wright, Virginia Woolf, and Ralph Ellison.

It is a harrowing portrait of a terribly debilitating disease that affects close to one in 10 Americans. The essay is slight in page length, but massive in its courage and resonance. Try reading it as a companion piece to poet Randall Jarrell's works *Blood for a Stranger, Losses,* and *Little Friend, Little Friend.* Jarrell also suffered, but unlike Styron, he never recovered, and killed himself by stepping in front of a moving car at the age of 50.

## E: The Education of Henry Adams, *by Henry Adams*

This was the big winner in the Modern Library 100 Best Nonfiction sweepstakes, so it has to be the best, right? Adams's book is an autobiography (in third person) that charts the change in the American landscape from the Civil War to World War I. Lyrical prose and a distinct literary flair separate this work from the hordes of dry tomes from writers, historians, and politicians.

**Biblio-Trivio**

Henry Adams is the son of American diplomat Charles Francis Adams, the grandson of America's sixth president, John Quincy Adams, and the great-grandson of America's second president, John Adams. And to the delight of commuter students everywhere, he also introduced the seminar style of instruction while teaching at Harvard.

Adams's ironic sense of humor shines through in the book's indictment of an educational system that doesn't prepare an intelligent man for the chaos of modern life. It is a cynical bildungsroman that worries about the destruction of the values of the past and a future predicated on corruption and greed. Sound familiar?

## F: Backlash: The Undeclared War Against American Women, *by Susan Faludi*

There is nothing like controversy to cleanse the soul, and if you belong to a co-ed book club, get ready to rumble. This book caused a stir when it was released in 1991, and it is the kind of galvanizing work guaranteed to provoke passion one way or the other.

Faludi's main tenet is that there was a pronounced backlash in the '80s against the strides the women's movement made in the previous two decades. She attacks the idea that all career women yearn for a husband and are on the brink of a total meltdown. She also analyzes the suspect methodology in the Harvard-Yale study that produced the famous statistic about the odds of women over 30 getting married being lower than the chance of death by terrorist. She also leads a tour of antifeminine myths commonly held in the workplace, popular culture, health, and politics.

What separates Faludi's book from other tracts with a clear agenda is that she is a Pulitzer prize–winning journalist, and her extensive research shows (there are more than 80 pages of citations). It is an exhaustive work that many people aren't going to buy into because of her hard-line feminist stance, but she does make some intriguing points based in fact. If your book club is feeling ambitious, compare it to its opposite, *Who Stole Feminism?: How Women Have Betrayed Women,* by Christina Huff Sommer. In both books, note how easily and rapidly the media repeat faulty, bombastic rumors and statistics.

## *G:* **The Guns of August,** *by Barbara Tuchman*

This is a vivid portrait of the events that lead up to the original "War to End All Wars." In summer 1914, Europe was a powder keg, and Tuchman takes the reader through the opposing forces that lead to the war. She covers the month leading up to the war and the first month of fighting.

**Biblio-Trivio**

World War I is often overlooked in our culture, but all of the seeds of later conflicts were planted in it. The losses were horrifying: Almost 8.5 million soldiers were killed, 10 million civilians died from causes indirectly related to the war, and there were 37 million total casualties. Perhaps the worst legacy of World War I was that the treaties that were formed in Versailles (and elsewhere) were not effectively enforced by the victorious powers, which lead to a chaotic Europe and the resurgence of nationalism in Germany.

Tuchman's nonfiction reads like a great novel, as she captures the people involved brilliantly. She also conveys how the world changed—the nineteenth century became a thing of the past with the technological advances of World War I. Gone are the colorful costumes and romance of warfare, replaced by flamethrowers and phosgene gas. Read it with *All Quiet on the Western Front* to get the total picture.

## H: A Brief History of Time, *by Stephen Hawking*

This is a landmark best-seller by one of the true geniuses on the planet. It is a fascinating look at scientific concepts most of us never consider, and it is written clearly and concisely. Try to pick up the 1998 revised copy, because technological advances have proven Hawking's theoretical predictions of just 10 years ago.

This book asks big questions like: Where did the universe come from? Will it ever end? When was the beginning of time? Are there boundaries in space? What is a wormhole, and what does it mean to time travel? Hawking's book will have your head spinning about concepts that, no matter how foreign, are important to everyone who walks the Earth. *A Brief History of Time* will offer a challenge to your book club, because most people aren't prepared to think in terms of alternate dimensions or theorize on the origins of the universe. Hawking's book is accessible, though, and it might spark a whole new strain of conversation. If you are looking for something totally different and thought-provoking, look no further than the deepest black hole.

**Pro's Prose**

"Well, what's there to say about capital punishment? I'm not against it. Revenge is all it is, but what's wrong with revenge? It's very important. If I was kin to the Clutters, or any of the parties York and Latham dispensed with, I couldn't rest in peace till the ones responsible had taken that ride on the Big Swing."

—From an interview with Dick Hickock in *In Cold Blood,* by Truman Capote

## I: In Cold Blood: A True Account of a Multiple Murder and Its Consequences, *by Truman Capote*

Keep this in mind as you read through the best true-crime book ever written: Before Capote penned it, writing about crime was considered second-rate, and there was no such thing as creative nonfiction. The man invented a style of writing in which journalism meets literature: Factual events are lyrically told in prosaic style. Capote spent years researching the unprovoked murder of the Clutters and immersed himself in the town of Holcomb, Kansas, interviewing everyone the four family members ever knew, including the prisoners (one of whom became his lover inside the penitentiary). It is a chilling book, and Capote is so thorough that it feels like the crime unfolded in our hometown, with perpetrators and victims we knew.

A discussion of capital punishment always seems to stem from this novel, and the funny thing is, either side could make a claim that this book illustrates their case. It is a masterpiece.

## *J:* The Undisclosed Self: With Symbols and the Interpretation of Dreams, *by Carl Jung*

The 1990 edition, translated by R. F. C. Hull includes two of Jung's later major works. *The Undisclosed Self* deals with the wary existence between the individual and mass society. The father of analytical psychology believed each human is comprised of the conscious and the unconscious elements of the human psyche. The study of the unconscious enlightens one's self-knowledge because it is in the unconscious where one will find the potential for good and evil.

Jung felt that dreams were the expression of the unconscious, and repressed, ignored, or unexplored elements of the individual come out in those dreams in symbols. The symbols are a link to the basic collective human essence, which has been lost. This might sound like a dry read, but it can lay the groundwork for a wild evening of dream exploration. Sometimes, the book club needs to put the cognitive arguments in a sack and delve into the subconscious. After reading Jung's theories, you will have a deeper appreciation for the nether regions of the brain, even if you don't buy all of his theories. Question: What makes up an individual?

## *K:* Savage Inequalities: Children in America's Schools, *by Jonathan Kozol*

It has been a long time since the *Brown* v. *Board of Education* decision struck down the "separate but equal" system of schooling, but to spend time in the nation's poorest school districts, one would never know. Kozol's searing look at the lack of resources, funding, manpower, and basic fundamental needs (from toilet paper to textbooks) in the American public education system.

Most folks have an inkling that poor school districts have less to work with, but the inequalities are so egregious that it's hard not to feel utter hopelessness for the situation. Kozol doesn't pull any punches; he wants to horrify and shock his readers into recognition.

**Pro's Prose**

"There is no systematic justice for poor children. Rich children don't have to perform miracles to survive and poor children shouldn't have to either."

—From a speech by Jonathan Kozol

The dangerous environmental issues alone should be enough to rouse the comfortable, but the same situations can be found across the country today. The hardest question Kozol poses is, how can we blindly abandon so many children? They didn't ask for the world they inhabit. Is it racism? Ignorance? Apathy? If "throwing money" at the schools isn't the answer, what is? Is the "American dream" a realistic concept for the kids who try to get an education in these schools? More important, what can be done? Be prepared for some tough questions after reading *Savage Inequalities*.

## L: The Lives of a Cell: Notes of a Biology Watcher, by Lewis Thomas

Essays about biology and cell life might not sound too exciting at first, but Thomas' writing is lyrical and captivating. He covers a variety of topics, including medicine, death, and the essence of life. Thomas was a longtime physician who taught at numerous colleges, including a stint as the dean of the School of Medicine at Yale. Thomas's joie de vivre shines through in every essay, and it is a remarkable reminder of the scientific wonders of life. Rarely do we take the time to think about the natural brilliance of the microscopic cell, which contains DNA, the genetic material with the coded instructions for the self-reproducing cell that makes us who we are.

If your book club selects Thomas' work, you might be surprised at how easy it is to become immersed in these biological essays. It is a funny, poetic book with a lot of praise for the world we share, which might be just the ticket after *In Cold Blood* or *Bury My Heart at Wounded Knee*.

## M: The Prince, by Niccolo Machiavelli

Oh, what a tangled web we weave, when first we practice to deceive, and shred files, and destroy evidence, and lie to Congress, and erase subversive recordings, and plot coups d'état, and rub out the opposition, and extort voters, and steal confidential material. In 1512, after Machiavelli was fired from his position of secretary to the Second Chancery of the Signoria by Lorenzo de' Medici, he penned a work that is still the primary treatise on power politics. Machiavelli believed that leaders are not bound by ethical norms and can acquire and maintain power in any way they see fit. *The Prince* has often been regarded as a defense of the despotism of such rulers as Cesare Borgia, but it is so prophetic and realistic, that it can be related to kings, tyrants, czars, or presidents.

It isn't hard to relate his theories to today's world; look at it in terms of your office politics. It's fascinating to think how accurate Machiavelli is, and the question remains: Is ethical behavior essential for worthy political leadership? Read this as a companion piece to a biography of any controversial world leader of the last 400 years.

# *N:* Beyond Good and Evil: Prelude to a Philosophy of the Future, *by Friedrich Nietzsche*

God may be dead, but Nietzsche lives on through his challenging, thought-provoking, mind-altering works like this one. Beach reading this isn't. It is a thorough examination of Nietzsche's ideas, thoughts, and overall philosophy in nine parts (still under 300 pages, though). Each part is sure to spark intense reaction, because he subverts the standard tenets and definitions of Christian morality.

### Pro's Prose

"It must be understood that a prince ... cannot observe all of those virtues for which men are reputed good, because it is often necessary to act against mercy, against faith, against humanity, against frankness, against religion, in order to preserve the state."

—From *The Prince,* by Niccolo Machiavelli

Here is one example: He believed that traditional Christian values of right and wrong represented a slave mentality purported by leaders who know that nonthreatening "good" behavior (i.e., humility, compassion, charity) serves their best interests because the "herd" will follow its religious rules of conduct in hopes of achieving the rewards of the next life. Nietzsche felt that so-called "evil" behavior (individual power and strength) is the key to a liberated life in the real world, because it is the power that unlocks creativity, originality, and independence. Examples of people who were models who lived according to Nietzsche's "will to power" and created their own value systems were Socrates, Michelangelo, and Jesus Christ, among others.

Nietzsche's influence on Western thought in the last century is astounding. Hitler used it as justification for his anti-Semitic actions, even though Nietzsche praised the quality of the will of Jewish people. Nietzsche is a radical thinker who has been condemned for his scathing views on Christianity, his elitism, and his blatant misogyny, but his basic philosophy is remarkably complex and sure to provoke the members of your book club. Try to find *Pandora's Box* or *The Awakening of Spirits,* by Frank Wedekind, or *Papa Hamlet,* by Arno Holz and Johannes Schaff; these German works were direct descendants of Nietzsche.

### Novel Ideas

Read *The Origin of Species* with the Jerome Lawrence/Robert E. Lee play *Inherit the Wind*, which was based on the Scopes Monkey Trial of a teacher in Tennessee who violated the Butler Act and taught Darwin's theory of evolution. After that, rent the great Stanley Kramer film version with Spencer Tracy and Fredric March, who delivers the famous line, "I am more interested in the Rock of Ages than the ages of rocks."

### Pro's Prose

"So I say to you, my friends, that even though we must face the difficulties of today and tomorrow, I still have a dream. It is a dream deeply rooted in the American dream that one day this nation will rise up and live out the true meaning of its creed—we hold these truths to be self-evident, that all men are created equal."

—From the "I Have a Dream" speech by Martin Luther King Jr.

## *O:* The Origin of Species, *by Charles Darwin*

Another controversial work that manages to get lambasted by creationists on a regular basis, this landmark work is still an engaging read about the theories of evolution and natural selection. A case could be made that the scientific theories in Darwin's book shook the fundamental beliefs of Christianity like no other since Copernicus wowed the world with his subversive heliocentric universe ideas.

Darwin's book doesn't have the gift of prosaic language, but it is such an important book that it shouldn't be skipped. Rumor has it that the book sold out in one day upon publication in 1859, and it hasn't lost any of its relevance. It is only a book of science, so what is everybody so afraid of? If you have never read it, choose the *Origin of Species* and try to decipher one thing: Why all the hullabaloo?

## *P:* Parting the Waters/Pillar of Fire, *by Taylor Branch*

Any book club that is interested in the civil rights movement should read the first two books of Branch's *America in the King Years* trilogy (the third book isn't completed as of this writing); they are two of the most comprehensive works on the subject. *Parting the Waters* is the Pulitzer Prize–winning first book, and it is stunning in its ability to juggle a wide cast of characters involved in the struggle for equality. From the pulpits of Atlanta, to the streets of Birmingham and Montgomery, to the manicured lawns of Hyannis Port, Branch captures the remarkable events in America's recent past. It is an all-encompassing work, but it is clear and concise within each chapter. *Parting the Waters* covers the early formative years of the movement through the march on Washington, and Martin Luther King Jr. is the centerpiece of the book.

Even though this is a familiar story, Branch's books take the reader much deeper than the notorious television footage of Bull Connor's riot squads. The levels of hostility the protesters faced at every turn, the internal strife amid the greatest gains, and the amazing ability of Dr. King to stay focused in the eye of the hurricane are detailed to perfection in *Parting the Waters,* and *Pillar of Fire* picks up right where *Parting the Waters* leaves off. Branch conducted exhaustive research, and if the civil rights issue is your bag, look no further.

## Q: Red Lobster, White Trash, and the Blue Lagoon, *by Joe Queenan*

**Novel Ideas**

The book might be too frivolous for your book club, but at least get a copy of the original Joe Queenan article, "How Bad Can It Be?" which appeared in the September 1996 issue of *GQ*. The book is basically more of the same.

Admittedly, this isn't a deep work of much social significance, but it is riotously funny and completely accurate on more than one occasion. Queenan spent 18 months toiling in the brainless mire of places like Branson and Atlantic City, watching films like *Cannonball Run II*, eating at restaurants like the Red Lobster, listening to John Tesh and Billy Joel, and filling himself with the Robert James Waller experience. It's snotty, cynical, elitist, and a real hoot, especially when he realizes things are bad, but not as bad as he hoped they would be. A great moment is his observation that crummy books use highbrow quotes in their opening. And to that I say, "Whether I shall turn out to be the hero of my own life or whether that station will be held," never mind.

## R: The Rise and Fall of the Third Reich: A History of Nazi Germany, *by William Shirer*

It will probably take your book club two or three months to get through this massive book, but it is still the one to beat. Historian Shirer spent more than five years sifting through the documents marking Hitler's plans of world domination. It starts with the early days of the Nazi party and follows their horrifying reign through the Nuremberg Trials and beyond. It is an incredible book that documents the great tragedy that defined the twentieth century. It is one of the best histories ever written, period. If your group happens to be spending a year studying the effects of Nazism or something along those lines, may I also suggest *Hitler's Willing Executioners: Ordinary Germans and the Holocaust,* by Daniel Goldhagen.

## S: A Bright and Shining Lie, *by Neil Sheehan*

This is another massive book about a war, only this time the battlefields have been shifted to the jungles of Vietnam. This is a fascinating account of the war through the eyes of Lt. Col. John Paul Vann, an All-American hero type, who quickly became fed up with the brutality, corruption, and ineptness of the South Vietnamese regime and America's unwillingness to look at the actuality of what was taking place on the battlefield. He set out to do something about it. He left the military and returned to Vietnam as a civilian worker in the pacification program, and rose to become the first civilian with a general's command in war.

**Pro's Prose**

"Now is time, quite literally, to separate the men from the boys. I have been disappointed in several instances to find advisers who are obviously feeling sorry for themselves and mentally wringing their hands ... Get your counterparts and their troops out from behind the barbed wire and aggressively on the offensive, both day and night. The enemy has never been more vulnerable to effective military action than he is today."

—From *A Bright and Shining Lie,* by Neil Sheehan

This is a different kind of book about Vietnam because Vann is a military man, yet avoids polemics on either side. It is primarily a book about how little the military leadership knew about the Vietnam War. John Vann was a courageous American who understood Vietnam, and this is his tragic story. One question is certain to arise within your book club: Why didn't anyone listen?

## *T:* The Mole People: Life in the Tunnels Beneath New York City, *by Jennifer Toth*

It might not be easy to locate enough copies of this book for a discussion, but it would be worth it because this is journalism as it should be. Toth brings an incredible subterranean world to light, one that is both horrifying and alluring, and she does so with class and dignity. It will be clear to the reader that she is haunted by her experiences, but she presents the lonely souls as fully realized people. Who are the mole people? They are folks who live far beneath the streets of Manhattan in all sorts of abandoned tunnels. Some of them are regular working folk who can't afford rent, some are homeless drifters, some are full-time denizens who rarely see the light of day, but almost all of them belong to an underground community of one kind or another.

No good journalism is risk-free, and Toth comes across a few frightening characters, but what stands out is the sense of family amid the death, violence, and despair. Toth also works in historical and literary examples of underground living to accompany the story of the "houseless" residents underneath New York City.

## *U:* Up from Slavery, *by Booker T. Washington*

This is his 1901 autobiography that was controversial then, and remains so today. It is the story of his learned life and what education could do for all black Americans. Washington attended school wherever and whenever he could, including the off-hours as he worked in a salt furnace and in coal mines. He eventually ended up at a new school for blacks, the Hampton Normal and Agricultural Institute. Eventually, he was picked to organize and be the principal of the Tuskegee Institute, which became a major center for African-American education. He became a renowned orator, and his famous compromise speech urged blacks to accept their inferior social standing and work toward self-reliance through education. The speech was a hit with whites, but many blacks, most notably W. E. B. Du Bois, completely disagreed with his accommodating tactics.

There have been differing views of Washington since the turn of the century, in part because of his behind-the-scenes lobbying against inequality. He has also been viewed as a consummate diplomat and politician who knew that education was the main key to success and getting along was essential to improving educational conditions. What does your book club think of Booker T. Washington's views?

**Novel Ideas**

Read *Up from Slavery* in conjunction with *The Souls of Black Folk,* by W. E. B. Du Bois, to get a feel for both sides of an argument that is just as relevant today.

## V: Very Special People, *by Frederick Drimmer*

This is the warm story of a group of human oddities, more commonly misnamed "freaks." Drimmer tells a slew of authentic tales about the amazing lives of people born with physical deformities who go on to triumph over incredible odds. The cast of characters includes: Tom Thumb, a fully developed man who stood only 25 inches tall; a Burmese family that suffered from extreme hairiness; Jane Bunford, a 7'7" woman who may have been five inches taller but for a curvature of the spine; and Harry Williams, a man born without legs who could walk on his hands like most people do on their feet.

**Biblio-Trivio**

Born in Siam, Chang and Eng were brothers developed from a single egg that didn't divide completely. They became legends in their native country and were brought to America and created an act with physical movements in unison that included somersaults. They made a pile of money, bought property in the Blue Ridge foothills of North Carolina, got married, and were the characters in a spoof written by Mark Twain.

Drimmer's book is bubbling with humanity and chock-full of touching, inspirational yarns. If you are looking for an off-the-wall selection, this is the one.

## W: Working: People Talk About What They Do All Day and How They Feel About What They Do, by Studs Terkel

Pulitzer prize–winning writer/radio host/commentator Terkel offers an oral history about—what else—working. His countless interviews provide a rich tapestry of one of the common experiences we all share: time on the job. His interviewees range from hooker to miner, blue-collar to white-collar, big bucks to puny wages, high profile to menial; all sorts of working lives are covered in this oral slice of Americana. It was written almost 30 years ago, but the hopes, dreams, joys, miseries, satisfactions, problems, thrills, and despairs know no time boundaries. This book always relates well to book clubs because of its universality, and the war stories about the daily grind will fly. I wholeheartedly endorse picking up a copy of Terkel's interviews on cassette to add authenticity to your monthly meeting.

## X: The Autobiography of Malcolm X, by Alex Haley, Based on Interviews with Malcolm X

This is one of the most important works to come out of the civil rights era, and its power and relevance has not faded one iota. It is an impressive look into a full life and the inner development of a man. At times, it seems like Malcolm was three completely separate men. As a young man, he watched his father's murder at the hands of the KKK and became involved in a dead-end life of crime. In prison, he became a dedicated follower of the Nation of Islam and a controversial separatist leader. And, finally, a unifying presence.

After a visit to Mecca, and other places around the world, Malcolm X denounced his past teachings that whites are evil and began preaching unity. He was assassinated by men alleged to be connected with the black Muslims. Malcolm X lived a uniquely complex American existence. He proved that there are second acts, and even a third. His book is insightful in its examination of human behavior, and the transformation of the last chapters is remarkable. He nails many truths about race in America, but ultimately he delivers a unifying message. A question to ask yourselves if you decide to pick up this book: Is circumstance or environment the main cause in most human decisions?

### Pro's Prose

"Whites can help us but they can't join us. There can be no black–white unity until there is first some black unity. We cannot think of being acceptable to others until we have first proven acceptable to ourselves."

—From a speech by Malcolm X

## Y: Young Men and Fire, *by Norman Maclean*

This work took 14 years to complete, and it is a story of bravery. Thirteen smoke jumpers died in a 1949 summer forest fire in the Rocky Mountains at Mann Gulch, Montana. It was a breathtaking fire brought on by lightning, the type of natural disaster that comes along once in a generation. It was a fire of 2,000°F, 300 feet deep, and 200 feet tall. Maclean captures the event in this harrowing nonfiction work that grips like the best of fiction. Maclean knows his subject, and the examination of the forces that led to the deaths is thorough and detailed. There are no maudlin digressions about the meaning of life or mawkish sentimental passages. It is the story of man against nature and what nature wrought. It is a must for any group with outdoors lovers, but it has an ethereal power that will remind any reader how powerless we are in the scheme of things. There are many undertones in this book, including the mysteries of death and spirituality.

## Z: A People's History of the United States: 1492–Present, *by Howard Zinn, and* A History of the American People, *by Paul Johnson*

Zinn's tome is the famous leftist history book of the marginalized voices that also built our great nation and Johnson's is an optimistic look at America's greatness from a conservative outsider. Both offer different points of view than the average high school textbook; just remember to keep each author's staunch political views in mind.

Both Zinn and Johnson are going to tweak those on the opposite side, but both works are complex, thought-provoking looks at America. Read them both, hash it out, but keep one thing in mind: many book clubs around the world wouldn't be allowed to read whatever they want, no matter how radical. Reality bites, so bite it right back. Take a big chunk out of any of these great nonfiction works. It may seem a bit more labor-intensive than fiction, but I guarantee you'll enjoy what you get out of it.

**Jane Err**

Don't skip certain titles, in this list or anywhere else, because they don't jibe with everyone's viewpoint in your book club. First off, if all the members fall in line on hot-button issues, political affiliations, or professed world-views, your book club is going to be a big ho-hum. Second, if your book club has a wide range of individuals, choosing intelligent tomes with strident theories sparks exciting debate. It is the quality of the writing and the potential for deliberation that is most important.

## The Least You Need to Know

➤ Creatively written nonfiction reads like the best of novels.

➤ Try to find companion pieces in the literary world to get the full scope.

➤ Books with a distinct point of view will spark debate, but it is good to bring material espousing the other side for balance.

➤ All subjects, from Abbevillian culture to zygapophysis, can be found in the nonfiction universe if you look hard enough.

# Chapter 18

# People Are People, So What Should I Read?

## In This Chapter

➤ Does everyone have a story to tell?

➤ Harry S, a True-Man

➤ Miles smiles on the written word and his remarkable career

➤ An interview with Anaïs Nin's confidant

➤ Do Julia Roberts and Jerry Springer explain the rise of memoir?

Biographies, autobiographies, and memoirs are like opinions: Everyone has one, just very few of them are worth hearing about. Okay, maybe that's harsh. Everybody has interesting stories to tell—the thing with books is the author has to be very good at telling them. Great writers can turn semi-interesting lives into gold, but it is the rare combination of an intellectual and creative link between subject and author that promises an enthralling read. Jack Perkins and Harry Smith notwithstanding, personal tales are tough to handle one after another if you are used to fiction. They are often long, and, unfortunately, dry, but the cream of the crop offers stories that fit into that most overused of clichés, "stranger than fiction." When you find a biography, auto-biography, or memoir that is worthwhile, keep these questions in mind:

➤ How did the author's life impact his or her given field of strength?

➤ Is there a link between the subject's life and my own?

➤ How would the world be different if this person never existed?

➤ How did they differ in their personal/private life?

➤ What did the writer do to bring this person's life to life? (A bad writer could turn Salvador Dalí into Al Gore.)

# The Big Cheeses

1. ***Truman,* by David McCullough.** This is one of the best presidential biographies because it is an interesting story of both a man's life and the changes America underwent during his lifetime. It is a thorough look at one of the more engaging presidents of the twentieth century, before television, spin doctors, and handlers robbed the personality of our leaders. Harry Truman is a fascinating character and a politician who actually had character. McCullough captures the amazing life of the man who was in charge as America underwent its postwar changes, but who grew up in small-town nineteenth-century America. President Truman was a man of integrity who was faced with the awesome decision of whether or not to drop the atomic bomb on Japan. Interestingly, McCullough tells us that whether or not to send troops into Korea was the decision Truman felt was the most important.

**Biblio-Trivio**

Harry S Truman was the last of a dying breed. He did not attend college because of his family's financial situation. President Truman was, however, a voracious reader and loved to debate on a wide range of topics. One other tidbit: The "S" in Harry S Truman doesn't stand for anything. He had no middle name; his parents gave him the initial to appease two family members.

Truman emerges as an honest, loyal (to a fault, you could say) family man who tried to do what he thought was right. He isn't as glamorous or high-profile as some other presidents, but look at his record as compared to JFK, for instance. Truman was the president at the beginning of the Communist takeover in Europe, prompting the Truman Doctrine; he ordered the armed forces to desegregate the military after Congress refused to do so; and he kept plugging along in his famous "Whistle-Stop" campaign of 1948, which led to the biggest presidential upset of the century.

Truman was a forthright man from Independence, Missouri, an irascible figure with more character than we have come to expect from our presidents in these cynical times. McCullough tells his life story with clarity, humor, and flair. He is one of the finest chroniclers of history we have, and I would also like to recommend his books *Mornings on Horseback,* a biography of Teddy Roosevelt, and *The Great Bridge,* the astounding saga of the building of the Brooklyn Bridge. The latter is a brilliant work on an amazing feat of engineering that rivals the best science-fiction or adventure novels.

**Pro's Prose**

"A President has to expect those things."

—Harry S Truman's comment after two Puerto Rican nationalists tried to assassinate him

2. *No Ordinary Time,* **by Doris Kearns Goodwin.** This is a superb book by one of our nation's finest historians. Goodwin captures the chaos inside the Roosevelt White House as the Great War raged on continents across the ocean. The wide cast of confidants, advisers, family members, would-be lovers, and interlopers who were around at all times provides an oddly amusing narrative in contrast to the war. Goodwin's commitment to examining the lives of the Roosevelts, and only occasionally the battlefields, makes this book an original work that has the scope and drama of a nineteenth-century British novel.

**Biblio-Trivio**

Eleanor Roosevelt was a committed civil rights activist. One famous incident that shows her resolve happened when she resigned from the Daughters of the American Revolution because they wouldn't allow African-American opera singer Marian Anderson use of their facilities. Any book club interested in Eleanor Roosevelt should start with her books *It's Up to the Women* (1933) and *This I Remember* (1949).

The relationship between Franklin and Eleanor Roosevelt was also quite astounding, ahead of its time as an equal partnership on the intellectual/political/intellectual level, but run-of-the-mill in its infidelity fault-line. Eleanor never wavered on her commitment to social justice, and her dedication to the causes of women, labor, and minorities lay the groundwork for the future movements. Her worldview was quite contemporary. Goodwin captures the fractured intimacy and inner lunacy of the Roosevelt White House during the time of World War II. Don't wait 'til next year; pick up Goodwin's book for your reading group today.

3. *Coolidge: An American Enigma,* by Robert Sobel. If your book club is going to spend time examining the head honchos, why spend all the time on the ones you are most familiar with? Sobel reexamines the man who was unaffectionately known as "Silent Cal," and comes to some rather different conclusions. Was he a do-nothing president and big business pawn whose ardent belief in the free market helped bring about the stock market crash of 1929? Or was he (as Sobel believes) a man who stuck by his Jeffersonian principles that government should keep from meddling in the economy and who had no way of predicting the future? His impact on the country wasn't overwhelming, to be sure, but he did bring in a budget surplus every year, which was given back through tax cuts, and he cut the national debt by a third (sounds like a recent stump speech). Sobel makes the case that Coolidge was a man of great integrity who washed out the stink left over by the Harding administration.

**Pro's Prose**

"I want your vote. I need it. I shall appreciate it."

—The simple reply Coolidge gave to his constituents when shaking hands in the early local-level days of his political career.

What is most interesting about Sobel's book is the way it forces the reader to reconsider the impression of Coolidge that has almost become fact. Sobel has been criticized for relying on Coolidge's thin autobiography (all of his papers were destroyed) and for making big jumps in his conclusions, but like all smart book clubs you'll be bringing in outside materials to look at all the sides of the equation. What is interesting, though, and worthy of discussion, is the role historians play in all this. Shouldn't people know that Coolidge was a decent, responsible man, even if they have disdain for his economic policies? If he were scandal-ridden we would know about that, so why is his personal integrity overlooked? Which is more important, the mark of a man or the mark of a presidency? Is it important to know Coolidge was devastated when his son died at an early age? Did he lead us to the stock market crash? And, if so, does that still mean history books shouldn't include Sobel's account of his general decency?

Now, if you still have a hankering for some presidential reading, the following list ought to help you satisfy your craving. These books are not all biographies, but they do come under the heading of nonfiction; otherwise I would recommend books like Gore Vidal's *Lincoln*, which is an incredible work of historical fiction, or Harriet Beecher Stowe's *Uncle Tom's Cabin*, which had major Civil War implications. The one thing they all share is that they're fascinating works about the toughest job on the planet.

➤ *American Sphinx: The Character of Thomas Jefferson,* by Joseph J. Ellis

➤ *In the Time of the Americans: FDR, Truman, Eisenhower, Marshall, MacArthur—The Generation That Changed America's Role in the World,* by David Fromkin

➤ *John Quincy Adams and the Foundations of American Foreign Policy,* by Samuel Flagg Bemis

➤ *Flawed Giant: Lyndon B. Johnson, 1960–1973,* by Robert Dallek

➤ *What It Takes: The Way to the White House,* by Richard Ben Cramer

➤ *Woodrow Wilson, American Prophet,* by Arthur Walworth

➤ *Florence Harding: The First Lady, the Jazz Age, and the Death of America's Most Scandalous President,* by Carl Sferrazza Anthony

➤ *All the President's Men,* by Carl Bernstein and Bob Woodward

➤ *George Washington: A Biography,* by Washington Irving

➤ *The Life and Writings of Abraham Lincoln,* by Abraham Lincoln, Philip Van Doren Stern (Editor)

**Pro's Prose**

"He was a reluctant Vice President. He had hoped and planned for the presidency, but fate or the limitations of his time, place, and personality had cast him in the second spot. And he despised it. From his earliest days in the Texas Hill Country, he had aspired to be the best, to outdo friend and foe. He needed to win higher standing, hold greater power, earn more money than anyone else. Some inner sense of want drove him to seek status, control, and wealth. Being less than top dog made him feel rejected and unworthy."

—From *Flawed Giant: Lyndon B. Johnson,* by Robert Dallek

# Oh, Those Arty Types

1. *Oscar Wilde,* **by Richard Ellmann.** This book won the Pulitzer Prize in 1989, and Ellmann is one of the finest biographers of our time (his book on James Joyce is also generally considered a masterpiece). In this look at the dramatic life of Wilde, Ellmann manages to relate to the audience why the infamous Irishman deserves a spot with the best writers of the era. The numerous Wilde

quotations are judiciously woven throughout the book and his sharp, relevant humor shines. Ellmann gives shape to an ultimately tragic life that rivals any fictional screenplay Tinsel Town scribes could concoct.

### Pro's Prose

"Morality is simply the attitude we adopt toward people who we personally dislike."

—Oscar Wilde

Wilde was at the center of a sensationalized sodomy trial in 1895; he was convicted and sentenced to two years of hard labor in prison. The Victorian middle class was scandalized. He emerged penniless and spiritually washed out. Wilde was convicted at the peak of his career, which never got back on track. Ellmann presents the later years of his subject's life in touching fashion, and it is easy to understand why Wilde is considered a martyr in some circles. If your reading group is interested in reading about who's doing the writing, this is one of the best and would make a fine companion piece to *The Picture of Dorian Gray*. One question to consider: What is it about Wilde and his life that seems so contemporary?

2. *Jackson Pollock: An American Saga,* by Steven Naifeh and Gregory White Smith. Born in Cody, Wyoming, Pollock was a painter who went on to become one of the preeminent leaders of the abstract expressionist movement.

### Biblio-Trivio

Abstract expressionism was a movement in the mid-twentieth century that was concerned primarily with the spontaneous declaration of the individual through painting. Generally, abstract expressionism ignores conventional forms and recognizable images and is characterized in terms of the concepts behind the art rather than a specific look.

This is a biography of a man who was in the forefront of modern art. It gives the reader the sense of how an artist's life becomes part of his work, and it makes the case for Pollock to be ranked among the best of the last half-century. The authors did exhaustive research and explain how Pollock fits in the bigger construct of modern art. Pollock was famous for using a technique in which the artist lays a big canvas on the floor and drips paint and enamel from a stick, trowel, or something similar, to produce intricate, vivid patterns of color.

The authors have been criticized for their limited understanding of art history and critiques of Pollock's work, but a quick trip to the art history section of the library should help dig up counterpoints. Overall, it is a biography that will introduce your book club to a lesser-known American giant in the art world.

### Novel Ideas

Every time there is a modern art exhibit, some yahoo will loudly proclaim, "I could do that," or the even more zinging, "My kid could do that." If you aren't said yahoo, and even if nobody in your sophisticated book club is *that guy,* it would still be a funky exercise to do a little abstract expressionist painting during the meeting when you discuss this book. It doesn't matter if you're any good or not, it is all about the experience. Grab a canvas (bedsheet will do), some paints, and a tree branch and have at it. Now, what can your kid do again?

3. *Miles Davis: The Autobiography,* **by Miles Davis, Quincy Troupe (Contributor).** The last time Jack Nicholson won an Oscar he thanked Miles Davis. Why? Well, this is strictly conjecture, but it may have something to do with the fact that Davis is the only cultural icon in the last few decades who is absolutely twice as cool as Jack. (Okay, maybe that's not it, but the man *is* cool.) This autobiography is fascinating, in no small part because the man who rarely spoke lays it all on the line, and I do mean all. This tour de force takes readers through his career, from the early days with Charlie Parker and Dizzy Gillespie to his work with John Coltrane and his recording of *Porgy and Bess.* It also details all his lost drug years where he treated his body like a punching bag, which isn't as interesting to many jazz fans as the numerous stories and details of the working life. But give Davis credit, he wanted to tell the entire story, and a full life is a full life.

Davis's book is worth reading just to see how much influence he has wielded on America's homegrown art form. From his early days in bebop through the fusion movement that exploded basically because that's what Miles was doing, it is a revelatory journey. All jazz fans, or fans of virtuosos, should pick the autobiography of a man who truly deserves to be called a genius, a very cool genius.

Following are some more arty books for you to peruse:

➤ *The Professor and the Madman,* by Simon Winchester
➤ *Harriet Beecher Stowe: A Life,* by Joan D. Hedrick

### Jane Err

I don't have to tell you that the reading group should have *Kind of Blue, Miles Smiles, Sketches of Spain,* or the *Birth of the Cool* on the turntable because it would just be taking up valuable tree space, right? What I will say is that if you want a counterpoint to the often caustic book by Davis himself, get *Miles Davis: The Definitive Bio,* by David Chadwick, which gives balance to what his career meant to others.

### Novel Ideas

Admittedly, *Why Sinatra Matters* is a slim essay, but it captures the essence of the young Sinatra and the immigrant dream. Throw on Ol' Blue Eyes and read it in conjunction with *Unto the Sons,* by Gay Talese, or *EB: A Boy … a Family … a Neighborhood … and a Lost Civilization, Memories of Growing Up in Brooklyn NY in the '40s and '50s,* by Bert Kemp. Both fit with the young Sinatra Hamill recalls.

➤ *Out of Sheer Rage: Wrestling with D. H. Lawrence,* by Geoff Dyer

➤ *Orson Welles: The Road to Xanadu,* by Simon Callow

➤ *Why Sinatra Matters,* by Pete Hamill

➤ *Robert Frost: The Years of Triumph, 1915–1938,* by Lawrence R. Thompson

➤ *Speak, Memory: An Autobiography Revisited,* by Vladimir Nabokov

➤ *Midnight Dreary: The Mysterious Death of Edgar Allan Poe,* by John Walsh

➤ *Henry and June: From a Journal of Love: The Unexpurgated Diary of Anaïs Nin 1931–1932,* by Anaïs Nin

➤ (Tie) *Pryor Convictions: And Other Life Sentences,* by Richard Pryor and Todd Gold (and) *How to Talk Dirty and Influence People: An Autobiography,* by Lenny Bruce

## Memoirs, All Alone in the Spotlight

Anyone who follows the literary world at all knows that the memoir has become all the rage in the last few years. Everyone who thinks he has a story to tell seems to be getting a six-figure deal and a book contract. Every publisher in the free world is searching for the next *Angela's Ashes,* which was written by Frank McCourt and has sold somewhere in the range of eight trillion copies. No subject is taboo anymore, either: Had a willing sexual relationship with your father? C'mon aboard. Heroin addiction? Tell us your story. Play a central part in a presidential scandal? Why not? And the list goes on and on and on.

*Memoir* is described in the dictionary as an account of something noteworthy, or a narrative composed from personal experience. An autobiography is a biography by the person him- (or her-) self. So, anybody who has ever done anything "noteworthy" in his life is qualified. It's that noteworthy part that tends to get a little fuzzy, but what the heck?

# The One and Only Interview

To discuss the recent memoir phenomena, I have brought in an expert. Tristine Rainer is one of the preeminent scholars of memoir writing and teaching in the country. She has long been involved in the world of letters and has recently written *Your Life as Story, Discovering the "New Autobiography,"* and *Writing Memoir as Literature* (1998). She also wrote the definitive work on contemporary journal writing entitled *The New Diary: How to Use a Journal for Self-Guidance and Expanded Creativity,* which was published in 1979. She is also founder and director of the Center for Autobiographic Studies, a nonprofit organization devoted to the creation, appreciation, and preservation of autobiographic works.

Tristine was kind enough to sit down for a chat about what is unique to the memoir and why there has been such an eruption in the last few years.

**Patrick Sauer:** What makes a good memoir?

**Tristine Rainer:** A work in which you can hear the distinct voice of the author, in which you know the writer not only through what they reveal about their life, but also in how they see and process the world coming at them. A good memoir also has depth of perspective; that is, the narrator in the present has an understanding of and has given coherent meaning to the events with which the protagonist, in the past, had to struggle. A good memoir is candid and authentic; the writer allows himself or herself to be vulnerable.

**PS:** What should a book club be looking for in the memoir?

**TR:** The book club should be looking for the unique message and perspective that this writer offers, and at how he or she has chosen to tell the story. Has the author chosen only a slice of his or her life? Has the author devoted the book to one thematic question and illuminated this aspect of

**Jane Err**

If your book club is in the market for a first-person account of substance abuse, I recommend Jerry Stahl's *Permanent Midnight: A Memoir.* It is a brutally funny dark tale of a life of drugs, degenerate behavior, and sitcom writing. Stahl wrote for *Alf,* and his observations about Hollywood on horse are black comedy at its finest.

**Novel Ideas**

Both of Tristine Rainer's books, *Your Life as Story* and *The New Diary,* would make great monthly selections for your book club because of her expertise in the techniques of writing. Or you could take it to the next level and use her books as the jumping-off point for writing your own stories. Even if they are for book club eyes and ears only, it's an entirely different process and could lead to all sorts of self-awareness and discovery.

human experience through deep personal exploration? How does the author deal with the problem of truth in memoir? Is there a disclaimer that allows the author to use his or her imagination where memory fails? How does the author deal with the problem of invading the privacy of others?

**PS:** Besides the obvious point, how do memoirs differ from fiction?

**TR:** The "new autobiography," which is the type of literary memoir now being published, may be indistinguishable from the novel stylistically. It is written in scenes with dialogue and with story and character development. The memoirist may make up dialogue that he or she can't remember, or may even rearrange chronology. However, novelists make up events that never happened, whereas the memoirist in writing nonfiction has a contract with the reader not to invent events that never took place.

**PS:** Why is memoir so popular right now?

**TR:** People feel a need for intimacy and authenticity in their lives that is increasingly difficult to find, especially in the United States where mobility and divorce have atomized families. Also, so much of what we read and see through the media is processed to the point of inauthenticity, so readers crave to know what really happened, not what someone has dreamt up. Last, contemporary personal life has become so complicated that people read memoirs to see how someone else has been able to deal with the mystery of living a life.

**PS:** How can book clubs use the occasional memoir?

**TR:** Book clubs should look for memoirs written by noncelebrities as well as the heavily promoted celebrity memoir that is usually written by a ghost or a cowriter.

### Biblio-Trivio

The Center for Autobiographic Studies hosts workshops and an annual retreat. The Web site provides extensive resources for persons interested in autobiographic writing as well as a useful bibliography of memoirs. Visit www.storyhelp.com. or write:

Center for Autobiographic Studies
260 S. Lake Avenue, Suite 220
Pasadena, CA 91101-3002
Phone: 818-754-8663

Why not plan your next vacation in sunny Southern California learning the art of the memoir? Who knows, if it's half as big as *Angela's Ashes*, you can take a permanent vacation.

Tristine also offers a few of her favorite memoirs of the last few years that don't fall into the heavily promoted celebrity category:

➤ *Paula*, by Isabel Allende

➤ *I Know Why the Caged Bird Sings*, by Maya Angelou

➤ *Growing Up*, by Russell Baker

➤ *Shot in the Heart*, by Mikal Gilmore

To which, I would like to add the following works:

➤ *Spinster*, by Sylvia Ashton-Warner

➤ *An American Childhood*, by Annie Dillard

➤ *The Color of Water: A Black Man's Tribute to His White Mother*, by James McBride

➤ *Out of Africa*, by Isak Dinesen

➤ *Memories of a Catholic Girlhood*, by Mary McCarthy

➤ *Good-Bye to All That*, by Robert Graves

➤ *Witness to a Century*, by George Seldes

➤ *Depth Takes a Holiday: Essays from Lesser Los Angeles*, by Sandra Tsing Loh

➤ *The Duke of Deception*, by Geoffrey Wolff

➤ *This Boy's Life*, by Tobias Wolff

➤ *All Over but the Shoutin'*, by Rick Bragg

**Pro's Prose**

"When I was a boy, I used to wonder where my mother came from, how she got on this earth. When I asked her where she was from, she would say, 'God made me,' and change the subject. When I asked her if she was white, she'd say, 'No. I'm light-skinned,' and change the subject again. Answering questions about her personal history did not jibe with Mommy's view of parenting twelve curious, wild, brown-skinned children."

—from *The Color of Water*, by James McBride

**Biblio-Trivio**

Geoffrey and Tobias Wolff are brothers, and they have both written books about the men their mother married. *The Duke of Deception* is Geoffrey's story of their biological father, a charming man who created a persona that was far from the truth, whom he lived with after Tobias and their mother had left.

Tobias ended up in Washington State, across the country from Geoffrey with a ruthless stepfather right out of a Dickens book. Individually, they are both excellent, but together they paint an entire picture of a bizarre family life. (The movie of Tobias's book with Robert De Niro and Leonardo DiCaprio isn't bad either.)

In general, nonfiction books are less popular with book clubs, but memoir is the opposite. Partially that has to do with the trendiness of the genre, but I also think it has to do with a cultural shift toward a theoretically level playing field. An example is the movie *Notting Hill,* which features Julia Roberts playing a movie star who wants to be a regular person. In a more debased sense, shows like *Jerry Springer* have given the average person (by economic and social parameters, anyway) the chance to go on television and let the whole world know what he's done.

Somewhere in the middle, the memoir has carved a niche for itself. It gives regular people (for example, Frank McCourt, a teacher) the chance to create a narrative of their life, and since anything goes now, the more sordid the better (*The Kiss*). Factor in all of the airtime that has to be filled in the cable universe, which gives all sorts of people the opportunity to be on television, and the democratic ethos of the Internet, and, voilá, every Johnnie-lunchpail can be a star.

The question is, does everyone have a story to tell?

### The Least You Need to Know

➤ Great authors can tell interesting stories about bland people, but rarely is it the other way around.

➤ A memoir is best if you can hear the distinct voice of the author.

➤ The Center for Autobiographic Studies Web site (www.storyhelp.com) offers all sorts of useful info for those who want to tell their story.

➤ A level media playing field has conributed to the rise of the memoir.

# Part 5

# My Group Wants to Party All the Time

*"It will be dawn soon. I think the party's over."*

—George, *in* Who's Afraid of Virginia Woolf? *by Edward Albee*

*Now that your reading group is a best-seller, it is time to toast your efforts. This part has a few party ideas, and field trips to get the full reading experience. It also kicks around other formats, including film and theater, that can be used once in a while to recharge the book club batteries.*

# Chapter 19

# Food for Thought

---

### In This Chapter

➤ How to keep members' stomachs happy and minds focused

➤ Foodie lit that's fit for consumption

➤ Oysters and eggs, together again!

➤ Barbecue sauce of the cowboy gods

➤ Christmas on ice

---

Now that we've covered all the serious topics, it's time to get to the good stuff—it's party time!

## A Final Reminder

Before we begin to make the arrangements, let's repeat the golden rule one more time:

*The time must be spent discussing the book.*

I promise this is the last time you will have to hear that phrase, because from here on, we are going to pull out all the stops.

## Biblio-Trivio

The "stops" in "to pull out all the stops" are organ stops. These control the pipes, which give the organ its great range of tones. To pull out all the stops is to use the organ to its fullest capacity, achieving maximum volume of sound. In general usage, therefore, the expression means to use all the available resources to their fullest extent.

It is important to keep the golden rule in mind at this juncture because this is where book clubs can get away from their original purpose. Dinners can be great fun, but they are a lot of work, and it should never become a burden to anyone, financially or in terms of time. Either way, here are a few tips for keeping the gastronomic and the literary in perfect harmony:

## Novel Ideas

One host of a book club meeting I heard about served milk in martini glasses with vanilla wafers and handed out white plastic bowlers. They were discussing *A Clockwork Orange,* by Anthony Burgess, and they watched selected scenes from Stanley Kubrick's film version. Simple and effective.

➤ **Keep it relevant.** Oftentimes, if the meal isn't related to the book, it becomes the center of attention and creativity is stifled in favor of grandiosity. Hot dogs, peanuts, cold beers, and Cracker Jacks are apropos for reading Mark Harris's *Bang the Drum Slowly,* a great novel (and flick) about the grand old game, but ahi tuna isn't. Even something as simple as bagels with cream cheese for *Call It Sleep,* by Henry Roth, adds to the New York flavor. It is the crafty relation to the book that makes whatever you serve unique, and it keeps the tome as the central focus.

➤ **Keep it rare.** Only have full meals every so often and divvy up the workload. If your reading group has nine members, have three meals a year, prepared by teams of three, and serve finger foods or hors d'oeuvres for the other gatherings. That way, more thought and preparation can go into the night, and it will be more of a treat than an expectation.

➤ **Keep it relaxed.** Full meals are fine, but it should be a relaxed atmosphere. Keep the fine china, silver candlesticks, and cloth napkins in the oak hutch where they belong, unless this is the way all of your group members eat every meal at home. Paper plates, plastic utensils, and disposable cups make folks feel right at home. Subconsciously, fancy dinners make the average diner more reserved and tentative.

➤ **Keep it real.** You'll know if your meals/cocktail hours aren't working, and if you know it, chances are the other members in your group know it as well. Whatever works is the best way to do it, but just because one month was spent eating boiled lobster and clam chowder while dissecting *The Bostonians,* by Henry James, doesn't mean any other month has to be the same. If it is too much and the discussions are suffering, scale it back to bread and water, which reminds me of another reading group meeting. The selection was Manuel Puig's *Kiss of the Spider Woman* (which takes place in prison), and the host served her book club bread, water, and cold black beans. She also held the meeting in her basement with a single low-wattage bulb and the members sat on a cold concrete floor. Realistic, I'd say.

# Cooking Up Some Good Reading

Ah, food—glorious food. Lots of leisure activities involve some form of sustenance—cake at birthdays, popcorn at movies … why can't reading groups get in on the action?

The answer is you can—and in more ways than one. There are books about making food, books about people who make food, and fictional tales woven around the glory of gastronomical pursuits. In the following sections, we take a look at a few foodie books to delight more than the taste buds.

**Jane Err**

*Do not,* I repeat, do not sell anything at your book club meetings. Nobody likes to be hit up at any time, but it is inappropriate at the monthly meetings and can sour everyone before the discussion gets underway, which leads to personal animosity and ruins the meeting. Leave the Amway, your kids' band popcorn, the church raffle tickets, and the Boy Scouts magazine drive at home. This isn't the place for *Let's-Make-a-Deal.*

## *Books for Cooks and Food-Lovers Alike*

The first list of books consists of titles that are about what food means in our lives by the people who have lived the culinary-literary duality. These tomes can be enjoyed by your reading group because one central question is always worth discussing, how does food impact our lives? Can't live without it, but the meal is also the basic centerpiece of all human gatherings. Could your reading group survive without grub?

The following books were written for those who love food and want to understand what it means to us as humans.

➤ *Nobody Knows the Truffles I've Seen*, **by George Lang.** Lang's life story is well worth the time and effort. He was raised in a happy Hungarian home, forced into a Nazi labor camp, came to the United States, and started as a vegetable peeler and cooked his way up to an enormously successful restauranteur. It's a powerful tale peppered with lots of humor.

➤ *The Gourmet Atlas*, **by Susie Ward (introduction).** A fascinating tome about the historical origin of foods and their social, political, and cultural implications.

➤ *Food in History*, **by Reay Tannahill.** Tannahill has written an intriguing book about how food shapes society, including how pepper contributed to the fall of the Roman Empire and what cinnamon had to do with the discovery of America.

➤ *Tender at the Bone: Growing Up at the Table*, **by Ruth Reichl.** Former *New York Times* restaurant critic, Reichl pens a memoir about how food has influenced her life. Engaging storytelling abounds, and the recollections of her mother's cooking are priceless.

➤ *Honey from a Weed: Fasting and Feasting in Tuscany, Catalonia, the Cyclades and Apulia*, **by Patience Gray, John Thorne.** This is a tapestry of the author's love of the Earth and its natural gifts, lyrical tales of places and people.

➤ *The Making of a Chef: Mastering Heat at the Culinary Institute of America*, **by Michael Ruhlman.** Journalist Ruhlman talked his way into the Harvard of cooking schools to try and learn how to turn potatoes into art. The high-energy, boot-camp, whirlwind lifestyle at the CIA is intriguing, and Ruhlman's journey will be identifiable because he went into the world of chefs as a neophyte. A must for anyone who loves four-star restaurants.

➤ *The Man Who Ate Everything and Other Gastronomic Feats, Disputes, and Pleasurable Pursuits*, **by Jeffrey Steingarten.** A collection of wry, funny essays from the food critic at *Vogue*. Steingarten had to learn to love all the foods he had previously abstained from (maybe the kids should read it, too).

**Pro's Prose**

"My goal was both humble and presumptuous: I wanted to learn how to put myself in the service of the potato. This was to me the key phrase, in the service of, the axis, the unmoving shaft, of a statement with many ramifications. Is great cooking really art? Are chefs artists? What is wrong with flash and flamboyance? How could the lowly potato become so important in a meal as to be the one thing my uncle remembered decades later?

"Also, I love to eat potatoes."

—Excerpt from *The Making of a Chef*, by Michael Ruhlman

## *Books That Cook*

These are works of fiction in which food plays a predominant role in the narrative. Any of this culinary literature would make a fine selection/ dinner choice. *Bon appétit.*

➤ *Like Water for Chocolate,* **by Laura Esquivel.** A love story set in Mexico with a young woman who is forbidden to marry Pedro, her true love, because tradition dictates she must care for her mother until she dies. Pedro marries Tita's older sister just to be near her, and she uses the sensuality of food to convey her feelings. It comes complete with recipes to tempt your own object of desire.

➤ *Reef,* **by Romesh Gunesekera.** This is the affecting story of Triton, a young Sri Lankan chef who is so focused on pleasing his master's stomach that he is totally immune to the revolution taking place in society. The lush descriptions of Sri Lanka and of Triton's meals are outstanding.

➤ *The Butter Did It: A Gastronomic Tale of Love and Murder,* **by Phyllis Richman.** Richman's mystery takes place in the world of upscale Washington, D.C., restaurants. When an aristocratic chef drops dead from a heart attack, the death is ruled a murder, and food critic Chas Wheatley begins snooping around the high-profile kitchens for clues. Richman is a restaurant critic, so the authentic flavor of this culinary caper makes it stand out.

➤ *Fried Green Tomatoes at the Whistle-Stop Café,* **by Fannie Flagg.** Flagg's book is a reading group favorite because of its warm recollections of the Whistle-Stop Café and its honest look at sexism, racism, and agism. The two main female characters, Idgie and Ruth, run the café that serves anyone, whether they have money or not. The two women form a strong, loving bond. Flagg never spells out if they are lovers—what does your group think?

**Pro's Prose**

"My other half, Wilbur, and I ate there the other night, and it was so good he says he might not ever eat at home again. Ha. Ha. I wish this were true. I spend all my time cooking for the big lug, and still can't keep him filled up."

—Excerpt from *Fried Green Tomatoes at the Whistle-Stop Café,* by Fannie Flagg

## Call Me Ish-*Meal*

The rest of this chapter is strictly devoted to the filling of bellies, wounding of livers, and lifting of spirits. Some of these ideas are small and easy to implement, others are larger party ideas that might only happen once in the length of your reading group. For instance, you may decide to have a blow-out every other anniversary. A big open-invitation read-aloud, costume party with a Shakespearean actor walking around in tights and a breastplate delivering sonnets as you all gnaw on a mutton chop. Or maybe a well-chosen combination of wine and cheese will suffice?

It is natural for book club members to pitch in for birthdays, anniversaries, graduations, weddings, etc., especially after a couple of years when everyone becomes close friends, but it may not be the best route to take. I heard from a long-time (over 15 years) book club that kept track of the occasions and had a toast, but instead of buying gifts, flowers, etc., everyone gave a card to the honoree and a donation (totally confidential) into a coffee can that was kept separate. Every year, on the month before the book club's anniversary, they counted the coffee coffers and threw themselves an appropriate party, night at the theater, restaurant excursion, etc. It had a twofold benefit: There wasn't the constant pressure to have to donate and keep up with the Joneses, and, more important, it provided an outing the members looked forward to like kids at Christmas.

## The Great Gatsby Roaring Soiree

Break out those flapper dresses, skirts above the knee, sequined skullcaps, pin-striped suits, or whatever accouterment you need to get ready to roar like it's 1925. The rich and powerful in Gatsby's world threw lavish parties, drank the finest champagne, and lived without a care in the world, well, that is until it all collapsed both literally and literaturely.

Here's a recipe guaranteed to get you started in the morning:

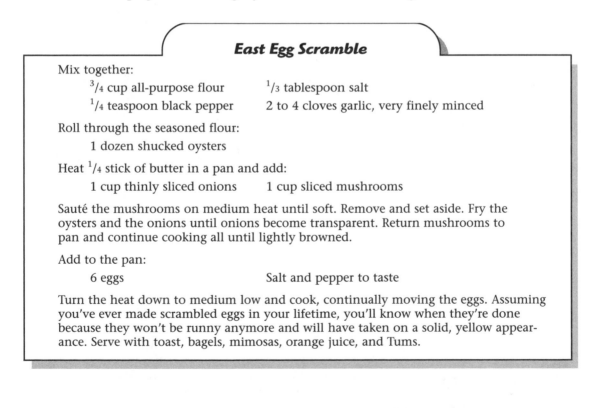

### East Egg Scramble

Mix together:

| $3/4$ cup all-purpose flour | $1/3$ tablespoon salt |
| $1/4$ teaspoon black pepper | 2 to 4 cloves garlic, very finely minced |

Roll through the seasoned flour:

1 dozen shucked oysters

Heat $1/4$ stick of butter in a pan and add:

| 1 cup thinly sliced onions | 1 cup sliced mushrooms |

Sauté the mushrooms on medium heat until soft. Remove and set aside. Fry the oysters and the onions until onions become transparent. Return mushrooms to pan and continue cooking all until lightly browned.

Add to the pan:

| 6 eggs | Salt and pepper to taste |

Turn the heat down to medium low and cook, continually moving the eggs. Assuming you've ever made scrambled eggs in your lifetime, you'll know when they're done because they won't be runny anymore and will have taken on a solid, yellow appearance. Serve with toast, bagels, mimosas, orange juice, and Tums.

For dinner clubs, I would like to recommend any of the following entrees:

➤ Oyster stew

➤ Filet mignon

➤ Cornish game hens

➤ Anything rich people eat

Serve with the Manhasset recipe that follows.

## The Joy Luck Club Feast

Ordering Chinese from your favorite restaurant is one quick way of getting this meal underway, but the communal sense of the novel can come alive if the book club takes part in preparing a Chinese dinner.

Plus, homemade grub is made with love, not MSG. Try the following Hot-Sour Soup recipe at your next book club meeting.

### Pro's Prose

"The bar is in full swing and floating rounds of cocktails permeate the garden outside until the air is alive with chatter and laughter and casual innuendo and introductions forgotten on the spot and enthusiastic meetings between women who never know each other's names."

—Excerpt from *The Great Gatsby,* by F. Scott Fitzgerald

### Manhasset

1$^1$/$_2$ ounces blended whiskey

1$^1$/$_2$ teaspoons sweet vermouth

1$^1$/$_2$ teaspoons dry vermouth

1 tablespoon lemon juice

Lemon peel

Mix and serve in a cocktail glass with ice.

Also consider the classic martini, nonalcoholic champagne, or seltzer with lime.

### Hot-Sour Soup

Serves 4

4 dried black mushrooms

2 bean curd cakes

2 tablespoons cornstarch

5 cups beef stock (but feel free to use vegetable if you're not a carnivore)

1 tablespoon sherry

1 egg, lightly beaten

$^1/_4$ pound pork

1 scallion

$^1/_4$ cup water

2 tablespoons cider vinegar

Pinch salt

1 teaspoon soy sauce

$^1/_4$ teaspoon pepper

Sesame oil

Soak dried mushrooms, reserving 1 cup of soaking liquid; thinly slice mushrooms, pork, and bean curd. Mince scallions. Blend cornstarch and water to a paste.

In a large saucepan, bring stock and a cup of mushroom-soaking liquid to boil, add pork and mushrooms and simmer, covered, for 10 minutes.

Add bean curd and simmer, covered, three more minutes.

Stir in sherry, vinegar, salt, soy sauce, and pepper. Thicken with cornstarch paste.

Slowly add beaten egg, stirring gently once or twice. Remove from heat. Sprinkle with a few drops of sesame oil and minced scallion.

### Biblio-Trivio

There is an ancient Chinese belief that music is meant not to amuse but to purify one's thoughts and also that sound influences the harmonies of the universe. There is still a cult of classical *qin* music that follows the tradition. A qin is a long zither possessing a repertory calling for great subtlety and refinement in performance. Why not visit the world music section of the local music store and pick up a collection of qin music to play in the background?

### Sesame Chicken

1¹/₂ pounds boneless, skinless chicken breasts

1 tablespoon soy sauce

2¹/₂ teaspoons Chinese five-spice powder

2 teaspoons sesame seeds

Several red lettuce leaves (about 5 should do it)

1 tablespoon maple syrup

1 tablespoon dry sherry

1 teaspoon chopped fresh ginger

3 tablespoons flour

Salt and pepper

¹/₂ teaspoon peanut oil

1 large, ripe tomato, cut into wedges

Preheat oven to 350°. Cut chicken into pieces about 1 × 2 inches.

Mix soy sauce, maple syrup, sherry, ginger, and Chinese five spice together. Add chicken and marinate 20 minutes, turning once.

Meanwhile, place sesame seeds on a baking tray and toast in oven for 10 minutes or until slightly brown.

Drain chicken, reserving marinade. Coat chicken in flour seasoned with salt and pepper (don't be shy with the pepper). Shake off any excess.

Heat oil in a medium nonstick skillet. Add chicken and brown, about two minutes per side. Spoon marinade over chicken.

Reduce heat and sauté another minute, or until chicken is cooked through. Remove from heat and roll chicken in sesame seeds.

Wash and dry lettuce leaves. Line a serving plate with leaves, and spoon chicken on top. Garnish plate with tomato wedges.

Serve with: Lung Ching (Dragon Well) Green Tea, Lu An (Clear Distance) Black Tea, or Shot Lee Low (Pear Wine).

## All the Pretty Horses Smokeout Barbecue

This Texas-meets-Mexico meal is for the hearty eatin' and hard livin'. All varmints remember not to bring your pistols to the chuck wagon.

Southwest five-alarm chili and hot apple pie are essential for the Cormac McCarthy party. The stakes could be raised even higher if the discussion of *The Border Trilogy* were held under the stars by a campfire. Read all three books and treat yourselves right, *comprende?*

Pretty much whatever you can get from the text works, but remember that it isn't a contest. Cheese, crackers, and intelligent conversation is better than foie gras and silence.

---

### Barbecue Sauce for Ribs, Chicken, Squirrel, Possum, or Varmint of Choice

$1/2$ cup chopped onion

2 cloves garlic, crushed

$1^1/2$ cups chopped dill pickles

$1/4$ cup firmly packed brown sugar

2 tablespoons dill pickle juice

2 teaspoons salad oil

2 cups ketchup

$1/8$ teaspoon black pepper

$1/4$ teaspoon Tabasco sauce (more for fire)

$1/8$ teaspoon liquid smoke

Few dashes bitters

In a medium bowl, mix together all ingredients.

Brush on any critter you can wrassle up, pardner.

To wash down the vittles try: water from a canteen, boiled coffee, mescal tequila (with lime), bourbon whiskey straight from the bottle, Lone Star beer, or blended lime and sugar water.

---

## Black Bean Burritos

1 tablespoon olive oil

1 pound boneless chicken breasts, baked and shredded

2 jalapeño chiles, seeded and minced

1 clove garlic, minced

Tabasco sauce

1 green bell pepper, chopped

1 cut shredded Monterey Jack cheese

Optional: guacamole, salsa, sour cream

1 large onion, diced

1 tablespoon chili powder

1 teaspoon ground cumin

1 large sweet potato, baked and peeled

1 can whole-kernel corn, drained

1 red bell pepper, chopped

1 can black beans, drained

Flour tortillas

The juice of one lime

Season chicken an hour beforehand with lime juice, chili powder, and Tabasco.

Preheat oven to 350°.

Heat oil in a large iron skillet or frying pan. Add onion and chicken, stirring until golden brown.

Add chiles, chili powder, garlic, cumin, and Tabasco, stir until hot, add 1 tablespoon water and stir; remove from heat.

Stir in sweet potato, beans, corn, peppers, and lime juice.

Add filling to tortillas, add cheese if desired, fold all sides, and sprinkle with a quarter of the lime juice.

Cover burritos with foil and bake 30 minutes.

Serve with guacamole, salsa, or sour cream, if desired.

### Pro's Prose

"They stood holding the horse. They had not been invited forward. The dog when it struck the circle of light stopped in its tracks and then backed away slightly and stood waiting. The men were watching them. One of them was smoking a cigarette, and he raised it to his lips and sucked thinly at it and blew a thin stream of smoke toward the fire. He made a circling motion with his arm, his finger pointed down. He told them to take their horses around and into the trees behind them. Nuestros caballos, estan alla, he said."

—Excerpt from *The Crossing* (Part two in *The Border Trilogy*), by Cormac McCarthy

# Seize the *Holi*-Day

Holidays are another opportunity for book clubs to have a little fun, so here are a couple of small party ideas to liven up the bibliophile gathering.

## *A Bloody Good Halloween Party*

Before we mix up some ghoulishly delightful treats, please allow me to offer five more scary story selections from which to choose:

1. "The Premature Burial," a short story by Edgar Allan Poe
2. *Queen of the Damned,* by Anne Rice
3. "A Horseman in the Sky," a short story by Ambrose Bierce
4. *Roald Dahl's Tales of the Unexpected,* by Roald Dahl
5. "The Monkey's Paw," a short story by W. W. Jacobs

Of course, any Halloween party could have bowls of candy or caramel apples, but why not try something a little different?

### Bloody "Anne" Rice Pudding

$^3/_4$ cup medium-grain white rice

$^1/_4$ teaspoon salt

$^1/_2$ cup sugar

1 cup raisins

$^1/_2$ cup dark raspberry syrup (this is the blood, get it?)

$1^1/_2$ cups water

4 cups whole milk

$^1/_2$ teaspoon vanilla

1 cup red cinnamon candies

In a large, heavy saucepan, combine the rice, water, and salt.

Bring to a simmer over medium heat, then reduce the heat to low, cover, and simmer until the water has been absorbed (about 20 minutes). Gradually stir in the milk and sugar.

*continues*

*continued*

Cook, uncovered, over medium heat for 35 minutes, stirring occasionally. You will know the pudding is ready when the rice and milk have melded into a thick, oatmeal-like state. Remove from heat, then stir in the remaining ingredients.

Serve warm.

### Biblio-Trivio

The ancient Druids believed that Saman, the lord of the dead, called forth the evils spirits on the night before Hallowmas (All Saint's Day), and so they lit great fires to scare off the spirits. The ancient Celts also followed the practice, which has stayed alive through centuries. Jack–o'–lanterns also evolved from the practice. Originally, the scary carvings coupled with a lit candle were used to ward off the ghosts and witches.

If you want some spirits for your spirits, give this a try:

### Count Dracula's Bloody Mary Substitute

1¹/₂ ounces vodka

3 ounces tomato juice

1 teaspoon lemon juice

¹/₂ teaspoon Worcestershire sauce

A healthy shot of Tabasco or a healthy drop of horseradish

Dash celery salt

Lime wedges, celery sticks, or dill pickle

Combine all ingredients (except lime wedges, celery sticks, etc.) in a large pitcher. Stir until thoroughly mixed. Pour into tall glasses and serve with a wedge of lime, celery stick, or dill pickle to garnish.

If you are in the mood for something different, add Clamato juice, lose the tomato juice and lemon, and you've got the Bloody Caesar.

# Yule Have a Great Time

Don't let the rash of boring office parties, animated specials with sappy endings, and holiday ads that start on Labor Day get your book club down next December. Here are a few lesser-known holiday selections to get you in the spirit of the season:

➤ *Holidays on Ice,* by David Sedaris

➤ *The Silent Stars Go by: A True Christmas Story,* by Philip Lee Williams

➤ "One Christmas" and "A Thanksgiving Memory," by Truman Capote

➤ *Southern Christmas: Literary Classics of the Holidays,* edited by Julie Long, Thomas Payton

➤ *The Greatest Gift,* by Phillip Van Doren Stern

Of course, no party in the winter months would be complete without the old staple. That's right, it's nog time.

## A Boy and His Nog

6 eggs, separated, yolks and whites and reserved

$^1/_2$ cup light rum

1 teaspoon vanilla

1 cup whipping cream

$^1/_2$ cup sugar

2 cups milk

$^1/_2$ cup bourbon

$^1/_4$ teaspoon salt

Ground nutmeg for garnish

In a small mixing bowl, beat egg yolks until blended. Gradually add $^1/_4$ cup of the sugar and beat at high speed until thick and yellow.

Stir in milk.

Stir in rum, bourbon, vanilla, and salt. Chill thoroughly.

In a medium bowl, whip cream. In a separate medium-sized bowl, and with clean beaters, beat egg whites until soft peaks form.

Gradually add remaining sugar to egg whites, and fold in yolk mixture and whipped cream.

Pour into glasses, sprinkle with nutmeg, and serve.

If you want to make a non-alcoholic version, substitute another cup of milk for the booze.

Be careful when using raw eggs—always make sure you check the expiration date to ensure that they are fresh. There's nothing like a little salmonella to ruin the holiday spirit.

### Biblio-Trivio

The first fully Americanized Santa Claus appeared in 1823 in Clement Clarke Moore's poem *A Visit from Saint Nicholas* (a.k.a. *The Night Before Christmas*), but he was an elf in Moore's poem. The jolly fat man we know now evolved from two sources. He was rotund in Thomas Nast's drawings for the holiday issues of *Harper's* from the 1860s to the 1880s. Santa Claus became human size in illustrations for a Coca-Cola ad campaign in 1931, and its influence has dictated the Santa we see in thousands of similar campaigns every year.

### The Least You Need to Know

➤ Dinners and snacks that fit thematically with a book are more appropriate than elaborate feasts.

➤ There are numerous books about food that would make for interesting monthly selections.

➤ Instead of giving gifts for every occasion, pool donations and do something on the book club's anniversary.

➤ Holiday parties can be a good time, but they are a better time if the literary discussion still takes place.

# Chapter 20

# The Moviegoers

## In This Chapter

➤ Why couch potatoes shouldn't feel guilty

➤ How to view a film in terms of its merits as an adaptation

➤ Walker, Movie Ranger

➤ Picks about flicks

➤ Did Altman Carver a turkey?

A bedtime story.

Once upon a time, there were no large halls in which various members of the community could pay $9 to gather together and munch on $5 bags of popcorn, have their eardrums rattled by THX speakers, laugh at the wacky antics of a fat man's intestinal problems, and cheer when the bad guy "gets his" from the long end of the good guy's peacemaker. There were no megaplexes with 18 screens of animated monkeys, computer-generated blizzards, or handsome young couples who aren't quite sure if they're meant for each other, but by gum the audience sure wanted to see it happen. Once upon a time, there was no such thing as the movies.

People everywhere flocked to literary clubs, children quoted Chaucer not Carey, women dreamed of Poe not Pitt, men wanted to be Thom Hardy, not Tom Cruise. Books were king, and we were a nation of well-read, cultured intellects in a constant state of theorizing and analyzing, a celebration of cerebration.

And it was good.

# I Found It at the Movies

Let's be honest, that never happened. Sure, there was a pre–moving image point in history when folks probably did read a bit more than they do now. But as a professor of mine once said, there was never a time when everyone was sitting around reading Henry James all the livelong day.

There is, however, a school of book club thought that believes watching filmic versions of chosen texts goes against the very reason for joining book clubs in the first place. Many members join because they either …

➤ Want a monthly forum dedicated to the analysis of literature, far away from the nonstop barrage of the visual media, or,

➤ They don't feel that they read enough and want to encourage their habit.

**Pro's Prose**

"To stuff our minds with what is simply trivial, simply curious, or of a low nutritive power, is to close our minds to what is solid and enlarging, and spiritually sustaining."

—Frederic Harrison

It is an admirable stance, trying to maintain the book club purity by banning the use of audiovisual aides, but you may be missing out on an interesting outlet for discussion.

If you have no interest in movies at this time, feel free to skip the rest of the chapter. If you are interested in watching cinematic adaptations of your favorite prose, proceed with an open mind. Even if your reading group only engages in the activity about as often as a Merchant-Ivory production is number one at the box office, it can be a refreshing and rejuvenating evening if you feel that the meetings have become a bit stale.

If you are on the fence about whether or not movies should be worked into your reading group's milieu, there are safeguards to ensure that the soul of the novel is not stained by the guts of the VCR.

# There's No Place Like Home

If your reading group follows the standard pattern and has a monthly meeting in the home of a member, it is quite easy to integrate a movie-watching night. Assuming at least one member owns a television and a VCR (or its crystal-clear cousin the DVD), all that is required is reserving the adaptation of the book at your video store. But there are a few practical issues that have to be discussed.

➤ **Time.** The average movie is two hours long, and many literary films are longer, so how is that going to fit into the average length of your book club's meeting? Should the meeting be stretched to four hours, or will an additional meeting be necessary? You all know how hard it is to accommodate everybody's schedule, so having two meetings may be impossible, but how many people can stay focused on a single topic for four-plus hours?

➤ **Procedure.** This is the biggest quandary facing a club, because the most intellectual way of discussing a cinematic adaptation is to compare and contrast the book and the movie. The way to view a movie that doesn't work very well is to read the book, hold the discussion, and then watch the movie just for fun. What's the point? It eliminates the essence of the practice of debate, and it subconsciously tells members that watching the movie is outside of the book club and some of them will in turn skip it. But if the movie is viewed first, again, some members will avoid reading the book. If you have a conscientious group, these issues won't affect the occasional film, but if you have trouble with situational-illiterateeism, films might exacerbate the problems.

➤ **Importance.** Unless your reading group is designed to be a read-and-watch organism all the time, either the book or the movie may become the center of importance, which again begs the question: What's the point? If half the group doesn't care to comment on the movie, and the other half wants to skirt the text, the discussion is going to go absolutely nowhere and could demoralize the group rather quickly.

**Jane Err**

Although it might seem like a sound idea, don't ask everyone to watch the movie choice on his own. First off, not everyone will watch it (guaranteed), and the time and effort spent formulating the discussion questions will be all for naught. Second, the inverse is also true—it becomes an easy escape for those who want to skip reading the book. They'll focus on the movie without any repercussions. Lastly, it takes away the communal joy of watching and dissecting the movie together.

If you set a few ground rules, however, these situations can be resolved before they become a nuisance. Once you get into the habit of enjoying a night at the movies, coupled with the days at the novel, it can be a rewarding experience. You have nothing to fear.

**Pro's Prose**

"But I rather like it. This swift change of scene, this blending of emotion and experience—it is much better than the heavy, long-drawn-out kind of writing to which we are accustomed. It is closer to life. In life, too, changes and transitions flash by before our eyes, and emotions of the soul are like a hurricane. The cinema has divined the mystery of motion. And that is greatness."

—Excerpt from *A Conversation on Film with Leo Tolstoy*, reprinted in Roger Ebert's *Book of Film*

# Rules to Read (and Watch) By

If you want to watch a movie every now and again, it can be a simple, fun diversion, but if you want to get the most out of your reading/watching experience, you have to prepare your discussions in a way that analyzes both ends of the equation. It has to be more than the average, "I liked the book much better," because that nugget of wisdom has about as much originality as a *Rocky IV* novelization. The golden rule is still the central focus, but it gets a bit of tweaking in the reading/viewing club:

> *The time must be spent discussing the book.*

becomes

> *The time must be spent discussing the book and the merits of its adaptation.*

What this means is that a normal book discussion can take place, but when it comes to the movie, it should be analyzed in terms of how it relates to the novel upon which it is based. The adaptation is the key, and a debate about which choices the screenwriters and directors made that work (and don't) will be much more interesting than a rehashing of why the book is better. Try to navigate the murky waters through one of these periscopes.

## *Edward Scissorhands Snips Again*

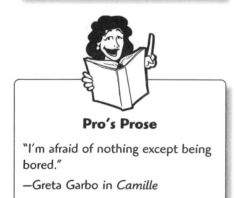

**Pro's Prose**

"I'm afraid of nothing except being bored."

—Greta Garbo in *Camille*

The greatest challenge to a screenwriter is, of course, what to keep and what to jettison. The toughest assignment is taking a novel like *L.A. Confidential*, which runs almost 500 pages, or *War and Peace*, which tips the scales at around 1,600 pages, and slicing it into a two- to three-hour screenplay that runs between 120 and 180 pages. Is it better to aim for the spirit of the book? Or to try and jam as much plot as possible into the script?

James Ellroy's *L.A. Confidential* is a great example of editing the text while keeping the essence of an author's prose. Screenwriter Brian Helgeland comes close to capturing the novel on its highest levels, but there is the argument that the various story lines are condensed too much. Which camp are you in? There is the flip side examination as well, as in a short story like Mary Orr's *The Wisdom of Eve,* which was adapted by Joseph L. Mankiewicz into *All About Eve.* Does the writer flesh out the story fairly, or is it just "adapted" for its premise? Questioning the merits of the adaptation can provide hours of unfiltered debate, especially when you can work in passages from the text that bolster your views of the movie. Find sections, characters, dialogue bits, etc., that worked very well (or failed miserably) in the movie to reinforce your stance on adaptation.

**Novel Ideas**

Try to spend at least the first half of your reading/viewing discussion focusing on the writing, both prose and screenplay. It takes practice to pay close attention to the nuances of the dialogue while watching the camera magic, but it is the screenplay that is the rewritten version of the novel.

## Who's That Girl?

If you're like most bibliophiles, there has been a character in a book that you fell in love with, only to see some other mutant creature inhabiting his or her name and lifestyle up on the big screen. Why is that? If the filmmakers choose a particular text for an adaptation, why change the way the characters live and breathe in their celluloid universe? It's an intriguing point to wrestle with, because oftentimes movie stars can't be anything but their movie star image, even if the attempts at faithfulness to the prose are sound.

A brilliant example is Audrey Hepburn's turn as Truman Capote's lonely, lovable heroine Holly Golightly in *Breakfast at Tiffany's.* Hepburn doesn't ignore the sad undertones of the novella, but her beauty and sparkling personality changed the very nature of what was being shown on the big screen. It is a relatively accurate adaptation (other than the weirdly insipid Asian Mickey Rooney). It is, however, generally misregarded as a warm romantic comedy, mainly because of movie fans' unabashed love of Audrey Hepburn and, to a lesser degree, George "I love it when a plan comes together" Peppard. Another example is Judy Garland's portrayal of Dorothy, which is the familiar image in our collective psyche. Try reading L. Frank Baum's *Wizard of Oz* and imagining your own version of Dorothy—not so easy, is it? But ask yourself: Does Judy Garland do Baum's character justice? You make the call.

## The End

One of Hollywood's favorite tricks is to change the spirit of an author's work, and often this involves rewriting the ending, usually to give it an upbeat bent. There isn't a whole lot to discuss in this arena; 99 times out of 100 the producers of the film just don't get it. What can be discussed, however, is why this practice has become so common. Find a movie that had the ending changed, say *The Natural,* and open up the discussion as to why they changed it. It might only be a discussion for one

**Novel Ideas**

One movie that exemplifies this is the infamous and vilified film adaptation of Jim Carroll's *The Basketball Diaries*. Ironically, the movie has a "just say no to drugs" type of ending in contrast to the ambiguity of the original text.

**Novel Ideas**

If you have an independent theater nearby, they are more likely to work out some kind of a group discount. You'll know they're independent if the newspaper ad doesn't have a corporate logo across the top. Other places to check are local revival houses, college campuses, or film societies. If this is impossible, weekday matinees are usually cheaper and less crowded, and some theaters offer senior and/or student discounts.

evening, but it is a worthy topic that might otherwise go ignored. Why do we insist on happy endings? Or, do we? When do filmmakers overstep their bounds? The debate could include other examples that may not have glaring omissions or commissions, but are clearly the filmmaker's vision and don't attempt to be faithful to the author. Whose property is it? If the members of the group don't see the novel in the same light, isn't the movie an extension of the variety of possible interpretations?

# There's No Place Like the Movie Haus, Either

Open up your newspaper and scan the local movie listings; odds are fairly high that there is an adaptation or two. From the latest military thriller from Tom Clancy to a Stephen King gore-fest to an Elizabethan character study, adaptations of novels constitute a major portion of movies that are released every year. Austen, Balzac, James, Nabokov, Conrad, Chekov—you name it, they have probably been turned to celluloid in the last few years, or they will be coming soon to a theater near you.

Kurt Vonnegut said that the reason there aren't as many young people trying to write the Great American Novel as there used to be is because they are all making movies. True or false, there has certainly been an upswing in literary adaptations over the last decade. If you have the means and can schedule it, take the reading group to see a movie on the silver screen. That is how movies were meant to be seen, and a postfilm, postread discussion over coffee and pie can make for a great afternoon or evening.

Getting out to the movies at least once a year comes highly recommended for two reasons. One is that book clubs enjoy the social, yet still intellectual, outing, and the other is that if the book is a challenging favorite, and the movie is equally stimulating, it is a pleasure that gets to be lived twice.

# Books for the Movie Fan in All of Us

We will get to titles that fall into the reading/ viewing milieu, but first let's look at three book titles *about* the movies. The following books truly show why we live on a globe of movie devotees, enamored since 1895 when the Lumière brothers sent that speeding train across the screen at the Grand Café in Paris.

**Pro's Prose**

"The fact *is* I am quite happy in a movie, even a bad movie. Other people, so I have read, treasure memorable moments in their lives ... What I remember is the time John Wayne killed three men with a carbine as he was falling to the dusty street in *Stagecoach,* and the time the kitten found Orson Welles in the doorway in *The Third Man* ..."

—Excerpt from *The Moviegoer,* by Walker Percy

1. *The Moviegoer,* **by Walker Percy.** This is the story of Binx Bolling, a spiritually deprived New Orleans stockbroker who spends his days in tawdry affairs with secretaries or at the movies, which deliver the "treasurable moments" his real life is missing. The big screen offers excitement and adventure, both of which are lacking in his mundane universe. Binx finds that the movies provide a greater sense of reality, which is, of course, impossible. It's just celluloid, right?

   Percy's novel is a challenging existential novel from the get-go, asking is "real life" any more real than life in the movies? Binx decides one Mardi Gras to find what is out there, and his joyously wry journey takes him through the chaos of the French Quarter. It is a novel about taking irrational risks, of the mind and spirit as well as the body. With the proliferation of children and adults whose existence and memories are wrapped up in the movies, television, and the Internet, it is a timely tome that will open up all sorts of topical discussions. Can anyone find meaning in the universe? Or do the movies suffice for the average Joe?

2. *The Player,* **by Michael Tolkin.** If there is one thing we can all agree on in this country it is that Hollywood is the sleaze, sex, and sin capital of the world and that those in the film industry are a step below the Mafia in terms of a collective moral compass. All right, so the illicit visions we have of La-La-Land are a vast exaggeration, but it's fun to believe the Wild-Wild-West ethos of "anything goes to get what you want" still reigns supreme in Tinsel Town. Tolkin's novel is the story of an executive, Griffin Mill, a rich, ruthless studio exec who ends up murdering a screenwriter after his paranoia leads him to believe the writer has it in for him.

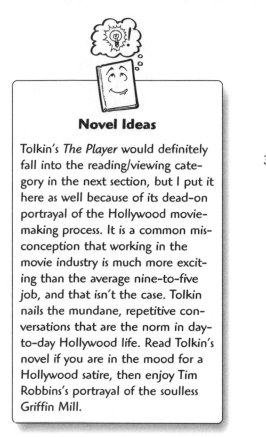

**Novel Ideas**

Tolkin's *The Player* would definitely fall into the reading/viewing category in the next section, but I put it here as well because of its dead-on portrayal of the Hollywood movie-making process. It is a common misconception that working in the movie industry is much more exciting than the average nine-to-five job, and that isn't the case. Tolkin nails the mundane, repetitive conversations that are the norm in day-to-day Hollywood life. Read Tolkin's novel if you are in the mood for a Hollywood satire, then enjoy Tim Robbins's portrayal of the soulless Griffin Mill.

This book is a scathing dark comedy with the banal dialogue that rings out through studio hallways across the Southland. It was written by an insider, and if your group has any interest in the ridiculous inner-workings of the studio system, wrapped around a murder mystery, this is the book for you. This is a novel for "people who hate the movies we make."

3. ***Roger Ebert's Book of Film,* edited by Roger Ebert.** Chicago's rotund film critic has been in the forefront of America's cinema culture for a long time; he and his late partner Gene Siskel made the phrase "two thumbs up" a staple of movie marketing and promotion. This lengthy hodgepodge of writing about various facets of the movie world is a film fan's dream. It isn't a book club type book per se, but if your reading group wants to make reading/viewing the focal point, it is a great place to start. It includes sections on directors, technique, sex and scandal, early days, and going to the movies. Some of the essays are striking. For instance, Tolstoy's grasp of what movies are going to mean to the future is eerily accurate. There are also famous writings from heavyweights like John Updike's ode to Doris Day, "Suzie Creamcheese Speaks,"

and Gore Vidal's critique of the so-called auteur theory of filmmaking, "Who Makes the Movies?" The book also includes such diverse writers as Pauline Kael, Charlie Chaplin, F. Scott Fitzgerald, David Mamet, H. L. Mencken, and Preston Sturges.

**Bibio-Trivio**

The *auteur* theory is a French term that means the director is the primary creative force, i.e., author of a film.

Ebert's book was written by a man who loves movies and wants other people to love movies equally. Perhaps you want to form a reading group devoted to the study of literature in film and examine the long history of the adaptation. If so, this book is a great jumping-off point, because of the variety of historical analysis, expert opinion, criticism, praise, fiction, dissection, and simple remembrances of movies that have touched the viewing public on a personal level. It would take some judicious pruning to pick X number of essays for a night of discussion, but it could be a lot of fun to debate the experts' views on the role of motion pictures in our lives. If nothing else, *Roger Ebert's Book of Film* is one that any movie lover will revere.

**Pro's Prose**

"He was only thirty-three. I learned a long time ago that life wasn't always fair. But it shouldn't cheat that much."

—Excerpt from *My Belushi Pals* (March 7, 1982), by Mike Royko, reprinted in *Roger Ebert's Book of Film*

What follows is a list of some more books about the movies and movie-making folks that your book group might enjoy:

➤ *Hollywood,* by Charles Bukowski

➤ *The Comedy Writer,* by Peter Farrelly

➤ *The Day of the Locust,* by Nathanael West

➤ *The Studio* and *Monster,* both by John Gregory Dunne

➤ *The Last Picture Show,* by Larry McMurtry

➤ *What Makes Sammy Run?* by Budd Schulberg

➤ *Adventures in the Screen Trade,* by William Goldman

➤ *The Picture,* by Lillian Ross

➤ *Easy Riders, Raging Bulls: How the Sex-Drugs-And-Rock-'N'-Roll Generation Saved Hollywood,* by Peter Biskind

➤ *The Last Tycoon,* by F. Scott Fitzgerald

➤ *Spike Mike Slackers and Dykes,* by John Pierson

# Viewing/Reading Lists

Perhaps stories of Hollywood, or about the movies in general, aren't your ball of string, but your reading group is interested in cinematic adaptations of literary favorites for their own sake. Fair enough. Don't forget, it's a natural impulse to want to see the movie version of a book that was just completed, so unless you absolutely loathe the cinema (which would put you in the .0000000001 percent of

### Novel Ideas

If your reading group is watching a movie at home, serve popcorn in bags. Nothing says flicks like corn in a bag with lots of butter.

the population), don't feel guilty for making it either a common practice or an occasional treat. Just make sure that the discussion is about the strengths/weaknesses of the adaptation and not a movie review.

## Let's All Go to the Movies

The following seven selections are worthy of an examination by your reading group. Try to take the time to figure out why the director and screenwriter chose to adapt the book in the fashion they did. Also, keep in mind the following question: Why are some adaptations so successful and some totally miss the point?

1. *Great Expectations,* **by Charles Dickens.** Dickens has long been a favorite of filmmakers, in no small part to his tightly constructed plots. There is even a common literary theory that prognosticates that Dickens would be a screenwriter were he alive today because of his vivid style. Whether or not you think this hypothesis holds water, he has been adapted to film more than 80 times. In David Lean's 1946 version of *Great Expectations,* the lonely young Pip is well acted and doesn't whitewash the brooding, ominous undercurrents of the novel.

### Biblio-Trivio

Look for a young Alec Guinness, Mr. Obi Wan Kenobi himself, playing Herbert Pocket in David Lean's *Great Expectations.* Magwitch might have been a bit more congenial staring down the green end of a Jedi light saber.

If you like Dickens (and who in his right mind doesn't?), Lean's 1946 cinematic take on this classic novel is regarded by many as one of the best films ever made. It maintains a distinct British feel. The opening graveyard sequence is filmic gold.

2. *The Magnificent Ambersons,* **by Booth Tarkington.** Both the book and the movie have received high praise, but Orson Welles's film has become the one best known to the national audience. If you haven't read the story of the three generations of a Midwestern American aristocracy's fall from grace, it might be

time to rediscover this somewhat forgotten classic. It chronicles a family's battle to maintain their social standing against changing economic times. It is an underappreciated work that shows the "good old days" might not have been as good as nostalgia would make us believe. It is also a solid adaptation, although the movie-going audience can only dream of what might have been.

### Biblio-Trivio

RKO took the film out of Welles's hands and recut it with additional shots, dialogue, and an upbeat ending. They edited nearly 45 minutes of film from 131 minutes down to 88 without Welles's consent, and the original surviving footage was destroyed. It still made the highly respected *Sight and Sound* once-a-decade list of the "Greatest Films of All Time" on more than one occasion, but cineasts dream of the chance to see the movie that never was.

Welles's genius is renowned (it reportedly took him nine days to write the screenplay), but Tarkington's is equally impressive, and he never had to watch a publishing house destroy his vision. Question: What exactly is magnificent about the Ambersons?

3. ***The Godfather*, by Mario Puzo.** If you ask the average person (past the age of 18) on the street what the greatest movie ever made is, Francis Coppola's classic will be the answer that most often rolls off his or her tongue without a moment's thought. The organized crime saga is a beautifully crafted family tale of blood and loyalty inside the Mafia vacuum. There are so many famous scenes, passages, and characters that it is hard to choose a single moment of brilliance that captures all the levels of the film, but the baptism massacre comes awfully close. A sacred Catholic ritual provides an airtight alibi for ruthless murder, which is the twisted sense of propriety and family that runs through the Corleone blood.

The interesting thing about the Mario Puzo novel is that many film scholars think the screenplay is far superior. There is a standard axiom that great books don't make great movies because the best literature is multilayered, internal, and based in the ethereal meaning of humanity, whereas popular fiction is driven by a thrilling narrative. Leonard Maltin calls *The Godfather* "pulp fiction raised to the highest level," which is by no means an insult. If your group

**Pro's Prose**

"This book is to be neither an accusation nor a confession, and least of all an adventure, for death is not an adventure to those who stand face to face with it. It will try simply to tell of a generation of men who, even though they may have escaped its shells, were destroyed by the war."

—Prologue, *All Quiet on the Western Front,* by Erich Maria Remarque

**Pro's Prose**

"I must be crazy to be in a looney bin like this."

—Jack Nicholson as Randle McMurphy in *One Flew Over the Cuckoo's Nest*

decides to take on both the film and page-turning versions of *The Godfather,* ask yourselves the following: It is a masterpiece on film, but is it also a masterpiece on the page? It is a crime novel, but is Puzo's book in the same league with Dostoyevsky's *Crime and Punishment?* Can the movie be better than the book?

4. ***All Quiet on the Western Front,* by Erich Maria Remarque.** The first great antiwar novel of the twentieth century is still a powerful work with the 1930 movie adaptation that holds up equally. It is the story of a group of German soldiers in the last chaotic days of the original "Great War," World War I. Remarque had been a German soldier, and the intense hell he describes is an authentic record of the atrocities from a conflict that has taken a backseat to the Second World War and Vietnam War. The adaptation plays it fairly close to the vest, which is the right decision with Remarque's harrowing prose.

Both the film and the novel are stark reminders that there are no "heroic" war stories, only the stories of men trying to stay alive amid bloody carnage. It seems in these salad days that there has been an upswing in life-affirming war yarns, so this might be the right time to visit these bleak battlefields. Films and novels that claim to be antiwar should never be placating, and the final scenes of *All Quiet on the Western Front* are haunting and disturbing, not pacifying. Ask your group whether the visual imagery of the movie depiction of war is more or less harrowing than the image created in their own heads.

5. ***One Flew Over the Cuckoo's Nest,* by Ken Kesey.** This story of rebellious Randle Patrick McMurphy and his stay in a mental institution has become one of the flashpoint novels of the 1960s and one of the films from Hollywood's last "golden age" in the 1970s. It is a story of man-against-man, man-against-the-system, man-against-society, and man-against-himself. The casting of the angry youth Jack Nicholson was about as close to Kesey's character as humanly possible.

One book club exercise that can be done with *One Flew Over the Cuckoo's Nest* is to compare and contrast the book with the second adaptation of it, the stage play starring Kirk Douglas that ran on Broadway for more than 10 years, before Milos Forman's film. Dale Wasserman adapted it for the stage. It is an interesting way to look at the evolution from the inner-narrative of prose to the dialogue of stage, to the imagery of film.

6. *Last Exit to Brooklyn,* **by Hubert Selby Jr.** Selby is one of America's best unheralded authors, a true original whose stories of urban grit don't fit into any Disneyfied version of America. He writes in a jagged stream-of-consciousness style using freestyle paragraph breaks, punctuation, and spelling. His books are an edification in pain—these are people who know only sadness. Selby never robs his downtrodden characters of their humanity, even if their instincts are to rob themselves.

**Novel Ideas**

Compare the narrator's voice in the novel and in the film version of *One Flew Over the Cuckoos Nest*. There is a distinct difference, and it is one of the restructured parts of the screenplay. Is there a palpable difference in your reactions to the film as opposed to the book? Could the narrator of the book be the narrator of the movie? Is this the way an adaptation should be, rewritten for the screen with the soul of the novel? Or, does the novel's narrator have a different story to tell?

The film version doesn't water down the human suffering or despair. It is tough and unrelenting in its depiction of Selby's raw universe. Some of the members of your book club might abhor it, some may think it's genius. The trick in your discussions is to find out why. It's interesting that Selby's book takes place in the 1950s, which was the last time of American coasting on an ocean of prosperity and peace. Ask yourselves if the environment for Selby's story could just as easily be taking place today.

7. *Short Cuts* **(based on stories and a poem by Raymond Carver).** Another cast of unsavory characters, but in this weirdly human (at its best it feels like watching life) tapestry of a movie, they aren't all desperate or depressed. They are just—human. The master of minimalism, Raymond Carver, is shifted to Los Angeles by Robert Altman in a three-hour look at the way humans cross each other's paths, for good, bad, and indifference. It is a hard movie to categorize, just as Carver's fiction doesn't fit into conventional descriptive parameters. Altman has thrown the accidental encounters, near misses, and general messiness of everyday life into a pot and seasoned it with the disconnected characters Carver pulled from the shadows.

### Biblio-Trivio

Hubert Selby Jr. has a major cult following, and in 1989 he went on a spoken word tour in Europe with Henry Rollins, which was recorded on a live album. His latest album is *Blue Eyes and Exit Wounds* with acclaimed poet/writer Nick Tosches. Selby's novel *Requiem for a Dream* is being made into a movie by director Darren Aronofsky. Selby makes a cameo as a cab driver in the film version of *Last Exit to Brooklyn*.

### Pro's Prose

"Bill and Arlene Miller were a happy couple. But now and then they felt they alone among their circle had been passed by somehow, leaving Bill to attend to his book-keeping duties and Arlene occupied with secretarial chores. They talked about it sometimes, mostly in comparison with the lives of their neighbors, Harriet and Jim Stone. It seemed to the Millers that the Stones lived a fuller and brighter life."

—Excerpt from "Neighbors," by Raymond Carver, one of the stories in *Short Cuts*

This is a great film for a discussion of whether or not it works as an adaptation, because many critics felt that Altman's characters are too rootless and harbor less hope than Carver ever intended. Others felt Altman hit the nail on the head. Either way, the stories are incredible, the acting and directing is first-rate, and both celluloid and source material will provide for hours of dissection. And what could be better than that?

Now, if those weren't enough to get you started, I've listed some more great books that have been translated to the big screen—it's up to you to decide how well, though.

➤ *For Whom the Bell Tolls* (1943), by Ernest Hemingway

➤ "The Man Who Shot Liberty Valance," a short story by Dorothy M. Johnson

➤ *A River Runs Through It,* by Norman Maclean

➤ *2001: A Space Odyssey,* by Arthur C. Clarke

➤ *A Simple Plan,* by Scott B. Smith

➤ *The Shop Around the Corner* (adapted from the play *Parfumerie,* by Nikolaus Laszlo)

➤ *Paths of Glory,* by Humphrey Cobb

➤ *The Butcher Boy* (1997), by Patrick McCabe

➤ *The Big Sleep,* by Raymond Chandler

➤ *Sophie's Choice,* by William Styron

➤ "The Lady Eve," a short story by Monckton Hoffe

➤ *Rope,* by Patrick Hamilton

➤ *Frankenstein* (1931), by Mary Wollstonecraft Shelley

➤ *The Sweet Smell of Success,* a novella by Ernest Lehman

➤ *The Grifters,* by Jim Thompson

➤ *Gone With the Wind,* by Margaret Mitchell

➤ *Smoke Signals* (adapted in part from stories in *The Lone Ranger and Tonto Fistfight in Heaven,* by Sherman Alexie)

➤ *Devil in a Blue Dress,* by Walter Mosley

➤ *East of Eden* (1955), by John Steinbeck

➤ *Leaving Las Vegas,* by John O'Brien

➤ "Rashomon," a short story by Ryunosuke Akutagawa

➤ *Wise Blood,* by Flannery O'Connor

➤ *The Age of Innocence* (1934 and 1993, both worthy), by Edith Wharton

➤ *Once Upon a Time When We Were Colored,* by Clifton L. Taulbert

➤ *Detour* (1945), by Martin Goldsmith

➤ *Naked Lunch,* by William S. Burroughs

---

### The Least You Need to Know

➤ Reading/viewing nights can add a breath of fresh air to your book club.

➤ The key is to discuss the film in terms of its merits as an adaptation.

➤ Pay close attention to the filmmakers' attempts to capture the author's voice, tone, characterization, and dialogue.

➤ Many small books become great movies—seek them out with the help of a knowledgeable film buff.

# Chapter 21

# The Play's the Thing

---

## In This Chapter

➤ Enjoying literature with legs

➤ Seven suggestions to see a show sans a slew of scratch

➤ This land is your land, young theater lover

➤ Why is Biff crying again?

➤ Bill knows personality

---

Many reading groups take the time to watch and analyze films along with their book selection, but the glory of the theater is often overlooked as an equally rewarding reading/viewing experience. This is unfortunate, as a live play is exciting and, much like a reading group, a living, breathing organism with a life all its own. The other great benefit to plays is that not only can they be read, as you would any other form of literature, they can be performed aloud by you and your fellow members—and your living room can be turned into a mini Globe Theater.

Selecting the occasional play as an alternative to a novel will give your reading group a literary experience of a different kind. In this chapter, we'll take a look at how plays can spice up your book club—after all, all the world's a stage, isn't it?

# Literature with Legs

Plays are the happy medium between the internal bliss of an exciting novel and the communal gratification of a thrilling adaptation on the big screen. They are also a whole lot more. They are literature with legs.

At your next book club gathering, take the following survey:

> ➤ All those who have seen a professional production in the last six months stand up.

All of your fellow book clubians will most likely oblige, so add this addendum:

> ➤ All those who have seen a professional production in the last six months that doesn't include singing mammals, isn't based on a Hollywood movie with dancing teenagers, features no aged 1970s sitcom stars, doesn't have the names Lloyd or Webber in its playbill, has long stretches of actors actually talking about their lives, is based on a work you could theoretically buy and read for yourself, and at no point includes any big rousing number complete with fireworks, prancing kitchen utensils, or crooning chimney sweeps.

Are you still standing?

### Biblio-Trivio

During the warm months in the Elizabethan theaters, the open-air structures featured a stage that jutted out into a pit, which was a standing-room-only area for the lower-class visitors. The upper-class boxes were situated in three galleries around the theater. Sounds more like the bleachers as opposed to luxury boxes at Camden Yards. Unfortunately, the same crowds don't take in the Bard and the ballpark very often these days.

At some point, honest-to-goodness drama became a thing for academics, bluebloods, and devotees, but it has been a long time since the average American took in a couple of productions a year. It's too bad, because the legitimate theater makes perfect sense to go along with a reading group. One of the main reasons folks join book clubs is so they can be part of a social, yet intellectual, group of people that get together once a month and do something completely out of the ordinary. What is more stimulating than a well-written play with feisty actors and an attentive audience?

# Why Not Godot See a Production?

The main reason people say they don't go see plays is the cost. It is a legitimate concern. There are, however, a few ways to bring down the cost of attending the best local theater in your area.

1. **Group discounts.** Ideally, theaters want to sell the seats before the show opens; that way they are ensured of a full-length run. If it's a small, local theater, call the producer of the production. If it's a large play, try the theater manager, because if it isn't a hugely expensive production (and most standard plays aren't), they might be able to give your book club a fair price.

2. **Offer repeat business.** If you know that your book club is interested in making this a regular habit, get a hold of the upcoming season's schedule and work out a long-term deal. If you can guarantee a crowd of 12 three or four times over the course of a year, the odds are fairly good that a discount will be available.

3. **Same-day tickets.** This can be much tougher, but if you have a relatively small group with good planning ability, it is often possible to get reduced "rush" tickets the day of the show based on performances availability. Keep abreast of the box office, especially if it is a long-running production or it's near the end of the run. If the houses are only half-full, why not try for the cheap seats?

   The problem with this is, of course, that quality productions with limited runs are often sold out and it will be very tough to get a bunch of tickets. Day-of-the show tickets are normally sold only one or two at a time.

4. **Preview performances.** Previews are a great way to see top-shelf plays for bottom-shelf prices. Usually there are performances within the two or three weeks before the actual opening that can be had for much less. It's more than a dress rehearsal, because the director rarely stops the show. Sometimes actors don't have a total feel for the material yet, but if your reading group isn't too accustomed to regular theater trips, it probably will go unnoticed. Try to get a preview as close as possible to opening night, but keep in mind that lots of theater-lovers with less cold cash take advantage of the preview option.

5. **College productions.** The local colleges in your area have theater departments that produce a number of plays over the course of a semester. The drawback is that many of the students are probably not career actors and will not have the same abilities as a seasoned professional to interpret the material. The benefits are that the productions are usually

**Novel Ideas**

Keep track of the weather. Anytime there's a blizzard, major thunderstorm, tornado warning, freezing temperature, etc., the crowds get smaller. If your book club is made up of spontaneous, spur-of-the-moment types with heavy rain-resistant coats, it is often the best chance to get reduced-price, same-day seating.

very cheap, often a few bucks or even free, and there may be a standout who will go on to bigger and better things and you can say you saw him when.

6. **Smaller theaters.** If your reading group is near a large city, there are smaller 99-seat theaters that put up productions for the love of the work, and tickets are almost always under $20. People work in these venues to hone their writing, acting, or directing skills, and their love of the craft is readily apparent. It is just a matter of poking around: checking local newspapers, calling theater departments or stopping by to look at the walls of flyers, stopping at artists' hangouts like coffee shops, indie bookstores, and so on. You won't find these theaters in metropolitan areas only—lots of small towns and tucked-away villages love the communal sense of theater, whether it's a local year-round theater group or a summer stock theater.

### Biblio-Trivio

Summer stock began primarily because indoor theaters didn't have air conditioning and would often shut down in the humid summers. Actors would form companies in the regions where folks spent their summers and put on plays. It was a standard tradition in the summer evenings, and many famous thespians like Paul Newman started off that way before air conditioning filled the movie houses.

7. **Discount tickets.** Larger cities often have outlets that sell cut-rate tickets for same-day performances. In New York City, for example, TKTS locations in Times Square and the World Trade Center (the latter has much smaller crowds) sell for all of Broadway. Also, Hit Show Club Vouchers, 630 Ninth Avenue at 44th Street, 8th Floor, offers vouchers for up to 50 percent off. Chicago has a similar booth, and other cities have their own programs. Sometimes certain shows discount weeknights or matinees, or offer senior or student savings. Small theaters have their own deals as well, it is just a matter of getting lucky.

# Great Theaters Around the Country

America has a cornucopia of good theaters, and your book club should try to take in a production if you get the chance. Seasons are posted months ahead of time, so all you have to do is align the elements: title, cost, date, and transportation.

Following are some of the best theaters and companies.

**Eastern time zone:**

➤ Coconut Grove Playhouse, 3500 Main Highway, Miami, FL 33133; 305-442-2662

➤ Pittsburgh Public Theater, 6 Allegheny Square, Pittsburgh, PA 15212; 412-323-8200

➤ Actors Theatre of Louisville, 316 W. Main Street, Louisville, KY 40205; 502-584-1265

➤ Woolly Mammoth Theater, 1401 Church Street NW, Washington, DC 20005; 202-234-6130

**Central time zone:**

➤ The Guthrie Theatre, 725 Vineland Place, Minneapolis, MN 55403; 612-347-1100

➤ Arkansas Repertory Theatre, P.O. Box 110, 601 Main Street, Little Rock, AR 72203-0110; 501-378-0405

➤ Steppenwolf Theatre Company, 1650 N. Halsted, Chicago, IL 60614; 312-335-1888

➤ Dallas Children's Theater, 2215 Cedar Springs, Dallas, TX 75201; 214-978-0110

**Novel Ideas**

If your book club finds itself in Washington, D.C., you might also want to see what production is taking place at historic Ford's Theater at 511 Tenth Street. Close your eyes, and with a little imagination, you can take yourself back to the infamous night of April 14, 1865.

**Biblio-Trivio**

Steppenwolf is the outstanding Chicago theater company founded on a commitment to the principles of ensemble collaboration and artistic risk. The ensemble members include such stalwarts as Joan Allen, John Malkovich, Laurie Metcalf, and cofounder Gary Sinise.

**Mountain time zone:**

➤ Denver Center Theater Company, 1050 13th Street, Denver, CO 80210; 303-893-4000

➤ American Living History Theatre, P.O. Box 752, Greybull, WY 82426

➤ Arizona Theatre Company, P.O. Box 1631, Tucson, AZ 85702-1631; 520-884-8210

➤ Billings Studio Theater, 1500 Rimrock Road, Billings, MT 59102; 406-248-1141

**Western time zone:**

➤ American Conservatory Theater (A.C.T.), 30 Grant Avenue, 6th Floor, San Francisco, CA 94108; 415-439-2469

➤ Intiman Theatre Company, 201 Mercer Street, Seattle, WA 98109; 206-269-1901

➤ Oregon Shakespeare Festival, P.O. Box 158, Ashland, OR 97520; 541-482-2111

➤ The Victory Theater, 3326 West Victory Boulevard, Burbank, CA 91505; 818-843-9253

**Biblio-Trivio**

Since its founding in 1965, A.C.T. has staged more than 200 productions and performed to over six million people throughout the United States, Japan, and Russia. A.C.T. also has an actors' training program, and former students include Denzel Washington, Annette Bening, and Winona Ryder.

# Drama Queens (and Kings)

Another great way to enjoy theater is to act it out right there in the den. That's right, break out the footlights (flashlights will do), stage blood, prop swords, commedia dell'arte masks, Kabuki makeup, or whatever it takes to turn your living room into a living theater.

This might sound like a corny idea, but plays are written to be read aloud. Even if it's simply assigning parts to various members, it will still bring the play to life in a much more visceral way than a discussion.

The only thing your reading group members have to remember is that they need to have read the play before the meeting. You will be more likely to read certain scenes or monologues because it would take up too much time to read the entire work. I highly recommend getting volunteers to act out certain poignant moments in the drama, though, because it is fun and it gives the heightened language of the theater context. It doesn't have to be anything elaborate, and it could be prepared in a couple of hours. Think of it as the research that would normally be done if you were presenting a novel. It isn't about the acting; it's about understanding the text in its naturally implied state.

## Always Go with the Favored Heavyweights

The following two plays aren't going to blaze any new trails, but it is quite possible that the members of your reading group haven't read these twentieth-century classics aloud, so the beauty and complexity of the language and ideas has never been experienced to the fullest. Assigning characters to members of your reading group will give everyone a chance to inhabit the role and try to understand the author's intentions and the deeper meanings that are sometimes lost on the page.

**Jane Err**

Don't bypass Ashland, Oregon, if you love the theater. The Oregon Shakespeare Festival runs most of the year (February through October in 1999), and the performances are plentiful and usually riveting. There are both Shakespeare and contemporary productions and the community loves its theatrical niche. The whole town gets behind the festival, and it is well worth the trip.

**Novel Ideas**

Try acting out important scenes or passages from great plays, and then discussing them individually; it is the best of both worlds.

Living room performances aren't going to take place very often, but great dramatic works are certainly literary and shouldn't be overlooked simply because of their format. Since staged readings are most likely going to be a rare occurrence, I suggest one of these two heavyweight dramas.

### Biblio-Trivio

The word *drama* comes from a Greek word meaning "to do," "ideas of action."
So, in the words of the famous Greek God of Swoosh, "Just Do It."

### Pro's Prose

"I'm one dollar an hour, Willy! I tried seven states and couldn't raise it. A buck an hour, do you gather my meaning? I am not a leader of men, Willy, and neither are you; you were never anything but a hard working drummer who landed in the ashcan like all the rest of them! I'm not bringing home any prizes any more and you're going to stop waiting for me to bring them home!"

—Biff Loman in *Death of a Salesman,* by Arthur Miller

Enjoy trodding the boards and reading the words.

1. *Death of a Salesman,* **by Arthur Miller.** This masterpiece is one of the most important works of the last hundred years. It is the story of a salesman, Willy Loman, and it created a new standard for tragic tales of average folks. Willy refuses to see the forest for the trees and his family life is in shambles and his career isn't as important as he fools himself into believing it is. It is a tragedy of the common man, poetic and moving, and Miller's depiction of the family is brilliant. Willy's son Biff's recognition of his own failure is sad, poignant, and heart-wrenching.

   One interesting thing to consider while enjoying the story of Willy Loman, is that it is generally recognized for its realistic portrayal of a flawed everyman, but Miller used expressionism to delve into Willy's memory. Miller changed standard theatrical constructs and allowed his characters to slip in and out of Willy's mind. Take time to discuss how memory works within novels, and compare it to Miller's usage and how it relates to your own sense of memory.

2. *Waiting for Godot,* **by Samuel Beckett.** Originally written in French, this classic play had its world premiere on January 5, 1953, in the small Left Bank Theatre de Babylone in Paris. It slowly built momentum, and it is now regarded as one of the standard-bearers of the stage. It is a play that falls into the category of what British scholar Martin Esslin labeled the "theater of the absurd" in 1961. It is a style of theater that ignored basic dramatic conventions, and threw

standard logic, characterization, plotting, language, and structure out the window. This is the story of two tramps, Vladimir and Estragon, who are waiting by a tree on a country road for a character named Godot to show up. They don't know who he is, what he wants to see them for, or if he even exists in the first place. The plot is slim, because Beckett wants to examine metaphysical questions of the nature of human existence.

Beckett's play can be tricky because its themes are layered deeply in the work and need to be extracted, but they are complex and could open unique lines of discussion. Don't we all at various times wait for things to happen while in the meantime life passes right on by? What is it that we're waiting for in the first place?

### Pro's Prose

"Let us not waste time in idle discourse! Let us do something, while we have the chance! It is not every day that we are needed. Not indeed that we personally are needed. Others would meet the case equally well, if not better. To all mankind they were addressed, those cries for help still ringing in our ears! But at this place, at this moment in time, all mankind is us, whether we like it or not. Let us make the most of it, before it is too late!"

—Vladimir in *Waiting for Godot,* by Samuel Beckett

## Bill, Bill, Bill, and More Bill

There has been a Shakespeare renaissance at the movies over the last 10 years, but his work is still best viewed/read/performed on the stage. The Bard's influence on Western culture cannot be overestimated. In his latest tome, *Shakespeare: The Invention of the Human,* literary critic/Bard authority Harold Bloom states, "personality, in our sense, is a Shakespearean invention." His colossal book basically promotes the idea that human personality was created through the depth, self-creation, and interior lives in Shakespeare's works. Shakespeare was the first to examine what it is to be human, and thus he invented personality, which has a fundamental tenant of existence since he penned his plays 400-odd years ago. Whether or not you agree with Bloom's central thesis (and you have to read the book to formulate an opinion), it certainly goes a long way to explaining why Shakespeare has remained the world's greatest and most popular playwright.

One great way to enjoy Shakespeare is to read one of his plays at home, perform it aloud (as much of it as you have time for, that is) at a reading group discussion, and see the play live at a local theater. This will give each member of your group the chance to really dig into the material, which can be tough to understand with the King's English and all. Find copies of the play with footnoted definitions and explanations (I suggest the Signet Classic series). The following two Shakespearean plays are the ones most often mentioned by reading groups, so they obviously must be much ado about something.

### Jane Err

Don't overlook the original play-wrights like Sophocles, Aeschylus, Euripides, and Aristophanes; all modern plays flow from their work. Anyone seriously interested in examining drama should have a copy of Aristotle's *Poetics* on his or her body at all times. It is the most fundamental study of drama ever written, and it has influenced all dramatic works of the last 2,000 years.

### Novel Ideas

If you want to see a beautiful film with amazing images, try to catch Kenneth Branagh's 1996 *Hamlet,* shot in brilliant 70mm (and is best on the big screen). If you want to see great acting and Shakespeare performed at its finest, watch Laurence Olivier's 1948 masterpiece of *Hamlet.*

➤ *Hamlet,* **by William Shakespeare.** The most popular Great Dane this side of Marmaduke, this brilliant tragedy is one of the most important works ever penned, period. It is the story of the Danish Prince Hamlet, who is told by the ghost of his father that his death was no accident. The father says he was poisoned by Hamlet's uncle, his brother Claudius, who is now the King. Hamlet swears revenge on Claudius and vows to avenge his father's death. He decides to fake madness until the proper time arises to murder Claudius. This is one of the central questions of debate from scholars to schoolchildren: Did Hamlet go insane in the membrane, or was it just an Oscar-worthy performance?

As in all great tragedies, everyone ends up in a pine box. Claudius, Hamlet, his mother, Gertrude, his girlfriend, Ophelia—you name 'em, they're dead. The language Shakespeare uses is harrowing at times, touching at others. So many of the words throughout his works have become part of everyday vernacular, like "good night, sweet prince," and "to be or not to be." The impact of Shakespeare on writing throughout the ages is always a worthy subject. Ask yourselves: Is he the most important single author in history? It would also be fun to find a modern-day tragedy of family violence and death (*Affliction,* perhaps?) and compare how the stories are similar and different. *Hamlet* could even be used for a discussion of your own family history, but hopefully the sibling rifts and rivalries never lead to literal skeletons in the closet like Hamlet's did.

➤ *Romeo and Juliet,* **by William Shakespeare.** One thing to consider right off the bat: Is this the "greatest love story ever told," as it is often called? Like *Hamlet,* it is a tragedy, but it is also a story rooted in love, not revenge. Is it a tragedy in the same way as *Hamlet?* Is it sadder to die at a young age having known true love? Or is Hamlet's cruel fate the deeper curse?

By now, most people are familiar with the story of the star-crossed lovers, Romeo the Montague and Juliet the Capulet, members of rival families in Verona. Romeo sneaks into a Capulet party and falls in love at first sight of the fair maiden Juliet. They meet that night and exchange some of the most flowery, yet beautiful, language ever uttered by gaga teenagers.

Since this is a tragedy, the relationship doesn't turn out as well as planned. Romeo mistakenly believes Juliet is dead, so he commits suicide in her tomb. She was only asleep, trying to fool her parents so she can run away with her one true love. Upon awakening, she finds Romeo, and decides to join him in the afterlife by stabbing herself with his dagger. All isn't really well that ended well, but it sparks the question: How far would you go to prove your love to another? Is it better to have loved and lost (even for a couple of days) than to have never loved before? Or does a dagger in the heart supersede the mushy stuff?

**Pro's Prose**

"For murder, though it have no tongue, will speak
With most miraculous organ. I'll have these players
Play something like the murder of my father
Before mine uncle: I'll observe his looks;
I'll tent him to the quick: if he but blench,
I know my course. The spirit that I have seen
May be the devil; and the devil hath power
To assume a pleasing shape ..."

—Hamlet in *Hamlet,* by William Shakespeare

## Book Club Kinda Plays

Whatever play your reading group chooses, I can't emphasize enough how much more you will get out of it if scenes are performed. It is a change of pace and there may be a master thespian among the book club. Great plays are as rich and textured as great novels, and they can foster a sense of community when everybody works together to bring them to life.

➤ *A Streetcar Named Desire,* by Tennessee Williams

➤ *Patient A,* by Lee Blessing

➤ *Medea,* by Euripides

➤ *Desire Under the Elms,* by Eugene O'Neill

➤ *Agamemnon,* by Aeschylus

➤ *A Raisin in the Sun,* by Lorraine Hansberry

➤ *The Miser,* by Molière

**Novel Ideas**

If your group really enjoys analyzing plays, try to find an academic book called *Backwards and Forwards: A Technical Manual for Reading Plays,* by David Ball. It is a practical, informative work that is short (96 pages), but very helpful in showing how to look at plays. Ball uses *Hamlet* as his main illustration.

**311**

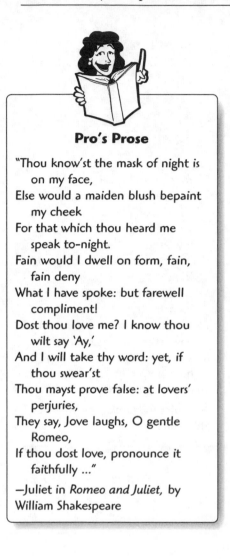

**Pro's Prose**

"Thou know'st the mask of night is on my face,
Else would a maiden blush bepaint my cheek
For that which thou heard me speak to-night.
Fain would I dwell on form, fain, fain deny
What I have spoke: but farewell compliment!
Dost thou love me? I know thou wilt say 'Ay,'
And I will take thy word: yet, if thou swear'st
Thou mayst prove false: at lovers' perjuries,
They say, Jove laughs, O gentle Romeo,
If thou dost love, pronounce it faithfully ..."

—Juliet in *Romeo and Juliet,* by William Shakespeare

➤ *The Chairs,* by Eugene Ionesco
➤ *Blood Wedding,* by Federico García Lorca
➤ *Three Sisters,* by Anton Chekov
➤ *Glengarry Glen Ross,* by David Mamet
➤ *A Doll's House,* by Henrik Ibsen
➤ *King Lear,* by William Shakespeare
➤ *All My Sons,* by Arthur Miller
➤ *One for the Road,* by Harold Pinter
➤ *The Piano Lesson,* by August Wilson
➤ *A Midsummer Night's Dream,* by William Shakespeare
➤ *Cyrano de Bergerac,* by Edmond Rostand
➤ *The Miss Firecracker Contest,* by Beth Henley
➤ *Suburbia,* by Eric Bogosian
➤ *The Real Thing,* by Tom Stoppard
➤ *Death and the King's Horseman,* by Wole Soyinka
➤ *Vyrozumeni (The Memorandum),* by Vaclav Havel
➤ *The Heidi Chronicles,* by Wendy Wasserstein
➤ *Our Town,* by Thornton Wilder
➤ *Look Back in Anger,* by John Osborne
➤ *Macbeth,* by William Shakespeare
➤ *Pygmalion,* by George Bernard Shaw
➤ *Angels in America,* by Tony Kushner
➤ *Who's Afraid of Virginia Woolf?* by Edward Albee

### Biblio-Trivio

Arthur Miller's 1949 Pulitzer Prize–winning drama *Death of a Salesman* is significant for a number of reasons. It is one of the first major dramatic works to feature a pathetic failure in the lead (literally, a "Low Man," Willy Loman). The true nature of tragedy was hotly debated. Some critics felt that Willy was unworthy of the pathos of classic tragic heroes like Oedipus. Miller (and audiences for decades have agreed) argued that any character willing to do whatever it takes to salvage a sense of personal dignity is a worthy tragic hero.

### The Least You Need to Know

➤ Drama should be performed aloud, that's why it's written.

➤ One great way to attend shows for less is to go to preview performances.

➤ No matter where you go in America, a great theater isn't too far away.

➤ Even if you read plays aloud, members have to read them beforehand for effective discussions.

➤ Once and for all, Shakespeare is the man.

# Chapter 22

# Of Tender Verse and Narrative Terse

## In This Chapter

➤ Why ignoring poetry is a bad idea all around

➤ The slam dunk funk

➤ A Whitman sampler

➤ Oh, Henry, you loveable scribe

The most surprising thing I found out while working on this *Idiot's Guide* is that more than a few groups adamantly oppose any other form of literature besides the novel. But why on earth would seemingly intelligent and rational reading groups ignore two of the greatest formats that stimulate ideas, emotions, and discussions: short stories and poetry? In this chapter, we'll explore the beautiful prose in these literary forms that no group should miss.

### Biblio-Trivio

Poetry is one of the oldest art forms in the history of mankind. Ancient poetry was originally fused with song (hip-hop, circa eighth century B.C.E.), but it became an independent form in the Western world by the classical era, sixth to fourth centuries B.C.E. Wherever poetry has existed separate from music, it has substituted linguistic rhythms in place of the musical ones. It is primarily the rhythms that differentiate poetry from its prose cousin.

## To Rhyme or Not to Rhyme—That Is the Question

There are a few standard arguments against reading poetry.

➤ **Argument:** "It isn't like reading a novel; it's too short."

**Rebuttal:** Poems have a full structure within themselves. It isn't the length of something that determines whether or not it has scope, it is the ideas and emotions the piece encompasses. Plus, most books of poetry have an overall feeling to them that can be examined in terms of its whole as well as its individual parts.

➤ **Argument:** "Poetry is more about structure and format than language."

**Rebuttal:** No, it's not. Language is language, whether it's curt, flowery, obscene, long-winded, or written to follow a certain metrical pattern. The structure in poetry is different than the novel, but they both share one thing—it is the way that language is used that's important. In many cases, structure dictates that poems be efficient and powerful in their brevity, which is not the case with a lot of novels. Small ideas can be stretched to 500 pages, and massive ideas can be packed into a few lines.

### Novel Ideas

Picking up a collection of a single poet's work offers your book club the opportunity to study a single author's career in ways that aren't possible with a novelist. For instance, a collection of Emily Dickinson gives the reader a chance to view her work at different stages in her career within a single book—and it can be done in only a meeting or two.

➤ **Argument:** "I just don't *get* poetry."

**Rebuttal:** This is the weakest dispute of them all. What exactly is there to *get* about poetry? Have you ever met anyone who read Melville and then said, "Oh, I get literature"? There is no secret decoder ring that poets and poetry buffs are issued if they pass an exam in the dark of night in a warehouse on the outskirts of the concrete jungle. Poetry is another form of literature, and it isn't something that is either gotten or not. Like novels, there is all kinds of poetry. Some of it will speak to you like a great book; it's just a matter of finding it.

➤ **Argument:** "Poetry doesn't offer the same experience as a novel."

**Rebuttal:** You are right, every poem offers its own experience, just the same as every novel does. People who haven't read any poetry often use this argument, or its less subtle cousin, "I don't like poetry." They would never say, "I don't like literature," but for some reason poetry is beneath them. Their loss.

I am not advocating turning your meeting into Poet's Corner, or even that a single gathering revolve around a single collection or author (*Beowulf* being the notable exception, of course). I am advocating the use of poetry to buttress the monthly selection, or as a way to expand the content of the discussion. I would say, however, that if your book club has never had a meeting devoted to poetry, try it, because it might stir an entirely new set of topics and emotions and liven things up a bit.

## Living Room Laureates

One way to introduce poetry into your reading group is to have a night of poetry readings. You can do this in a couple of ways. You can have a "classic" night of poetry, where each member brings in a couple of poems on any subject, by any author, of any length and style, to read aloud and discuss.

**Pro's Prose**

"'Don't teach my boy poetry,' an English mother recently wrote the Provost of Harrow. 'Don't teach my boy poetry; he is going to stand for Parliament.' Well, perhaps she was right—but if more politicians knew poetry, and more poets knew about politics, I am convinced the world would be a little better place to live on this Commencement Day of 1956."

—Excerpt from Senator John F. Kennedy, in an address to the annual meeting of the Harvard Alumni Association, June 14, 1956

**Jane Err**

Consider keeping the poems you and your fellow members write closed to criticism. The point of the exercise is to help each of you find poetry topics that hit home and to get the group more comfortable with poetry in general. Criticizing each other's poems may leave one or all with negative feelings that could possibly break up your reading group before it gets started.

**317**

### Novel Ideas

To get an idea of what a poetry slam feels and sounds like, rent Marc Levin's dynamic 1998 film *Slam.* It is about an African-American man, Saul Williams, who is sent to prison and uses poetry as an outlet for ideas, emotions, and preserving his sanity. Obviously, it has a much deeper plot than an average poetry slam, but much of the verse was written by the actors, actual poets, and the resulting tone and style is comparable to the standard poetry slam. It's a generalization, but you will get an idea of what slams are all about.

### Jane Err

Don't attend a poetry slam expecting to come away with poetry for discussion at your group. The poems are recited rapidly and most likely won't be handed out in hard copy. Consider it more of just a plain-fun reading group outing, or as research for a slam in your own kitchen.

Start by analyzing the basic structure. Is it written in a unique style? If so, how does the structure help define the poem? Is it part of a collection of similar themes? Does it have a beginning, middle, and end? Is there a central tenet to the poem?

The trick is to take the questions normally suited for analyzing literature and reshape them for poetry. Start with the basics: who, what, where, when, and how? After a few poems, you will start to see the same patterns found in literature. Researching the time in which poems were written is also important, because they are often a visceral response to a poet's environment.

If you have a brave and creative group, you may want to have everyone try to come up with one original poem to read. Make copies for every member in the group and see what develops. Looking at your original poems structurally will help you better understand famous poems and make them more accessible.

Meetings of this sort are an opportunity for members to become immersed in poetry by immediately finding something with which they connect, whether it be someone else's words or their own.

## Slam It Home

Another way to add poetry to the mix is to attend a poetry slam. For the uninitiated, a poetry slam is sort of like hyped-up, competitive, lyrical Ultimate Fighting match. It's verse as vocal contact sport. Poetry slams were very popular a few years back, and while the hype has cooled down somewhat, they are still readily available. They are usually held in coffee shops or bars, or on and around college campuses.

Basically, what happens is poets in the house compete against each other, with the audience deciding the winner. On occasion, there are more formal poetry slams with official judges, but it isn't a regular occurrence. I have seen slams where poets were allowed to bring in their own material, and ones where they were given topics and had to write and perform on the spot, which is always more fun to watch. If it is a poetry slam worth its salt, the contestants really get into it and it is like nothing you are used to seeing. Imagine a street fight through words, gestures, volume, and voice.

The poetry isn't always top-of-the-line (although there are occasionally some great writers), but the energy, excitement, and emotion makes for a great evening. Here's another golden opportunity to get the book club out of the house.

# Poets You Should Know

The following is a brief list of poets if you're interested in dipping a toe into the lyrical waters of poetry.

## Langston Hughes

Hughes was a prominent figure in the Harlem Renaissance of the 1920s. He eschewed classical forms for musical rhythms of jazz and the oral traditions of black culture. The multitalented Hughes had a wide-ranging career that included a stint as a reporter in Madrid for a Baltimore newspaper covering the Spanish Civil War. Hughes wrote in genres across the board, but it is his poetry that is his signature work. He used his poetry as a vehicle for protest in the numerous political and social causes in which he was involved.

A few Hughes's poems to consider are …

➤ "The Weary Blues"

➤ "Sylvester's Dying Bed"

➤ "The Negro Speaks of Rivers"

➤ "50-50"

➤ "Theme for English B"

**Pro's Prose**

"I've known rivers:
I've known rivers ancient as the world and older than the flow of human blood in human veins.
My soul has grown deep like the rivers"

—From "The Negro Speaks of Rivers" by Langston Hughes

## Emily Dickinson

Dickinson is America's greatest female poet, whose intellectual musings covered all sorts of topics that define human existence, including love, hatred, the nature of life and death, war, sexuality, and the meaning of art. Dickinson often used iambic tetrameter, common in church hymns. (Iambic tetrameter is a meter that features eight syllables per line with every second syllable being stressed.)

**Pro's Prose**

"I heard a fly buzz—when I died—
The stillness in the room
Was like the stillness in the air—
Between the heaves of storm—"

—From "465," by Emily Dickinson

Dickinson is often believed to have been a severe recluse, but that isn't quite the truth. It was the persona her first editors created to match with stereotypes of nineteenth-century female authors. Although Dickinson never married and kept select company, she had numerous friends and often entertained at her home in Amherst, Massachusetts.

### Biblio-Trivio

The brilliant Lorraine Hansberry play *A Raisin in the Sun* was the first drama by a black woman to be produced on Broadway and win the New York Drama Critics' Circle Award in 1959. Its title comes from the Langston Hughes poem "Harlem": "What happens to a dream deferred? Does it dry up like a raisin in the sun ..."

Instead of titles, Dickinson was fond of numbering her poems. Although she wrote more than 2,000 poems in her lifetime, only 10 were published while she was alive. Try numbers "214," "249," "341," "1670," and "465."

## William Blake

Blake was an English poet of great significance. He dreamed up an intricate mythology and used symbolic characters to address social concerns that troubled him. His

### Pro's Prose

"Pity would be no more
If we did not make somebody poor
And mercy no more could be
If all were as happy as we."

—From "The Human Abstract," by William Blake

two works, *Songs of Innocence* and *Songs of Experience*, offered two opposing forces in the singular human soul. Both works use the same style, address much of the same subject matter, and in a few cases offer the yin-and-yang to a particular theme. Throughout his career, Blake would develop these themes—that imagination leads to innocence, but experience is the key to imagination.

Blake was also known for his elaborate illustrations that challenge the reader to decipher the complex dialogue between word and picture. Blake was a believer in the imagination and wanted his work to express inner visions, not what one observes in the world. He is a true original and a night of his works will offer numerous conversation pieces.

Here is a smattering of Blake's best:

➤ "Little Girl Lost"

➤ "HOLY THURSDAY"

➤ "AH! SUNFLOWER"

➤ "The Human Abstract"

➤ "The GARDEN of LOVE"

## Walt Whitman

Perhaps no poet has had as much influence on other twentieth-century writers than the old warhorse from New York City. His masterwork, *Leaves of Grass,* was a break from the standard sentimental verse of the time. Whitman emphasized the individual and brazenly praised the human body and the power of the senses. In the preface, he declared that he was a new kind of poet who had created a new kind of democratic literature for the people.

*Leaves of Grass* is one of the poetry classics, but it may not have come about if Whitman hadn't lost his job editing the influential *Brooklyn Eagle.* His position was taken from him for his support of the Free-Soil Party, a group organized in 1848 on a platform of opposing the extension of slavery. The Free-Soil motto was "free soil, free speech, free labor, and free men."

Enjoy a Whitman sampler:

➤ "Song of Myself"

➤ "When I Heard at the Close of the Day"

➤ "Crossing the Brooklyn Ferry"

➤ "A Sight in Camp in the Daybreak Gray and Dim"

➤ "To a Locomotive in Winter"

**Pro's Prose**

"Flow on, river! Flow with the flood-tide, and ebb with the ebb-tide!
Frolic on, crested and scallop-edged waves!
Gorgeous clouds of the sunset! Drench with your splendor me, or the men and women generations after me!
Cross from shore to shore, countless crowds of passengers!
Stand up, tall masts of Manhatta! Stand up, beautiful hills of Brooklyn!"

—From "Crossing Brooklyn Ferry," by Walt Whitman

## Carl Sandburg

Sandburg is another multifaceted writer who, in addition to his poetry, wrote an authoritative six-volume biography of Abraham Lincoln that is still considered one of

the finest. Sandburg used Walt Whitman as his model in a time of dormant American poetry and helped revitalize the genre by using free verse, a style that ignores meters and rhymes, features lines of varying length and cadence, and tries to capture the free rhythms of natural human speech. Sandburg was a realist who wrote of the brutality and vitality of urban life in his hometown of Chicago. He was a member of the Industrial Workers of the World, a socialist action organization, but unlike some strictly socialist writers, Sandburg generally had optimism for the future of America based in no small part in his faith in the average citizen.

Sandburg gave Chicago a much-needed facelift at a time when it had the reputation as a typically overgrown industrial city. He also ushered in a blunt, political wave of poetry, founded in his idealized socialist society. Sandburg even went as far as writing a poem defending Sacco and Vanzetti, two infamous anarchists of the 1920s. In his poetry are all the makings of good, heated reading group discussion.

From the Bard of the City of the Big Shoulders, I offer the following:

➤ "Cool Tombs"
➤ "Chicago"
➤ "Old Times"
➤ "Our Prayer of Thanks"
➤ "I Am the People, the Mob"

## William Carlos Williams

No poet has grown in stature over the last few decades as greatly as Williams. He wrote in distinctly American speech about ordinary situations and average subjects in order to communicate directly with the world. Williams's work was based in the common sensory experience and was also rooted in the idea that all arts are local and the sensory experiences needed to write poetry are all around us. Williams's poetry was very influential to poets like Allen Ginsberg.

Interestingly, Williams didn't start out as a poet. He went to the University of Pennsylvania Medical School

and practiced medicine in New Jersey. He used to write verse in between patients during his internship in New York City.

Here is a selection of Williams's wondrous words:

➤ "The Widow's Lament in Springtime"

➤ "At the Ball Game"

➤ "The Young Housewife"

➤ "Burning the Christmas Greens"

## Sylvia Plath

What exactly is the link between pain and creativity? It is a common precept, and Plath certainly lived the life of a tortured artist. Her poems are renowned for their brutal passages and imagery and repeated theme of self-destruction. Plath stands on the front line of writers who transformed their pain, anguish, and heartbreak into works of art. The odd thing about Plath is that she lived a relatively routine life on the outside. Her poetry collection *Ariel,* written a year before her suicide, has many of her finest poems, and it is notable that some of the poems reflect an obsession with death.

Reading Plath's poetry should open up some interesting avenues for debate, because of the obvious pain she spills out onto the page. Question: What exactly is the link between pain and creativity?

Here is a Plath-ora of poems (get it?):

➤ "Lady Lazarus"

➤ "Elm"

➤ "Blackberrying"

➤ "Fever 103°"

➤ "Daddy"

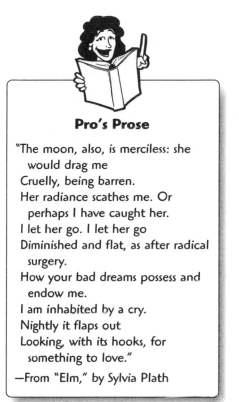

**Pro's Prose**

"The moon, also, is merciless: she would drag me
Cruelly, being barren.
Her radiance scathes me. Or perhaps I have caught her.
I let her go. I let her go
Diminished and flat, as after radical surgery.
How your bad dreams possess and endow me.
I am inhabited by a cry.
Nightly it flaps out
Looking, with its hooks, for something to love."

—From "Elm," by Sylvia Plath

If that wasn't enough for you, never fear. The world of poetry isn't lacking in abundance and talent. Whether your group likes rhyme or free verse (or both), the following list of poets should help you get into the lyrical mood. Keep in mind, this is a very short list and it includes primarily twentieth-century poets.

### Novel Ideas

Try opening the *Norton Anthology of Poetry* or *Modern Poetry* to get a much fuller picture of the world of poetry and for some inspiration for your group.

### Novel Ideas

Bibliophiles should make sure to catch Brian Lamb's program *Booknotes* on C–SPAN, Sundays at 8 and 11 P.M. EST. It is usually centered on nonfiction works, but the interviews about the writing processes can be quite interesting. Also, on its sister network, C–SPAN 2, from Saturday at 8 A.M. to Monday at 8 A.M., is *Book TV*, with all sorts of authors, conferences, lectures, readings, etc. Check out the lineup and other important info at www.booktv.org.

➤ Allen Ginsberg
➤ William Butler Yeats
➤ Seamus Heaney
➤ Robert Pinsky
➤ Cecil Day-Lewis
➤ Rita Dove
➤ Jim Ragan
➤ Louise Erdrich
➤ Pablo Neruda
➤ Robert Frost
➤ Adrienne Rich
➤ Richard Hugo
➤ Robert Penn Warren
➤ Amiri Baraka
➤ Henry Wadsworth Longfellow
➤ Charles Bukowski
➤ Sharon Olds
➤ W. H. Auden
➤ Anne Sexton
➤ T. S. Eliot

## America's Concise Contribution

As with poetry, short stories are also underused by reading groups. Too often, they are viewed as lesser works because, well, why didn't the author write a novel?

Great short stories equal their novel counterparts in every way except one: length. Length is irrelevant, otherwise *War and Peace* and *Infinite Jest* would be the only books worth reading. Pick up John Updike's "A&P" sometime. Updike communicates more in the story's ultra-short one-and-a-half-page length than some books ever portray in hundreds of pages.

Interestingly, short stories are a format that has been crafted and perfected in America. There have been "short stories" around forever, but it is a form that has really resonated with American authors. It isn't even possible to give an exact definition of what a short story is. Some scholars follow the standard that a short story adheres to a general fiction of a certain length, while others claim that the modern version evokes mood and divulges character. The latter is the type of story that has roots in American literary soil (this, of course, is not to say that there aren't brilliant short story writers from all over the world).

Short stories are another way to enjoy fiction, so analyze the content of the work, and don't feel guilty because it isn't a novel. If your book club deems short stories not worthy of dissection, you are missing out. I even heard one author say that the short story is where the best writing is, because anyone can be long-winded and digressive, but it takes a sharp mind to be concise. Edgar Allan Poe was such a mind, and he was the first modern master of the short story. He gained a worldwide reputation for his stories, and, ever since, Americans have been the primary virtuosos of the small tale. So, raise the Stars and Stripes, break out those back issues of *The New Yorker,* and revel in the complete work that can usually be finished in under an hour. Here are a few writers that are known primarily as short-story authors, and for good reason. Their prose is lovely, poignant, riveting, and certainly worthy of your group's attention.

## O. Henry

O. Henry is the pseudonym of William Sydney Porter, a prolific writer of short stories, whose most famous work, "The Gift of the Magi," is still a Christmas favorite today. O. Henry's signature was to use an ironic twist of circumstance, or an odd coincidence that produces a surprise ending to the story (the trading of hair for a watchband and a watch for combs for Christmas gifts).

**Pro's Prose**

"And it seemed as though in a little while the solution would be found, and then a new and glorious life would begin; and it was clear to both of them that the end was still far off, and that what was to be most complicated and difficult for them was only just the beginning."

—Last sentence in "The Lady With the Pet Dog," by Anton Chekhov

**Pro's Prose**

"And here I have lamely related to you the uneventful chronicle of two foolish children in a flat who most unwisely sacrificed for each other the greatest treasures of their house. But in a last word to the wise of these days let it be said that of all who give gifts these two were the wisest. Of all who give and receive gifts, such as they are wisest. Everywhere they are wisest. They are the magi."

—Ending excerpt from "The Gift of the Magi," by O. Henry

Despite the fact that he gives a full narrative often with a clever twist, there is a school of criticism that O. Henry's stories are too formulaic. Ask your group if short stories should only be brief encounters that clearly show a moment in time, or if they deserve a neat ending. What makes a short story effective in the first place?

### Biblio Trivio

O. Henry served three years in a penitentiary for an embezzlement conviction.

## Raymond Carver

We touched on Carver in the movie section, but he is certainly worthy of another plug; he is that darn good. Carver's stories couldn't be any farther away from O. Henry's in every aspect, and yet they are two of the best writers in the short-story pantheon. Go figure. Carver used an often-bleak Pacific Northwest backdrop for his stories, the same area where he was born and worked on and off as a young man in the same sawmills where his father toiled. Carver wrote minimalist stories, some that don't reveal anything about a character (including name), except for what is happening in the moment, and others of greater scope. Almost every one, however, has someone on the fringes of life scraping by, paying bills, getting drunk, laughing, crying, dreaming, dying—you know, real people.

Carver's sparse landscapes, lives, and language usage give the stories a depth that usually manifests itself in some minor revelation by a character. Carver certainly has his detractors—many find his work overtly depressing and repetitive—but he also has a legion of staunch supporters among literary critics and fans alike. It would be worth selecting one of his collections to get the experience of reading short stories based in a state of emotion, which is often detached and subtle. Question: Where do the characters in his stories go from here?

### Pro's Prose

"... that night he lay awake for a long time. Once he got out of bed and looked out the window at the mound of wood which lay in the backyard, and then his eyes were drawn up the valley to the mountains. The moon was partially obscured by clouds, but he could see the peaks and the white snow, and when he raised his window, the sweet, cool air poured in, and farther off he could hear the river coursing down the valley."

—From "Kindling," by Raymond Carver

## Alice Munro

Canadian short story-author Munro has made a career out of telling the stories of small-town folk rebelling against the repressive, banal realities of their lives. They are the kind of people who want more, but either don't know what it is or how to get it. They aren't generally part of any community; they sort of exist in a netherworld all their own. It is the exploration of the lonely rural life, simultaneously empty and eccentric, that is the driving force behind her works.

### Biblio-Trivio

Munro's first collection of short stories came out in 1968. She won Canada's prestigious Governor General's Award for fiction and has been a respected voice for our neighbors to the north ever since.

Munro also zeroes in on the moments of experience, rather than a large arc. The intensity of her stories can be truly revelatory.

Like the poetry list, the next two lists are short, so you may have to do more legwork in finding your personal saviors. However, they should give you some firm footing on the road to short storyville. The first is a list of short-story collections that will be fodder for endless discussion with your group:

➤ *The Progress of Love*, by Alice Munro

➤ *What We Talk About When We Talk About Love*, by Raymond Carver

➤ *The Four Million*, by O. Henry

➤ *A Doctor's Visit: Short Stories*, by Anton Chekhov

➤ *What Was Mine*, by Ann Beattie

➤ *Here We Are in Paradise*, by Tony Earley

➤ *Song of the Silent Snow*, by Hubert Selby Jr.

➤ *Close Range: Wyoming Stories*, by Annie Proulx

➤ *Lost in the City*, by Edward P. Jones

➤ *Self-Help*, by Lorrie Moore

➤ *The Things They Carried*, by Tim O'Brien

Here is a list of individual stories to keep an eye out for, some of which were written by well-known authors. Many classic scribes penned short stories as well as novels— Melville, Hemingway, Fitzgerald, and Cather, for starters—so if you or your reading group have a favorite writer that you keep returning to, see what is out there in the world of shorts. Also, consider bringing in a short story for the monthly meeting to offer a comparison to the novel the author penned:

➤ "The Rube's Waterloo," by Zane Grey

➤ "King of the Bingo Game," by Ralph Ellison

➤ "The Lottery," by Shirley Jackson

➤ "Welcome to the Monkey House," by Kurt Vonnegut Jr.

➤ "The Daring Young Man on the Flying Trapeze," by William Saroyan

➤ "Luck," by Mark Twain

➤ "The Bride Comes to Yellow Sky," by Stephen Crane

➤ "Death in the Woods," by Sherwood Anderson

➤ "Friend of the Family," by Kay Boyle

➤ "The National Pastime," by John Cheever

---

### The Least You Need to Know

➤ Just because poetry adheres to structural demands, it isn't any less worthy or relevant of reading group discussion than prose.

➤ Attending a poetry slam is a way to get your book club excited about the verbal verse.

➤ Short stories often capture a moment in time of direct intensity.

➤ Bring in a short story by the same author as a companion piece to the novel to compare and contrast.

# Chapter 23

# Take a Vacation ... Bring a Book ... and the Book Club

## In This Chapter

➤ Beach bibliophiles

➤ The Angry Ocean vs. Artificial Seaweed

➤ Thoreau your hands in the air and wave 'em like you just don't care

➤ Hitting the open road

➤ Finding the literary treasures in your town

We're coming to the end of our long, arduous journey. By now the book club of your dreams could become a reality within days. Or you have been following the book step-by-step and are thoroughly immersed in a productive reading group. Where do we go from here, you say? What could possibly be left to concern ourselves with after all the hard work? What else is there?

It's time to take a vacation.

Or maybe not a vacation, but let's at least get that hard-working reading group of yours some fresh air. You've all been hunkered away in a locked study intently reading the monthly selections, and quite frankly, you could use some sun. Hold your next meeting in the great outdoors. In this chapter, I'll show you how and where to go to get the most of a reading group excursion to the great outdoors.

# Beach Blanket Book Club

As I mentioned earlier, a lot of book clubs take the summer off, but it isn't an absolute necessity. Sure, time is scarce, the kids are home, it's too hot to prepare meals, but does a rise in the mercury mean you enjoy reading any less? What could be better than a tall glass of iced tea, a comfortable couch, and an air conditioner on full blast?

A book club on the beach, that's what.

## *It's Too Darn Hot*

The main reason people cite for not holding book club meetings in June, July, and August is because too much time is spent at the beach. Fair enough, but most folks go to the same beaches and summer homes week after week, month after month, and year after year, so start a smaller summer group right there on the sand.

**Novel Ideas**

It sounds like a hassle to start a whole new book club just for the summer, but there is one great advantage: new blood. At some point, you will get tired of hearing Mary use the word "contextual," and you won't care if you ever hear Joe say, "In my opinion, there hasn't been a good novel written since before the advent of television. It's like Marshall McLuhan said ...." The summer offers the chance to hear some fresh views.

It comes down to this: If you enjoy the book club experience, why waste three months? Keep it simple—get three or four folks and meet under an umbrella by the ocean or on the porch of a cabin in the mountains, or at the side of a local pool. Wherever you want to be for the warm months is the best place for your summer reading group. Reading groups know no boundaries, and wouldn't it be a shame if the lazy days of summer (ironically, the season of the year with the most abundant time for leisurely reading) were the source of your book club's demise because you got out of practice?

Don't let the freedom to assemble, the freedom to think, the freedom to thumb through a mass-market romance novel while eating a rapidly melting fudgesicle in the blazing sun, ever go to waste, because the next thing you know, it's *1984* all over again.

And don't forget, it is a scientific fact that heat and sun can turn your brain to mush if you allow it to remain dormant for a long period of time. I read it in a book called *Old Wives' Tale*.

## *Pass the Hawaiian Tropic and the Tropic of Cancer, Please*

What to read on those lazy, hazy, crazy days of summer? In the spirit of the warm weather, I give you the following:

**Pro's Prose**

"'Who controls the past,' ran the party slogan, 'controls the future: who controls the present, controls the past.'"

—From *1984*

1. *The Beach,* **by Alex Garland.** This book will soon be on every teenage girl's Christmas list, because Mr. Leonardo DiCaprio himself is starring in the movie version. As for the novel, it is quite an achievement for the debut effort by Garland. It is the story of Richard, a young, disaffected wanderer who is roaming the globe to avoid pesky things like family, work, and the standard existence that passes for life these days. He meets up with all sorts of odd characters of his ilk, including a guy who uses the moniker Daffy Duck and gives Richard a hand-drawn map before killing himself.

   Richard follows the map, and, after a grueling trip, finds a stretch of beach that is home to a bunch of pot-smoking nomads with a bizarre community all their own. Lurking in the highlands are Thai commandos guarding the fields of marijuana. It has the solid plotting of a thriller, but it delves much deeper into the human psyche. It reads like Joseph Conrad's *Heart of Darkness* if he had written it after seeing *Apocalypse Now* in the early 1990s at the height of grunge. It is a wild, hallucinatory reshaping of both Coppola and Conrad and the '90s' nihilism. Pay particular attention to the small-group dynamics, and compare the adult "behavior" to the kids' behavior in *Lord of the Flies*.

2. *Cape Cod,* **by Henry David Thoreau.** The original beach book from the original lay-around-all-day-doin'-nothing beach bum. Thoreau understood that the study of nature and the meditation of philosophical constructs will free one's mind in ways that pushing a rock up a hill simply won't. He had fascinating ideas about all sorts of topics, and *Cape Cod* won't disappoint. Just because you're sitting in the sand doesn't mean you have to have your head in it.

### Biblio-Trivio

In 1846, Thoreau chose jail over paying the poll tax, which was used to fund the Mexican War. He clarified his rationale for the Big House in his 1849 essay "Civil Disobedience" (a.k.a. "Resistance to Civil Government"). His famous essay included theories on passive resistance, a method of protest that was picked up by Mohandas Gandhi and used as a tactic against the British, and then by civil rights leaders like Dr. Martin Luther King Jr. in the fight against segregation in the United States.

In *Cape Cod,* Thoreau waxes philosophical as he takes long, meditative, beach-combing walks in the 1850s. *Cape Cod* features various essays on everything from how a lighthouse works to what part of the clam to avoid to what happens in local villages when there is a shipwreck to his favorite topic, the utter bliss of total solitude.

Some of you are probably saying, "Thoreau? That doesn't sound like beach reading." Don't be fooled. This is great reading about the beach that will illuminate your ocean-side surroundings if you happen to be sitting there, or make you yearn for its sandy nirvana if you're stuck in an office building in downtown Toledo. Sounds like beach reading to me.

### Pro's Prose

"I would rather sit on a pumpkin, and have it all to myself, than to be crowded on a velvet cushion. I would rather ride on earth in an ox-cart with a free circulation than go to heaven in the fancy car of an excursion train and breathe malaria all the way."

—Henry David Thoreau

3. *Against the Tide: The Battle for America's Beaches,* by Cornelia Dean. Dean is science editor at *The New York Times,* and this is her attempt to explain how coastal erosion is not going to be halted, no matter what Mr. Wizard contraptions we build to stop it. There are all sorts of engineering mechanisms and methods that have been used to try to prevent the natural happening, including artificial beds of seaweed (which sounds like something Q would have dreamt up for a James Bond adventure in Maui). Dean explains that a huge amount of tax

dollars have been spent trying to curb the incurable, mostly in the name of protecting private property. Dean's work is interesting and accessible; if you've never spent one second thinking about coastal erosion, this is the place to start. There are numerous probing questions that can be extracted from this book, and they will take on a much deeper relevance if you happen to be staring out at the ocean. Why do we think we can stop the processes of nature in this instance? Would we try and stop rain from falling?

**Novel Ideas**

Coastal erosion might not sound like a thrilling topic for a leisurely read, but Dean's book is an examination of a scientific issue that isn't written like a textbook. If you happen to read it with your new beach group, take a stroll by sections of waterfront property to get a bird's-eye view of what she is describing. Heck, just watch the tides come in and out; that's a front-row seat to coastal erosion.

Here are a few more beach-themed books for you to check out with your fellow sandy-toed bibliophiles:

➤ *Beach Music,* by Pat Conroy

➤ *A Pirate Looks at Fifty,* by Jimmy Buffet

➤ *The Tempest,* by William Shakespeare

➤ *Jaws,* by Peter Benchley

➤ *Brighton Beach Memoirs,* by Neil Simon

➤ *Somewhere off the Coast of Maine,* by Ann Hood

➤ *Shore Stories: An Anthology of the Jersey Shore,* edited by Richard Youmans

➤ *The Nearest Faraway Place: Brian Wilson, the Beach Boys, and the Southern California Experience,* by Timothy White

➤ *North Shore Chronicles: Big Wave Surfing in Hawaii,* by Bruce Jenkins

➤ *Robinson Crusoe,* by Daniel DeFoe

# Day Trippin'

Another way to enjoy the warm months is to take the book club on a day trip, or, if you prefer, a summer outing. There is always more free stuff and festivals going on in the summer months than the gray wintry ones, so why not combine the monthly meeting with an outing? One of the following excursions may be just the airing out that your group needs.

## Music, Maestro: Symphony in the Park

Most small towns, suburbs, and cities have a symphony in the park performance at some point during the summer. This is a great opportunity to get really good seats, because you'll be there a couple of hours ahead of time for your monthly discussion.

**Pro's Prose**

"My plan has always been to keep adding to that mess in the trunk and, if I make it to my eighties and am still functioning in the brain-cell department, to retire to a tropical island, buy an old beach house, hire several lovely native girls as assistants, ship in a good supply of rum and red burgundy, and then spend my golden years making a complete picture out of the puzzle pieces in the old steamer trunk. That to me is the way any good romantic would look at his life: Live it first, then write it down before you go."

—Excerpt from *A Pirate Looks at Fifty* (epilogue), by Jimmy Buffet

You can pack a picnic basket with fancy French cheese and stone-ground wheat crackers, fresh fruit, pasta salad, biscotti, or you could forgo the yuppie grub and get foot-long dogs with kraut and extra mustard. A meeting followed by the symphony under the stars is as romantic as it is intellectual. I would suggest reading *Amadeus,* a play by Peter Shaffer, for your reading group symphony excursion. Make no bones about it, this would make for a fine evening.

## Drivin' Down a Country Road

Take that same picnic basket, load up the car, and hit the high road. A drive to the closest wilderness area, say within one hour, gives your book club the opportunity to get away from the everyday calamities like traffic, phones, obnoxious neighbors, and all the other nuisances. Even if it is only for an afternoon or at a park that isn't all that far from the house, a quiet discussion amidst fresh air and sunshine will do wonders.

Surprisingly, this isn't as uncommon as you might assume. A few book clubians told me that they like to have picnic-style meetings every so often, whether it be at a park in town or a bit of a drive. May I suggest *A Country Year: Living the Questions,* by Sue Hubbell, a woman who lived in the Missouri Ozarks for 12 years and became a beekeeper to make a living. Hubbell is a naturalist who takes time to question the wonders of nature and the failures of humans. It is a graceful account of why the small details of nature shape our lives.

## Around the Pool

Poolside meetings are a great way to enjoy the sun, get a tan, and talk lit crit. Most towns and cities have a public pool available in the summer months, or, even better, maybe one of your members happens to have one in his or her own backyard. This is a great alternative to the beach if you don't live within reasonable driving distance from the ocean blue, or just aren't all that fond of getting sand between the pages of your books.

### Biblio-Trivio

The origin of the phrase "make no bones about it" is unknown, but it may have come from the days when soup was the primary meal of many people. If the soup was made without bones, it was thought to be delicious and simple to eat. If it contained bones, however, complaints were frequently made by the connoisseurs because pieces of bone would upset their stomachs.

I would like to suggest E. L. Doctorow's *The Waterworks,* which has absolutely nothing to do with swimming pools but is a cunning Gothic novel about New York City Tammany Hall politics and the city's waterworks.

## Museum Musings

If it is too hot, a trip to an air-conditioned museum is just the ticket. This is a good idea at any time of the year, because all you have to do is find out what local exhibits are on display and choose the appropriate literature.

Authors and poets have been dazzled by visual artists and vice versa since the inception of art itself. Reading groups can call and make arrangements for a guided tour, and then have a meeting and lunch on the museum's grounds afterward. In the warmer months, museums frequently have evening performances by local artists, so that could be part of the package as well.

### Novel Ideas

There are book clubs that have been known to meet at the clubhouse an hour or two before tee time, and then play together in a couple of foursomes. If you have a golfing crowd, this might be the way to go. Have the meeting over a nice breakfast and you'll be hitting the links by 9 or 10 in the morning, still beating the crowds and the heat.

### Jane Err

Try to avoid having kids in the pool while the meeting is taking place, because it is too distracting. Hire somebody to watch them for an hour before they are allowed to swim if necessary while you and your cohorts kick around your brilliant insights.

### Pro's Prose

"Everybody wants to understand painting. Why is there no attempt to understand the song of the birds? Why does one love a night, a flower, everything that surrounds a man, without trying to understand it at all?"

—Pablo Picasso

To go along with your excursion, I suggest *Camille Claudel: Une Femme,* by Anne Delbee. It is a fictionalized biography of French feminist sculptor, and lover of Auguste Rodin, Claudel. It is a unique look at the relationship and her devotion to art.

If you happen to have a book club event in a museum that includes children, I would like to encourage the selection from the *Mixed-Up Files of Mrs. Basil E. Frankweiler,* by E. L. Konigsburg. It is the story of two precocious children who move into the Metropolitan Museum of Art.

## Take a Walk on the (Literary) Wild Side

Okay, these would all take a lot of planning and effort, not to mention costs, but I wanted to throw a few at you in case your book club has a discretionary fund or has saved its pennies to go on a little group vacation:

➤ Take a boat trip down the Mississippi River to try and capture the spirit of what it was like for Huckleberry Finn and Jim. There are actually historical week-long steamship cruises if you happen to be a Twain freak.

➤ A drive up California's Pacific Coast Highway, stopping in all the little farm towns you can find to get a beat on Steinbeck country. Along the way, you can hit the Henry Miller library/ museum in a forest near Big Sur.

➤ Take the subway up to Harlem, get off at 125th Street, head toward Malcolm X or Adam Clayton Powell boulevards, and walk around the neighborhoods. In Harlem you will find the former homes of Claude McKay, Countee Cullen, and Langston Hughes, not to mention the famous Apollo theater and Sylvia's soul food restaurant.

➤ Drive the mysterious route of Edgar Allan Poe. He attended the University of Virginia for a year, returned to his birthplace of Boston and began writing, moved to Baltimore, and then spent time in Philadelphia and New York City (the Bronx) editing periodicals. Each city has some sort of marker that he lived there, so it would be a great chance to check out the eastern seaboard while following Poe's footsteps.

➤ If your reading group is in the mood to visit a bright-light city that is gonna set your soul on fire, why not take a literary excursion to Las Vegas? You can start with Hunter S. Thompson's classic, twisted, drug-soaked ride through Sin City, *Fear and Loathing in Las Vegas*. Follow that up with John O'Brien's heartbreaking story of suicide, *Leaving Las Vegas*, and end with Nicholas Pileggi's *Casino*, a page-turning history of the rise and fall of the Chicago mob in Vegas.

➤ Perhaps your group has the time and money to go overseas. I would recommend celebrating Bloomsday (June 16) in Dublin and walking the *Ulysses* path. Celebrations throughout Dublin, including readings and performances, abound, both official and unofficial (an interesting mix, to say the least). There are numerous reenactments on the trail of Leopold Bloom, and the pubs are packed all day with costumed folks in the spirit (and spirits) of the occasion. For more information check out www.ireland.com.

➤ Hop on a motorcycle and travel through the South á la *Easy Rider*. Along the way you can stop in Jackson, Mississippi, home of Eudora Welty, and see where *The Optimist's Daughter* got her start. From there you can visit Mr. Faulkner's old stomping grounds and continue on to Milledgeville, Georgia, where Flannery O'Connor raised her pigeons and wrote her classics.

Continue on to the Big Easy and enjoy a hurricane (a refreshing, yet walloping alcoholic drink) in the hot spot where average, run-of-the-mill folks like John Kennedy Toole, Truman Capote, Tennesee Williams, and Anne Rice honed their craft.

**Jane Err**

Don't go to Monterey expecting to see *Cannery Row*. It is a gaudy tourist trap with more Steinbeck novelty items than you can shake a plastic *Grapes of Wrath* sno–dome paperweight at. If you want the real deal, go out to the strawberry or garlic fields and ask to be a hired hand for a day, or try the museum in Salinas.

**Novel Ideas**

If you enjoy hiking, backpacking, or camping in the wilderness, do yourself a favor and pick up *My First Summer in the Sierras*. It is John Muir's account of his maiden voyage into the Sierra and Yosemite. His vibrant, poetic descriptions of the Sierra Nevada and the effect they have on his emotions are quite powerful. Perfect reading for that shade break going up the mountain or down the long trail.

Following are some more book ideas for those of you who want to spend your summers in the great outdoors. Happy trails.

➤ *My First Summer in the Sierras,* by John Muir
➤ *The Ends of the Earth: The Selected Travels of Paul Theroux,* by Paul Theroux

**Pro's Prose**

"One who has some artistic ability may know how to do a thing, and even show how to do it, and yet fail in doing it after all; but the artist and the man of some artistic ability must not be confounded. He only is the former who can carry his most shadowy precepts into successful application."

—Edgar Allan Poe

**Pro's Prose**

"If a man does not keep pace with his companions, perhaps it is because he hears a different drummer. Let him step to the music which he hears, however measured or far away."

—Henry David Thoreau

➤ *Light and Color in the Outdoors,* by M. G. J. Minnaert, translated by Len Seymour
➤ *Coming Into the Country,* by John McPhee
➤ *Walden,* by Henry David Thoreau
➤ *Into the Wild,* by John Krakaur
➤ *Pilgrim at Tinker Creek,* by Annie Dillard

## It Starts at Home

If your book club can't make any of these "little" jaunts, there is more than likely a literary benchmark relatively close to the exact spot you are in right now. Maybe a famous writer came through town at one time, or a nearby city was the setting for a novel, or a local scribe penned a story about a place you've been to 100 times. The point is, a place doesn't have to rival the Globe Theater to be important; it's the experience of seeing firsthand the inspiration for a writer's work. Even if the author is unknown, there is something intriguing about reading his work and then getting a feel for what he saw, be it a mountaintop, a river, a corner bar, or his front porch. Dig a little bit, and you are guaranteed to find something.

Maybe your members would hate the idea of spending time in a park because the noise, bugs, and distractions would detract from the standard deep conversation. That's perfectly acceptable. Or maybe your reading group has already flown to Ireland to take a walking literary pub tour, and that's acceptable as well.

If you can find one, call a local literary historian to come in and give a guest lecture on works from the region. It's common to find tenured English professors at the closest college who have studied and read the writings of local authors. Another way to find a speaker is to get the names of authors in the area who have written books, because they often know a lot about the local scene. Even if all they do is come in and share some anecdotes, it would still make for an entertaining evening.

Book clubs are what you make of them, because great literature will always be there. Just have fun and keep reading.

**The Least You Need to Know**

➤ If you don't want a summer hiatus from your book club, pack them up and head for the beach; or, if the rest of your regular group wants a break, find a summer group to share your warm-weather reading with.

➤ Outdoor meetings are a way to keep the book club together during the summer months.

➤ With some careful time and financial planning, your group can take a storybook vacation together.

➤ There is a spot of literary importance in your hometown, it just takes digging to find it.

➤ Have fun and keep reading!

# Further Suggested Book Club Kinda Books

- ➤ *Going After Cacciato*, by Tim O'Brien
- ➤ *Into the Wild*, by Jon Krakauer
- ➤ *The God of Small Things*, by Arundhati Roy
- ➤ *Foxfire*, by Joyce Carol Oates
- ➤ *A Civil Action*, by Jonathan Harr
- ➤ *This Side of Brightness*, by Colum McCann
- ➤ *Cavedweller*, by Dorothy Allison
- ➤ *The Book of Ruth*, by Jane Hamilton
- ➤ *Travels With My Aunt*, by Graham Greene
- ➤ *The Wedding*, by Dorothy West
- ➤ *The Kingdom and the Power*, by Gay Talese
- ➤ *Stones from the River*, by Ursula Hegi
- ➤ *Amy and Isabelle*, by Elizabeth Strout
- ➤ *The Night in Question*, by Tobias Wolff
- ➤ *Freedomland*, by Richard Price
- ➤ *CivilWarLand in Bad Decline*, by George Saunders
- ➤ *Memoir from Antproof Case*, by Mark Helprin
- ➤ *Outerbridge Reach*, by Robert Stone
- ➤ *Quinn's Book*, by William Kennedy
- ➤ *Paradise Lost*, by John Milton
- ➤ *The Egoist*, by George Meredith
- ➤ *Matilda*, by Mary Wollstonecraft

- ➤ *Phineas Finn,* by Anthony Trollope
- ➤ *Ivanhoe,* by Sir Walter Scott
- ➤ *On Liberty,* by John Stuart Mill
- ➤ *Citizen Soldiers,* by Stephen E. Ambrose
- ➤ *Tess of the d'Urbervilles,* by Thomas Hardy
- ➤ *Complete Prose of Woody Allen,* by Woody Allen
- ➤ *Cat's Cradle,* by Kurt Vonnegut Jr.
- ➤ *Give War a Chance,* by P. J. O'Rourke
- ➤ *Birds of America,* by Mary McCarthy
- ➤ *Nobody's Fool,* by Richard Russo
- ➤ *About a Boy,* by Nick Hornby
- ➤ *The View from the Ground,* by Martha Gellhorn
- ➤ *Go,* by John Clellon Holmes
- ➤ *Ask the Dust,* by John Fante
- ➤ *The Age of Grief,* by Jane Smiley
- ➤ *The Best of Plimpton,* by George Plimpton
- ➤ *Enduring Love,* by Ian McEwan
- ➤ *The Best American Short Stories of the Century,* edited by John Updike, coedited by Katrina Kenison
- ➤ *Emperor of the Air: Stories,* by Ethan Canin
- ➤ *Dinner at the Homesick Restaurant,* by Anne Tyler
- ➤ *Bridget Jones's Diary,* by Helen Fielding
- ➤ *The Screwtape Letters,* by C. S. Lewis
- ➤ *City of Night,* by John Rechy
- ➤ *The Plague,* by Albert Camus
- ➤ *Moon Palace,* by Paul Auster
- ➤ *The Blindfold,* by Siri Hustvedt
- ➤ *Fall on Your Knees,* by Ann-Marie MacDonald
- ➤ *Stigmata: A Novel,* by Phyllis Alesia Perry

# Index

## A

About a Boy, 342
absenteeism, 54
Adams, Henry, 240
The Adventures of Huckleberry Finn, 4, 23, 179
The Adventures of Tom Sawyer, 179-180
Affliction, 152
African-American, 159-161
  authors
    Ellison, Ralph, 159
    Hurston, Zora Neale, 159
    Wideman, John Edgar, 160
  books, 161
    Brothers and Keepers, 160
    Invisible Man, 159
    Their Eyes Were Watching God, 159
Against the Tide: The Battle for America's Beaches, 332-333
The Age of Grief, 342
The Age of Innocence, 204
aggressors (personality type), 74-75
Alcott, Louisa May, 139
Alexie, Sherman, 169

Alice's Adventures in Wonderland, 7
All Quiet on the Western Front, 296
allegory, 100
Allen, Woody, 342
Allende, Isabel, 140
Allison, Dorothy, 131, 341
Almanac of the Dead, 169-170
Alvarez, Julia, 137
Amazing Grace, 91
Amazon.com, 48
  top five bestsellers list, 48
Ambrose, Stephen, 342
American books, 199
  Gotham tales, 203-205
    The Age of Innocence, 204
    The Bonfire of the Vanities, 203
    The New York Trilogy, 204-205
  New England, 200-203
    The Country Doctor, 200-201
    Outerbridge Reach, 201-202
    A Prayer for Owen Meany, 201

  Old West, 198-200
    Dancing at the Rascal Fair, 199-200
    The Handyman, 198-199
    The Portable Western Reader, 198
American Psycho, 18, 223
Amis, Martin, 193-194
Amsterdam, 194
Amy and Isabelle, 341
analyzing books, 208-210
  main characters, 208
  patterns, 209
  red herrings, 210
  settings, 208
  styles, 210
And the Band Played On: Politics, People, and the AIDS Epidemic, 82, 237
Angelou, Maya, 24
Animal Dreams, 130-131
antiheroes, 99
Are You There God? It's Me, Margaret, 138
Armstrong, William H., 178
Asian authors, 165-168
  Ishiguro, Kazuo, 166
  Tan, Amy, 165-166
  Yamamoto, Hisaye, 167

*Ask the Dust,* 342
Austen, Jane, 193
Auster, Paul, 204-205, 342
authors
  African-American, 159-161
    Ellison, Ralph, 159
    Hurston, Zora Neale, 159
    Wideman, John Edgar, 160
  Asian, 165-168
    Ishiguro, Kazuo, 166
    Tan, Amy, 165-166
    Yamamoto, Hisaye, 167
  biographies, researching, 92-93
  Hispanic, 161-164
    Castedo, Elena, 163
    Diaz, Junot, 163
    García Márquez, Gabriel, 100, 162-163
    Hijuelos, Oscar, 164
  Native American, 168-171
    Alexie, Sherman, 169
    Erdrich, Louise, 170-171
    Silko, Marmon, 169
  short stories
    Carver, Raymond, 326
    Henry, O., 325
    Munro, Alice, 327

autobiographies
  *The Autobiography of Malcolm X,* 250
  *Miles Davis: The Autobiography,* 259

**B**

*Backlash: The Undeclared War Against American Women,* 240-241
Banks, Russell, 152
barbecues (recipes), 278-280
Barker, Pat, 51
Barnes & Noble
  top 10 bestsellers list, 49
  Web site, 49
baseball, books about, 148
  *Men at Work,* 149
  *The Natural,* 148
  *Shoeless Joe,* 148
Bassani, Giorgio, 196
*Bastard out of Carolina,* 131-132
*The Beach,* 331
beaches (as location of meetings), 330-333
Beat generation, 41, 88, 113, 183-184
Beckett, Samuel, 190, 308
*Beloved,* 75, 128
benefits of reading groups
  brain capabilities, 10-11
  conversations, 9-10

family as members, 16
friends as members, 19
home meetings, 33
personal, 6-8
pleasure reading, 13
positive effects on your children, 12
publicly, 8
socially, 9
*The Best American Short Stories of the Century,* 342
*The Best of Plimpton,* 342
*Beyond Good and Evil: Prelude to a Philosophy of the Future,* 245
Biblio Bytes Web site, 70
biographies
  *Coolidge: An American Enigma,* 256
  *Jackson Pollock: An American Saga,* 258-259
  *No Ordinary Time,* 255-256
  *Oscar Wilde,* 257-258
  *Truman,* 254-255
*Birds of America,* 342
Blake, William, 320-321
*The Blindfold,* 342
*Blood Thirst: 100 Years of Vampire Fiction,* 223-224
Blume, Judy, 138-139
*The Bonfire of the Vanities,* 203
book clubs, *see* groups
*The Book of Ruth,* 341
Book Spot Web site, 70
bookmarks, 103

books
　by African-American
　　authors, 159-161
　　*Brothers and Keepers,*
　　　160
　　*Invisible Man,* 159
　　*Their Eyes Were
　　　Watching God,*
　　　159-160
　American, 199
　　Gotham tales,
　　　203-205
　　New England,
　　　200-203
　　Old West, 198-200
　analyzing, 208-210
　　main characters,
　　　208
　　patterns, 209
　　red herrings, 210
　　settings, 208
　　styles, 210
　by Asian authors,
　　165-168
　　*The Joy Luck Club,*
　　　165-166
　　*The Remains of the
　　　Day,* 166
　　*Seventeen Syllables
　　　and Other Stories,*
　　　167
　autobiographies
　　*The Autobiography of
　　　Malcolm X,* 250
　　*Miles Davis: The
　　　Autobiography,* 259
　baseball, 148
　　*Men at Work,* 149
　　*The Natural,*
　　　148-149
　　*Shoeless Joe,* 148

biographies
　*Coolidge: An
　　American Enigma,*
　　256
　*Jackson Pollock: An
　　American Saga,*
　　258-259
　*No Ordinary Time,*
　　255-256
　*Oscar Wilde,*
　　257-258
　*Truman,* 90, 254-255
　borrowing, 52
　British, 193-195
　　*Amsterdam,* 194-195
　　*Emma,* 193
　　*Money: A Suicide
　　　Note,* 193-194
　children's
　　middle-schoolers,
　　　178-181
　　teenagers, 181-185
　　young children,
　　　176-178
　Christmas-related, 282
　classics, 111-123
　cost considerations of
　　group, 46
　father/son, 152-154
　　*Affliction,* 152
　　*The Great Santini,*
　　　153
　　*Independence Day,*
　　　153
　fiction
　　detective stories,
　　　214
　　mysteries, 211-219
　fishing, 146
　　*Moby Dick,* 147
　　*The Old Man and the
　　　Sea,* 146

　*A River Runs
　　Through It,* 147
　food-related, 271-273
　　*The Butter Did It: A
　　　Gastronomic Tale of
　　　Love and Murder,*
　　　273
　　*Food in History,* 272
　　*Fried Green Tomatoes
　　　at the Whistle-Stop
　　　Café,* 273
　　*The Gourmet Atlas,*
　　　272
　　*Like Water for
　　　Chocolate,* 273
　　*The Making of a
　　　Chef: Mastering
　　　Heat at the
　　　Culinary Institute of
　　　America,* 272
　　*Nobody Knows the
　　　Truffles I've Seen,*
　　　272
　　*Reef,* 273
　　*Tender at the Bone:
　　　Growing Up at the
　　　Table,* 272
　great outdoors, 337
　Hispanic, 161-164
　　*Drown,* 163
　　*The Mambo Kings
　　　Play Songs of Love,*
　　　164
　　*One Hundred Years
　　　of Solitude,* 162-163
　　*Paradise,* 163
　horror, 221-230, 233
　　*Dr. Jekyll and Mr.
　　　Hyde,* 225-226
　　*Red Dragon,* 228-229

*The Silence of the Lambs*, 228
*The Trial*, 225
Irish, 190-192
  *The Country Girls Trilogy and Epilogue*, 191-192
  *Murphy*, 190
  *The Snapper*, 190-191
Italian, 197
  *The Garden of the Finzi-Continis*, 196-197
  *Reeds in the Wind*, 195-196
  *Unto the Sons*, 197
movie adaptations, 286, 293, 298-299
  *All Quiet on the Western Front*, 296
  *The Godfather*, 295-296
  *Great Expectations*, 294
  *Last Exit to Brooklyn*, 297
  *The Magnificent Ambersons*, 294
  *One Flew Over the Cuckoo's Nest*, 296
  *Short Cuts*, 297
murders, 227-230
  *Crime and Punishment*, 227-228
  *Red Dragon*, 228-229
mystery, 208-219
by Native American authors, 168-171
  *Almanac of the Dead*, 169-170

  *The Lone Ranger and Tonto Fistfight in Heaven*, 169
  *Love Medicine*, 170
nonfiction, *see* nonfiction books
presidential readings, 257
purchasing for groups, 47, 52
science-fiction, 230-233
  *The Left Hand of Darkness*, 231-232
  *The War of the Worlds*, 230
tough-guy books, 150
  *L.A. Confidential*, 150
  *Lonesome Dove*, 151
  *Population 1280*, 151
vampire, 222-224
  *Blood Thirst: 100 Years of Vampire Fiction*, 223-224
  *Dracula*, 222-223
bookstores
  finding members for reading groups, 25-26
  as location of meetings, 38-40
BookWire Web site, 69
brain capabilities, improvements from reading, 10-11
Branch, Taylor, 246
*Brave New World*, 10 116-117
*Breakfast at Tiffany's*, 289

*Bridget Jones's Diary*, 342
*A Brief History of Time*, 242
*A Bright and Shining Lie*, 247-248
British books, 193-195
  *Amsterdam*, 194-195
  *Emma*, 193
  *Money: A Suicide Note*, 193-194
*Brothers and Keepers*, 160
Brown, Dee, 237-238
Burroughs, William S., 184
*Bury My Heart at Wounded Knee: An Indian History of the American West*, 237-238
*The Butter Did It: A Gastronomic Tale of Love and Murder*, 273
buying books, *see* purchasing books

## C

Camus, Albert, 342
Canin, Ethan, 342
*Cape Cod*, 331-332
Capote, Truman, 35, 242
Carroll, Lewis, 7
Carver, Raymond, 297-298, 326
Castedo, Elena, 163
*Cat's Cradle*, 342
*Catch-22*, 118-119
*The Catcher in the Rye*, 23
Cather, Willa, 140
*Cavedweller*, 341

Center for Autobio-
graphic Studies, 262
  Web site, 262
characters (movie adap-
tations), 289
*Charlotte's Web*, 175
charters, setting goals,
63
childcare issues, 33
children's reading
groups, 173-174
  dinner-table reading
groups, 174
  goals, 185
  ideas to ensure participation, 174-175
  middle-schoolers,
178-181
  teen-agers, 181-185
  young children,
176-178
Childress, Alice, 24
Chinese dinner (recipes),
276-277
choosing
  leaders for groups,
63-64
    celebrities, 67-68
    democracy, 65-66
    dictatorship, 64-65
    Internet, 69-70
    professional, 66-67
    public radio, 69
    socialism, 66
  members, 16
    bookstores, 25-26
    classmates, 23-24
    co-workers, 20-22
    community mem-
bers, 22-23
    family members,
16-18

friends, 18-20
gym acquaintances,
26
posting at local
merchants, 26
strangers, 26-28
Christie, Agatha, 208,
212
Christmas (party ideas),
282-283
*Citizen Soldiers*, 342
*City of Night*, 342
*A Civil Action*, 341
*CivilWarLand in Bad
Decline*, 341
classic literature, top 10
bestsellers lists,
111-123
Classifieds for Free Web
site, 28
classmates, choosing for
reading groups, 23-24
climax, 99
co-workers, choosing for
reading groups, 20-22
*Cold Mountain*, 4
*The Communist
Manifesto*, 238
community centers
finding members for
reading groups,
22-23
as location of meet-
ings, 36-37
*The Complete Prose of
Woody Allen*, 342
concentration when
reading, 86-87
concrete definition of
reading groups, 6

*A Confederacy of Dunces*,
132-133
Conroy, Pat, 153
conversation benefits,
9-10
*Coolidge: An American
Enigma*, 256
cost considerations
  books, 46
  food for meetings,
52-53
  ideas for saving
money when attend-
ing plays, 303-304
*The Country Doctor*,
200-201
*The Country Girls Trilogy
and Epilogue*, 191-192
country (as location of
meetings), 334
*Crime and Punishment*,
227-228
cultural identity, 158,
172

## D

*Dancing at the Rascal
Fair*, 199-200
*Darkness at Noon*,
119-120
*Darkness Visible: A
Memoir of Madness*,
239-240
Darwin, Charles, 246
Davis, Miles, 259
day trips (location of
meetings), 333-334
Dean, Cornelia, 332-333
*Death of a Salesman*, 308

debates, 97-98
Deledda, Grazia, 195
democracy (leadership style), 65-66
detective stories, 214
    *see also* mystery books
Diaz, Junot, 163
Dickens, Charles, 294
Dickinson, Emily, 319-320
dictatorship (leadership style), 64-65
A Different Light bookstore Web site, 69
digressors (personality type), 75-76
*Dinner at the Homesick Restaurant,* 342
dinner considerations, 270-271
dinner-table reading groups, 174
disadvantages
    family as members, 17-18
    friends as members, 19
    home meetings, 34-35
Doctorow, E. L., 97
Doig, Ivan, 199-200
Dostoyevsky, Fyodor, 227-228
Doyle, Roddy, 135, 191
Doyle, Sir Arthur Conan, 212, 215-216
*Dr. Jekyll and Mr. Hyde,* 225-226
*Dracula,* 222-223
Drimmer, Frederick, 249-250

*Drown,* 163
*The Duke of Deception,* 264

### E

Ebert, Roger, 292-293
editing of text (movie adaptations), 288-289
*The Education of Henry Adams,* 240
*The Effect of Gamma Rays on Man-in-the-Moon Marigolds,* 24
*The Egoist,* 341
Ellis, Bret Easton, 223
Ellison, Ralph, 159
Ellmann, Richard, 257-258
Ellroy, James, 150
*Emma,* 193
*Emperor of the Air: Stories,* 342
Empowerment Theory, 127
ending of movie (movie adaptations), 289
*Enduring Love,* 342
entrees for dinner clubs, 275
Erdrich, Louise, 170-171
Esquivel, Laura, 273
ethereal definition of reading groups, 6

### F

*Fall on Your Knees,* 342
Faludi, Susan, 240-241

family as members of reading groups, 16-18
    benefits, 16
    disadvantages, 17-18
Fante, John, 342
father/son books, 152-154
    *Affliction,* 152
    *The Great Santini,* 153
    *Independence Day,* 153
Faulkner, William, 117-118
feedback, giving to group members, 102
feminism, 133-137
fiction books
    detective stories, 214
    mysteries, 208-219
        *The Hound of the Baskervilles,* 215-216
        *The Intuitionist,* 217
        *The Maltese Falcon,* 216
        seeking advice on titles, 218
        *The Talented Mr. Ripley,* 216
Fielding, Helen, 342
first group meeting, 104-105
    importance of details, 105
    reading required materials, 105-106
fishing books, 146
    *Moby Dick,* 147
    *The Old Man and the Sea,* 146
    *A River Runs Through It,* 147

Fitzgerald, F. Scott, 113
Flagg, Fannie, 273
food
  cost considerations of
    group, 52-53
  food-related books,
    271-273
    *The Butter Did It: A
      Gastronomic Tale of
      Love and Murder,*
      273
    *Food in History,* 272
    *Fried Green Tomatoes
      at the Whistle-Stop
      Café,* 273
    *The Gourmet Atlas,*
      272
    *Like Water for
      Chocolate,* 273
    *The Making of a
      Chef: Mastering
      Heat at the
      Culinary Institute of
      America,* 272
    *Nobody Knows the
      Truffles I've Seen,*
      272
    *Reef,* 273
    *Tender at the Bone:
      Growing Up at the
      Table,* 272
Ford, Richard, 153
*Foxfire,* 341
Francis, Dick, 214
Frazier, Charles, 4
Freedom Factor Theory,
  126
*Freedomland,* 341
*Fried Green Tomatoes at
  the Whistle-Stop Café,*
  273

friends as members of
  reading groups, 18-20
  benefits, 19
  disadvantages, 19

## G

García Márquez, Gabriel,
  100, 162-163
*The Garden of the Finzi-
  Continis,* 196
Garland, Alex, 331
Gellhorn, Martha, 342
GetSet Web site, 69
*The Ghost of Tom Joad*
  album, and *The Grapes
  of Wrath,* 122
*The Ghost Road,* 51
Ginsberg, Allen, 77, 79,
  184
*Give War a Chance,* 342
*The Giving Tree,* 176
*Go,* 342
goals
  children's reading
    groups, 185
  researching books,
    90-91
  setting, 60-63
    charters, 63
    group-oriented, 62
    personal progress,
      60-61
*The God of Small Things,*
  341
*The Godfather,* 295-296
*Going After Cacciato,* 341
Golding, William, 180
Goodwin, Doris Kearns,
  255-256

Gotham tales, 203-205
  *The Age of Innocence,*
    204
  *The Bonfire of the
    Vanities,* 203
  *The New York Trilogy,*
    204-205
*The Gourmet Atlas,* 272
*The Grapes of Wrath,*
  121-122
*Great Expectations,* 294
*The Great Gatsby,*
  113-114
great outdoors, books
  about, 337
*The Great Santini,* 153
Greene, Graham, 341
groups
  benefits
    brain capabilities,
      10-11
    conversations, 9-10
    personal, 6-8
    pleasure reading, 13
    positive effects on
      your children, 12
    publicly, 8
    socially, 9
  children's, 173-174
    dinner-table read-
      ing groups, 174
    goals, 185
    ideas to ensure par-
      ticipation, 174-175
    middle-schoolers,
      178-180
    teenagers, 181-185
    young children,
      176-178

concrete definition of reading groups, 6
cultural identity, 158, 172
ethereal definition of reading groups, 6
men's, 144-146, 154-155
  baseball books, 148-149
  father/son books, 152-154
  fishing books, 146
  tough-guy books, 150-151
mission, 6
movie adaptations, 286, 293, 298-299
  *All Quiet on the Western Front,* 296
  *The Godfather,* 295-296
  *Great Expectations,* 294
  *Last Exit to Brooklyn,* 297
  *The Magnificent Ambersons,* 294
  *One Flew Over the Cuckoo's Nest,* 296-297
  *Short Cuts,* 297
party ideas, 273-274
  barbecue, 278-280
  Chinese dinner, 276-277
  holidays, 280-283
  suggested entrees, 275

plays (performing), 306-307, 311
  *Death of a Salesman,* 308
  *Hamlet,* 310
  *Romeo and Juliet,* 310
  *Waiting for Godot,* 308
poetry, 315
  arguments against poetry, 316-317
  poetry slams, 318
setting goals, 62
short stories, 324-326
survey on plays, 302-303
vacations, 336-337
women's, 125
  books to include in group, 128-141
  feminist examination, 133-137
  mother/daughter groups, 137-142
  theories, 126-128
Guest, Judith, 181
guidelines (reading groups), 96
  debates, 97-98
  group feedback, 102
  leaving the group, 106
  literary terms, 99, 101
  replacing members, 103-104
  tension, 98
    bad, 98
    good, 98-99
Gunesekera, Romesh, 273
*The Guns of August,* 241-242

**H**

Haley, Alex, 250
Halloween (party ideas), 280-281
Hamilton, Jane, 341
*Hamlet,* 310
Hammett, Dashiell, 213, 216
*The Handyman,* 198-199
Harr, Jonathan, 341
Harris, Thomas, 228-229
Harrison, Jim, 136-137
Hawking, Stephen, 242
Hegi, Ursula, 341
Heller, Joseph, 118-119
Helprin, Mark, 341
Hemingway, Ernest, 146
Henry, O., 325-326
*Her First American,* 140-141
*A Hero Ain't Nothin' but a Sandwich,* 24
Highsmith, Patricia, 216
Hijuelos, Oscar, 164
Hispanic authors, 161-164
  Castedo, Elena, 163
  Diaz, Junot, 163
  García Márquez, Gabriel, 100, 162-163
  Hijuelos, Oscar, 164
*A History of the American People,* 251
holidays (party ideas), 280-283
  Christmas, 282-283
  Halloween, 280-281
Holmes, John Clellon, 342

Holmes, Sherlock, 211-212, 215-216
home (location of meetings), 32
    accessibility, 33
    availability, 33
    benefits, 33
    disadvantages, 34-35
Hornby, Nick, 342
horror books, 221-230, 233
   considerations when choosing, 222
   *Dr. Jekyll and Mr. Hyde*, 225-226
   *Red Dragon*, 228-229
   *The Silence of the Lambs*, 228
   *The Trial*, 225
Horror Writers Association Web site, 69
*The Hound of the Baskervilles*, 215-216
*How the Garcia Girls Got Their Accents Back*, 137
*Howl*, 79, 184
hubris, 100
Hughes, Langston, 319
Hurston, Zora Neale, 159-160
Hustvedt, Siri, 342
Huxley, Aldous, 10, 116-117

**I**

*I Know Why the Caged Bird Sings*, 24

*Im Westen Nichts Neues*, 25
*In Cold Blood: A True Account of a Multiple Murder and Its Consequences*, 34, 242-243
*Independence Day*, 153-154
Internet
  leaders for reading groups, 69-70
  posting for members, 28
interrupters (personality type), 73-74
interview on memoirs, 261-263
  favorites, 263
*Into the Wild*, 341
*The Intuitionist*, 217
*Invisible Man*, 159
Irish books, 190-192
  *The Country Girls Trilogy and Epilogue*, 191-192
  *Murphy*, 190
  *The Snapper*, 190-191
*Ironweed*, 75, 99
irony, 99
Irving, John, 201
Ishiguro, Kazuo, 166
Italian books, 197
  *The Garden of the Finzi-Continis*, 196
  *Reeds in the Wind*, 195-196
  *Unto the Sons*, 197
*Ivanhoe*, 342

**J**

*Jackson Pollock: An American Saga*, 258-259
James, Henry, 129-130
Jewett, Sarah Orne, 200-201
Johnson, Paul, 251
*The Joy Luck Club*, 165-166
Joyce, James, 112-115
*Julip*, 136-137
Jung, Carl, 243
Just-Because Theory, 128

**K**

Kafka, Franz, 225
Kennedy, William, 75, 99, 341
Kerouac, Jack, 183-184
Kesey, Ken, 296
*The Kingdom and the Power*, 341
Kingsolver, Barbara, 130-131
Kinsella, W. P., 148
Kittredge, William, 198
Koestler, Arthur, 119-120
Kozol, Jonathan, 91, 243-244
Krakauer, Jon, 341

**L**

*L.A. Confidential*, 150
*Lady Chatterley's Lover*, 121

Lang, George, 272
*The Last Best Place*, 168-169
*Last Exit to Brooklyn*, 297
Lawrence, D. H., 120-121
Le Guin, Ursula K., 231-232
leaders, choosing, 63-64
  celebrities, 67-68
  democracy, 65-66
  dictatorship, 64-65
  Internet, 69-70
  professional, 66-67
  public radio, 69
  socialism, 66
leaving a group, 106
Lee, Harper, 182
*The Left Hand of Darkness*, 231-232
*The Lesson*, 91
Lewis, C. S., 342
libraries (location of meetings), 37-38
*Like Water for Chocolate*, 273
literary critics, resources, 93-94
literary terms, 99-101
  allegory, 100
  antiheroes, 99
  climax, 99
  hubris, 100
  irony, 99
  magical realism, 100
  minimalism, 100
  motifs, 99
  stream of conscious-ness, 101
  symbolism, 100
*Little Women*, 139-140

*The Lives of a Cell: Notes of a Biology Watcher*, 244
local merchants, posting flyers for members, 26
location of meetings, 32-42, 330-337
  beaches, 330-333
  bookstores, 38-40
  community centers, 36-37
  day trips, 333-334
  group vacations, 336-337
  homes of members, 32-35
  in the country, 334
  libraries, 37-38
  museums, 335
  offices, 40
  poolside, 334
  restaurants, 40-42
  schools, 36
*Lolita*, 115-116
*The Lone Ranger and Tonto Fistfight in Heaven*, 169
*Lonesome Dove*, 151
*Lord of the Flies*, 180
*Love Medicine*, 170-171

## M

MacDonald, Ann-Marie, 342
Machiavelli, Niccolo, 244
Maclean, Norman, 147, 251
magical realism, 100

*The Magnificent Ambersons*, 294-295
main characters, 208
*The Making of a Chef: Mastering Heat at the Culinary Institute of America*, 272
Malamud, Bernard, 148-149
*The Maltese Falcon*, 216-217
*The Mambo Kings Play Songs of Love*, 164
*The Man in the Gray Flannel Suit*, 21
Marx, Karl, 238
Masculine Socialization Theory, 126
*Matilda*, 341
McCann, Colum, 341
McCarthy, Mary, 342
McCullough, David, 90, 254-255
McEwan, Ian, 194, 342
McMurtry, Larry, 151
meetings
  childcare issues, 33
  choosing a leader, 63
    celebrities, 67-68
    democracy, 65-66
    dictatorship, 64-65
    Internet, 69-70
    professional, 66-67
    public radio, 69
    socialism, 66
  cost considerations, 53
  dinner considerations, 270-271

first meeting, 104-105
  importance of
    details, 105
  reading required
    material, 105-106
location, 32-41
  beaches, 330-333
  bookstores, 38-40
  community centers,
    36-37
  country, 334
  day trips, 333-334
  group vacations,
    336-337
  homes of members,
    32-35
  libraries, 37-38
  museums, 335
  offices, 40
  poolside, 334
  restaurants, 40-42
  schools, 36
rules, 43
  absenteeism, 54
  borrowing books,
    52
  cost considerations
    of books, 46
  frequency of meet-
    ings, 44
  purchasing books,
    47, 52
  reading of materi-
    als, 55
  tardiness, 54
  time of meetings,
    45-46
Melville, Herman, 147
members
  choosing, 16
    bookstores, 25-26
    classmates, 23-24

co-workers, 20-22
    community mem-
      bers, 22-23
    family members,
      16-18
    friends, 18-20
    gym acquaintances,
      26
    posting at local
      merchants, 26
    strangers, 26-28
  personality types
    aggressors, 74-75
    digressors, 75-76
    excessive talkers,
      72-73
    interrupters, 73-74
    professors, 77-78
    regressors, 76-77
    wallflowers, 78-79
*Memoir from Antproof
Case,* 341
memoirs, 260
  interviews, 261-263
*Men at Work,* 149
men's reading groups,
  144-146, 154-155
  baseball books,
    148-149
  father/son books,
    152-154
    *Affliction,* 152
    *The Great Santini,*
      153
    *Independence Day,*
      153
  fishing books, 146
  tough-guy books,
    150-151
mental exercises for
  reading, 88-90

Meredith, George, 341
merits of movie adapta-
  tions, 288
  characters, 289
  editing of text, 288
  ending of movie, 289
middle-schoolers (book
  selections), 181
  *Lord of the Flies,* 180
  *Sounder,* 178
  *Tom Sawyer,* 179
*Miles Davis: The
  Autobiography,* 259
Mill, John Stuart, 342
Miller, Arthur, 308
Milton, John, 341
minimalism, 100
mission of reading
  groups, 6
*Moby Dick,* 147
*A Modest Proposal,* 27,
  99-100
*The Mole People: Life in
  the Tunnels Beneath New
  York City,* 248
*Money: A Suicide Note,*
  193
*Moon Palace,* 342
Morrison, Toni, 128-129
mother/daughter
  groups, 137-141
motifs, 99
movie adaptations, 286,
  293, 298-299
  issues to discuss, 286
  merits of adaptation,
    288-290
    characters, 289
    editing of text,
      288-289
    ending of movie,
      289

titles
  *All Quiet on the Western Front*, 296
  *The Godfather*, 295-296
  *Great Expectations*, 294
  *Last Exit to Brooklyn*, 297
  *The Magnificent Ambersons*, 294-295
  *One Flew Over the Cuckoo's Nest*, 296
  *Short Cuts*, 297
*The Moviegoer*, 291
Munro, Alice, 327
murder books, 227-230
  *Crime and Punishment*, 227-228
  *Red Dragon*, 228-229
*Murphy*, 190
museums (location of meetings), 335-336
*My Antonia*, 140
mystery books, 208-219
  *The Hound of the Baskervilles*, 215-216
  *The Intuitionist*, 217-218
  *The Maltese Falcon*, 216-217
  seeking advice on titles, 218
  *The Talented Mr. Ripley*, 216

**N**

Nabokov, Vladimir, 115
Naifeh, Steven, 258-259

Native American authors, 168-171
  Alexie, Sherman, 169
  Erdrich, Louise, 170-171
  Silko, Leslie Marmon, 169-170
*The Natural*, 148-149
*The New Diary*, 261
New England books, 200-203
  *The Country Doctor*, 200-201
  *Outerbridge Reach*, 201-202
  *A Prayer for Owen Meany*, 201
*The New York Trilogy*, 204-205
newspaper ads, finding members for reading groups, 28
Nietzsche, Friedrich, 245
*The Night in Question*, 341
*No Ordinary Time*, 255-256
No Sweating Theory, 127
*Nobody Knows the Truffles I've Seen*, 272
*Nobody's Fool*, 342
noir novels, 213
nonfiction books, 235-237
  *And the Band Played On: Politics, People, and the AIDS Epidemic*, 82, 237
  *The Autobiography of Malcolm X*, 250

*Backlash: The Undeclared War Against American Women*, 240-241
*Beyond Good and Evil: Prelude to a Philosophy of the Future*, 245
*A Brief History of Time*, 242
*A Bright and Shining Lie*, 247-248
*Bury My Heart at Wounded Knee: An Indian History of the American West*, 237-238
*Cape Cod*, 331
*The Communist Manifesto*, 238
*Darkness Visible: A Memoir of Madness*, 239-240
*The Education of Henry Adams*, 240
*The Guns of August*, 241-242
*A History of the American People*, 251
*In Cold Blood: A True Account of a Multiple Murder and Its Consequences*, 35, 242-243
*The Last Best Place*, 168-169
*The Lives of a Cell: Notes of a Biology Watcher*, 244

*The Mole People: Life in the Tunnels Beneath New York City*, 248
*The Origin of Species*, 246
*Parting the Waters/ Pillar of Fire*, 246
*The Prince*, 244
*Red Lobster, White Trash, and the Blue Lagoon*, 247
*The Rise and Fall of the Third Reich: A History of Nazi Germany*, 247
*Savage Inequalities: Children in America's Schools*, 243
*The Undisclosed Self: With Symbols and the Interpretation of Dreams*, 243
*Up from Slavery*, 248-249
*Very Special People*, 249-250
*Working: People Talk About What They Do All Day and How They Feel About What They Do*, 250
*Young Men and Fire*, 251

## O

O'Brien, Edna, 191-192
O'Brien, Tim, 341
O'Connor, Flannery, 90
O'Rourke, P. J., 342
oasis factor, 27

Oates, Joyce Carol, 341
Oe, Kenzaburo, 168
offices (location of meetings), 40
*The Old Man and the Sea*, 146
Old West books, 198-200
  *Dancing at the Rascal Fair*, 199-200
  *The Handyman*, 198-199
  *The Portable Western Reader*, 198
*On Liberty*, 342
*On the Road*, 183-184
*One Flew Over the Cuckoo's Nest*, 296-297
*One Hundred Years of Solitude*, 162-163
Oprah's book club, 68
*Ordinary People*, 181-182
*The Origin of Species*, 246
Oscar Wilde, 257-258
*Outerbridge Reach*, 201-202

## P

*Paradise*, 163
*Paradise Lost*, 341
Parker, Dorothy, 135-136
*Parting the Waters/Pillar of Fire*, 246-247
Partners and Crime Web site, 218
party ideas, 273-274
  barbecues, 278-280
  Chinese dinners, 276-277

  holidays, 280-283
    Christmas, 282-283
    Halloween, 280-281
  suggested entrees, 275
patterns (analyzing), 209
*Paula*, 140
*A People's History of the United States: 1492–Present*, 251
Percy, Walker, 291
personal goals of progress, 60-61
personal benefits, 6-8
personality types of members
  aggressors, 74-75
  digressors, 75-76
  excessive talkers, 72-73
  interrupters, 73-74
  professors, 77-78
  regressors, 76-77
  wallflowers, 78-79
*Philadelphia Fire*, 160
*Phineas Finn*, 342
physical surroundings, 88
*The Plague*, 342
Plath, Sylvia, 323
*The Player*, 291-292
plays, 302-303
  best theaters, 305-306
  cost-saving ideas, 303-304
  performing in reading groups, 306-311
    *Death of a Salesman*, 308
    *Hamlet*, 310

*Romeo and Juliet,* 310

*Waiting for Godot,* 308

plays, 313

Plimpton, George, 342

Poe, Edgar Allan, 211

poetry, 315-324

arguments against poetry, 316-317

poetry slams, 318

poets, 319-324

Blake, William, 320-321

Dickinson, Emily, 319-320

Hughes, Langston, 319

Plath, Sylvia, 323

Sandburg, Carl, 321-322

Whitman, Walt, 321

Williams, William Carlos, 322-323

Poets and Writers Web site, 28

poolside (location of meetings), 334

*Population 1280,* 151

*The Portable Dorothy Parker,* 135-136

*The Portable Western Reader,* 198

*The Portrait of a Lady,* 129-130

*A Portrait of the Artist As a Young Man,* 114-115

Powell's

top five bestsellers list, 51

top 10 classics list, 122

Web site, 50

*A Prayer for Owen Meany,* 201

presidential readings, 257

Price, Richard, 341

prices, *see* cost considerations

*The Prince,* 244

professional (leadership quality), 66-67

professors (personality type), 77-78

public benefits, 8

public radio, leaders for reading groups, 69

purchasing books, 47, 52

Puzo, Mario, 295

## Q-R

Queenan, Joe, 247

*Quinn's Book,* 341

Radcliffe Publishing, top 10 classics list, 123

*Ragtime,* 97-98

Rainer, Tristine, 261-263

Random House Web site, 69

reading

focusing on task, 91-92

author biographies (researching), 92-93

literary critics, 93-94

goals, researching books, 90-91

level of concentration, 86-87

mental exercises, 88-90

physical surroundings, 88

required material for meetings, 105-106

reading groups, *see* groups

reasons for reading

dinner-party disaster, 4-5

intellectual workout, 5

Rechy, John, 342

recipes, 274-282

barbecues, 278-280

Chinese dinner, 276-277

*Red Dragon,* 228-229

red herrings, 210

*Red Lobster, White Trash, and the Blue Lagoon,* 247

*Reeds in the Wind,* 195-196

*Reef,* 273

regressors (personality type), 76-77

Reichl, Ruth, 272

*The Remains of the Day,* 166

Remarque, Erich Maria, 296

replacing group members, 103-104

researching
  authors, 92-93
  books, 90-91
resources
  literary critics, 94
  scholarly journals, 94
restaurants (location of
  meetings), 40-42
Richman, Phyllis, 273
*The Rise and Fall of the
  Third Reich: A History of
  Nazi Germany*, 247
*A River Runs Through It*,
  147
*Roger Ebert's Book of Film*,
  292-293
*Romeo and Juliet*,
  310-311
*A Room of One's Own*,
  134-135
Roosevelt, Eleanor, 255
Roy, Arandhati, 341
Ruhlman, Michael, 272
rules (meetings), 43
  absenteeism, 54
  borrowing books, 52
  cost considerations of
    books, 46
  frequency of meet-
    ings, 44
  purchasing books, 47,
    52
  reading of material,
    55
  tardiness, 54
  time of meetings,
    45-46
Russo, Richard, 342

## S

Salinger, J. D., 23
Sandburg, Carl, 321-322
Saunders, George, 341
*Savage Inequalities:
  Children in America's
  Schools*, 243-244
scholarly journals,
  resources, 93-94
schools (location of
  meetings), 35-36
science-fiction books,
  230-233
  *The Left Hand of
    Darkness*, 231-232
  *The War of the Worlds*,
    230-231
Scott, Sir Walter, 342
*The Screwtape Letters*, 342
See, Carolyn, 198-199
Segal, Lore, 140-141
Selby Jr., Hubert, 297
Sendak, Maurice, 177
settings
  analyzing, 208
  goals, 60-63
    charters, 63
    group-oriented, 62
    personal progress,
      60-61
Seuss, Dr., 177
*Seventeen Syllables and
  Other Stories*, 167
Shakespeare, William,
  145, 309-311
Sheehan, Neil, 247
Sheer Numbers Theory,
  126
Shilts, Randy, 82, 237
Shirer, William, 247

*Shoeless Joe*, 148
*Short Cuts*, 297-298
short stories, 324-328
  authors
    Carver, Raymond,
      297-298, 326
    Henry, O., 325-326
    Munro, Alice, 327
  favorites, 327-328
*The Silence of the Lambs*,
  228
Silko, Leslie Marmon,
  169-170
Silverstein, Shel, 176
Simon Says Web site, 69
slams, poetry, 318
Smiley, Jane, 342
Smith, Gregory White,
  258-259
*The Snapper*, 190-191
Sobel, Robert, 256
social benefits, 9
socialism (leadership
  style), 66
*Sons and Lovers*, 120-121
*The Sound and the Fury*,
  117-118
*Sounder*, 178-179
Steinbeck, John,
  121-122
Steingarten, Jeffrey, 272
Stevenson, Robert Louis,
  225-226
*Stigmata: A Novel*, 342
Stoker, Bram, 222-223
Stone, Robert, 201-202
*Stones from the River*, 341
strangers, choosing for
  reading groups, 26-28
  Internet postings, 28
  newspaper ads, 28

stream of consciousness, 101

Strout, Elizabeth, 341

styles, analyzing, 210

Styron, William, 239-240

Sunday Paper Web site, 28

Swift, Jonathan, 27, 99

symbolism, 100

## T

*The Talented Mr. Ripley*, 216

*Tales of a Wayside Inn*, 8

Talese, Gay, 197, 341

Talk City Web site, 69

talkers (personality type), 72-73

Tan, Amy, 165-166

Tannahill, Reay, 272

tardiness to meetings, 54

Tarkington, Booth, 294-295

teenagers (book selections), 184-185
  *On the Road*, 183-184
  *Ordinary People*, 181
  *To Kill a Mockingbird*, 182

*Tender at the Bone: Growing Up at the Table*, 272

tension
  bad, 98
  good, 98-99

Terkel, Studs, 250

theaters, best locations, 305-306

*Their Eyes Were Watching God*, 159

theories, women's groups, 126-128
  Empowerment Theory, 127
  Freedom Factor Theory, 126
  Just-Because Theory, 128
  Masculine Socialization Theory, 126
  No Sweating Theory, 127
  Sheer Numbers Theory, 126
  Trend-Watcher Theory, 127

*This Side of Brightness*, 341

Thomas, Lewis, 244

Thompson, Jim, 151

Thoreau, Henry David, 331-332

*Three by Flannery O'Connor*, 90

*Through the Looking-Glass*, 7

time (meetings), 45-46

*To Kill a Mockingbird*, 182

Tolkin, Michael, 291-292

Toole, John Kennedy, 132-133

Toth, Jennifer, 248

tough-guy books, 150
  *L.A. Confidential*, 150
  *Lonesome Dove*, 151
  *Population 1280*, 151

*Travels with My Aunt*, 341

Trend-Watcher Theory, 127

*The Trial*, 225

Trollope, Anthony, 342

Troupe, Quincy, 259

*Truman*, 90, 254-255

Tuchman, Barbara, 241-242

Twain, Mark, 23, 179-180

Tyler, Anne, 342

## U–V

*Ulysses*, 112-113

*The Unbearable Lightness of Being*, 16

*The Undisclosed Self: With Symbols and the Interpretation of Dreams*, 243

*Unto the Sons*, 197

*Up from Slavery*, 248-249

Updike, John, 342

Usedbooks.com, 52

vacations with group, 336-337

vampire books, 224
  *Dracula*, 222-223

*Very Special People*, 249-250

*The View from the Ground*, 342

Vonnegut Jr., Kurt, 342

## W

*Waiting for Godot,* 308-309
wallflowers (personality type), 78-79
*The War of the Worlds,* 230-231
Ward, Susie, 272
Washington, Booker T., 248-249
Web sites
  Amazon.com, 48
  Barnes & Noble, 49
  Biblio Bytes, 70
  Book Spot, 70
  BookWire, 69
  Classifieds for Free, 28
  A Different Light bookstore, 69
  GetSet, 69
  Horror Writers Association, 69
  Partners and Crime, 218
  Poets and Writers, 28
  Powell's, 50
  Random House, 69
  Simon Says, 69
  Sunday Paper, 28
  Talk City, 69
  Usedbooks.com, 52
*The Wedding,* 341
Welles, Orson, 294-295
Wells, H. G., 230-231
West, Dorothy, 341
Wharton, Edith, 204
*Where the Wild Things Are,* 177
White, E. B., 107, 175
Whitehead, Colson, 217

Whitman, Walt, 321
Wideman, John Edgar, 160
Will, George, 149
Williams, William Carlos, 322-323
Wilson, Sloan, 21
Winfrey, Oprah, 67-68
Wolf, Leonard, 223
Wolfe, Tom, 203
Wolff, Geoffrey, 264
Wolff, Tobias, 341
Wollstonecraft, Mary, 341
*The Woman Who Walked into Doors,* 135
women's reading groups, 125
  books, 128-141
  feminist examination, 133-137
  mother/daughter groups, 137-141
  theories, 126-128
Woolf, Virginia, 134-135
*Working: People Talk About What They Do All Day and How They Feel About What They Do,* 250

## Y–Z

Yamamoto, Hisaye, 167
*Yertle the Turtle,* 177
young children (book selections)
  *The Giving Tree,* 176
  *Where the Wild Things Are,* 177-178

*Young Men and Fire,* 251
*Your Life as Story,* 261

Zindel, Paul, 24
Zinn, Howard, 251